GLOBAL GREEN POLITICS

In light of growing urgency in tackling the global environmental crisis, there is a need for new visions and strategies to ensure a more sustainable and just world. This book provides a comprehensive overview of Green perspectives on a range of global issues, including security, the economy, the state, global governance, development and the environment. Drawing on academic literature on Green political theory, combined with insights from real world practice and the author's own extensive personal experience, it provides a timely and accessible account of why we need to embrace Green politics in order to tackle the multiple crises facing the world today. Presenting alternative visions and concrete strategies for achieving change, this book will be of interest to activists and policymakers as well as to students of the environment, development and politics.

PETER NEWELL is a professor of International Relations at the University of Sussex, UK. He has worked on the political economy of the environment for over twenty five years as a researcher, teacher and activist. As well as holding academic posts at the universities of Sussex, Oxford, Warwick and East Anglia in the United Kingdom and FLACSO Argentina, he is a board member of Greenpeace UK, Carbon Market Watch in Brussels and the Greenhouse think tank in the United Kingdom and is co-founder of the Rapid Transition Alliance.

an invaluable and pioneering guide to how to think globally in the twenty-first century, and how to understand and navigate our uncertain and turbulent times.'

John Barry,
Queens University Belfast

'At last, here is a critical introduction to global Green politics from one of the field's most versatile intellectual pioneers. Grounded in a deep appreciation of the inextricable interconnections between social and ecological systems, this book offers a clear normative vision, a penetrating critique of business and politics as usual and a set of practical strategies for sustainability transitions. Younger generations can now take heart!'

Robyn Eckersley,
University of Melbourne

'Newell's incisive analysis brings a vital Green lens to the study of global politics that has been largely neglected by mainstream scholars of international relations. *Global Green Politics* provides powerful insights and critiques that arise from taking an expressly ecological perspective on humanity's most pressing global concerns.'

Jennifer Clapp,
University of Waterloo

GLOBAL GREEN POLITICS

PETER NEWELL
University of Sussex

CAMBRIDGE
UNIVERSITY PRESS

CAMBRIDGE
UNIVERSITY PRESS

University Printing House, Cambridge CB2 8BS, United Kingdom

One Liberty Plaza, 20th Floor, New York, NY 10006, USA

477 Williamstown Road, Port Melbourne, VIC 3207, Australia

314–321, 3rd Floor, Plot 3, Splendor Forum, Jasola District Centre, New Delhi – 110025, India

79 Anson Road, #06–04/06, Singapore 079906

Cambridge University Press is part of the University of Cambridge.

It furthers the University's mission by disseminating knowledge in the pursuit of education, learning, and research at the highest international levels of excellence.

www.cambridge.org
Information on this title: www.cambridge.org/9781108487092
DOI: 10.1017/9781108767224

First published 2020

Printed in the United Kingdom by TJ International Ltd. Padstow Cornwall

A catalogue record for this publication is available from the British Library.

ISBN 978-1-108-48709-2 Hardback
ISBN 978-1-108-72057-1 Paperback

Contents

Acknowledgements

Like many books, the idea for this one existed in my head for many more years than I care to admit. It finally came to fruition in my first and only academic sabbatical to date, during the academic year 2017–18. It was a daunting task. Re-connecting with, as well as discovering afresh, bodies of work on Green politics written over the last forty years was at once overwhelming and awe-inspiring. This meant surveying literatures that were abundant in some areas but very sparse in others. Gaps had to be filled in, developing a Green political account of world politics through extending key concepts, examining real world praxis and working from core principles. I hope I have done those bodies of work justice in trying to build the foundations of a global Green politics.

During the period in which the bulk of the writing took place, awareness of the scale and urgency of our planetary predicament was heightened by the publication of the Intergovernmental Panel on Climate Change (IPCC) special report in October 2018 on the impacts of global warming of 1.5°C above preindustrial levels that warned of the need for 'transformative systemic change' and, as if to underscore the severity of the warnings, was followed by a series of droughts, floods and severe weather events around the world. This was the trigger for new mobilisations such as the Extinction Rebellion and the declaration of a state of climate emergency by many cities and councils and several governments of which the UK government was the first, as well as an increase in divestment from fossil fuels and direct action against ecologically destructive projects. Although climate change is seen as the meta-issue of our time for many understandable reasons, we are also now living through a sixth mass extinction event, in which insect populations that sustain food systems have been devastated and our oceans are acidifying, warming and full of plastic waste. And yet 'business as usual' continues as if none of this constitutes an indictment of a wasteful, inequitable and unsustainable system.

The time is ripe for Green politics and alternative visions of global politics organised around principles of equity, ecology, peace and democracy. Our collective survival depends on it, even if policy and business elites use all the power at their disposal to deny that this is the case. As the prominent Green thinker E. F. Schumacher (1974:31) said, 'Perhaps we cannot raise the winds. But each of us can put up the sail, so that when the wind comes we can catch it.' In some small way, this book hopes to raise awareness of Green perspectives on world politics that have been so sorely missing from policy and academic debate.

For their support in writing the book, I would like to thank my colleagues in the School of Global Studies at Sussex and members of the department of Politics and International Studies at the University of Queensland, where I was lucky enough to spend some of my sabbatical: in particular Matt McDonald and Richard Devetak for their support and the hospitality extended to me and my family. For inspiration through their work in this area and for their collegiality, I want to mention the brilliant Mat Paterson and John Barry. And for the grounding in the messy realities of doing Green politics in practice, I want to thank campaigners and fellow board members at Greenpeace, Carbon Market Watch and the Green think tank Greenhouse, and co-founder of the Rapid Transition Alliance and my partner in crime in all things Green, Andrew Simms.

For twice weekly injections of community, camaraderie, friendship and exercise, I would like to thank Lewes F.C Vets and the endless dedication of manager Pete Bull to building 'equality F.C' across gender, age and ability. For their professional guidance in seeing the book through to production I would like to thank Matt Lloyd and all the production and marketing team at Cambridge University Press. Thanks too to Leah Good and Gerardo Torres for cross-checking references and helping to produce the index for the book.

I am forever indebted to Rahul Moodgal for an incredible life-long friendship through good times and bad. For love, support and all the things that make all of this worthwhile and possible, I want to thank my family, my wife Lucila and children Ana and Camilo, whose world we continue to fight for at all costs.

Abbreviations and Acronyms

BECCS	Bioenergy with carbon capture and storage
BP	British Petroleum
BRIC	Brazil, Russia, India, China
CAP	Common Agricultural Policy
CBD	Convention on Biodiversity
CDM	Clean Development Mechanism
CEO	Chief Executive Officer
CERES	Coalition for Environmentally Responsible Economies
CFCs	Chlorofluorocarbons
CGG	Commission on Global Governance
CIF	Climate Investment Fund
CND	Campaign for Nuclear Disarmament
CO_2	Carbon Dioxide
COP	Conference of the Parties
CSD	Commission on Sustainable Development
CSR	Corporate Social Responsibility
EC	European Commission
ESG	Earth Systems Governance
EU	European Union
FAO	Food and Agriculture Organization
FDI	Foreign Direct Investment
FTAA	Free Trade Area of the Americas
G8	Group of Eight Countries
G20	Group of Twenty Countries
GATS	General Agreement on Trade in Services
GDP	Gross Domestic Product
GEF	Green European Foundation
GEJ	*Green European Journal*
GHG	Greenhouse Gas

GM	Genetically Modified
GMO	Genetically Modified Organism
GND	Green New Deal
GNP	Gross National Product
GPI	Genuine Progress Indicator
HDI	Human Development Index
HSBC	Hong Kong and Shanghai Banking Corporation
IEA	International Energy Agency
IFC	International Finance Corporation
ILO	International Labour Organization
IMF	International Monetary Fund
IPCC	Intergovernmental Panel on Climate Change
IPE	International Political Economy
IPEE	International Political Economy of the Environment
IPR	Intellectual Property Rights
IR	International Relations
IT	Information Technology
LDCs	Least Developed Countries
LETs	Local Exchange Trading Schemes
LGBT	Lesbian, Gay, Bisexual and Transsexual
MAI	Multilateral Agreement on Investment
MDB	Multilateral Development Bank
MDGs	Millennium Development Goals
MEA	Multilateral Environmental Agreement
MEP	Member of the European Parliament
MLK	Martin Luther King
MNC	Multinational Corporation
MNE	Multinational Enterprises
MST	Movement of the Landless
NAFTA	North American Free Trade Agreement
NASA	National Aeronautics and Space Administration
NATO	North American Treaty Organization
NEF	New Economics Foundation
NETS	Negative Emissions Technologies
NGO	Non-Governmental Organisation
NIEO	New International Economic Order
NPT	Non-Proliferation Treaty
NVDA	Non-Violent Direct Action
NWS	Nuclear Weapons States
ODA	Overseas Development Assistance

OECD	Organisation for Economic Co-operation and Development
OPEC	Organization of Petroleum Exporting Countries
REDD	Reduced Emissions from Deforestation and forest Degradation
RTA	Rapid Transition Alliance
SAP	Structural Adjustment Policy
SDGs	Sustainable Development Goals
SME	Small and Medium-sized Enterprise
SPS	Sanitary and Phytosanitary
SRI	Socially Responsible Investment
TNC	Transnational Corporation
TREMs	Trade-Related Environment Measures
TRIPS	Trade-Related aspects of Intellectual Property Rights
TRWC	The Real World Coalition
UK	United Kingdom
UN	United Nations
UNCED	United Nations Conference on Environment and Development
UNCTC	United Nations Centre on Transnational Corporations
UNDP	United Nations Development Programme
UNEP	United Nations Environment Programme
UNFCCC	United Nations Framework Convention on Climate Change
US	United States (of America)
USAID	United States Agency for International Development
WEO	World Environment Organisation
WIPO	World Intellectual Property Organization
WRI	World Resources Institute
WSSD	World Summit on Sustainable Development
WTO	World Trade Organization
WWF	World Wide Fund for Nature

1

Global Green Politics

For the Common Good

Introduction

Environmental issues are now firmly on the global political agenda. Major UN summits and even meetings of the G8 most powerful economies in the world often feature environmental issues, especially climate change. Having now had nearly fifty years of international environmental diplomacy, unsurprisingly 'the environment' is part of everyday parlance in the practice and teaching of global politics. The same cannot be said for Green politics and perspectives on key global issues coming from more radical Green positions. Despite the potential contributions of Green thinking to an understanding and explanation of the underlying causes and potential solutions to the multiple crises engulfing global politics around war, poverty and social inequality or climate change, Green perspectives on global politics issues have rarely been articulated or brought together and have yet to gain traction. In a modest way, this book seeks to remedy that.

It is certainly the case that environmentalism has made real headway in changing law and government policy, driving multilateral treaties on environmental protection and changing consumer and corporate behaviour (Mol 2003). Yet the ecological crises deepens, and with politics and economics as usual we continue to surpass planetary boundaries at an alarming rate with little prospect of shifting the trajectory. States and corporations clearly take the lion's share of the blame for our planetary predicament and what has been described as the 'anthropocene' – a new geological epoch in which human forces are dominant in shaping the biosphere (Steffen et al. 2007). For many people, academics and activists alike, environmentalism also has to take some share of the blame. Questions are asked about the long-term effectiveness of what has been referred to as the 'environmentalism of the rich' (Dauvergne 2016) and the 'corporatization of activism' (Dauvergne and LeBaron 2014), a reference to the growing engagement of many mainstream, as well as formerly more radical groups, with market environmentalism. This practice refers to working with the corporate sector through brand activism, certification schemes and roundtables, for example, selling ecoconsumerism and lifestyle politics, while allegedly ignoring the underlying and structural drivers of environmental degradation. On the one hand, this is understandable given the urgency of the crisis we face and the desperate and evident need for short-term changes that mean being strategic, working with those that hold the power to change things now and 'going with the grain'. On the other hand, this diagnosis suggests that the politics of incrementalism is not enough. Time no longer allows for powerful corporate and state elites to dictate the pace and terms of change. Bolder envisionings and articulations of alternatives, new strategies and politics are required, even if grounded in relatively old traditions in some cases. I will argue that Green politics, extended and more clearly articulated to deal with today's global politics, has a key role to play in this regard.

Why 'global' green politics? Is not all Green politics intrinsically global? On one level, yes. There are very few issues, especially environmental ones, that can be thought of as wholly local, when they are intrinsically tied to global ecosystems through water and carbon cycles, for example, as well as produced through complex internationalised economic chains of production. The same might be said of the interconnections across scales and actors that produce economic and security challenges, such that scholars sometimes refer to 'glocal' politics (Rosenau 1997). Likewise, Green Party manifestos around the world are often strongly internationalist in their outlook. Core elements of Green politics concerning ecology, peace and feminism are necessarily global and universal struggles, whose goals cannot be achieved locally, or in isolation from global politics, if they are to be sustained and impactful. At first glance then, it would seem obvious that all Green politics are global, rooted in the classic axiom 'Act locally, think globally'.[1] Environmental and social concerns that underpin Green political theory (GPT) transcend sovereign borders, and responsibilities to others are often expressed in global (as well as intergenerational) terms. In this sense, Green articulations of political community are intrinsically global.

Nevertheless, insights from Green politics are remarkably absent from discussions and debates in global politics and from academic enquiry about them. The neglect is often mutual. In practical terms, foreign policy is also often down-played or given scant attention in Green Party manifestos, where emphasis tends to be placed on economic localism and the decentralisation of political power as a reaction against global power structures (GEJ 2015). In the academic world, the underexplored links between International Relations (IR) and (political) ecology and the failure to acknowledge the existence and potential contributions of more radical ecological literature, observed twenty years ago (Laferièrre and Stoett 1999), remain valid today. This is the case despite important, but scattered, contributions over a period of forty years from IR scholars such as Paterson

(2009), Katz-Rosene and Paterson (2018), Hovden (1999), Helleiner (1996), Eckersley (2004, 2010), Laferièrre and Stoett (1999, 2006) and a small body of pioneering work from the 1960s to the early 1980s (Falk 1971; Sprout and Sprout 1965; Ophuls 1973; Pirages 1977, 1984). We continue, nevertheless, to lack a systematic application of perspectives derived from different strands of Green politics to a broad range of key areas of global politics.

This neglect is not withstanding a vast literature on global environmental politics and a growing acceptance of *environmentalism* (about which more below) but not of *ecologism*, which questions the ability of the current economic and political system to achieve ecological or social, let alone economic, sustainability (Dobson 1990). There has been a lack of application of Green politics as source of critical, strategic thinking and as a normative project regarding global politics at a time when, I would argue, Green perspectives on global politics are urgently required. Green insights (as opposed to more narrowly conceived environmental ones) are sorely missing in many debates about security, economy, development and global governance, let alone sustainability. This book seeks to fill that gap.

The central claim here then is that Green politics offers up a rich and distinct set of critiques, visions and utopias and the strategies for achieving them, aimed at transforming global politics in more equitable and sustainable directions. As well as thinking globally and acting locally, this book explores whether there is also scope to act, as well as think, globally and to engage with debates and issues in global politics more fully from the standpoint of Green politics. It is hoped this will be of benefit both to those interested in global politics and International Relations, and to Green thinkers and activists looking for tools and resources to further develop critiques, visions and strategies for transforming global politics.

This is the aim of this book: to draw on different strands of Green thinking to articulate Green perspectives on key aspects of contemporary global politics, in terms of critiques of the existing unsustainable world order and visions of how alternative worlds might be imagined and constructed and also in terms of the strategies that will get us from where we are now to where Greens would like us to be. This is not just a question of looking at the theory and practice of Green foreign policy (GEJ 2015), or Green (international) political economy where there have been some important contributions (Helleiner 1996; Katz-Rosene and Paterson 2018) but a more encompassing attempt to define and evaluate a Green view of global politics: a set of normative commitments, explanatory resources and proposals for change.

To do all this, I have built upon contributions from Green writers, academics, practitioners and philosophers. I have also sought to articulate and extend Green views on issues based on my own interpretation of core principles and values, surmising what a Green perspective might look like and so helping to fill in the gaps in an account of Green global politics. This work of induction, creative interpretation and extrapolation from core principles and real world practice has been necessary precisely because of the absence of such accounts to date. For Green thinkers, politicians and activists, I also hope to showcase scholarship which intersects with, supports, reinforces, as well as challenges, Green politics. Providing resources, food for thought, and the views of critical friends is done in the spirit of advancing the project of showcasing and promoting Green thinking in contemporary politics.

I recognise the immense value of work whose main purpose is to situate ecologism alongside other 'isms', whether liberalism, socialism, feminism or anarchism, as a comparable school of thought (Dobson 1990; Barry 1999) and I adhere to Hayward's claim that: 'One of the most urgent intellectual tasks of our time is to understand the implications of ecology for social and political thought' (1994: 1).

Rather than assessing the value of ecologism in relation to existing bodies of thought, however, my aim here is to systematically develop an ecological account of global politics. What I am offering then is not a new theory of International Relations. It is the articulation and extension of Green political analysis, thinking and solutions from the local and national to the global, notwithstanding the immanently 'global' nature of Green politics. My starting point, building on the contributions of others, is to articulate a Green view of world politics that challenges many mainstream perspectives in IR, while not proclaiming to offer a new theory of IR. It is not preoccupied with a theory of the international, or how and when and why institutions form, or of when wars occur or peace prevails, or why the current system of states persists. Being clear about this runs the risk, of course, of making it even easier for the gatekeepers of the discipline of IR to further ignore the potential value and contributions of Green thinking to IR as they have done to date so successfully.

In the world we inhabit today, we would do well to move beyond refining accounts of interstate relations while the world of which they are a part descends further into ecological crisis. This view relates closely to Laferièrre and Stoett's observation that: 'Realists seemingly foreclose the future (and deny social freedom) by postulating an historical recurrence of violent conflict and studying human behaviour through an epistemology of control ... such philosophical straightjackets are destined to deny the autonomy of subjects and to dissuade alternative thinking' (1999: 101). Their self-fulfilling presentations of the world as a natural and unshakeable order of things inevitably serve the beneficiaries of the current order, invoking Robert Cox's (1981) suggestion that theory is always for someone, for some purpose. Addressing the question of who theory is for, the call here is for a practice and activist turn in IR. It builds on Burke et al.'s insight that: 'International Relations, as both a system of knowledge and institutional practice, is undone by the reality of the planet. We must be in tension with *status-quo* struggles within our disciplines, and transgress academic boundaries to create conversations with activist networks and movements engaged in struggle against oppressive regimes and systems' (2016: 501).

To be clear then, this book does not seek to establish Green politics as a 'great pillar' of the discipline alongside Realism, Liberalism, Marxism and Constructivism, even if it implies critiques of those perspectives and offers other ways of thinking about global politics. The book rather serves as a set of resources for making sense of the world from a Green perspective, as well as offering tools and ideas for how to change it. This is unlike Pirage's attempt, for example, to 'suggest an ecological approach to international relations . . . that provides an efficient and useful alternative to realism, liberalism, and critical international relations theory' (1997: 53). I do not claim that ecologists provide a superior understanding of the international system, even if the starting points of their enquiry should force a reconsideration of the conduct and goals of global politics. This is not, in other words, a macro theory of world order and change, but it does aim to articulate a normative and critical perspective on world affairs that departs from many existing perspectives.

Indeed, for many Greens the ecological order which sustains all life on Earth constitutes a meta-order within which the entire international system of states and other actors is just one component, and certainly not the only one that exercises agency. Many Green accounts that speak to global politics and IR start with the need to put humanity in its place: to locate human and international society within the wider ecosystem of which it is a part. As Pirages puts it: 'An ecological approach to explaining the evolution of the international system and the emergence of global issues begins with the observation that *Homo sapiens* is but one species among millions sharing the global ecosystem . . . ecological factors continue to shape human societies, human conflicts, the international distribution of power, and the nature of emerging global issues' (1997: 53). Furthermore, 'The traditional theoretical approaches to international relations, centered on men [sic] and their motives, are increasingly obsolete in the face of the relentless ecological and technological changes that are transforming the state system into a global one' (Pirages 1997: 54).

Here I proffer an account of global politics that is explicitly and unapologetically socio-ecological: neither reducing understandings of global politics to their ecological base, nor assuming that there can be a global politics that exists outside of ecological systems which sustain it and make it possible. Rather, it is attentive to ways in which social and ecological systems are intertwined in ways that are currently driving ecological devastation and social inequality but which might be transformed along more sustainable and socially just lines.

The Neglect of Green Politics in International Relations

There is now a vast literature across many disciplines including sociology, economics, development studies, political science and International Relations dealing
with questions of global environmental change (cf: Grubb 2014; Redclift and
Benton 1994; Corry and Stevenson 2018). Testimony to this is found in the ever
proliferating numbers of journals dedicated to publishing work pertaining to
different aspects of the ecological crisis. These include *Global Environmental
Change, Environmental Politics, Environmental Ethics, Global Environmental
Politics, Nature, Capitalism Nature Socialism*, and *The Journal of Environment
and Development, Ecology and Conservation* to name just a few. In relation to
global politics specifically, there is also now over thirty years of work on environmental politics and the greening of different aspects of world politics covering
global environmental institutions (Young 1998, 2010; Brenton 1994; Biermann
2014) and the global economy (Clapp and Dauvergne 2011; Newell 2012; Kütting
2005; Speth 2008; Christoff and Eckersley 2013) in particular.

Nevertheless, interestingly, surprisingly but also problematically, there has been
a lack of systematic engagement with a Green perspective in International Relations, the discipline that you might imagine to be best placed to explain global
politics (Agathangelou 2016). Despite early engagements by IR scholars addressing ecological questions, most notably Sprout and Sprout (1965), Richard Falk
(1971) and Dennis Pirages (1984), the neglect has been notable. As Chandler et al.
(2017: 18) recently wrote: 'International Relations is inherently the discipline that
has the responsibility for considering global processes, and that this is a responsibility it has thus far failed to shoulder', despite the fact that ecological metaphors
have, on occasion, been invoked to furnish an alternative account of world politics,
such as Thomas Kuehls' 'rhizomatic'[2] approach to world politics. In 2016 Burke
et al. in calling for 'planet politics' ask provocatively: 'If the biosphere is collaps-
ing, and if International Relations has always presented itself as that discourse
which takes the global as its point of departure, how is it that we – IR's scholars,
diplomats and leaders – have not engaged with the *planetary* real?' (Burke et al.
2016: 501). Furthermore:

We contend that International Relations has failed because the planet does not match and
cannot be clearly seen by its institutional and disciplinary frameworks. Institutionally and
legally, it is organised around a managed anarchy of nation-states, not the collective human
interaction with the biosphere. Intellectually, the IR discipline is organised sociologically
around established paradigms and research programmes likewise focused on states and the
forms of international organisation they will tolerate; it is not organised to value or create
the conceptual and analytical changes that are needed. The problems lie in the way we
think and are trained; in the subjects and approaches our discipline values and rewards.

(2016: 501)

The prerequisites for a sustainable society might be thought to include stability, order and peace, which form central preoccupations for the discipline of IR. Yet as Laferièrre and Stoett suggest: 'While structural realism has produced an interesting debate over the implications of shifts in Great Power parity, it has yet to seriously consider the shifts inherent in an even more fundamental context of human affairs – the biosphere itself' (1999: 97). As we will see in Chapter 3, from an ecological point of view, stability and security, pursued through Realist strategies that give pride of place to state-based militarism, are illusory. Likewise, if the order to be preserved is the global capitalist economy, peace and sustainability will remain a distant prospect.

Mainstream scholars of IR would remain suspicious about the value of Green perspectives on global politics, however. Although we do not know, because Realists ignore these concerns as peripheral, it is likely they would view notions of ecological limits and self-restraint on the part of societies as dangerous and regressive, heightening vulnerability to enemy attack, all the while overlooking that they are accelerating towards their own (and everyone else's) destruction through an unquestioning commitment to militarism and industrialism. Insofar as they accept evidence of increasing environmental threats, the extent of their contribution would likely be to call for the expansion of military forces and budgets in order to extend the arenas and issues to be secured through force. This notion follows from the fact that Realism serves as 'the intellectual defence *par excellence* of the military establishment' (Laferièrre and Stoett 1999: 103), thereby managing to disregard the military's own role as a source of insecurity by consuming resources at an unsustainable rate (as discussed in Chapter 3) as well as its ties to industrialism (through a military-industrial complex discussed in Chapter 5). This gives lie to the notion of autonomous state action in pursuit of rationally determined national interests (somehow abstracted from state strategies) in a global capitalist economy.

With the exception of a few notable interventions (Paterson 2009; Katz-Rosene and Paterson 2018; Eckersley 2010; Laferrière and Stoett 1999; Helleiner 1996; Pirages 1997) then, Green perspectives rarely feature in IR as an academic discipline. Most IR textbooks ignore Green politics as a standalone perspective or theory of global politics,[3] even if the 'environment' features as another 'issue area' of International Relations. Part of the answer to this lies in Steve Smith's (1993) explanation of why the environment is on the periphery of IR, alongside issues such as gender and race. According to him, it fails to speak to the 'big' issues of the day, as defined by global elites. It occupies a vulnerable position on the international agenda, easily displaced by other issues. It is an issue area just like any other, no more compelling than others with which it competes for attention (such as hunger and health); and it does not transcend the state-system despite claims of one-worldism. For Smith, the environment is not an integral component of theory, or in any way disruptive of, or subversive of, conventional theoretical categories. Realism regards environmental issues as 'low politics' (or even lower than low politics); high politics will inevitably re-assert itself and scholars need to focus on where the action is, taking their cue from global elites.

Taking the environment seriously means moving away from the state as the key unit of analysis, Smith argued, while the predominance of pluralist thinking by environment scholars has left many key concepts and assumptions uncontested. While disagreeing with much of his intervention, and agreeing with the critique of Saurin (1996) and others about its dismissive approach to the importance of environmental issues, interestingly Smith's observation that this marginalisation was due, in part, to the dominance of liberal institutional thinking among scholars of global environmental politics, was and in many ways remains valid. The hegemony of that perspective, and its comfortable fit with key assumptions and biases of the discipline, partially helps to explain the neglect of Green perspectives (Newell 2008; Clapp and Helleiner 2012). Hence, as Laferièrre and Stoett note: while the 'formal study of global politics has acknowledged the environment . . . little IR theory explicitly incorporates ecological principles' (1999: 2).

Although there is perhaps more progress to report in terms of the embrace of ecological ideas by critical theories of IR than by Realism and Liberalism, it is also true that the awareness remains limited. The section below on International Political Economy (IPE) and ecology suggests that in this area of the discipline of IR, this has, to some extent, changed. Even there, it remains the case that it is more often than not scholars who work on the environment and ecological politics who are using concepts and theories from (international) political economy rather than IR and IPE scholars revising their theoretical approaches or empirical focus in the light of insights from ecological thinking.

What this overlooks is the scope for Green politics to offer distinctive, critical and radical perspectives (even if not new overarching theories of IR) on questions of world (dis)order, anarchy, war and security, economy and what mainstream scholars would define as the terrain of 'high politics', as well as the everyday global politics as the majority of the world experience them: as social exclusion, poverty, discrimination of various kinds and lack of access to resources. IR has largely failed to seriously register or entertain the implications of thinking ecologically (Katz-Rosene and Paterson 2018), preferring to treat the environment within traditional and dominant theoretical categories and perspectives. Hence even though 'Ecology could provide a radical language that could alter the usual conceptions of peace/order/justice etc found in IR theory' (Laferièrre and Stoett 1999: xii), IR theory continues to neglect the value of ecological thought to political theory, apart from the obvious interests of mainstream IR in questions of *geo*politics and how resource abundance and imbalances can reconfigure the balance of power or exacerbate war through scarcity.

Laferièrre and Stoett's (1999) book *International Relations and Ecological Thought* broke important ground in showing how radical ecological thought in particular relates to key theories in IR of Realism, Liberalism and Critical theory (covering a range of (neo) Marxist, Feminist and Postmodern approaches). Many of their critiques of the neglect of ecological thought in IR remain frustratingly pertinent today, despite the steady consolidation of global environmental politics as a subfield of the discipline. Writing about the discipline in the late 1990s Laferrière and Stoett argue:

> the searching and challenging body of ecological thought which had emerged during the preceding decades (and indeed centuries) had yet to have a substantive impact. When IR theorists did discuss ecological issues, they did so from a very conservative understanding of the ecological problematique, reformulating classic problems of scarcity and collective action. This is still largely the case.
>
> *(1999: xi)*

The neglect was, and I will argue, still is, mutual. Ecological thought, they proposed 'needs to take explicit consideration of international questions into account and at present there is great room for such conceptual development. In other words, it is not just the study of ecology that can enrich our perspective on IR theory; ecologists would do well to familiarise themselves with IR as well' (1999: xiii). Ecologists have been even less willing or able to incorporate the vital questions raised by the condition of international politics into their work. 'Much of the ecological literature produced in this century reads as though it were written with a political system roughly the size of Thoreau's Walden Pond in mind' (Laferrière and Stoett 1999: 2) they noted, suggesting that there is paradoxically 'relatively little discussion of international political dynamics within ecological thought, and, similarly, little recognition within IR theory of the complex process by which ecological degradation occurs and how it may affect global relations' (1999: 72). Dobson's (1990) classic book on *Green Political Thought* contains just one short passage on the challenges posed by international politics for ecological thought. Moreover, the 'international' dimension of ecopolitical thought is rarely discussed specifically,[4] and although much of the global *problematique* is arguably implicit within ecology, it remains necessary for ecologists to tackle theories of international relations directly.' Ecologists, it is noted:

> have generally declined the task of treating international politics seriously. It too often appears to be assumed that, once the proper ecological 'society' (the geographic and demographic and legal limits of which are rarely defined) is created, the global political system will simply sort itself out. Sovereignty, territoriality, interstate competition: all of these remnants of the Westphalian order will simply wither or fall into harmonious place

along with the other ordering principles (sustainability, non-hierarchical societies, decentralization, participatory democracy etc) of a new ecological society.

(Laferrière and Stoett 1999: 157)

Yet, they argue, 'the generalised attack on nature', 'compels an interdisciplinary rapprochement between IR theory and ecological thought' (Laferrière and Stoett 1999: 5). Though my concern here is not with what Green politics contributes to IR theory per se, but to the understanding and practice of global politics more broadly, they are right to suggest that: 'ecological thought is arguably well-positioned to help IR theory refine its own understanding of order, peace, security and power (its traditional explananda). In fact, ecological thought can play a role in shaping both the normative commitments of IR theory (which are rarely articulated explicitly) and its conceptions of political process' (Laferrière and Stoett 1999: 5).

IPE and Ecological Thought

IPE has shown itself more open to engaging with ecological concerns than the broader discipline of IR within which it sits (Stevis and Assetto 2001). Yet in spite of important progress being made in the study and practice of the international political economy of the environment (IPEE) (Clapp and Helleiner 2012), the challenge of revealing and acting upon the intimate relationship between the very foundations, constitution and governance of the international political economy and the 'nature' of contemporary patterns of global environmental degradation continues today (Newell and Lane 2018).

The agreement of the seventeen UN Sustainable Development Goals (SDGs) in 2015 embodied an attempt to articulate a new universal vision of development applicable to all states. And yet, as we will explore further in Chapter 7, despite the overall consensus underpinning the goals and indicators, the mere acceptance of the SDGs does not do away with the ways in which the prevailing organisation of the global economy may actively undermine the realisation of goals around the provision of food security, access to water and energy, and attempts to address climate change, still less the impact that the primacy that will be given to economic growth might have on the achievability of all other goals.

Similarly, the Rio+20 summit in 2012 generated heated debates about what forms of institutional and governance reform are required for sustainability, reigniting debates about the need for a World Environment Organisation, for example, but without regard to the systematic and structural drivers of environmental degradation and social exclusion. This is reflected in recent overviews of the academic literature on IPEE (Clapp and Helleiner 2012; Kütting 2014) which underscore how IPE analysis of the environment in the last two decades has remained largely focused on the treaties, institutions and regimes that are concerned explicitly with the intersection of the economy and the environment to the neglect of the environmental implications of larger structural trends in the global political economy. In this regard, there is a fundamental misdiagnosis both of the problem and where power lies. Saurin (1996) claims that the processes of global environmental change are subversive of both the theory and the practice of international relations, yet 'international political analysis continues to be conducted as if environmental goods and bads are produced, accumulated and therefore regulated by public organisations. They are not' (Saurin 2001: 80). As he put it earlier: 'bluntly stated, a focus on inter-state relations is largely irrelevant to the explanation of global environmental degradation, nor is the elaboration of inter-state relations likely to lead to any reversal of such degradation' (1996: 85).

There is, however, now a huge literature on the relationship between key elements of the global economy and their compatibility or otherwise with different notions of sustainable development (Clapp and Dauvergne 2011; Newell 2012; Christoff and Eckersley 2013). The intensification of specific patterns of production, exploitation and consumption have been shown to be intensifying environmental harm and the patterns of social inequality associated with them. In particular, the globalisation of the world food economy (Clapp 2011) and intensification of farming production and the timber trade (Lister and Dauvergne 2011), as well as the scramble for new fossil-fuel energy frontiers, emerge as critical contemporary drivers of resource exhaustion alongside the industrialisation of fishing that has decimated ocean stocks (De Sombre and Barkin 2011).

IPE should also be well placed in its dependency theory iterations at least, to be able to capture and explain the symmetries and interrelatedness of development and underdevelopment and how the former is premised on the latter (Gunder Frank 1966; Cardoso and Faletto 1979). Ideas about ecologically uneven exchange (Roberts and Parks 2008; Hornborg 1998) represent important progress in this regard as noted below, as do more historical accounts of the accumulation of ecological debts through (colonial and postcolonial) extractivism by means of the circulation of resource economies in favour of the global North (Patel and Moore 2018). Dependency approaches, however, remain committed to a modernist and materialist ethic of economic development and prosperity (Laferrière and Stoett 1999) and, as developed by Latin American thinkers, are principally concerned (understandably) with matching the material wealth of the global North but without reflection on the ecological viability of such a world.

Given the increasing role of the private sector in environmental governance: in particular the embrace of market-based mechanisms, voluntary approaches and public–private partnerships (Newell 2008), looking at the role of corporations in global environmental politics (Falkner 2008; Levy and Newell 2005; Dauvergne

2018) opens up the possibility for introducing Green thinking about economic alternatives to business as usual. Both in terms of their influence financially and politically, as well as their ecological footprint, they dwarf the role of state environmental agencies that remain the point of reference for mainstream IPE theorising.

One manifestation of this power, which political economists have sought to explain, is the way in which capitalism seeks to create new opportunities for accumulation, even in the form of responses to the problems generated by its own production and consumption (Mansfield 2004; Sullivan 2013; Büscher and Fletcher 2015). Literatures on so-called neoliberal nature, including those from 'ecological political economy' (Gale and M'Gonigle 2000), explore the diverse ways in which both nature and its degradation are converted into accumulation strategies (Smith 2006). Given that environmental issues are produced by the same global political economy that provides the ideological, institutional and material context in which responses to the ecological crisis have to be forged, this may be unsurprising. Recognition of this fact takes us to the heart of the contradictions and opportunities that we observe in global attempts to manage environmental crises that are shaped by the social relations, institutional configurations and practices of power that we observe in other areas of the global political economy (Newell 2008). What is surprising, however, is that whereas the problematic nature of these power relations and dependencies form the basis of Green political thinking about the need to transform the state, economy and sustainability, as we will see in later chapters, such connections are not often explicit in mainstream accounts of IPE and global environmental politics.

This reiterates the necessity of incorporating the insights of ecology within IPE and IR (Helleiner 1996; Katz-Rosene and Paterson 2018) as part of a Green account of global politics. In part, this is about taking seriously the inseparability of the environment and economy, and is where ecological economics or Green economics might be well placed to make a contribution (Kütting 2014; Cato 2008, 2011), as discussed further in Chapter 4. Ecological economics departs from the neo-classically informed discipline of environmental economics (Barbier and Markandya 2012) by critiquing its lack of attention to limits to growth, the modes of valuation (of costs and benefits) and discounting of future costs and the values and interests that are downplayed by framing environmental problems in those terms (Costanza 1991; Söderbaum 2000). Ecological economics assumes that the environment and the economy are inseparable and that the environment provides key functions for economic systems (resources, sinks, amenities and life-support mechanisms for consumption) reflected in concerns with 'ecological debt' (Simms 2005) and 'ecological footprints' and the abuse and exploitation of 'free resources' by capitalist investors. Attempts to map ecological flows have immense value in highlighting issues of ecological debt, uneven development and responsibility (Costantza 1991) and the long 'shadows' cast by global patterns of consumption (Dauvergne 2008). Ironically, however, the very metrics of valuation developed have formed part of the technical arsenal of market liberals to price nature and, as such, have become the means through which the marketisation and commodification of nature have taken place (Gómez-Baggethun and Ruiz-Pérez 2011). Greens need to proceed with caution here around the ways in which in neo-liberalism calls to value nature more highly are interpreted and enacted.

Hence while ecological economics usefully challenges policy orthodoxy about growth and the valuation of natural resources, Green economics is more resistant to the idea of greening the economy through more appropriate pricing (Cato 2011). The social ecology of Murray Bookchin (1994), discussed further in the next chapter, broadens the analytical lens still further by seeing environmental degradation as a product of the degradation of humans, resulting from capitalist expansion and its associated regulation through hierarchical forms of social control (for example, patriarchy and racism), a strand of thinking that has been taken up by scholars of environmental justice (Bullard 2005; Agyeman et al. 2003; Sikor and Newell 2014). There is also an important difference, therefore, between thinking ecologically (Katz-Rosene and Paterson 2018) and the articulation of a Green IPE informed more explicitly by Green political thought alongside efforts to advance the notion of a Green economy not subject to the contradictions of 'green growth' proposals. Work within this tradition is clearly more normatively driven and explicit in its critique of globalisation (Speth 2003, 2008; Woodin and Lucas 2004; Trainer 1996), and of the viability and sustainability of dominant ideas about growth (Blewitt and Cunningham 2014), strongly contesting the ecological viability of 'green growth'. I discuss this further in Chapter 4.

Global Politics in the Anthropocene: Does This Change Everything?

Frustration with the ongoing neglect of questions of ecology by IR scholars and practitioners manifests itself in recent calls, introduced above, for a 'Planet politics' in IR, 'a dialogue about both the limits of IR, and of its possibilities for forming alliances and fostering inter-disciplinarity that can draw upon climate science, the environmental humanities, and progressive international law to respond to changes wrought by the Anthropocene and a changing climate' (Burke et al. 2016: 499).The starting point for this group of scholars is that:

Global ecological collapse brings new urgency to the claim that 'we are all in this together' – humans, animals, ecologies, biosphere. To survive, we must ask questions that are intimately connected to capitalism, modernity, and oppression. We must ensure that our diplomacy, our politics, and our institutions are open to those who will bear the brunt of ecological change . . .The planet has long been that space which bears the scars of human will: in transforming *the* world into *our* world, we damaged and transformed it to suit our purposes. It now demands a new kind of responsibility, binding environmental justice and social justice inextricably together.

(2016: 500)

They ask:

Can we match the planet with our politics? We are concerned that International Relations, as both a field of knowledge and a global system of institutions, is failing the planet. A state-centric world obsessed with bargaining, power and interests, which talks arrogantly of an atmosphere divided into 'carbon space' divided by national borders, and in which the state is the handmaiden of a capitalism which sees nature as mere material in wait of profit, is failing the reality of the planet . . . our fundamental image of the world must be revolutionised. Our existence is neither international nor global, but planetary. Our anthropocentric, state-centric, and capital-centric image of international relations and world politics is fundamentally wrong; it perpetuates the wrong reality, the wrong commitments and purposes, the wrong 'world-picture'. In its obsession with power, it fails to understand the true power of a 'social nature' that is transforming the living reality of the planet.

(2016: 504)

For many scholars, it is the Anthropocene condition – the new geological epoch transformed by the dominance of human forces in which we are said to be living – which produces new socio-natures which require a different sort of IR (Newell and Lane 2018). The nature, timing and significance of the Anthropocene are all contested and there is a need to proceed with caution and care amid some of the hubris and hyperbole in this debate. In the first instance, there are ongoing debates over its precise timing (Lewis and Maslin 2015; Steffen et al. 2007; Zalasiewicz 2015). But wherever we place the start date and for whichever reason, Burke et al. suggest (2016: 502) that: 'The Anthropocene represents a new kind of power – "social nature" – that is now turning on us. This power challenges our categories and methodologies. It demands we find accomplices in our discipline and beyond it. It demands a new global political project: to end human-caused extinctions, prevent dangerous climate change, save the oceans, support vulnerable multi-species populations, and restore social justice'. More fundamentally,

Both the discipline of International Relations, and international state practice, are underpinned by a silent Cartesian assumption that humanity and nature are radically separate: that the human is not really an animal, that social affairs go on independent of the biosphere, and that the environment exists to provide services for humanity. Rather, our movement into the Anthropocene forces an ontological shift: human activity and nature are so bound together that they are existentially indistinguishable, into a complex but singular 'social nature'.

(Burke et al. 2016: 510)

For others, most notably Jason Moore, the 'capitalocene' more accurately describes this condition. He argues that the notion of the Anthropocene, while capturing something of the changed relation between humanity and the global environment due to fossil-fuel use and technological change, actually 'creates more fog than light' (Moore 2014: 2). By attributing epochal change to the *Anthropos* – humanity in general, it becomes impossible to determine the motive force driving the shift to coal and steam and then later to oil and internal combustion during the 'great acceleration' (Malm and Hornborg 2014; Moore 2011a, 2011b). As Malm and Hornborg put it: 'transhistorical – particularly species wide – drivers cannot be invoked to explain a qualitatively novel order in history', and the relocation of environmental impacts from natural causes to human activities then falls back on generic and innate human traits, such as the ability to control fire (2014: 65). The capitalocene framing has, in turn, been critiqued by those concerned that it closes down the possibilities of change. Lewis and Maslin argue: 'epochs, as formal geological units of time, typically last for millions of years. So unless we think that capitalism will structure human societies for such a vast amount of time, any such name is a mistake. Saying capitalism is now so durable that we measure it on geological timescales closes possibilities of change rather than opening them up' (2018a: 60).

Others have invoked the phrase 'Eurocene' (Burke et al. 2016) or the 'Manthropocene' (Raworth 2014) to offer more socially, geographically and temporarily specific accounts than the generic 'Anthropocene' narrative. The Anthropocene implies that we have never been human, leading others to call for a post-human International Relations (Cudworth and Hobden 2011; Youatt 2014). This 'decentering of humankind' (Clark 2014: 25) requires that attempts to interrogate the politics and power driving the development of the new epoch recognise the inseparability of society and nature, global political economy and the environment. Thus, it has been claimed a broadly Earth systems or world ecological (Moore 2011a, 2011b) perspective needs to be brought to the analysis of environmental change in the Anthropocene and of global politics more broadly (Newell and Lane 2018).

As noted above, here my concern is not with the fate of IR as a discipline or its ability as such to address (or not) the ecological crisis we face. It is to address and explore the rather more pressing and important question of what Green politics has to offer an account of today's global politics and alternative envisionings of it. The debates above do, nevertheless, provide an entry point for such an intervention. Their insights form a useful basis for Green perspectives that develop a more socio-ecological account of the crises we face and the implication of key actors such as the state and capital in driving it, as well as alternatives for addressing it. In many ways then, this book picks up those embryonic strands of literature on ecology and ecological thought, Green Politics and both IR and IPE and seeks to pull them together and extend them to explore their potential and value as a source of critique, strategic engagement and normative vision in relation to key areas of contemporary global politics – namely security, economy, the state, global governance, development and environment.

What will be become clear in Chapter 2 is that Green politics is itself a product of strands of thought in feminism, anarchism, pacificism and, to a lesser extent, critical theory – all of which have, to different degrees, articulated their own theories of IR. In many ways, different traditions of Green politics are informed by strands of pacifism and idealism, liberal ideas around ethics and global cosmopolitanism, strands of critical IPE (dependency thinking, world systems theory concerning the maldistribution of power and resources in the global economy), (eco)-Marxism on the unsustainability of capitalism, and socialism, anarchism and feminism on questions of hierarchy, patriarchy and social exploitation.

It also offers something distinct, not just derived from the fusion of those insights but through its emphasis on the totality of human relations within a broader ecology upon which we are dependent. This fuller and more holistic account of socio-nature (Castree and Braun 2001), post-human IR (Cudworth and Hobden 2011) or the web of life (Moore 2015), offers a fundamental point of departure from mainstream IR accounts, as well as more critical ones including Marxist, Feminist, Queer and post-structuralist literature where questions of ecology are also often neglected. As Burke et al. put it (2016: 513), for example: 'Feminism – the fourth great paradigm in IR – has long questioned the ontological and moral centrality of the state and the ethical commitments of international society's institutions, but remains largely (and understandably) anthropocentric and humanist.' Green inflections on these perspectives cannot afford to be so.

A Green global politics requires that we recentre ecology as constitutive of International Relations. There is no IR that is not ecological, nor lies outside of ecology. Interstate relations, war, trade are only possible because of specific socio-ecological materialities and flows that determine their viability. They take place upon and are inserted within broader canvases and cycles of world socio-ecological history (Moore 2011b). There is no IR, no interstate system, no war or trade or investment flow that is not built on, embodies and, at the same time, disrupts ecologies upon which it depends. Ecology sets the limits of the possible in a very profound and basic sense. IR scholars might recognise it as structural power in that it shapes the context within which others make decisions (Strange 1998). And yet the consequences and implications of this fact, for it is an a priori fact, for questions of welfare, security, let alone sustainability, are systematically ignored in theory and in practice. The key question for Greens in many ways is what sort of global politics do we want and, critically, do we have the global ecology able to support and sustain it without compromising the systems that support life for all living creatures on the planet?

Ecological systems make and remake global politics and vice versa. Ecological crises are certainly changing the conduct and possibilities of global politics, as I explore in the chapters on security, economy and development, for example, reconfiguring the trajectories of wealth creation and the arenas of conflict and competition. Indeed, order, security, peace and freedom can only be fully realised, in the long term at least, within thus far ignored ecological constraints. Green politics does not have a monopoly on ecologism of course, but it does, unlike many other approaches, hold it centrally in its philosophy, values and politics, and more so than other accounts of the world it offers a chance of addressing the collective blindness regarding our current predicament.

Why Now?

On a personal level, as someone involved in both Green and environmental politics for more than thirty years since the age of sixteen, my interest in combining personal, political and intellectual and research interests is part of an ongoing journey. It is one that is brought into sharp focus by a deep frustration with the obvious need for Green thinking and politics and its failure to meaningfully penetrate mainstream political discourse, or even large parts of academia. As a teenager studying geography, I remember clearly being taken to a talk by someone from Friends of the Earth (an organisation I ended up working for later in life) about the destruction of the rainforests. I was shocked and appalled at the degree of destruction being ravaged upon Amazonian rainforests and the role of governments and corporations in accelerating it and profiting from it. Yet, even to my young mind, near-term accounts of the cause of the problem that ranged from corrupt officials, problematic land tenure regimes to greedy ranchers and poorly enforced regulations fell short of a convincing and adequate account of how and why it was acceptable, legal and profitable to destroy the global commons in this way.

It was shortly afterwards that my attention turned to Green politics. Attending an event in 1989, I picked up a copy of the manifesto of the UK Green Party and was blown away with its clarity of vision and clear and profound critique of what was so wrong with our polluted, heavily armed, racist and patriarchal world, combined with bold and radical proposals to change it. I have been involved in the environmental movement and Green politics ever since. I remain, though, a critical friend, frustrated at times by infighting within the movement, however understandable given the diversity and plurality of visions, strategies and agendas which fall under its broad umbrella (see Chapter 2). And I have been equally frustrated by what feels at times like a naivety about power and a failure to embrace the importance of multiple theories of change, including near-term ones, over the preference for articulating distant utopias and a preference for purism and 'one-solution' politics over an acceptance of the inevitability of the messy politics of negotiation and trade-offs, albeit with their attendant dangers of co-optation.

At other times I have been outraged and shocked at the complicity of some sections of the environmental movement in processes of exclusion, dispossession and rights violations in the pursuit of narrow environmental aims and a corporatisation of the movement, enabling greenwashing and more sinister forms of silencing and censorship of protest. Furthermore, I have been frequently overwhelmed by the systematic bias, neglect and deliberate and non-deliberate blindness to Green ideas in mainstream politics, whether around unshakeable commitments to economic growth, the maintenance and expansion of nuclear weapons, the normalisation of destructive patterns of consumption or production and every day violence, or the ways in which environmental problems can so often be invoked to consolidate a politics of control and disenfranchisement, dispossession and engender forms of anti-democratic politics in which state and corporate elites tighten their stranglehold over social and political life. In spite of these, I have remained overwhelming still passionate and positive about the possibilities of other, more socially just, peaceful and sustainable worlds, glimpses of which can be captured in struggles and practices of alternative communities and spaces of dissent and resistance the world over.

On a practical level, I would argue there is an urgent need for a multilateralist, internationalist, inclusive and equitable and sustainable global politics. In this sense the desire to articulate more clearly, coherently and forthrightly a Green global politics is born of a disaffection with mainstream politics and the failure of 'grey' politics to address the multiple and interrelated economic, social and ecological crises the world currently faces.[5] There is a clear and ever more urgent need to combat and keep in check global militarism, neo-liberalism and patriarchy, and the social relations which bind and sustain them, reproducing a world of barbaric violence and inequality that is pushing us beyond planetary boundaries (Rockström et al. 2009) and the safe social operating space for humanity (Raworth 2017). Science, as well as lived experience, show us clearly the failures of industrialism as usual as a driver of the Anthropocene condition from the industrial revolution to the great acceleration (Steffen et al. 2015a) to today's globalised world.

On a strategic level, there is also a sense of opportunity for Green politics. Old fault lines of Left and Right are fraying and being reconfigured by potentially toxic mixes of nationalism, populism and xenophobia, and scepticism about the ability of current political and economic systems to offer adequate responses to society's problems is high. There is a receptiveness to ideas about transitions to sustainability with governments, cities and businesses adopting this language and an open questioning of the excesses of capitalism, with calls even among proponents of neo-liberalism to rein in its more reckless elements though 'capitalism with a human face', philanthro-capitalism (Bishop and Green 2009), social enterprise and corporate social and environmental responsibility.

There is also an increasingly acknowledged need to pursue alternative indicators and metrics of growth, as well as to reframe the very goals of development around prosperity, well-being, *buen vivir* and the like, rather than growth per se (Jackson 2017). In some circles, the idea that growth is not an end in itself has gained purchase. This includes attempts within the UN by agencies such as the United Nations Environment Programme (UNEP) to start a conversation about re-orienting the financial system towards the goals and needs of sustainability (UNEP 2015). This movement has a longer history with the United Nations Development Programme (UNDP) and others producing human development reports and indices alongside the narrower economic ones of the World Bank to provide a fuller and more meaningful evaluation of societal well-being, albeit an inadequate one for Greens because of the frequent neglect of ecological considerations. The fact that the new development goals are titled the 'Sustainable Development Goals' is not a coincidence and reflects a growing acknowledgement that our future development will have to be sustainable if it is to have a future at all. Interestingly then, there has been a growing, perhaps even grudging, acceptance of many Green ideas without acknowledging them as Green. This would include prosperity without growth, community building and solidarity economies, resilience and (food, energy and water and ecological) security, strengthening local economies, devolution and projects of participatory democracy. In so far as emulation is the highest form of flattery, Greens should be delighted. And yet there is clearly such a long way still to go before Green ideas, many of which have been around for decades if not centuries in some cases, receive the attention and support they deserve.

Structure

The basis of the research and the analysis throughout the book includes knowledge and experience acquired over the last twenty-five years of researching global environmental politics and the political economy of the environment, as well as teaching on courses on environment and development, global governance and global political economy at a range of institutions and for an array of different audiences. It is also informed by working with, and for, an array of environmental NGOs and social movements over those years. In addition, the book draws on the literature on Green political theory and philosophy, the practice of Green Party politics and Green movements and discussions with key individuals involved in different types of Green politics.

Each chapter is structured in the same way to explore in turn Green critiques, alternatives and strategies with respect to key areas of global politics: security, economy, the state, global governance, development and environment. The decision to address the environment as an issue area last is a deliberate albeit surprising one. It makes the point that Green politics is about constructing a different world and not only protecting the environment and, moreover, that if we had a Green state and system of global governance, a Green economy, security and development, we wouldn't need a separate policy domain dedicated to protection of the environment as if this were somehow detached from all these other policy areas. Hence as well as providing Green perspectives on current global politics and their failings (A), and visions of what an alternative might look like (B), each chapter seeks to engage with the more challenging task of addressing strategies for getting from A to B. The next chapter provides an overview of different strands of Green thinking that will be drawn upon throughout the rest of the book in developing an account of global Green politics.

Notes

1   The phrase 'Think global, act local' has been attributed to Scots town planner and social activist Patrick Geddes, although the work of Barbara Ward and others popularised it.
2   Rhizomes are forms of vegetation that exist below the surface of the soil that spread horizontally. Kuehls (1996) uses them as an analogy to challenge conventional ideas about the nature of political sovereignty.
3   The exceptions Paterson (2009) and Eckersley (2010).
4   A rare exception in this regard is Laferièrre and Stoett (2006).
5   Greens often distinguish their agenda from that of 'grey' parties and politics that offers more of the same in terms of unsustainable development and economic growth at any cost (Porritt 1989; Icke 1990).

2

What Is Green Politics?

Conventionally, the history of Green politics is described as a product of a specific historical confluence of movements and events forged in the late 1960s and early 1970s with Europe at its epicentre (Pepper 1984; Spretnak and Capra 1984). Often in somewhat ahistorical and Eurocentric terms, these accounts describe increasing social reflexivity and awareness about the possibility of destroying life on earth through nuclear war or ecological degradation, and a growing recognition that prevailing modes of organising economic, social and political life were making that more likely, if not inevitable.

This conjuncture in many ways constituted a reaction to what has been referred to as the 'great acceleration' (Steffen et al. 2015a) and the tides of optimism brought about by post-war growth, the development of the welfare state, mass employment and mass consumerism under Fordism, and huge technological breakthroughs in relation to agriculture (the green revolution), space technology and the arms race, for example. It signalled growing unease about the darker side of these developments and the notions of progress they embodied (Beck 1999), underpinned by growing industrialism and militarism. This was the fertile soil in which critiques of the orientation of societies around goals of endless growth based on industrialism and wave after wave of technological advancement were able to take hold and find a voice in early Ecology and Green parties from the 1970s onwards.

Indeed, the rise of Green parties is attributed to the growing popularity of post-materialist values and concerns with the quality of life (Inglehart 1990) and close links to the new social movements of the 1960s and 1970s around peace and feminism. This was reflected in the 'new politics' grounded in ecology, concern for the developing world, unilateral disarmament and direct democracy in all areas of society (Poguntke 1989). Green parties have tended to thrive in countries with advanced welfare states, strong traditions of labour corporatism and regular participation of left-wing parties in government (Burchell 2002). The politicisation of

21

environmental problems and evidence of the damage and disruption they cause was undoubtedly also a driving factor in the rise of Green politics (Rüdig 1990). Evidence of environmental decline, combined with exogenous shocks manifested in acid rain, ozone depletion and growing concerns with climate change during the 1980s – the threat of which the Toronto conference in 1988 likened to nuclear war – as well as industrial disasters such as Bhopal and Chernobyl, certainly played their part in raising awareness of environmental issues and the politics of ecology (Brenton 1994).

Depending on how we define Green philosophy and politics, a much longer and more global history can be told. Key reference points for Green thinking include the teachings of Mahatma Gandhi, the writings of the Reverend Martin Luther King, the ecological knowledge of Native American and indigenous communities and the struggles of women's, human rights, peace and environmental movements the world over (Rocheleau et al. 1995; Carruthers 1996). Eco-feminists often pay homage to the Chipko movement in India (Shiva 1998) or the green belt movement in Kenya under Wangari Maathai. These origins are often referred to in relation to contemporary projects around the rights of nature, related to Pachamama in the Bolivian context and ideas about *buen vivir* in Ecuador and elsewhere (Gudynas 2015), where the rights of nature are enshrined in the constitution (Bell 2016).

In terms of historicising Green ideas, Richardson notes: 'Green political ideas are hardly new. Xenophon, among other ancient Greeks, is alleged to have set out the main principles of the Gaia hypothesis on which much Green thinking is based, over 2000 years before James Lovelock developed the modern, scientific version' (Richardson 1995: 4). Indeed, many indigenous and non-western cosmologies that date back centuries take many of the principles and ethics of Green politics as given regarding stewardship, intergenerational equity, living within means, respecting nature and defending the commons (McLuhan 1973; Yashar 2005; Carruthers 1996). The idea of intergenerational equity, for example, has roots in Islamic law and African customary law (Laferrière and Stoett 1999).

Green thinking in many ways forms part of broader and long-established critiques of modernity. The domination of non-human nature by states and their unbridled commitment to material growth has its roots, according to Laferrière and Stoett, in the 'momentous intellectual and political developments of the seventeenth century, where Newtonian science and the nation-state arose as twin pillars of modernity' (1999: 3). The emergence of technocentric thought is traced to the earlier development of rationalism and the scientific revolution of the sixteenth century onwards (Pepper 1986). These formed the basis of 'cornucopian' thinking and the belief in the right, and indeed destiny, of humans to conquer and control bountiful nature that has been the target of so much Green critique. Subsequent theory reflected this such that 'Utilitarian theories of the late eighteenth and early nineteenth centuries were logical consequences of the materialistic and mechanical "re-designing of the world"' (Laferrière and Stoett 1999: 3).

Schumacher (1974) argued that 'anti-environmental values' stemmed from the nineteenth century, grounded in ideas about evolution, competition, natural selection and survival of the fittest; Marxist ideas about the materialist base of history and what is called the 'treadmill of production' (Schnaiberg 1980); and ideas of relativism and scientism: the belief that valid knowledge is that which is ascertained through the natural sciences, the Cartesian–Newtonian paradigm.

Ecologism's roots can be traced to different strands of both romanticism and scientism. Romanticism is typically associated with the romantic movement of the eighteenth and nineteenth centuries that found expression in art, music and theatre, but which also articulated political expressions of anti-materialism that formed part of broader critiques of rationalism and the Enlightenment. Yet as Pepper (1986: 76) reminds us: 'it can be seen clearly as a reaction against material changes in society – changes in the mode of production which can be regarded as part of the emergence and expansion of industrial capitalism in the 18th century' and the degradation and despoliation that resulted. O'Riordan (1981) also traces the roots of modern environmentalism to the 'philosophies of the romantic transcendentalists of mid-nineteenth century America' that expressed a non-utilitarian view of nature's value that should be respected for its own sake and became manifest in the wilderness movement that emerged in the late nineteenth and early twentieth centuries (Newman 2011). The 'chain of being' cosmology, that ran counter to rationalism with its humility before nature, dates back to the Greeks (207 AD), even if its broader diffusion did not occur until the eighteenth century (Pepper 1986). Animism, likewise, attributed souls to animals and plants through a semi-religious ecological spirituality. Indeed, the American transcendentalists referred to trees as God's temples (Pepper 1986: 72). These currents form part of the pre-history of wilderness and conservation movements that led, for example, to the creation of national parks in the United States and the formation of groups such as the Sierra Club and the Audubon Society or the National Trust and Council for the Protection of Rural England in the United Kingdom.

Nevertheless, the rise and entrenchment of industrial society in the late eighteenth and nineteenth centuries supported and legitimated anthropocentric rather than eco-centric thinking based on the conquest of nature for human ends. Conservationist and preservationist groups can be traced back to the mid-nineteenth century, but environmentalism developed unevenly, peaking in western contexts at least, in the wake of periods of sustained economic, expansion as a reaction against the prevalence of materialistic values including the 1890s, 1920s, 1950s and early 1970s (Pepper 1986). Often, however, this was only to be subsequently displaced by more prevalent concerns with growth, employment and security.

The waves of consumerism and mass production that followed in the 'great acceleration' (see above, Steffen et al. 2015a) left little space for questioning the merits of industrial society. Indeed, Green values are often described as 'post-industrial' – ones that take hold once a certain level of industrial development has been achieved (Bell 1973; Inglehart 1990), a stage in a society's evolution when the economy shifts from producing and providing goods and products to one that mainly offers services. Notably, *The Ecologist*, upon launching itself in 1970, described itself as the '*Journal of the Post-Industrial Age*' (Pepper 1986). The experiences of pre-modern, contemporary indigenous and other struggles undermine the notion, however, that ecological values have to be presaged by advanced industrial development.

In many ways then, as O'Riordan (1981) argues, environmentalism represents a search for a mediation between several contradictory elements. The more spiritual dimensions of Green theory and practice exist in tension with the embrace of scientism by many in the Green movement. The work of Charles Darwin on the web of life, equilibrium and a systems view of nature (rather than elements of social Darwinism), on the one hand, and that of Thomas Malthus (1872) on the other, on the principle of population and what he called 'the fixed laws of nature' can be traced in a lot of Green philosophy and politics, for example. The scientific underpinnings of core ecological concepts around limits, tipping points and carrying capacity link questions of resource scarcity with population numbers. This finds expression in Hardin's tragedy of the commons (1968), concerns about the population explosion (Ehrlich 1975) as well as ideas central to Green economics (as we will see in Chapter 4) about limits to growth. For Hardin, the example he gave showed that open access led to overgrazing to the detriment of the common good. The implication being that private ownership or population restriction could avoid such a fate. The apparent need to respect 'natural laws' was further developed in his articulation of the 'lifeboat ethic', which is used as an argument against redistribution in a context of expanding population. He argued, for example that: 'Any nation that asserts the right to produce more babies must also assume the responsibility for taking care of them' (cited in Pepper 1986: 20). This led Ehrlich to form the 'Zero Population Growth Movement'. The acceptance of law and coercion to serve this goal was rightly denounced by other Greens as the 'New barbarism of the lifeboat ethic' (Commoner 1970). The determinism and reductionism of scientism and its uncritical embrace by some elements of the Green movement continues to provide cause for disquiet and disagreement over the diagnosis of the causes of the ecological crisis, and, therefore, where the appropriate solutions lie. In particular, it forms the basis of social ecology and eco-socialist thinking described further below that focus more on the maldistribution of resources in society and the social structures that sustain it.

In terms of the modern rise of Green politics, key turning points that are often highlighted include growing awareness of the impact of pollution, popularised in classic books such as Rachel Carson's *Silent Spring* (Carson 1965), which provided a damning indictment of the effects of pesticide use on the natural and human environment. Its concrete effect, according to Laferrière and Stoett (1999: 35), 'was to nudge governments and the (American) public away from classic, no-holds barred approaches to economic growth, and to lay a small stone in the path towards the reform environmentalism of the 1970s'.

Subsequent critiques of growth by Mishan (1967) in *The Costs of Economic Growth* and then the Club of Rome *Limits to Growth* report in 1972 (Meadows et al. 1972) laid the basis of a Green critique of industrialism as usual that went beyond environmentalism as concern for the environment devoid of a broader political project (see Chapter 4). Business-as-usual patterns of resource use, it predicted, would result in 'overshoot and collapse'. Hence a stabilised world model was needed that would be achieved through population and pollution control and an abandonment of economic growth as an overall goal. It advocated zero population growth and zero economic growth. We discuss the report in more detail in Chapter 4, including the critiques of it. What is important here, however, is the status it assumed for Greens as the bedrock and scientific rationale for their calls for a steady-state economy (Daly 1977).

The year 1972 was also when *The Ecologist* published their *Blueprint for Survival* (Goldsmith et al. 1972), another cornerstone of contemporary Green political thinking that combined key elements of Green philosophy to set out a programme for future (British) society to model, based on economic self-sufficiency, soft energy paths (Lovins 1977), appropriate technology (Schumacher 1974), decentralisation and population stabilisation. *The Ecologist* editor Edward Goldsmith went on to form a group called 'People' which was renamed The Ecology Party in 1975 and then the Green Party in 1985 (Richardson 1995). *Small Is Beautiful* meanwhile, by E. F. Schumacher (1974), outlined the basis of an alternative Green economics where people and planet, rather than profit, were placed centrally. This implied a shift of values that could re-organise the economy in more ecological and human-centred terms, such as 'Buddhist economics', improving fulfilment and quality of life as discussed further in Chapter 4.

Notwithstanding the role of the ancient Greeks noted above, a modern scientific basis for ecologism was to emerge from the publication of James Lovelock's book on *Gaia: A New Look at Life on Earth*, published in 1979. Lovelock advanced the idea that all life forms are interconnected and interdependent in a self-sustaining biosphere, that living organisms behave as a single entity – hence the reference to the Greek term *Gaia* meaning 'mother' (earth). In essence, humankind is part of nature, not above it. Harm to the latter is harm to ourselves as human beings are part of an intricate global ecosystem. Leading scientific journals such as *Science* and *Nature* refused to publish Lovelock's work at the time because of the controversial and unconventional approach it adopted. Perhaps unsurprisingly since, as Richardson puts it, Lovelock, in one foul swoop 'seemed to be challenging not only the orthodoxies of reductionism, Baconian science, Cartesian reason and religious dogmatism, but the political philosophies which rested on those orthodoxies' (Richardson 1995: 8).

The term *ecology*, often taken literally to mean the study or 'the science of the house', goes back much further, however. It is dated to the late nineteenth century and Ernst Haeckl is credited with first coining the term, which he defined as 'the total science of the connections of the organism to the surrounding external world' (Newman 2011: 150; Begon et al. 2006; Odum et al. 2004). This was the time the scientific community increasingly came to understand individual environments (water, soils, climate, forests) as part of a broader ecosystem, spawning both technical interest in how to manage and conserve ecosystems, as well as philosophical interests in how to appropriately value them.[1] Hence the scientific study of relationships among biological and non-biological processes making up ecosystems and the biosphere is closely related to the philosophy of ecology with its emphasis on the interconnectedness of human societies *within* the natural world. Conservationist and preservationist approaches developed, emphasising either utilitarian approaches to protecting nature in the interests of humans, or approaches based on 'intrinsic value' that sought to protect wilderness for its own sake. Hence more eco-centric, deep ecological and techno-centric, managerialist traditions co-exist under the broad umbrella of ecologism (O'Riordan 1981). How best to manage the commons and on whose behalf and according to which values has divided the environmental movement and global policymakers ever since.

Ecological thinking then can be understood very narrowly, and also quite broadly, even in its political manifestations. Like other political ideologies and perspectives, it has things to say across the whole gamut of issues facing society, and although there are elements of feminism, pacifism and anarchism in Green political theory, it has its own identity and intellectual heritage and, as I argue in this book, a coherent set of critiques, visions and strategies for achieving them in global politics.

In their early days, many Green parties were made up of diverse groups of ecologists and peace activists, anti-nuclear campaigners, feminists and development activists and elements of both radical Left groups and more conservative conservationists. This is captured in early formulations of the essence of Green politics such as the following:

It is an ecological, holistic and feminist movement that transcends the old political framework of left versus right. It emphasises the interconnectedness and interdependence of all phenomena, as well as the embeddedness of individuals and societies in the cyclical processes of nature. It addresses the unjust and destructive dynamics of patriarchy. It calls for social responsibility and a sound, sustainable economic system, one that is ecological, decentralized, equitable and comprised of flexible institutions, one in which people have significant control over their lives. In advocating a cooperative world order, Green politics rejects all forms of exploitation – of nature, individuals, social groups and countries. It is committed to non-violence at all levels. It encourages a rich cultural life that respects the pluralism within a society, and it honours the inner growth that leads to wisdom and compassion.

(Spretnak and Capra 1984: xvi–xvii)

In terms of the epistemological and philosophical foundations of Green politics, there are both elements of universalism (within deep ecology for example) and particularism (within Green anarchism for example), structuralism (within eco-socialism or Marxism for example) and determinism (in strands of eco-feminist thought for example). As Laferrière and Stoett (1999: 147) note:

ecological thought oscillates between foundationalist and antifoundationalist arguments, i.e. between logics of universality and particularity. In other words, just as it views suspiciously academic and political attempts at grounding a 'truth' in presumably universal 'foundations' (i.e. unshakeable assumptions about human nature or culture), it cannot accept a form of relativism that would offer no tangible guidelines in constructing a better world.

As they further suggest, the preference for 'linearity' and 'ahistoricity' in inter-national relations that are necessary in order for the 'efficient and manageable production of verifiable hypotheses about the world' come at the expense of dialectical and historical depth, whereas ecological holism compels a 'disregard' of social-scientific elegance (Laferrière and Stoett 1999: 159). As suggested in the Introduction in Chapter 1, a reading of ecology as foundational certainly exposes the limits of ideas of security, order and economy, neglecting, or worse still, denying the effect of any such foundation. Many Greens refer to three basic principles of Green politics: ecology, grassroots democracy and non-violence as those which are foundational (Spretnak and Capra 1984). In terms of its universal-ism Dobson notes: 'Ecologism thus has the potential to argue more easily than most ideologies that it is, literally, in everyone's interests to follow its prescrip-tions' (2007: 17). One of the key challenges lies in the fact that while this may be true in the long term, it is less clear that it is the case in the short term, particularly for elite and incumbent interests that profit from environmental destruction. The fact that, in the long term we are all dead (as Keynes once famously said) does not necessarily help mobilise near-term action.

From Environmentalism to Ecologism

In separating out the politics of the environment and environmental policy from Green politics, it is useful to start (though not end) with Dobson's distinction between environmentalism and ecologism. He notes: 'The big difference between single-issue environmental campaigns and Green politics proper is that the former treats symptoms while the latter deals with causes. Single-issue environmentalists rarely make a wide-ranging political analysis of the reasons for the problems they confront, while Green political activists most certainly do' (1991: 4).

This distinction finds echoes in the work of Murray Bookchin, explored further below where he suggests:

> From an outlook and movement that at least held the promise of challenging hierarchy and domination have emerged a form of *environmentalism* that is based more on tinkering with existing institutions, social relations, technologies and values than on changing them. I will use the word 'environmentalism' to contrast it with ecology, specifically with social ecology ... environmentalism reflects an 'instrumentalist' or technical sensibility in which nature is viewed merely as a passive habitat ... that must be made 'serviceable' for human use ... Environmentalism, in fact, is merely environmental engineering. It does not bring into question the underlying notions of the present society, notably that man must dominate nature.
>
> *(1980: 77)*

Many are critical of the robustness and utility of this binary distinction, where in reality there is significant overlap. As Barry puts it (1999: 4): 'such ideological accounts of green politics are unnecessarily restrictive and can become a hindrance to the future evolution of green politics'. There is certainly some exaggeration about the clarity of the distinction Dobson draws between environmentalism and ecologism. Environmentalists working on a suite of inter-related global threats such as climate change, biodiversity loss and ocean depletion do see common drivers and share critiques of the global economy and how and for whom it is organised. Having worked closely with many of them and been privy to strategy documents about challenges and future directions for advocacy, I am aware that many are full of such analysis. Yet the primary purpose of such organisations is not to explicitly articulate an alternative world view or global political critique of the current system, even if their near-term strategies are both informed by such a critique and seek to contribute to embedding alternative world views. Indeed, if many groups were to put such systemic critiques front and centre in their advocacy, they would run the risk of alienating some of their members and thereby reduce their effectiveness and ability to speak on behalf of a 'mass' of supporters and to secure near-term victories with state and corporate actors that currently hold power. They are in the business of protest politics rather than serving up macro theories, systemic critiques and articulating utopias, but they are often acutely aware of these and have sympathy with them and often see themselves contributing to them, albeit indirectly.

Nevertheless, it remains the case that for Greens, issues such as biodiversity loss, toxic pollution, climate change, ocean depletion and soil degradation are symptoms of structural and systemic problems. They constitute a failure of industrialism, whether organised along more socialist or capitalist lines (Porritt 1989). This is in opposition to Marxists, who insist that the 'root causes of the destructive character of capitalism are not to be found in growth, but in capitalist accumulation' (Vergara-Camus 2017: 1). The failure to value nature, respect limits and organise economies around 'need' rather than 'greed' has brought us to today's situation where we are surpassing planetary boundaries at an alarming rate. The 'planetary boundaries' model identifies nine major global ecosystem processes (climate change, ocean acidification, stratospheric ozone depletion, biogeochemical flows, freshwater, land system change, atmospheric aerosol loading and biosphere integrity/biodiversity) and thresholds 'within which humanity can exist safely' for each one (see Figure 8.1 in Chapter 8). A study in 2009 stated that three of these thresholds (climate change, ocean acidification and ozone) had been crossed (Rockström et al. 2009), while a 2015 study stated that the threshold for biosphere integrity had also already been crossed (Rockström et al. 2015).

For these reasons, all Greens take as given the unsustainability of the current system, even if they may disagree in their analysis of which social relations and ways of organising society have brought about this predicament and the specifics of which strategies should be adopted to construct a more sustainable society. The scale of the challenge Greens pose to conventional (global) politics should not be underestimated. Dobson (1990: 3) suggests that Green politics stems from 'the desire to restructure the whole of political, social and economic life'. He continues (1990: 13): 'ecologism argues that care for the environment presupposes radical changes in our relationship with it, and thus in our mode of social and political life'. As Porritt and Winner put it, Greens seek:

nothing less than a non-violent revolution to overthrow our whole polluting, plundering and materialistic industrial society and, in its place, to create a new economic and social order which will allow human beings to live in harmony with the planet. In those terms, the Green movement lays claim to be being the most radical and important political and cultural force since the birth of socialism.

(1988: 9)

Echoing calls for a *Planet Politics* discussed earlier, perhaps most radically as Dobson (1990: 9) states: 'Green politics explicitly seeks to decentre the human being, to question mechanistic science and its technological consequences, to refuse to believe that the world was made for human beings – and it does this because it has been led to wonder whether dominant post-industrialism's project of affluence is either desirable or sustainable.' In this regard, as Eckersley (1992: 10) suggests, Green politics introduces a dose of humility and compassion into our understanding of our place on earth and does so, in her view, by advancing ecocentric rather than anthropocentric world views.

It is, however, perhaps the proposition that human needs are not best met by continual economic growth that most clearly sets Green thinking apart from and in opposition to all other political ideologies. It is squarely opposed to one of the core givens of the modern age: that industrial growth is correlated with prosperity. As Porritt puts it: 'If you want one simple contrast between green and conventional politics it is our belief that quantitative demand must be reduced, not expanded' (1989: 13). Furthermore, from a Green point of view capitalism and communism are equally problematic because of their commitment to growth.

Both are dedicated to industrial growth, to the expansion of the means of production, to a materialist ethic as the best means of meeting peoples' needs, and to unimpeded technological development. Both rely on increasing centralisation and large-scale bureaucratic control and coordination. From a viewpoint of narrow scientific rationalism, both insist that the planet is there to be conquered, that big is self-evidently beautiful and that what cannot be measured is of no importance.

(1989: 44)

In this sense, as Dobson suggests, 'It makes no appreciable difference who owns the means of production if the production process itself is based on the assumption that its development need not be hindered by thoughts of limits to growth' (1990: 32). Greens refer to this as the ideology of industrialism – 'an adherence to the belief that human needs can only be met through the permanent expansion of the process of production and consumption' (Porritt quoted in Dobson 1990: 29). As the British Greens suggested in their 1989 European platform, 'Whether you call it capitalism, industrialism, socialism, liberalism or communism, every national economy in the world is based on the belief that more consumption is inevitably and incontrovertibly a Good Thing' (Green Party 1989).

Greens often propose an integrated approach to multiple economic, political and ecological crises that they view as interrelated and necessarily global in nature, as we can see throughout this book. They view short-term economic and techno-logical fixes as unlikely to address a myriad of problems that manifest themselves as different facets of a single crisis. This crisis is produced by industrial society and an economy structured around the need to serve capital as an end in itself. It manifests itself in growing inequalities that are intrinsic to capitalism (Piketty 2014; Di Muzio 2015) and which find expression in extractivism, resource conflict and war; expanding encroachments into the commons through legal and illegal land and resource acquisition and its ensuing dispossession of communities; the global integration of export-led economies serving the needs of richer consumers over domestic needs and self-sufficiency imperatives; and the increasing financialisation of the economy to overcome physical and spatial limits to capital and crises of underconsumption that result in volatility, speculation and indebtedness.

Which Shade of Green?

Despite some of the core areas of consensus around which most Greens would converge, such as the critique of industrialism and the unquestioning pursuit of economic growth at all costs sketched above, combined with certain shared foundational principles around grassroots democracy, ecology and non-violence, as well as common traditions and philosophies, there is a wide spectrum of positions that sit under the broad umbrella of Green politics and many tensions and areas of disagreement among them. 'Green' covers a spectrum of sometimes competing perspectives over values, politics and strategy. This passage from Lafierrière and Stoett nicely captures some of the fault lines between different ecologies:

An ecologist reflecting on the control of women (ecofeminism) should well frown at the thought that all nature could be subsumed under an extended self (deep ecology), while a critic of capitalism who sees its destructive ecological impact (eco-socialism) could legitimately wonder whether a radical project should begin with such slippery language as 'inherent value' (deep ecology). Alternatively, a theorist who situates ecological degradation squarely within long-standing, hierarchical patterns of authority (ecoanarchism) may react against perspectives openly sympathetic to the Gaia hypothesis and its reactionary overtones (deep ecology, bioregionalism).

(1999: 51)

It is also the case, however, that what divides ecologists is sometimes exaggerated to the point that we fail to appreciate the common ground which exists around core premises and values, even if preferred strategies and the accent placed on critique diverge strongly. Around the object of critique (modern industrial society and its ecocidal tendencies) and the scale of response required (transformational and systemic) there is much accord. Nevertheless, these different strands of ecological thinking, or ecologism, will be differentiated and distinguished from one another as and when they are introduced in the book unless referring generally to ecologism as an ideology at the broadest level — one to which most ecologists can subscribe (Baxter 1999).

Here I provide a brief typology of different strands of Green political thinking (also see Dobson 1990, 2007; Barry 1994; O'Riordan 1981; Clapp and Dauvergne 2011; Eckersley 1992; Laferrière and Stoett 1999).

Eco-socialism

I start with *eco-socialism*, a normative project which seeks to 'revise and reformulate the democratic socialist case in the light of the ecological challenge' (Eckersley 1992: 119). Its point of departure from traditional socialist theory and practice is in seeking to move beyond and challenge historical legacies of bureaucratisation, centralisation and in some cases authoritarianism, to transcend the central fixation on the working class as the only viable agent of radical social change and the productivism and growthism of traditional socialism (Pepper 1995). In so doing, it seeks to critique and transcend the legacies of Soviet-style socialism (Sarkar 1999). It expresses preferences for democratic self-management and production for human need, accepting that there exist both social and ecological limits to growth (Williams n.d.), although often still making the valid argument that lasting change and acceptance of anything resembling a conserver (as opposed to a consumer) society will require the support of working classes and trade union movements (Obach 2004). Despite its reluctance to embrace other aspects of ecocentrism, these moves do, however, place eco-socialism 'squarely within the spectrum of Green or emancipatory political thought' (Eckersley 1992: 126).

Eco-socialism, in most renditions, implies a key role for the state and, therefore, a rejection of some of the anarchism inherent in other strands of Green thinking (Pepper 1993). Eco-socialists (Weston 1986; Pepper 1993) tend to be much more positive about the role of the state, once free from its primary function in capitalist society to reproduce the conditions for its own existence. An ecological society, they claim, will require planning that will derive neither from wilderness living, as proposed by deep ecologists, or spontaneous autonomous action from below as eco-anarchists might imagine. It will require an 'enabling state' to bring it into existence, enforce its rules and ensure its survival (Pepper 1993). Moreover, capital will not be placed in the service of emancipatory goals without state intervention in the economy to set and enforce constraints on resource use, an argument with which many Greens could concur (see Chapter 5). The state, in an eco-socialist model, would sever its structural ties to capital and 'no longer be fiscally parasitic on private capital accumulation to fund its social and ecological reforms' (Eckersley 1992: 136).

As Ryle states:

Most ecosocialists, myself included, doubtless prefer to imagine a decentralized federation of autonomous communities, producers' collectives and the like, cooperating on the basis of a freely entered mutual association. If one is honest, however, about the objectives which an ecologically enlightened society would set for itself, it is difficult to avoid concluding that the state, as the agent of the collective will, would have to take an active law-making and enforcing role in imposing a range of environmental and resource constraints. More problematically, an ecosocialist transformation, which I regard as necessary if we are to transcend the contradiction between ecological imperatives and market 'laws', implies the necessity of replacing the current, highly centralized institutions of capitalist finance and production, and here the state must play an active role also.

(1988: 60)

In practice, state-based measures to ensure an equitable transition towards a conserver society have been adopted by many Green parties in their manifestos in relation to basic income schemes, work sharing and the redistribution of resources between richer and poorer countries. Greens are often also supportive of stronger and more effective forms of global governance, including of course for the environment (as we will see in Chapter 6) that imply a key role for the state. As Eckersley explains:

Without concerted eco-diplomacy resulting in a comprehensive array of treaties providing for macro-ecological controls and standards at the international level, Green economists will remain hard pressed to convince an effective majority of voters within their own nation that they must become ecological saints while individuals and corporations in other countries continue to engage in ecologically irresponsible practices.

(1992: 144)

Global governance can also check and provide safeguards against the excesses of local political elites in their abuse of the global commons as well as oversee the forms of global, as well as interregional, redistribution of resources that many Greens demand.

Many Green thinkers (Barry 1999; Gorz 1983; Eckerlsey 2004) foresee a central role for the state in managing a postindustrial conserver society. The emphasis is less on nationalising the means of production and more on their socialisation. For Greens and eco-socialists alike, there is a tension to be managed between the acknowledged need for planning and consensus building across society and the simultaneous desire for devolution and strengthened forms of participatory democracy. Likewise economically, undoing privatisation and breaking up monopolies as a precursor to community ownership would require significant state intervention. What is assumed perhaps, rather than explicitly articulated, is a Marxist understanding about the gradual withering away of the state as its core functions become less necessary in a socialist society.

We engage with this debate about the tension between centralisation and decentralisation more fully in Chapter 5 where ideas about multi-level governance and the notion that state power and authority might need to be expanded in some areas and retracted in others in the realisation of Green political visions. What is important to note here is that this belief in the state as a progressive agent of change sets eco-socialists apart from more decentralist, anarchist and libertarian strains of ecological thought discussed below.

The preface 'eco' distinguishes eco-socialists from other socialists who remain firmly committed to the project of economic growth, even if they want control of the means of production to rest in public and state hands to help ensure the redistribution of wealth towards the working class. For eco-socialists, there is something peculiar and unique to capitalism in terms of its propensity or structural requirement to devastate the Earth's natural resources (Baer 2018). Kovel, for example, calls capitalism 'the enemy of nature' (Kovel 2002). For Weston (1986) too, it is the accumulation of wealth and its concentration in the hands of a few that is the cause both of poverty and environmental degradation. Peace with nature, under this rendition, necessarily requires the end of capitalism. This stands in contrast to some Greens who foresee a role for a market economy and a private sector, albeit one operating on a different scale, subject to different rules-based frameworks and pursuant of very different ends to contemporary capitalist market-based society. As Daly and Cobb argue in their book *For the Common Good*:

> If one favours independence, participation, decentralized decision-making and small or human-scale enterprises, then one has to accept the category of profit as a legitimate and necessary source of income...If one dislikes centralised bureaucratic decision-making then one must accept the market and the profit motive, if not as a positive good then as a lesser of two evils...We have no hesitation in opting for the market as the basic institution of resource allocation.
>
> *(1989: 48–9)*

The aim for these Greens is to ecologise and democratise the institutions of the market economy: to retain and discipline rather than replace the price mechanism and private profit (Eckersley 1992). This would be done through support to local businesses, cooperatives and micro-finance institutions, for example, and to re-purpose them for ecological ends through taxation or other market-based incentives. As we will see further in Chapter 4, many Greens, in echoes of Polanyi, are keen to re-embed the market in frameworks of social control. Initiatives such as Local Exchange Trading Schemes (LETS) have been described in precisely those terms (Glover 1999). Hence private ownership and control of land, for example, would be placed not in the hands of the state but replaced by forms of community stewardship and trusteeship as part of processes of recommoning. This openness to a role for the market economy leads some on the Left to dismiss Greens as 'little capitalists' obsessed with the ecological impacts of production while failing to address questions of ownership and the social relations that keep such destructive modes of production in place (Pepper 1986).

There is an unhelpful struggle at times between ecologists and socialists around 'what comes first?': ecology or society – where both are intertwined, inseparable and dependent for their existence upon one another – or around which is *the* more important contradiction: the internal one between capital and labour, or the external one (often referred to as the second contradiction of capitalism) between capital and nature (O'Connor 1994). Pepper states, for example: 'we should proceed to ecology from social justice and not the other way around' (1993: 3). These divisions between 'Reds' and 'Greens' are apparent in real world politics, most notably and spectacularly in the experience of the German Greens (Frankland and

Schoonmaker 1992). But they surface in the contemporary context around competing understandings of Green transformations. For example, in discussing the UK Labour Party's plan for a low carbon economy as part of its Green transformation strategy, I asked of the strategy:

Can it go beyond a statist and productivist paradigm in which whatever the question, state-led growth is the answer? Or, more far-reaching still, could the embrace of the need for Green Transformations extend to questioning its unflinching commitment to economic growth at all costs and engage with ideas which place well-being and prosperity as the goals to be achieved which might open the way to seeing radical reductions in production and consumption of energy as possible and desirable, as well as necessary, to prolong life on a finite planet.

(Newell 2018)

Many Green parties have a Left faction within them, nevertheless, and there is scope to build on common ground between ecologists and socialists in so far as the former are more attentive to issues of distribution (of wealth and power) within society, equality among people (as well as other species) and questions of social justice. And the latter more cognisant and accepting of the need not just to change ownership structures and internal relations between classes but address the excesses and unsustainability of industrialism as usual, whether socialist or capitalist. Those exploring this potential include Weston (1986), Ryle (1988), Pepper (1993), Wall (2017) and Baer (2018). Ryle, for example, argues (1988: 6): 'The mere invocation of the word "ecology", crucial as it is, does not in itself determine in a positive sense the future development of social and economic reality … Ecological limits may limit political choices but they do not determine them.' Not organised along socialist lines or according to principles of social justice, all sorts of authoritarian, anarchic or apocalyptic and dystopian undemocratic post-capitalist futures remain possible. Hence, 'We should not assume that "ecology" can satisfactorily define the new politics we are trying to develop' (1988: 8). This conversation raises important questions for Greens about which forms of social relations might be ecologically viable and, consequently, takes us back to the questions social ecology seeks to address around justice, hierarchy and autonomy to which we now turn.

Social Ecology

Social ecology shares with eco-socialism the premise that the ecological crisis has its origins in society. Whereas for eco-socialists capitalist society is the focus of critique, for social ecologists, there is a range of social hierarchies (such as race, class and gender) that conspire to produce the current crisis. Social ecology is most closely associated with the work of Murray Bookchin who suggests that 'Ecology, in my view, has always meant social ecology' (Bookchin 1980: 76). It seeks to relate the ecological crisis explicitly to the organisation of the social order with its attendant hierarchies and patterns of exploitation. As long as hierarchy in human society persists, 'so the project of dominating nature will continue' he argued. He claimed that 'as long as hierarchy persists, as long as domination organizes humanity around a system of elites, the project of dominating nature will continue and inevitably lead our planet to ecological extinction' (1980: 76). To address this means 'changing the basic structure of our anti-ecological society'.

To my thinking, social ecology has to begin its quest for freedom not only in the factory but also in the family, not only in the economy but also in the psyche, not only in the material conditions of life but in the spiritual ones.

(1980: 76)

He continues:

solar energy, wind power, organic agriculture, holistic health and 'voluntary simplicity' will alter very little in our grotesque imbalance with nature if they leave the patriarchal family, the multinational corporation, the bureaucratic and centralized political structure, the property system, and the prevailing technocratic rationality untouched.

(1980: 78)

In many ways, social ecology developed by way of a response to and critique of deep ecology by placing questions of domination and exploitation at the centre of analysis. Much of it is defined as a rejection of deep ecology and totalising claims about the culpability of the mass of humanity for the ecological crisis. Bookchin opens his (1994) book *Which Way for the Ecology Movement?* with the story that provided the motivation for his intervention – a conversation with a biologist who argued strongly that humans were the problem – without any reflection on *which* humans were most responsible for the crisis. For Bookchin, an analysis of the ecological crisis devoid of an understanding of the social structures and patterns of domination along gender, racial, spatial and other lines results in either naive romanticism about a return to nature, or authoritarian responses aimed at control-ling generic human populations. These critiques relate to the discussion above about whether the Anthropocene condition should be more appropriately termed the 'capitalocene' or 'manocene' to give a (slightly) more precise sense of agency, responsibility and causality. Importantly, however, for social ecologists, 'while capitalism represents the pinnacle of control and exploitation, it remains one instance of a series of hierarchical patterns that have characterised human history' (Laferièrre and Stoett 1999: 64). Bookchin's work, in particular, is the inspiration for Saurin (1996) and others drawing on social ecology to emphasise the roots of ecological crises in multiple forms of hierarchy and exclusion in society. In framing the analysis beyond class and capitalism alone and instead around exclusionary hierarchies, social ecologists open up space for common ground with eco-feminists and eco-anarchists as discussed below. The focus in social ecology, unlike eco-socialism, is on a range of social hierarchies that, though related to capitalism, are not reducible to it. Bookchin suggests:

Neither sexism, ageism, ethnic oppression, the 'energy crisis', corporate power, conventional medicine, bureaucratic manipulation, conscription, militarism, urban devastation or political centralism can be separated from the ecological issue. All these issues turn around hierarchy and domination, the root conceptions of a radical social ecology.

(1980: 82)

Like social ecologists, 'Social Greens' for Clapp and Dauvergne (2011: 12) are defined by their view that social and environmental problems are inseparable. They draw on critical and radical traditions of social and ecological thought (often including Marxism, feminism and environmental justice scholarship) to sustain their critiques of industrialism and capitalism and as a basis for advocating for alternatives. They are also critical of bio-environmentalist and deep Green approaches offering generic critiques of anthropocentrism without taking into account questions of class, race and gender that strongly determine both degrees of culpability for environmental destruction, as well as exposure to its worst effects (Newell 2005).

Normatively, social ecologists call for municipalism. As Bookchin wrote: 'the living cell which forms the basic unit of political life is the municipality from which everything else must emerge: confederation, interdependence, citizenship and freedom' (1987: 282). 'Libertarian municipalism' would be achieved through 'a confederal society based on the coordination of municipalities in a bottom-up system of administration as distinguished from the top-down rule of the nation-state' (Bookchin 1992: 94–5). Here we return to the discussion introduced above about the role of the central state, at least on a temporary basis, in facilitating, enabling and protecting such spaces of democratic and economic experimentation.

Eco-Anarchism

As we will see in the discussion of the state in Chapter 5, Green critiques are heavily influenced by anarchist thinking and the work of people such as Peter Kropotkin whose ideas about 'mutual aid' were based on the recognition that 'life is not a survival of the fittest, but a cooperative cycle of biotic enrichment – survival of the most ingenious in a fully interdependent setting' (Laferrière and Stoett 1999: 65). Eco-anarchism affords a critique both of industrialism and its extractivism and the use of state violence to enable this and punish dissent, as well as presenting a vision of direct democracy in all areas of life through mutualism and cooperative self-governance and autonomy (Carter 1999).

Eco-anarchists have much in common with social ecologists in terms of their rejection of hierarchies and suspicion towards the state. Indeed, Robyn Eckersley (1992) locates social ecology and eco-communalism as two currents of eco-anarchist thought, albeit ones that attach different degrees of importance to social hierarchy and adopt different views of the types of eco-communities they would like to see. The former I have discussed above, although here I will draw out its connections to anarchism. Eco-communalism, meanwhile, is an expression of ecotopias organised along the lines of sustainable communities existing free of state laws and coercion and hence informed by anarchist thinking. Nisbet (cited in Eckersley 1992: 160–1) describes such communities as follows:

peaceful, not concerned with capture and forced adaptation, non-coercive, and seeking fulfilment through example or vision rather than through revolutionary force and centralization of power ... this – not the violent capture of government, army and police – is the most fundamental aim of the tradition of community in Western social thought I call ecological.

The notion of ecology invoked here relates to the use of the Greek word *oikos* meaning household and to the interdependencies of the household economy. This finds expression in ideas about 'cooperative autonomy' (Carter 1999) and 'mutual aid' that anarchists take from the work of Peter Kropotkin as noted above. Concretely, it is manifest in what Bahro calls 'liberated zones' (Bahro 1986) that would provide 'a supportive refuge from the destructiveness and alienation of industrialism' as well as the basis of a new 'biophile' culture (Eckersley 1992: 164). In such arrangements family and community are thought to be able to replace state functions involving welfare, security and protection and the polis would take the form of the self-regulating 'village republics' that Gandhi proposed or the *panchayat raj* (village assembly) model that operates in contemporary India as the lowest level of governance.

Such thinking is also apparent in proposals for bioregionalism (Sale 1985). These are areas that have common characteristics of soil, watersheds, climate, plants and animals and common human cultures such that human and non-human communities are integrated at the level of a particular ecosystem. Social ecologists, anarchists and deep ecologists have varying degrees of sympathy for bioregionalism. For anarchists, it holds out the promise of anarchist polities linked together by networking and information exchange rather than a formal state apparatus, while for deep ecologists it is seen as one way of realising on a regional level a vision of Leopold's 'land ethic', discussed further below.

Anarchists often view the state as an instrument of repression – a vehicle of class war for controlling working classes through police force, or as a centralising and faceless machine for extracting wealth and resources, dispossessing communities from the means of sustaining themselves autonomously. Anarchists hold both that anarchy is most compatible with an ecological perspective and that anarchism is inspired by ecology and the lack of hierarchies between species in ecological systems, described as characterised by 'unity in diversity, spontaneity and complementary relationships, free of all hierarchy and domination' (Bookchin 1982: 352); the non-hierarchical interdependence of living and non-living things (Eckersley 1992); and the 'natural' tendency towards intra-species cooperation (Kropotkin 1955). Bookchin, for example, argues that an anarchist society is a 'precondition for the practice of ecological principles' (1971: 71), while Woodcock (1983) suggests that anarchism depends on an acceptance of 'natural laws' such that anarchists see themselves as representatives of the 'true' evolution of human society. They oppose all forms of domination of the human and non-human world. For eco-anarchists, society is best transformed from below through popular struggles: direct action and direct democracy and local self-help and mutual aid initiatives aimed at building the political and economic autonomy of local communities (Carter 1999). In a more dystopian vein, echoes of this strand of thinking about the return to (local) community and rejection of all forms of conventional politics may be found in the work of writers from the Dark Mountain project whose devastating critique of the failings of modernity leads to preparations for ecological collapse and sowing the seeds of a new world in the damaged soil of a world in decline (Kingsnorth 2017).

Many eco-anarchist strategies imply the abolition of the state since it usurps the decision-making autonomy of local communities. As Bookchin suggests, 'we are committed to dissolving state power, authority and sovereignty into an inviolate form of personal empowerment' (1982: 340). This view explains their opposition to pursuing change through parliamentary means, grounded in a refusal to distinguish between ends and means. If the goal is the creation of an ecological society of inter-dependent but autonomous bioregions and communities, the means cannot involve further strengthening the state but rather the building of communes and alternative intentional communities.

Normatively, this chimes with the concerns of social ecologists for whom 'the logical proposition is to sever the chains of domination so as to establish truly democratic communities, communities of empowered individuals who will obviously have their own interests at stake, who will not be manipulated by authority, and who will rekindle their natural cooperative links which they were forced to shed hitherto' (Laferrière and Stoett 1999: 64). The communalism of Bahro (1986) and others speaks to this tradition. It highlights the need to disengage from conventional politics and what Bahro refers to as the 'march through the institutions' (1986: 87) because it envisages a deeper reorganisation of society than is possible via the state, one underpinned by the 'principle of a life beyond the currently valid norms and career path of civilisation' (1986: 87). The commune, he suggests, is 'anthropologically favourable' to other forms of human arrangement and constitutes 'the social form which most readily permits the control of social power' (1986: 87). This presages a line of thinking common to many strands of Green political thought about decentralisation of power as a means to control and check its concentration. Likewise, the economic function of the commune displaces economic efficiency in favour of ecological imperatives of reducing resource use and building social cohesion. Importantly, drawing on eco-feminist ideas sketched below, it assumes 'the feminine element' would permeate the regulation of community affairs as social bonds are strengthened through mutual cooperation, face to face interaction with community decision-makers and the emergence of a solidarity economy (Satgar 2014).

Party politics and efforts to secure power and achieve change through the state are, therefore, anathema to eco-anarchists. Expressing his fear that electoral gain becomes an end in itself, Bahro said that the 'party is a counter-productive tool' (1986: 210), and in the case of the German Greens he was writing about: 'The Greens have identified themselves – critically – with the industrial system and its political administration' (1986: 210). In terms of strategy, the preference is for direct action (Abbey 1990; Foreman and Haywood 1989), ecological resistance and the formation of alternative intentional communities (Seel 1997). The *Green Anarchist* magazine, established in 1984 in the United Kingdom, gives a flavour of the fusions of libertarian, socialist and ecological thinking that inform a Green anarchist perspective.

The nature of engagements among and between communes, and between communes and what remains of the state, is often left underspecified. Yet anarchists and social ecologists such as Bookchin are critical of ecologists who do embrace a role for the state, suggesting they promise the impossible by seeking to combine central planning without bureaucracy with forms of worker self-management and support for community self-help initiatives. But communes would need to reclaim and redirect resources currently amassed by the state and redirect them towards networks of communes if they are to fulfil their functions and maintain their autonomy. The means by which this would happen, or how and by whom and on what basis such negotiations would be undertaken, remains to be strategised. For Eckersley, ecological emancipation and the continued existence of the state are not incompatible. Indeed, she suggests 'the urgency of the ecological crisis is such that we cannot afford not to "march through" and reform' (Eckersley 1992: 154) existing institutions of democracy and mobilise the resources of the state towards a project of ecological transformation. She continues:

In view of the present rate of global ecological degradation, many threatened species habitats, species and tribal communities are unlikely to survive to see whether mutual aid and ecological restoration will indeed ensue from the ecoanarchists' strategy of withdrawing support from, or seeking to dismantle, hierarchical structures such as the nation state.

(Eckersley 1992: 172)

Similarly, eco-communalism, she suggests, 'needs to be supplemented by political engagement with state institutions if it is not to remain an ephemeral and/or marginal political phenomena' (Eckersley 1992: 163). She also questions the political naivety of some of the basic assumptions behind such proposals: 'Ceding complete political autonomy to the existing local communities that inhabit bior-egions will provide no guarantee that development will be ecologically benign or cooperative' (Eckersley 1992: 169). The point of departure has to be the fact that 'the maintenance of healthy and diverse ecosystems and bioregions is a matter of concern not only to the people who inhabit them' (Eckersley 1992: 178).

Ecofeminism

Though building on the same presumption of the interdependency and interrelat-edness of social and environmental processes and problems as eco-socialists, social ecologists and eco-anarchists, eco-feminists emphasise the commonality between forms of domination and oppression of women and those exercised over nature by patriarchal and capitalist systems of order and control (Collard and Contrucci 1988; Merchant 1990; Mellor 1992; Mies and Shiva 1993; Plumwood 1993; Rocheleau et al. 1995). Often based on claims of 'age-old' associations that have 'persisted throughout culture, language and history' (Merchant 1990: ixx), it is suggested that: 'The ancient identity of nature as a nurturing mother links women's history with the history of the environmental and ecological change'. The invoca-tion of Pachamama, Mother Earth, supports this view. The dualism between nature and culture, and the presumed superiority of the latter that underpins western civilisation's pillage of the former, features heavily in eco-feminist critiques of how, through reproduction and life-giving, nurture and child-rearing, women are represented as being closer to nature and, as a consequence, inferior.

Parallels are drawn between the brutalities visited upon the natural world and the everyday forms of violence and subjugation that women endure. A parallel is also drawn between the lack of value placed upon nature, despite it sustaining all economic life, and the lack of value placed on unpaid domestic and care work without which the formal economy would collapse. Hence, there is commonality in feminist and Green critiques of market society and its narrow and gendered view of what counts as productive and value-generating activity. Merchant suggests that

'Both the women's movement and the ecology movement are sharply critical of the costs of competition, aggression and domination arising from the market economy's modus operandi in nature and society' (1990: xxi).

While acknowledging the reality of the control many women have in large parts of the world over everyday household economies and choices regarding consumption that environmental campaigns aimed at promoting environmental consumerism have targeted, there are dangers associated with an essentialism that posits women as closer to nature that women then get burdened with the primary responsibility for environmental stewardship and subject to interventions by international agencies and donors, for example (Bretherton 1998). It is one thing to invoke the value of care and the ethics of nurturing, even claiming these as 'feminine principles' as some Greens do, as we saw above in discussions about the solidarity economy, but it is another to claim they are solely the preserve of women as some essentialising and binary accounts are prone to do.

Ecofeminism is, of course, a broad umbrella in and of itself and disguises differences between a multitude of feminisms subsumed beneath it. Differences around strategy and the politics of positionality and identity (around race and class, for example, in black feminism and socialist feminism) (Tong 1992) are important and provide a further basis for challenging the denial of difference found in many deep ecology accounts, for example. Feminist political ecology, for instance (Rocheleau et al. 1995) shows how in terms of the impacts of environmental degradation, patterns of causation as well as the politics of mobilisation, gender discrimination is intricately bound up with social cleavages of class, race and ethnicity as well as disability and sexuality. The emphasis on the intimate relationship between the organisation of society and the distribution of power within it and how environmental harms are experienced and distributed places some strands of ecofeminism very close to social ecology traditions described above. For, example, ecofeminists draw attention to three closely interrelated sets of structural power relations: North over South, men over women and humans over nature.

In many ways, ecofeminism seeks to articulate a pedagogy of the oppressed (Freire 1996), a view 'from below', by those oppressed by the dominant logic and organisation of capitalist patriarchy. Particular attention is paid to science, technology and governmentalities of control over women's bodies and natural systems which sustain and support life, such as soils, seeds and forests, but which are administered and enforced by states, corporations and military actors (Mies and Shiva 1993). Challenging these strategies of control and repressive social relations implies many of the proscriptions eco-anarchists advocate around cooperation, mutual aid and solidarity economies as well as recommoning and what Shiva calls resistance to the 'monocultures of the mind' (2011). At a philosophical level, ecofeminism shares much in common with foundational Green critiques of enlight-enment and cornucopian thinking with their ideology of the mastery of nature and its exploitation for human ends. This is the starting point for a lot of deep ecology thinking.

Deep Ecology

Deep ecology informs the spiritual and philosophical basis of key elements of Green political theory by seeking to embed humans in nature, rather than separate from it, guided by 'ecosophy'[2] as a guide to being, thinking and acting in the world (Naess 1972; Sale 1985; Leopold 1968). Grounded in environmental ethics, it calls for emotional, moral and eco-philosophical as well as intellectual responses to the ecological crisis, rejects narrower utilitarian approaches to valuing nature where 'privileges but not obligations' prevail and questions, as other Greens do, the damaging separation of humans from the land (Leopold 1968). It provides a strong critique of anthropocentrism and the arrogance of humanism (Ehrenfeld 1978) and emphasises heavily ecological concepts around biophysical limits, carrying cap-acity, scarcity, tipping points and the importance of sustainable population levels. Just as social ecology defines itself in opposition to deep ecology and environ-mentalism, deep ecology seeks to move beyond shallow ecology (Naess 1972) or environmentalism as it was juxtaposed with ecologism above (Dobson 1990). As well as pursuing a more general political project aimed at re-embedding humans in the natural world, deep ecologists share many concrete strategies in common with other Greens such as bioregionalism, decentralised communities, cultural as well as biological diversity and appropriate technology (Eckersley 1992). Sale (1985), in particular, argues for self-government through bioregions, linked and coordinated where necessary by a bioregion confederation. This would be critical to addressing critiques regarding the absence otherwise of mechanisms for redis-tributing resources between communities which are inevitably unevenly endowed with them.

The term 'deep ecology' was coined by the Norwegian philosopher Arne Naess. Points of departure include a 'rejection of the man-in-environment image in favour of the relational, total-field image' (Naess 1972: 95) in which intrinsic relations are key. This is combined with 'biospherical egalitarianism' – the equal right to live and blossom which, restricted to humans, 'is an anthropocentrism with detrimental effects upon the quality of humans themselves' (1972: 95). Deep ecologists also place emphasis on the crucial importance of diversity, symbiosis and complexity, as well as local autonomy and decentralization. 'Diversity' Naess wrote, 'enhances the potentialities of survival, the changes of new modes of life, the richness of forms'. While in words which resonate with Green critiques of the global economy, Naess suggests, 'The vulnerability of a form of life is roughly proportional to the weight of influences from afar, from outside the local region in which that form has obtained an ecological equilibrium' (1972: 95). This underpins calls for greater economic self-sufficiency explored in Chapter 4.

Deep ecologists Devall and Sessions suggest 'the well-being and flourishing of human and flourishing of human and nonhuman Life on Earth have value in themselves (synonyms: intrinsic value, inherent value). These values are independent of the usefulness of the nonhuman world for human purposes' (1985: 70). Leopold argues: 'The land ethic simply enlarges the boundaries of the community to include soils, waters, plants and animals, or collectively, the land' (1949: 101 [1968]). He further suggests, 'A land ethic of course cannot prevent the alteration, management and use of these "resources" but it does affirm their right to continued existence and, at least in spots, their continued existence in a natural state … In short, a land ethic changes the role of Homo sapiens from conqueror of the land-community to plain member and citizen of it' (1949: 202 [1968 version]). Deep ecologists advocate restricting human consumption and what 'we' [sic] take from nature to 'vital needs' (Matthews 1991). In this sense, no-one is given legal or moral dominion over the rest of nature. Indeed, as Warwick Fox argues (1990), nature is an extension of the human self.

Deep ecologists place a strong emphasis on ecological ethics (Curry 2011). As we saw above, Aldo Leopold articulates this in terms of a 'land ethic' which understands social instability, including violence and suffering, as rooted in human violence against the land. The call instead is to recognise 'a thing is right when it tends to preserve the integrity, stability and beauty of the biotic community. It is wrong when it tends otherwise' (1949 [1968]: 262). Calls for biospherical egalitarianism resonate strongly with concerns about animal rights and animal welfare which many Greens hold dear. These have been articulated further by a range of scholars, such as Tom Regan (1988) and mostly notably Peter Singer, whose classic book *Animal Liberation* (1995) provides perhaps the clearest statement in support of the rights of all living beings to be free from exploitation by other species.

This taps into deeper ideas within Green philosophy and politics about humility, holism and the hubris of the Anthropos. Ehrenfeld refers to this as the 'religion of humanism': 'a supreme faith in human reason – its ability to confront and solve the many problems humans face, its ability to rearrange both the world of Nature and the affairs of men and women so that human life will prosper' (1978: 5). This includes, of course, an all-pervasive faith in science and technology to overcome natural limits and even improve upon nature, one nurtured by late renaissance triumphs of science and technology but which Greens tend to be deeply sceptical about (see Chapter 4) including eco-feminists, as seen above.

There is a strong emphasis on 'ecological intuition', oneness with nature (Matthews 1991), 'a sense of place', protecting wilderness (a wilderness ethic), on the intrinsic value of all living beings and the embrace of 'eco-centrism' over 'anthropocentrism' (Eckersley 1992). Here 'value does inalienably inhere in the beings which possess it, and is not merely projected onto them from some external point of view' (Matthews 1991: 119). For Matthews (1991: 117) it is about 'intrinsic value that attaches to the cosmos as a whole on account of its status as a self'. She argues (1991: 118): 'If something is characterised as intrinsically valuable, then it is simply analytic that, other things being equal, it should not be destroyed or prevented from existing. It has a prima facie claim to our moral consideration.' This represents a direct challenge to utilitarian notions of value where the latter is determined by its perceived worth to humans. It challenges both utilitarian and mainstream economic thinking and underscores the importance of an emphasis on humility while opening space for post-human ways of thinking (Cudworth and Hobden 2011). In this sense, Greens' emphasis on holism often derives from a critique of 'Newtonian individualism' (Matthews 1991), emphasising that while humans are included in the web of life, they are not masters of it.

Deep ecologists refer to ecological history to show how previous 'civilisations' have fallen or survived according to their ability to live within natural limits (Ponting 2007; Chew 2001), replete with warnings about the 'tragedy of commons' (Hardin 1968) that befalls societies that over-use the commons. It is perhaps the furthest removed from direct engagement with world politics, and therefore, beyond describing some of the foundational ethical principles that it might articulate for ecologism or global ecological citizenship (observable for example in some aspects of Planet Politics (see Chapter 6), it features less in this book than many of the other strands of Green thinking summarised here.

In terms of strategy, deep ecologists, like other Green thinkers, embrace non-violence and economic simplicity as strategies against oppression in a lineage that flows back to Gandhi and others, as noted above. An emphasis on population control (Porritt 1989; Ehrlich 1975) and on bio-regionalism often also feature heavily in deep ecology or 'bio-environmentalist' thinking as Clapp and Dauvergne put it (2011). It shares with social ecology a critique of enclosure of the commons, private property regimes and the commodification of life – things which have served to break down mutual aid and interdependence among community members and replaced them with dependent consumer/supplier relations (The Ecologist 1993).

Deep ecology has faced critiques about the viability of bioregionalism when the boundaries of human communities rarely overlap with those of bioregions, thereby complicating the notion that a clear 'identity of interest' can be ascertained among communities in a bioregion. It is also heavily critiqued by social ecologists for its asocial and apolitical analysis (Bookchin 1994), uncritical 'rural romanticism' and embrace of neo-Malthusianism, as well as the alleged lack of humanity expressed by some deep ecologists who have articulated inhumane views regarding famines and the spread of HIV as inevitable, and even acceptable, features of the need to redress the imbalance in the relation between humans and the natural world. As Adams notes, (1995: 96) 'there is a new alliance between the neo-Malthusian science-based critique of population growth (with its apparently sound concepts such as "carrying capacity") that sees famines as somehow natural, and biocentric ideologies which identify people as organisms with no special rights, and that see intervention to sustain human lives at the expense of other organisms and inanimate objects as unacceptable'. It also forms the basis of Pepper's (1984) critique of the conservative, reactionary and potentially repressive forms of politics that fall under the banner of environmentalism. Nevertheless, leaving these critiques aside for a moment, the theoretical and practical contributions of deep ecology to today's Green politics are apparent in the activities of groups such as Earth First!, as well as movements such as Extinction Rebellion and in the ecological communities that seek to live by the principles expounded by Naess and others (Naess 1989; Sessions 1995; Drengson 1995).

(Global) Political Ecology

Besides these strands of Green political thought, other strands of theoretical thinking that are potentially useful to 'ecologising' global politics include political ecology in its various guises (Robbins 2004). This wide-ranging literature provides a set of resources for understanding the constitution of socio-natures, issues of access, justice and property as well as the ecological and social consequences of the conduct of International Relations by global elites (Newell and Bumpus 2012). This is especially true of political ecology's more globally articulated and theorised expressions, which go beyond the more traditional locally orientated focus of political ecology (Peet et al. 2011; Newell 2012; Sikor and Newell 2014).

Preceding many of these strands of work, there is also a body of work on 'global ecology' that developed as a response to the Rio summit in 1992 and its perceived failings. Writers in this tradition, such as Sachs (1993), Hildyard (1993) and Chatterjee and Finger (1994), whose work informs Green critiques of global governance developed in Chapter 6, were critical of the summit's attempt to safeguard industrialism and instead promote forms of global managerialism of common resources in the hands of state and corporate elites. *The Ecologist* (1993) book *Whose Common Future?*, a keystone text in Green politics, articulates many of these concerns (see Chapter 8). Global political ecology has also been used to understand patterns of global environmental inequality – or what Brand refers to as the 'imperial mode of living' (Brand and Wissen 2013) as well as patterns of ecologically uneven exchange (Roberts and Parks 2008) and the production of global environmental injustice (Sikor and Newell 2014).

Other political ecologies include post-structural (Escobar 1995; Stott and Sullivan 2000), Marxist (Blaikie 1985; Mann 2009), feminist (Rocheleau et al. 1995), urban (Heynen et al. 2006; Swyngedouw and Heynen 2003) and anarchist variants, each of which politicise and socialise our understandings of the social (gendered, class-based and racialised) and historical causes of environmental change and degradation and the politics of those whose knowledge (Forsyth 2003), institutions and power are brought to bear to 'address' them. They relate closely to, and draw from, the bodies of work outlined above in relation to eco-socialism and Marxism, ecofeminism and eco-anarchism, for example, broadly captured by the more general category 'social green' (Clapp and Dauvergne 2011).

More recently, work on the 'web of life' (Moore 2015) and the interrelated histories of ecology, society and economy (Patel and Moore 2018; Malm 2016) is useful for checking the neglect, oversight and ignorance of much thinking on global politics when it comes to understanding the role of ecology in shaping world history (Chew 2001). Mitchell (2014), for example, shows how the properties of fossil fuels such as coal, in terms of where they are located and the environments from which they have to be extracted and transported, were conducive to the exercise of working-class power to disrupt infrastructures through strikes and walk-outs in ways which led to welfare concessions.

Work on materialities, the new materialism and the agency of nature (Whatmore 2006; Hinchcliffe 2007), meanwhile, goes furthest in providing entry points for post-human global politics. Taken together, these ideas and literatures contribute to the idea that there is nothing outside of nature. They explore the porous and arbitrary nature of borders, actors, actants, networks and other categories in global politics when viewed from a socio-ecological perspective (Whatmore 2002). Although not taking a view on global politics per se, they helpfully show how all human history is ecological and how particular, historically specific, alignments of socio-ecological forces have brought about our current collective predicament.

On the other hand, insights from Bruno Latour's work on the *Politics of Nature* (Latour 2009) have been deployed to develop a post-human IR. According to Cudworth and Hobden (2011: 23), post-human IR 'should both understand our human condition as embedded in relations and practices with other species, for example, and acknowledge forms of power and domination over them'. Critical of the 'additive' approach that prevails in IR towards environmental problems, they seek to displace a human-centred (or humanocentric) Enlightenment project of control over nature with a focus on the biosphere. They are critical of a 'humanocentric' ontology for providing a 'poor and partial representation of international political structures and processes' (Cudworth and Hobden 2011: 20) and for reifying human/nature dualisms and limited understanding of agency in 'rationalist and human-referential terms' (Cudworth and Hobden 2011: 20). Like work on socio-natures referred to above, it seeks to challenge and transcend powerful dichotomies between the 'social' and 'natural' worlds in ways which go beyond questions of intra-human domination that social ecologists focus on, or the ways in which nature has become internal to the dynamics of capital accumulation (Castree 2003; Smith 2006).

Latour claims (2009: 75) that:

Since 'we have never been modern' we have always been living through a completely different history than the one we keep telling ourselves about: until the ecological crisis began to strike hard and strong, we could go on as though 'we' humans were living through one modernisation after another, jumping from one modernisation to the next . . . What happens if the very definition of the future has changed? If we now move from the position of taking into account a few beings to one of weaving careful attachments with an ever greater and greater list of explicated beings, where will we be? Attached at last!

As a species we humans have worked hard to produce forms of detachment which establish us as 'modern', 'human' and, therefore, superior to other inhabitants of planet Earth. That constructed and fragile detachment is rapidly unravelling in the face of ecological collapse as the folly of human-centred views becomes clearer by the day. Yet beyond establishing that 'we' have never (only) been human, post-human IR achieves most in indicating the narrowness of traditional IR and its blindness to global socio-natures. Notwithstanding the important emphasis on complexity and interconnectedness, in and of itself, it offers less in the way of a basis for articulating a more grounded and useable account of global Green politics.

Given this diversity of views within and beyond Green political theory, throughout this book I shall make clear, where relevant and practicable, strand of Green thinking I am referring.

Notes

1 The idea of an ecosystem is attributed to Tansley.
2 Naess (1972) proposed ecosophy – a philosophy of ecological harmony or equilibrium. One that is 'openly normative, it contains both norms, rules, postulates, value priority announcements and hypotheses concerning the state of affairs in our universe' (1972:99).

3

Green Security

If war is the answer, it must be the wrong question.[1]

For many practitioners and scholars of International Relations, security is the number one issue in global politics. The need to secure survival trumps all other imperatives where a 'state of nature' is said to prevail among nations (Aron 1966). This is constituted by an anarchical society (Bull 1977) in which no one central and overarching authority exists to restrain the actions of states, and thus states pursue the competitive politics of survival in absolute and relative ways (Wight 1977; Morgenthau 1948). Kenneth Waltz states: 'there is a constant possibility of war in a world in which there are two or more states seeking to promote a set of interests and having no agency above them upon which they can rely for protection' (1959: 227).

Maintaining order and avoiding war through the balance of power, securing hegemonic power or relying upon the restraining influence of multilateral institutions have been the driving preoccupations of academic International Relations since it's foundation in the wake of the First World War (Carr 1946; Krasner 1983; Keohane 1977). Such ideas about the 'nature' of the international system and the imperatives they impose on state behaviour have had a significant impact on the thinking and practice of foreign policy (van der Pijl 2014). The centrality of security as the *raison d'etre* of the nation-state, combined with the political nature of security itself, has led some to conclude that modern politics itself is a 'security project' (Dillon 1996: 12), given that the provision of security is central to legitimacy in all forms of political community. It seems appropriate, therefore, to begin our enquiry into the contribution of Green politics to global politics with this central concern.

Green thinking on security in many ways resonates among a growing body of scholars with the turn away from more limited and narrow conceptions of security as reduced to war, military power, 'weapons culture' and the role of the

'1; Buzan 1983). The notion that for large swathes of the
primary threat comes from their own state and not an
)1) shares a lot in common with Green critiques of state
n outlined in Chapter 5. The priority for many Greens is
ecurity, which may be juxtaposed with narrower pursuits of
nphasis in critical security studies on emancipation over
us on power and order (Linklater 1990) would resonate
vho ask critically at whose expense and on whose behalf
powei anu ᴗ.᪲   secured (Spretnal and Capra 1984). If security means the
absence of threats, then emancipation or 'development as freedom' as Sen (1999)
puts it, are vital to security. As Booth argues, 'emancipation, empirically, is
security' (1991: 323).

Yet in practice, militarism is often mobilised to protect the 'secure' and their
assets and not the dispossessed, who in their role as migrants and refugees are
constructed as threats to security (Buxton and Hayes 2016). For example, McDonald reveals how a 2003 Pentagon report proposed some states 'might seek to
develop more effective border control strategies to ensure that large populations
displaced by manifestations of climate change (whether rising sea levels or
extreme weather events) could be kept on the other side of the national border
[such that] people displaced by environmental disasters or environmental stress
may be positioned as threats to the security of the state rather than as those in need
of being secured' (2013: 46).

Despite the absolute centrality given to the politics of survival in orthodox
representations of IR noted above, ecological questions are largely neglected.
Ironically, Burke et al. suggest: 'IR is one of few disciplines that is explicitly
devoted to the pursuit of survival, yet it has almost nothing to say in the face of a
possible mass extinction event' (Burke et al. 2016: 517). 'Concepts of violence,
harm and (in)security that focus only on humans ignore at their peril the destruction and severance of worlds, which undermines the conditions of plurality that
enables life on Earth to thrive' (Burke et al. 2016: 518). Yet it is worth noting what
while the contributions of specifically Green thinking to debates and literature on
security and conflict has been lacking, there is now a vast literature on environmental security and environmental conflicts and the relationship between resources
and conflict (Dinar 2011; Matthew et al. 2010; McDonald 2012). Writers such as
Dennis Pirages noted two decades ago that: 'The greatest challenges to human
well-being in the next century are more likely to come directly from nature than
from the malignant designs of malevolent dictators' (1997: 55). There are
strands of work exploring (contentiously and at times problematically) the 'natural'
or environmental causes of conflict in places like Sudan (Darfur) and Syria and
cases of environmental conflicts, such as the 'cod wars' and the 'soccer war'

(Homer-Dixon 1999). Much of this work looks for evidence of the role of 'environmental' factors in causing or exacerbating wars (Homer-Dixon 1991).

   Below we will discuss the strategic considerations and dilemmas that flow from bringing environmental and security agendas together, recognising and acting upon the inter-relationships without further securitising ecological politics.

Critique

An eye for an eye only makes the whole world blind.[2]

Addressing the Sources of Violence and Conflict

As noted earlier in the book, the ecology movement has its base in the peace movement and many early environmental organisations were founded on the need to address the twin threats of nuclear holocaust and ecological collapse, captured most obviously in the name of the global NGO Greenpeace (Weyler 2004). Many Greens come from the peace movement and have been involved in protests at bomb bases such as Greenham Common in the United Kingdom and protests in Germany over the nuclear waste trade. The German Green movement, for example, was significantly shaped by opposition to nuclear power and the transport of waste. Greens campaign alongside, and are often members of, organisations such as the Campaign for Nuclear Disarmament or the Campaign Against the Arms Trade, and are involved in 'white poppy' campaigns aimed at remembering the losses of all combatants rather than celebrating military 'victories', for example, as well as the targeted disruption and use of direct action at arms fairs (Lucas 2015). Such actions directly challenge conventional ideas of national security pursued at the expense of others. The Greenham women argued, for instance, that while a country like the United Kingdom could survive a foreign invasion from a country like the USSR (at the time the main perceived threat invoked to justify the nuclear arms race), no one could survive a nuclear war or nuclear winter (Booth 1991). The community being protected and defended against nuclearisation was a global one, as befits the 'one worldism' of ecologism.

   Greens have also developed critiques of specific security policies such as the EU's Common Foreign and Security Policy for its links to NATO (North American Treaty Organisation) and 'opening the door to the militarisation of the EU' as Germany's Die Grünen put it (cited in Bomberg 1998: 77). A Green perspective on security taps into deeper traditions of anti-militarism and pacifism that are also gaining increasing attention in the academic study of IR (Jackson 2017). As Stavrianakis and Stern (2018: 3) suggest: 'While attention to security has grown exponentially over the last few decades, militarism – the preparation for and normalization and legitimation of war – has not received the widespread and sustained focus it warrants in mainstream or critical circles.' Furthermore, 'The prevalent emphasis on security has taken precedence over the study of the ways in which war and militarism continue to permeate societies the world over, in different forms and to different degrees' (2018: 4). This is not to overlook or diminish the value and significance of traditions of peace research, or the role of journals like the *Bulletin of Peace Proposals*, initiated in 1970, in which (de) militarisation was a key concern, in challenging the historic hegemony of war studies in the discipline of IR. 'War and society' approaches (for example, Shaw 1988) also allow us to see how military power shapes, and is shaped by, wider social relations. But renewed interest in pacifism and challenging militarism, in particular, suggest points of intersection with Green thinking, as well as the potential for Green politics to contribute to these debates to ensure that adequate attention is given to the ecological significance of anti-militarism and pacifism.

   For many Greens, the critique of prevailing approaches to security encompasses not only institutionalised violence and its embodiment in the state but the social and systemic sources of violence. The latter is taken to refer to everyday insecurity brought about by domination, patriarchy, masculinist culture (Mellor 1992; Plumwood 1993), competition, disaffection and alienation, fragmented communities and social disenfranchisement (Boyle and Simms 2009). The social and environmental roots of violence are often thought to lie in unemployment, dislocated families, disempowered communities, low social capital and disenfranchisement from political society, and resource and livelihood dispossession. As Laferrière and Stoett argue: 'The ecological understanding of peace compels an examination of all forms of violence, locating their sources at various societal levels; war is but one expression of violence and not a *sui generis* phenomenon' (1999: 58). Green approaches ask: how does violence come to be acceptable, morally defensible and perceived to be necessary, inevitable and even desirable? This means 'Paying attention to *how* people, institutions, practices, processes, and so on are militarized or rendered the subjects of security or securitized' (Stavrianakis and Stern 2018: 12). Or, as Mann stated in the late 1980s: 'in an age when war threatens our survival, it is as well to understand any behaviour, however mild in appearance, which makes war seem either natural or desirable' (Mann 1987: 35). To entirely misappropriate and rework a quote from former UK Prime Minister Tony Blair, it could be argued that Greens seek to be 'tough on war, tough on the causes of war'. Green perspectives offer, in other words, a more holistic, social and deeper understanding of the social and economic causes of conflict, violence and war in society (and not only international society) – and what fuels them and why they persist.

Green thinking encourages us not only to address these issues holistically but to address the causes of violence and insecurity. This means enquiring into the generative elements of war, conflict and violence. It means attending to the constitutive relations that enable, amplify and sustain armed conflict: the processes by which collective violence comes into being. Such policies would go beyond existing literature that frames war as an instrument, outcome or an instantiation of broader social, political and economic forces (Freedman 1994). While there are rich accounts of the diverse causal and constitutive mechanisms of war and its geopolitical consequences (Suganami 1996), these have left unaddressed the very conditions of warfare itself – the particular processes by which the emergent capacity for collective violence is actualised, directed and perpetuated; the social and cultural crucibles in which warfare is forged and shaped. The latter includes an appreciation of how individuals, communities and societies are marshalled into violent ends by mobilising and exploiting particular types of emotional reactions. Attention to the social and cultural politics of militarism necessarily blurs the boundaries between the domestic and the foreign, the civilian and the military, the public and the private and war and peace. It helps to address the problematic neglect of other key areas and interrelationships, such as the political economy of military institutions and their socioeconomic practices conducted in the name of development, or the connection between practices of militarisation, securitisation and mundane security practices in the name of counterinsurgency and public safety (Stavrianakis and Stern 2018).

Critique of Militarism

For Greens then, it is militarism in society that is the appropriate subject of critique. Militarism is defined by Stavrianakis and Selby (2013) as the social and international relations of the preparation for, and conduct of, organised political violence, an abiding and defining characteristic of world politics. For Mann, militarism is 'a set of attitudes and social practices which regards war and the preparation for war as a normal and desirable social activity' (1987: 35). In most classic conceptions of the state, a monopoly on the use of force is highlighted as a core state function and privilege (Weber 1978). Militaries are the means by which a state's energy foreign policies are sometimes pursued, as well as being among the largest consumers of fossil fuels and, therefore, part of the incumbent regime in many parts of the world.

Military expenditure often constitutes one of the largest demands on state finances and the often symbiotic relationship between energy and military regimes and complexes has led many scholars to propose the existence of a military-industrial complex (Koistinen 1980). The networks of funding and patronage that bind together universities, industry, technology providers and the military require a more relational and networked understanding of the role and autonomy of the state (Johnstone and Newell 2017). For example, given the close interrelationship between civilian and military uses of nuclear energy, it is not surprising that military actors play a critical, yet often under-acknowledged, role in setting the direction and pace of sustainability transitions (Cox et al. 2016). Hence although the state may seek to steer and align military forces, full control is often not exercised and power and dependency run in multiple directions. History underscores the ways in which states have depended on militaries for their survival in a literal sense but also seek to maintain their support for fear of military coups, the like of which we have seen throughout history and continue to see around the world today.

Militarism also operates as the social acceptance, celebration and embedding of military values throughout society, promoted and endorsed not just by the state but also by the outer reaches of civil and political society through the media, churches and schools (Gramsci 1971). Here the mass media play a key role in 'manufacturing consent' for war where their dependence upon access to state sources for reporting on foreign policy reproduces a 'propaganda model' (Herman and Chomsky 1994) that amplifies and normalises the preferred justifications of foreign policy articulated by state elites. Recent scandals about attempts by the arms industry to normalise the arms trade to school children, by spending millions of pounds annually on participation in educational events, roadshows and the provision of teaching materials including 'missile simulators', illustrate both the level of societal penetration that militarism has achieved (Doward 2018) and the perceived need to reinforce social legitimacy.

At a deeper cultural level, militarism relates closely to narratives of heroism (or Caeserism as Gramsci (1971) would put it) and great leaders, to cultures of machoism and the corresponding ridicule, ostracisation and punishment of pacifists and those who refuse to be conscripted into war. Green perspectives on security may have much in common with approaches which seek to address and counteract 'everyday militarism' (e.g. Bernazzoli and Flint 2010; Mabee and Vucetic 2018). Greens are critical of the hubris of control that characterises military approaches to 'managing' and 'containing' environmental threats, which they combine with an emphasis instead on humbleness and respect for the global ecosystems of which we are part. As Burke et al. note, 'the gravity of the changes to the biosphere that climate change will wreak grant the climate an independent agency that will exceed the agency of any state, group, or the state system itself' (Burke et al. 2016: 513). In academic terms, this positions nature itself as an actant and driver of security/insecurity in a way that places in doubt illusions of control that human security can be achieved while undermining the very ecological basis of our existence (Cudworth and Hobden 2011).

In this sense, there is a fundamental antagonism between the holistic and interdependent ecological thinking of Greens and the territorial, zero-sum, competitive focus of security thinking that takes as its premise the impossibility of collective security achievable by non-military means. The Green critique operates on a principled moral and ethical level around the value of human and non-human life (given the immense ecological destruction associated with military systems). As noted above, it also sees militarism as a social and cultural, as well as a political and economic phenomenon embedded and validated in the reproduction of everyday life. Rather than moments of spectacular exception, violence, distrust or competition, the breeding grounds of war are sown and nurtured in the soil of industrial society. Sustaining these critiques in the face of the realities of negotiating and exercising power has nevertheless proved very difficult, as seen most clearly in the experience of the German Greens, discussed further below.

In Green thinking militarism is a function of, and intrinsically linked to, the capitalist industrial society of which it is part, whose project it polices and whose strictures it is called upon to enforce 'at home' and 'abroad' in the service of the industrial state and its growth imperatives. Militarism was always thus. Mann notes that even in the 'age of the theorist–generals and diplomats [of Clausewitz and von Moltke, of Metternich and Bismarck] militarism became military science, harnessed to the logic of geo-political strategy, partaking in the scientific and technological developments of industrial capitalism' (Mann 1987: 38).

In Marxist and Leninist accounts, war is often thought of as evidence of the death throes of capitalism, in the way that Russia's involvement in the First World War created the possibility for the Russian revolution. War is understood as the highest stage of imperialism (Lenin 1996 [1916]), as well as serving as a diversion from domestic social struggle and class conflict. In Green thinking, contra Marxist accounts, industrialism is the key rather than capitalism per se. As Mann argued (1987: 47): 'militarized socialism *institutionalizes* global militarism in the lives of the people' to an even greater extent than capitalist powers. Think North Korea or China in today's world or the former USSR for examples of this.

Militaries and militarism provide, therefore, a key means by which states resource their economic expansion and growth, thereby maintaining and locking in unsustainable pathways. Oil wars (Kaldor et al. 2007) and conflicts over Suez or in Iran to prevent nationalisations of industries show the lengths powerful states will go to guarantee abundant supplies of natural resources, employing force where necessary (Rees 2001). Put most bluntly and polemically, having access to cheap energy requires states to be willing to fight wars where supplies of those resources are threatened with interruption. This is the violent cost of protecting and preserving industrial society, particularly in the core of the global economy, from its ecological contradictions. There is a direct link then between peace and economic self-sufficiency. Although this is an argument that Greens advance, China and many other countries such as India are actively seeking energy security through increased energy independence in order to reduce their dependence on supplies of imported energy, especially from regions of the world in conflict or considered to be politically volatile.

Beyond this deeper opposition to militarism, Greens are also critical of the organisation, maintenance and expansion of military complexes. Greens often articulate a critique of militarism in general and the military-industrial complex in particular (Porritt 1989; Commoner 1970). They illustrate how one sustains the other, as recent work in relation to the nuclear industry in the United Kingdom, for example, has shown, highlighting again the relevance of the notion of a 'deep state' (see Chapter 5). This work revealed how the importance of maintaining the civilian infrastructure for nuclear weapons capability is a key, if obscured, factor shaping UK civilian energy policy (Cox et al. 2016), signalling the militarization of energy policy and challenging the sanctity of the civilian–military binary that serves as a bedrock of the international nuclear order (Stavrianakis and Stern 2018).

The systematic state bias towards the ideology and practice of militarism, reflected in policy priorities and institutional access that results from these closely knit relations of power, points to another area of critique for Greens: namely, the (mis)allocation of state resources. Greens are often critical both of the scale of resources committed to militarism, as well as offering suggestions about how they might be redeployed. Globally, arms expenditure runs at around $1.7 trillion a year (SIPRI 2018). Andrew Smith, writing in the UK Green Party magazine *Green World*, asks:

What would happen if the government put peace and social justice ahead of militarism and war? What would happen if the level of resources currently being put into promoting military might were used to make the world a better place? This year alone, the UK will spend £37 billion on arms and the military. What if a similar figure was invested in promoting social and environmental justice and creating jobs in the renewable sector? There is a severe skills shortage in science, technology, engineering and maths (STEM) and a greater emphasis could see the UK as a global leader. However, at present the government spends 25 times more on research and development (R&D) for the military (£1.4 billion) as it does on R&D for renewable energy (£58 million). Every year, taxpayers subsidise arms companies to the tune of hundreds of millions of pounds to export their wares into war zones and to arm oppressive regimes. One estimate, from the Stockholm International Peace Research Institute puts the level of UK arms export subsidies at £700 million a year. These weapons don't just provide military support, they provide political support too, and give a sign of UK support for atrocities taking place across the world.

(Smith 2016)

This is only one example of how states provide arms companies and the military with a completely disproportionate level of political and financial support, while not investing enough in greener and more sustainable industries. There are clearly many others.

The neglect of militarism in the study of world politics is unsurprising, however, given as Stavrianaskis and Stern show (2018: 5–6): 'directly addressing particular wars and forms of militarism is intensely political and requires analysis of the role of the state and of organized violence as a social force, ongoing asymmetries in North–South relations, and the effects of a capitalist global political economy'. Green thinking, as we will see throughout this book, is well placed to make these connections between security, economy and the role of the state. Yet: 'A policy-oriented agenda such as human security has found it hard to make a critique of militarism bite: policymakers did not want to engage with the women of Greenham Common in the 1980s, and do not want to engage with anti-arms fair protestors today' (Stavrianaskis and Stern 2018: 5–6). Although Greens are often supportive of and involved in these forms of protest, they rarely have the ear of the military establishment, which can be relied upon to contest and ridicule the viability of disarmament proposals. For example, UK Labour Party leader Jeremy Corbyn found this to his detriment when the mainstream media paraded senior military officials to mock his stated reluctance to press the nuclear button and questioned his fitness for high office as someone closely involved in the peace campaigning organisation CND (BBC News 2015).

The nature of the military establishment is of course ever changing amid the evolving nature of threats, the proliferation of 'new wars' (Kaldor 2012) and the increased prominence of private military and security companies. The latter brings with it another set of challenges, including the lack of accountability and mechanisms of redress for the human, social and environmental impact of subcontracted and outsourced military operations or privatised forms of militarism. The advancement of militarism under the guise of development represents another. The project of liberal peace-building through statecraft and good governance, promoted by the development industry, serves to expand militarism globally. From this point of view, the expansion of the agenda whereby 'new issues have been added to the security agenda as part of the broadening move: poverty, sexual- and gender-based violence, health, borders and infrastructure' (Stavrianakis and Stern 2018: 7) creates ever more openings for the militarisation of everyday life. Green perspectives need to interrogate the ways in which, as Stavrianakis and Stern (2018: 7) suggest, 'the concept of militarism can be mobilized to offer a critique of military power or ideology, its preparation, effects and legacies'

The Ecological Costs of War and Militarism

A third area of critique is the impact of conflict and war on the planet. Whether through military training, weapon production, storage, disposal and, above all, armed conflict (but perhaps especially nuclear, chemical and biological testing and warfare), militarism has proved to a major cause of the most serious ecological degradation of the last century (Eckersely 2004). This ignominy includes the deliberate use of environmental damage as a tool of war through ecocide in Indochina (such as the use of agent orange to destroy forest cover and food crops in the Vietnam war), the burning of oil wells (in Kuwait 1990–1) and the deliberate contamination of waterways (Elliott 2004).

This critique of the environmental impact of militarism extends not just to the social and environmental devastation reaped by war and conflict but also to the everyday environmental impact and use of resources by the military, including chemical use and the vast amount of fossil fuels militaries consume. For example, the US military alone uses more oil than any other institution in the world. Every year US armed forces consume more than 100 million barrels of oil to power ships, vehicles, aircraft and ground operations (Union of Concerned Scientists 2017). Militaries are also both primary beneficiaries of fossil fuel subsidies and secondary ones, given that in several countries the military owns companies involved in fossil fuel production and distribution (Johnstone and Newell 2017).

By these means, militarism generates both longer-term security threats and 'everyday insecurity'. As Stavrianakis and Stern write (2018: 5): 'war and militarism have generated insecurity in a variety of forms – physical, gendered, food and health insecurity, to name just a few – through direct physical violence (attacks on civilian populations in both Syria and Yemen, for instance) and the attendant strategies thereof (starvation and famine, displacement)'. Militarism is identified as a key cause of insecurity by the United Nations Development Programme (UNDP) *Human Development Report*, which first articulated the concept of human security (UNDP 1994). In this report, UNDP sought to provide a redefinition of security in which concerns or threats at the individual level were institutionalised in the practice of security. These included 'safety from chronic threats such as hunger, disease and repression' and 'protection from sudden and harmful disruptions in the patterns of daily life'. As McDonald (2002: 277) suggests, 'Human Security has been viewed as a potential response to the growing insecurity of security: a situation wherein the continued prioritisation of military concerns at the state level in traditional discourses and practices of security has served to further individual insecurity and failed to respond adequately to the most pressing threats to individuals throughout the world'. While Greens would be sympathetic to the agenda behind human security of broadening understandings of threats and insecurities (O'Brien 2006), the, at times individualising, focus of human security approaches would be less helpful to their emphasis on collective planetary threats. They would also want to emphasise strongly the everyday generation of ecological insecurity via depleted and contaminated environments and the reduced access to resources and viable livelihoods induced by the routine operations of military systems.

Normative Vision

Ecological Security

The zero-sum, competitive logic which underpins conventional approaches to security is increasingly redundant for Greens, who argue it has been surpassed by the reality of multitudinous interconnections between and across societies thereby making them strongly interdependent, as well arguing that dependence upon a common ecosystem means acts of degradation against one group of human beings constitute acts of violence against us all. Advocates of 'planet politics' pose the challenge to traditional ideas and thinking about security in the following way:

Security comes from being more connected, not less. Gone are the days of billiard ball states and national security based on keeping the Other out or deterred. The Other is always already inside, so bound up with us in a common process that it no longer makes sense to speak of inside and outside. We cannot survive without accepting the cosmopolitan and enmeshed nature of this world. We are an array of bodies connected and interconnected in complex ways that have little to do with nationality. States will wither in the coming heat, freeze in the prolonged winters, and be lost under the rising oceans. We will not survive without the biggest and most complex system we know: the biosphere.

(Burke et al. 2016: 502)

The issue then is whether the Anthropocene changes how we understand security. Just as the end of the Cold War gave rise to new understandings and definitions of security,[3] so too appreciation that collective human security is only possible if humans are able to live within planetary boundaries surely resets the conversation once more. From an ecological and more holistic point of view, on an interconnected and mutually interdependent planet, violence against others and their environment is an act of self-harm. Devastating the water, forests, land or air in other parts of the world through military means necessarily, if spatially and temporally indirectly, comes back to bite the perpetrator through the global circulations of water and air pollution, climate change and the like, as well as through global circuits of exchange (such as food produced on contaminated land etc.). Zero-sum notions cease to make sense when there are only boomerang effects, and no winners, especially in an absolute sense. In this regard, as Burke et al. (2016: 513) suggest:

Little wonder that IR is ill-suited to make sense of the contemporary condition. Its dominant paradigms – realism, liberalism, and constructivism – are determinedly state-centric ... They may want more or less from the system, emphasise different causal principles, and have more or less hope, but they are unified by an investment in the institution of diplomacy and an anthropocentric ontology in which the field of human agonism, bargaining, and conflict, works at some distance from nature rather than being deeply, causally, enmeshed in its processes.

Instead, pacifism and non-violence have a central place in a normative vision of Green security (Spretnak and Capra 1984). Conflict resolution and peace-building are seen as the best ways for ensuring against future conflicts and managing existing ones: exiting the destructive cycle of violence and retribution. Yet, as a conference on 'Rethinking pacifism for revolution, security and politics' noted:

For the greater part of the past century, pacifism has occupied a marginal place in international relations scholarship, politics, activism, media, and the wider society. Pacifism is rarely used as the basis for normative theorising about the use of force, and is rarely drawn upon as an important source for thinking about resistance, revolution, security, counterterrorism, peacebuilding, national defence planning, humanitarian intervention, political institutions, and the like. In part, this is due to the persistence of a number of key misconceptions, including that pacifism represents a single homogenous position which rejects any and all forms of force and violence, that pacifism involves inaction in the face of injustice, that it is politically naïve about the reality of evil, and that it is dangerous because it invites aggression. Other important misconceptions revolve around the nature of violence and force, and its purported utility and necessity for engendering political change, civilian protection, and securing politics in the state. The marginal position of pacifism is a puzzling state of affairs, given the noted insights and advantages of pacifist theory in relation to dominant IR theories and popular beliefs, and to recent robust empirical findings documenting the success and positive effects of nonviolent movements compared to violent movements.[4]

Pacifism is often defined in negative terms, through its opposition to specific forms of harmful or destructive behaviour, such as the systematic and organised violence associated with war and armed conflict, or the taking of human life, or the use of violence more generally. A more positive approach would be to define pacifism in terms of its commitment to exclusively peaceful methods for dealing with conflict. Pacifism has a significant ethical dimension, involving a personal refusal to participate in or support the use of violence, particularly war and armed conflict. It also has important political implications, involving a rejection of political structures or forms of social organisation that depend upon or utilise violence. Pacifism is not only anti-war, for example, it can also be linked to the anarchist critique of the state (see Chapter 5) because it argues that the only way to eliminate war, armed conflict and other forms of political violence is to remove the capacity for institutionalised and systematic violence epitomised by the military structures and systems of the state (Atack 2001, 2017).

This latter point links nicely to anarchist traditions in Green Political Theory (GPT) outlined in Chapter 2, and reviewed further in Chapter 5, where anarchy is regarded more as an absence of constraints on autonomy, enabling the state to serve progressive functions rather than operate as a pathological driver of violence and war, and not as a condition, as it is understood in mainstream IR, that of necessity drives violence. Disassembling or 'de-capacitating' the power of the state to commit acts of war and to force and conscript civilians into conflict would in itself reduce conflict, given the extent of state sponsored violence and backing of ecologically destructive projects through force.

The move away from an economy organised along neo-liberal lines and its attendant repressions and requirements for violence might further enable a demilitarization of the state. State violence is often employed to enable extractivism in new frontiers. Witness the violence and repression frequently visited upon indigenous peoples and other 'environmental defenders' (Global Witness 2017) including activists such as the Arctic 30 from Greenpeace in Russia (Stewart 2015) and often involving global dispossessions through 'green grabbing' and 'land grabbing' (Fairhead et al. 2012) to find outlets for capital accumulation. Reduced dependence on resources would mean fewer oil and resource wars and fewer reasons to go to war, as outlined in the discussion above. Reduced overseas military presence would also dampen grievance-based radicalism and extremism which has scarred the world with cycles of aggressive imperialist ventures followed by terrorist backlash. There would be no sowing of the seeds of hate that imperial adventures cultivate. As George notes (2010: 167): 'People fight when they perceive that the distribution of vital necessities is unfair'. For example, reduced dependency on fossil fuels, their increasing scarcity and the volatility of their prices which drives states to intervene to protect their access to them, could reduce instability in the world, especially given their concentration in politically tumultuous regions.

A challenge to the general thrust of this argument from the point of view of the liberal peace doctrine (Doyle 1986) is that trade and economic interdependence among liberal states are a key means of securing peace. This builds on Kant's ideas in *Perpetual Peace* (1983 [1795]), where free commerce is seen as vital to the possibility of peace, as well as Woodrow Wilson's fourteen points where free trade policies lie at the core of peace. Kant suggests that: 'The spirit of commerce sooner or later takes hold of every people and it cannot exist side by side with war.' The idea is that 'Open commercial lanes will increase the chances of peace by increasing material bounty, directly reinforcing the (political) rapports of friendship. Enmity is dissuaded by the inevitable increasing of the "opportunity cost"; war becomes prohibitively expensive in an interdependent world economy, especially when cross investment prevails' (quoted in Laferièrre and Stoett 1999: 10). Problematically for Greens then, according to this view, peace and stability are said to rest on material growth. A corresponding implication is that the costs of going to war might be reduced for more autarkic societies.

Greens, however, might counter that, autarkic or not, if the state's military profile is substantively reduced, its ability to engage in warfare is compromised. As we will see in Chapter 4, Greens would also highlight the everyday, and at times structural, violence visited upon communities around the world as a direct result of the imperatives of expanding and globalising trade in an unequal world. Export-led extractivism has led to intense social conflict and violence the world over as a glance at a global map of environmental justice and resource conflicts makes clear (EJOLT 2018). This factor is overlooked in the liberal preoccupation with inter-state war that is largely a thesis about the reduced likelihood of war *between liberal states*, since it is evident that liberal states frequently engage in war with other types of regimes, as noted above. Critical Marxist-inspired accounts would also argue that it is the nature of capitalist powers to engage in imperialist ventures to expand opportunities for accumulation that brings them into conflict with other imperial rivals (Lenin 1996 [1916]). As noted above, Greens would extend this analysis and critique beyond the capitalist state per se to the industrial state.

More broadly, Greens would suggest, as Laferrière and Stoett do, that 'Historically, liberal peace has been indissociable from a belief in material progress – in other words, from the domination and use of nature by human beings' (1999: 126). They might also suggest that 'reciprocal vulnerability', which runs through much liberal thinking, can be recognised and acted upon in ways other than extending and deepening the chains of commerce over larger distances. It is an important argument for Greens to address, however. What is the basis, and what are the prospects, for perpetual peace when fewer material dependencies bind nations together? Can liberal values outlive the belief in sustaining an ever-expanding global economy?

Green thinking about what is to be secured, how and by whom, and in particular the need to address the causes of insecurity, resonates with academic work both from critical security studies (Booth 1991) as well as work on resilience (Brown 2016). Here, everyday security relates to freedom from violence, insecurity and deprivation. Security is tied to securing peoples' own ability to secure their supplies of food, water and energy grounded in an alternative notion of sovereignty as being about control over livelihoods rather than a territorial boundary, a process referred to elsewhere in the book as 'recommoning'. Consistent with traditions of human security and everyday security, Greens would seek to roll back 'securitisation', aiming instead at 'de-securitization' (Waever 1993). Reversing the 'slow violence' (Nixon 2011) of everyday degradation and resource depletion, or as Burke et al. (2016: 503) put it, future extinctions and assaults on civilisation, 'issues not from an exceptional event like war or terrorism, and not from a clash of states, but from the routine and extraordinary rhythms of human life, consumption, and industrialisation: from the encounter between humanity and ecology'.

Strategy

In pursuit of this broad, ambitious and quite radical normative vision, a range of strategies might be considered. The point of departure would flow from Eckersley's suggestion that 'it would be naïve for greens to believe that states can function without military and police forces. Once this is acknowledged, then from a democratic green perspective, everything should turn on whether those forces are deployed in legitimate ways to further legitimate ends' (2004: 25). As the editors of the *Green European Journal* suggest in their special issue on Green foreign policy: 'when one asks the Greens what foreign policy actually means to them, invariably the answer revolves around the same preoccupation: dealing with conflict, or the conditions of the use of force … In fact, the green vision is in essence so transnational and global that it seems "conflict" would be the only thing "foreign" to them.'

Ecologising Security

If ecological security is the normative vision for Greens, described above as securing the conditions for planetary survival through non-military means, what are the means for achieving this? What is the process of 'ecologizing security'?

For some environmentalists, highlighting the role of environmental factors in driving or exacerbating conflicts is a valuable political move in raising awareness about the importance of protecting the environment and moving it higher up the political agenda. Gaining the attention of the powerful security establishment could generate momentum and a sense of urgency and serve to mobilise significant state resources behind efforts to protect the environment. From invoking fears about waves of climate refugees from new arenas of conflict or areas of the world increasingly uninhabitable because of climate change, to projecting 'climate wars' over diminishing supplies of water or over remaining oil reserves (Dyer 2008), some in the environmental movement have been willing to invoke neo-Malthusian narratives about scarcity-induced conflict. The blurb on the cover of Harald Welzer's (2012) book *Climate Wars* reads, for example: 'Struggles over drinking water, new outbreaks of mass violence, ethnic cleansing, civil wars in the earth's poorest countries, endless flows of refugees: these are the new conflicts and forces shaping the world of the twenty-first century.' Indeed, some scholarly research has documented environment-induced conflict and sought to isolate primary drivers (Homer-Dixon 1991),[5] while NGOs such as International Alert have compiled lists of states they claim are at risk of armed conflict because of climate change, including Somalia, Nigeria, Colombia, Indonesia, Algeria and Iran (Smith and Vivekananda 2007). It is also the case, however, that shared resources can be a basis for cooperation. Hence, although there have been thirty-seven violent clashes between states over water since the Second World War, there have also been over 400 water agreements signed (George 2010: 173).

Nevertheless, it is easy to understand why there is a perceived need to emphasise the security dimensions of environmental threats. Commenting on the Falklands War between the United Kingdom and Argentina in 1982, the then UK prime minister Mrs Thatcher stated: 'It is exciting to have a real crisis on your hands when you have spent half your political life dealing with humdrum issues like the environment' (cited in Eckersley 2004: 21). Here, strategies might include both greening traditional security agendas, or seeking to recast the meaning and pursuit of security in some of the ways proposed above. In the case of the former, it is a question of attracting the attention of military strategists, a plan that brings its own risks and dilemmas (Deudney 1990). Many pronouncements from figures such as former UN Secretary-General Boutros Ghali, suggesting that the next war would be fought over water or calls for a UN Environment Security Council, demonstrate the growing recognition that environmental degradation poses a threat to national and international security. Indeed, Boutros-Ghali's successor Ban Ki-moon addressed the UN General Assembly about water wars in reference to crises in Kenya, Chad and Darfur, labelled the world's 'first climate change war' (George 2010: 178). Climate change, in particular, has been the focus of attention. The United Nations Security Council (UNSC) has held several debates on the international security implications of climate change in recent years and the UN General Assembly commissioned a report on this issue in 2009. Regional organisations have identified climate change as a current and growing security threat, while climate change has found its way into national security statements of key political institutions throughout the world, from the USA to the United Kingdom, Australia, Russia, Finland and Germany, among many others (McDonald 2013).

In turn, this has given rise to a series of critiques of resource determinism and neo-Malthusian narratives around conflicts over diminishing resources, as well as a cautioning against securitising environmental threats by constructing them in this way. Research positing these connections has been critiqued on a series of grounds including: that the correlations identified are spurious since they always rest upon coding and causal assumptions that range from the arbitrary to the untenable; that even if the correlations identified were significant and meaningful, they would still not constitute a sound basis for making predictions about the conflict impacts of climate change; and that such models reflect and reproduce a problematic ensemble of Northern stereotypes, ideologies and policy agendas (Selby 2014). Nevertheless, however problematic, such narratives remain attractive to military actors keen to find new roles for themselves, utilising the financial resources these would imply for them as protectors of water supplies and land for energy production around the world. Such is the danger of framing climate change as a 'threat multiplier' (rather than mono-causal driver as in some early accounts): implying and validating a need for military responses to contain threats to security that bypass public political discussion and potential contestation in favour of 'high politics' (Newell and Lane 2018). There is evidence indeed of military elites and disbanded troops seeking to secure a role for themselves in combatting environmental crime. For example, Duffy (2016) describes 'War by conservation' and the links that are posited between poaching and wildlife crime and the funding of terrorism ('the white gold of jihadi') as a means of justifying militarised incursions in other countries.

It is precisely the interest on the part of the military establishment that Greens are generally both suspicious and critical of, sparking their concern in linking these issues. In their book *The Secure and the Dispossessed*, Buxton and Hayes (2016) show 'how the military and corporations plan to maintain control in a world reshaped by climate change. With one eye on the scientific evidence and the other on their global assets, dystopian preparations by the powerful are already fuelling militarised responses to the unfolding climate crises'. Such activity is unlikely to form the basis of a progressive or effective response to global climate change. Dominant framings come from actors with a stake in protecting or expanding expenditure in their sector who benefit from threat proliferation thereby justifying their existence and indeed growth. The pitch to policy-makers is around climate adaptation and their ability to secure assets and infrastructures and protect borders. Climate mitigation is understandably actively neglected given the vast contribution of the military to global GHG emissions noted above.

Eckersley (2007) is optimistic, nevertheless, about the potential and need for 'ecological security'. As a concrete strategy this might include calls for a UN Ecological Security Council to deal with environmental emergencies and the deployment of 'green berets' as an environmental peace-keeping force to safeguard protected areas. The basis for this is that the UN Charter already confers on the Security Council the responsibility for maintaining peace and security. Again the issue is the difference between everyday, cumulative 'slow violence' (Nixon 2011) as opposed to spectacular emergency interventions, since both require very different types of response and where the former, in particular, would not be amenable to securitisation strategies.

Indeed, military threats are often thought of as discrete, deliberate, specific and zero-sum; characteristics which hardly apply to most environmental threats that are often diffuse, transboundary and unintended, and operate over longer time scales. Positing environmental threats such as climate change as security threats could encourage a military response: a response inconsistent with both the requirements for an effective solution to problems of environmental change and with proponents' goals of challenging existing discourses on security in global politics

(McDonald 2013). Simon Dalby, for example, points to 'the contradictions of linking the politically conservative language of security with the radical action programs demanded by more far-thinking environmentalists' (1994: 26). The former is highly unlikely to be able to tackle the underlying causes of environmental degradation and, as noted above, is heavily implicated in the everyday production of environmental harm.

The different logics and interests at play are apparent in competing framings of environmental security. While some focus on the threats that environmental issues, and particularly climate change, pose to long-term human security (Matthew et al. 2010; UNDP 2007), others emphasise the threat posed to the nation-state in terms of traditional concerns with sovereignty and territorial integrity (Campbell 2008). In other words, while the idea of environmental change as a security threat is gaining both academic and practical purchase, important differences in the logic of this link suggest radically different responses as a security concern. As Burke et al. (2016: 506) put it: 'These looming events are surely the greatest threat to international security in this century, whether we think in terms of state security, human security, or ecological security. We collectively face the profound, interwoven endangerment of the common worlds we inhabit and depend upon for survival'. Attempts to articulate, let alone precisely define, Green security will have to deal with the fact that security frames are socially constructed, context specific and ever changing (McDonald 2002: 288). Rather than seeking to ecologise security, Greens may want to make stronger claims for the democratisation of security or pursuing 'desecuritisation': the removal of issues from the security agenda and into the realm of normal politics, where they can be openly debated and discussed (Wæver 1993; McDonald 2013).

Ecological security, as the normative vision described above, is the least well embedded of the approaches linking environmental change to security (McDonald 2013; Pirages and Cousins 2005). This is perhaps because it is the most ambitious in seeking fundamentally to rebalance the relationship between people and the natural environment, orientating around the biosphere as the thing to be secured. For Pirages and Cousins (2005: 4) ecological security rests on: 'Preserving the following four interrelated dynamic equilibriums: 1) Between human populations living at higher consumptions levels and the ability of nature to provide resources and services; 2) Between human populations and pathogenic microorganisms; 3) Between human populations and those of other plant and animal species; 4) Among human populations.' Pirages and Cousins suggest that: 'insecurity increases wherever any of these equilibriums is disregarded either by changes in human behaviour or in nature' (2005: 4). There is also a recognition that moral obligation extends to other living beings, an ecological ethic or a form of eco-centrism wholly absent from other discourses of environmental security.

Ecological security is also the most controversial of the approaches because it highlights the need to revisit those political, economic and social structures that give rise to processes of environmental degradation in the first place, reframing the debate around the need for systematic structural change in our relationship to the natural environment (Barnett 2001; Dalby 2009). What it means to develop feasible political responses once security is (re)defined in these ways is often not specified.

Peace and Arms Control through Multilateralism

Besides seeking to contest and reframe what we mean by security and to engage with (as well as contest) the military establishment, Greens are keen to use the tools of multilateral diplomacy and international law to delimit the accumulation or use of weapons of mass destruction, as well as the arms trade in general. Greens have supported international treaties on nuclear non-proliferation, the control of biological weapons and recent efforts to ban the use of nuclear weapons. Efforts to reign in the use of such weapons have a long history of course. Bernard Brodie (1946) prayed that nuclear war would be unlikely enough 'to give society the opportunity it desperately needs to adjust its politics to its physics'. Yet despite the experience of Hiroshima and Nagasaki and Oppenheimer's comment in an interview on the horror their invention had unleashed on society – that 'Now I am become Death, the destroyer of worlds',[6] – the march to acquire and expand nuclear arsenals continues. What resulted at this time was a short-lived effort to think about nuclear world government and the banning of the weapons. Once the major power diplomacy in the UN Atomic Energy Commission failed in 1948, the fundamental irruptive power of the weaponry was left to the vicissitudes of militarism, power politics and interstate bargaining (Burke et al. 2016: 503).

Global nuclear governance now comprises a broad array of international organisations, treaties, initiatives, summits and networks responsible for the core areas of nuclear non-proliferation, nuclear disarmament and the peaceful uses of nuclear technology. These three pillars of nuclear order are all reflected in the 1968 nuclear Non-Proliferation Treaty (NPT), the centrepiece of the global non-proliferation regime. Building on this, forty-eight years later in October 2016, the First Committee of the United Nations overwhelmingly passed a resolution to begin negotiations towards a Treaty for the Prohibition of Nuclear Weapons. The resolution established an open UN negotiating conference that took place intermittently over twenty days from March 2017 to July 2017. Finally in July 2017, the final text on the Treaty was officially adopted at the UN (with 122 states in favour, 1 against, 1 abstention). The adoption of the treaty, also known as the Nuclear Weapons Ban Treaty, was much feted by peace activists and civil society organisations. These groups were awarded the Nobel Peace prize in 2017 for their efforts in bringing the treaty about.

On 20 September 2017, countries began signing the comprehensive treaty banning nuclear weapons. The treaty to prohibit nuclear weapons finally gives these weapons of mass destruction a similar legal status to biological and chemical weapons. The treaty prohibits signatories from: preparation of nuclear weapons, actual use and assisting other states or non-state groups in such actions. The United Kingdom, alongside other nuclear-armed states, boycotted the negotiations, con- tradicting government claims to support multilateral disarmament and despite polling indicating that 75 per cent of the UK population supported UK government participation (Pressenza 2017). Without the backing of many of the world's most powerful states and nuclear powers, questions remain about its effectiveness in any other than the symbolic realm.

In a long tradition of support for multilateral, cooperative and legal approaches to regulate or ban nuclear arms, Greens strongly supported the treaty and have formed links with peace movements to advance these goals. Civil society organisa- tions have recently sought alternative platforms in order to pursue a more open and public dialogue to bring 'democracy to disarmament' (Duarte 2009). Indeed, in 2013 they helped establish a new public-focused 'Humanitarian Impact of Nuclear Weapons' (HINW) initiative comprised of three unique consultative conferences co-organised by the International Campaign to Abolish Nuclear Weapons (ICAN) and attended by the majority of NPT signatory states. ICAN was launched in 2007 and comprised a diverse coalition of 440 CSOs in over one hundred countries. ICAN sees itself as a middle ground between the Global Zero Coalition (composed largely of former policy-makers, diplomats and military strategists), and Abolition 2000 (a largely unstructured assemblage of over two thousand organisations). This broader human security approach, connecting environmental, health and humanitarian law, shifts the focus away from the strategic narratives of nuclear deterrence and back to public opposition to nuclear weapons. The key focus of the Humanitarian Initiative, as both a consciousness-raising exercise in nuclear catastrophe and a new mechanism to advance nuclear disarmament, has gained significant and unprecedented legal traction.

The momentum towards peace appears to be coming from below, therefore. Recent human security initiatives such as the treaty bans on Landmines in 1997 and Cluster Munitions in 2008 were directly underpinned by the work of Transnational Advocacy Networks coordinating with governments in negotiations outside of formal channels. Successful CSO-led international campaigns helped to pass UN Resolution 49/75 on rethinking the legality of nuclear use, as well as lobbying the nuclear weapons states (NWS) to agree to an indefinite extension of the NPT in 1995. Continued alliances with peace movements and campaigns against the arms trade on these issues provide an obvious and important platform for the advancement of Green goals around security.

Alliances with civil society regarding financing for the arms trade provide another strategic avenue. Governments are clearly the primary clients and procurers of larger-scale weapons, although civilians in many countries have legal and illegal access to small arms that are also the subject of global regulatory initiatives. Banks, nevertheless, lend vast sums of money to arms manufacturers providing a point of leverage for activists who can pressure banks to divest their funds. For example, the 'Stop Barclays Coalition' has exposed the UK bank's involvement as a shareholder in several major arms firms including Raytheon, Boeing and Lockheed Martin. Following mass action in 2014, Barclays sold their shares in Elbit systems, an Israeli arms company that supplies most of the armed drones used in Gaza, although activists protest that they continue to hold shares in other major arms firms that supply Israel (CorporateWatch 2015).

The larger short- and longer-term goal has to be to resist and disrupt the 'normalization of nuclear weapons as a precondition of peace and security' (Stavrianakis and Stern 2018: 15) or, as Booth explains, to challenge 'the belief that there is ultimately no stronger basis for human coexistence than genocidal fear' (1991: 321). This brings me back to the theme touched upon earlier about the critical importance for Greens of being able to extend the boundaries of moral and political community, including and extending the progressive universalisation of cosmopolitan norms. This objective goes beyond cosmopolitan visions of liberal thinkers (Held 1995) to embrace an ethic of care and responsibility towards the planet and its non-human inhabitants consistent with the more ecocentric framings of security described above. It is about salvaging enlightenment ideals but free of the scientific and technological arrogance and illusions of mastery that accompanied them. For Greens, ideas of reciprocity, cooperation and mutual dependence should underpin security in ways which further undermine the boundaries that police domestic and foreign policy regarding communities of obligation (Walker 1993; Linklater 1998). Getting acceptance for alternative conceptions of security implies 'Changing the way people think about the role of the nation-state (particularly as security provider), creating situations in which particular security evocations become possible, empowering actors working towards changing the normative context, changing the way people think about responsibility and others in general' (McDonald 2002: 291).

Democratic Defence

Beyond engagement with the military establishment and efforts to pursue change and restraint through diplomacy and international law, Greens have also drawn on radical traditions of civil disobedience and non-violence that draw inspiration from the civil rights movement under Martin Luther King and '*satyagraha*' (truth force) strategies adopted by the followers of Mahatma Gandhi to oppose colonial rule. The aim of any non-violent conflict is to convert the opponent; to win over hearts and minds and persuade others of your point of view. Gandhi once said of non-violence: 'The essence of nonviolent technique is that it seeks to liquidate antagonisms but not the antagonists'.[7] Or, as Martin Luther King (MLK) said, 'the nonviolent resister does not seek to humiliate or defeat the opponent but to win his [sic] friendship and understanding'.[8] In non-violent conflict, the participant does not want to make their opponent suffer; instead, they show that they are willing to suffer themselves in order to bring about change. Among the techniques of non-violent protest are: peaceful demonstrations, sit-ins, picketing, holding vigils, fasting and hunger strikes, strikes, blockades and civil disobedience. The goal and the means both have to be non-violent. MLK pointed out: 'A boycott is never an end within itself. It is merely a means to awaken a sense of shame within the oppressor but the end is reconciliation, the end is redemption.'

Intellectually, support for civil disobedience and non-violence draws on the work of scholars such as David Thoreau or Gene Sharp, who identified 198 methods of non-violent action grouped according to the level of risk, preparation and forcefulness associated with them (Sharp 1960). His was an argument, not so much for the moral values of non-violent resistance in the vein of Gandhi or Luther King, as the sheer pragmatism and effectiveness of it, to which others have also drawn attention (Vinthagen 2015; Chenoworth and Stephan 2011). Indeed, in my experience of training for non-violent direct action (NVDA), Green groups often refer participants to this work to highlight the evidence base for the effectiveness of NVDA. The Extinction Rebellion movement also regularly cites Chenoworth and Stephan's (2011) work in defence of its claim that civil disobedience by a relatively small percentage of the population (three and a half per cent) can be sufficient to trigger revolutionary change. As noted above, leading Greens have been involved in direct action at arms bases such as Greenham Common in the United Kingdom, protests at arms fairs (Lucas 2015) and have sought to disrupt the movement and transportation of weapons (in Germany and the United Kingdom, for example), as well as being closely linked to the Campaign for Nuclear Disarmament (CND), the Campaign Against the Arms Trade and activism around the conversion of military technology for civilian and peaceful purposes, often referred to as 'swords into ploughshares'. Indeed, Green politicians often openly advocate the use of non-violent direct action (Bartley and Berry 2018).

The effectiveness of non-cooperation has, nevertheless, been questioned by critics who point to the limits of non-cooperation and civil disobedience. For example, Tharoor, reflecting on the Gandhian strategies of resistance in the context of colonialism in India, writes:

Other peoples have fallen under the boots of invading armies, been dispossessed of their lands or forced to flee in terror from their homes. Non-violence has offered no solutions to them. It could only work against opponents vulnerable to a loss of moral authority, governments responsive to domestic and international public opinion, governments capable of being shamed into conceding defeat. The British, representing a democracy with a free press and conscious of their international image, were susceptible to such shaming. But in Mahatma Gandhi's own day non-violence could have done nothing for the Jews of Hitler's Germany, who disappeared into gas chambers far from the flashbulbs of a war-obsessed press ... The power of non-violence rests in being able to say, 'to show you that you are wrong, I punish myself'. But that has little effect on those who are not interested in whether they are wrong and are already seeking to punish you disagree with them or not. For them, your willingness to undergo punishment is the most convenient means of victory.

(Tharoor 2016: 242–3)

There is plenty of counterveiling evidence for the effectiveness of strategies of civil resistance across a multitude of contexts and historical periods from Iran to the Philippines and Palestine. Chenoworth and Stephan (2011: 7) suggest that: 'between 1900 and 2006, non-violent resistance campaigns were nearly twice as likely to achieve full or partial success as their violent counterparts [...] the effects of resistance type on the probability of campaign success are robust even when we take into account potential confounding factors, such as the target regime type, repression and target regime capabilities'. The key to effectiveness is often mass participation. Higher levels of participation contribute to a number of mechanisms necessary for success, including enhanced resilience, higher probabilities of tactical innovation, expanded civic disruption (therefore raising the costs to the regime of maintaining the status quo) and loyalty shifts involving the opponent's erstwhile supporters, including members of the security forces. Here it is argued that 'Mobilization among local supporters is a more reliable source of power than the support of external allies, which many violent campaigns must obtain to compensate for their lack of participants' (Chenoworth and Stephan 2011: 10). Correspondingly, non-violent campaigns often fail to achieve their objectives when they fail to recruit a robust, diverse and broad-based membership.

Besides advocating non-cooperation as a strategy of civilian defence in case of invasion, the book *Democratic Defence* by Green Party candidate and long-time lesbian, gay, bi and trans-sexual (LGBT) activist Peter Tatchell (Tatchell 1985), offers a wide-ranging critique of forms of hierarchy (class, gender, race and sexuality) and oppression in military structures and invokes examples of alternatives around 'peoples' defence and citizen armies – with precedents going back to the Levellers and Chartists. This vision places democracy at the heart of efforts to demilitarize the military, and implies the need for proposals for Green security to re-orientate the military towards self-defence. The pursuit of non-violence and nuclear disarmament and restrictions on the arms trade would, in this rendition of Green strategy, go alongside the creation of a peoples' army (Tatchell 1985) and the repurposing of the Military-Industrial Complex for productive civilian and sustainable uses, such as the production of low-carbon energy. Dramatic shifts from civilian to military use and back again have historical precedents (Simms and Newell 2017) and would be seen as desirable from a Green point of view. Such shifts would include worker-led proposals for reconversions of production, such as the Lucas Plan in 1970s' Britain (Smith 2016). I discuss in the following Chapter 4 the importance to Greens of democratising control over, and access to, science and technology as part of moves to build a Green economy, but for Greens there is a link to peace and security too. Schumacher asked: 'how then could peace be built on a foundation of reckless science and violent technology?' (Schumacher 1974: 34). Greater social oversight and control over the development and deployment of technologies should spill over, in Green visions, to their applications in war and for the preservation of peace.

It is also important to note that there are important differences among Greens between pacifists and those who accept a role for conventional weapons capability as a transitional strategy away from nuclear weapons and to increase public acceptability that a country could defend itself in the event of an attack from a foreign power (Porritt 1989). Greens are generally hostile to military alliances such as NATO, but belief in coalition politics means they have had to make compromises that sit uncomfortably with their convictions. In power Greens have served in coalitions that have taken part in collective military ventures, causing deep divisions among their supporters and members (Frankland and Schoonmaker 1992). The experience of German Greens supporting military strikes when a member of a coalition, as well as Peter Tatchell and other Greens in the United Kingdom arguing for intervention in Syria, suggest these divisions persist. Green responses to the bombing of Syria in 2018 were more typical of Green approaches to security, with a focus on peace talks, sanctions, avoiding the cycles of violence and retaliation that bombing raids would provoke and calling for tighter regulation of the arms trade, which makes state violence towards their own citizens possible in the first place (Stavrianakis 2016). Indeed, despite all the bluster and brinkmanship shown by US President Donald Trump towards North Korean leader Kim Jong Un, at the time of writing, the prospects of peace are being advanced far more fruitfully and concretely through diplomacy and dialogue between the leaders of North and South Korea. Yet, as an article in the *Green European Journal*, reflecting on a range of contemporary crises and conflicts reflects: 'These examples raise fundamental questions with regards to the attitude of the Greens when the time for analysing the roots of a conflict is over and real actions are needed to stop a war and mend the peace.' Where Greens lack deference towards state sovereignty, especially when invoked to justify persecution of peoples, they may also lack the means to intervene militarily or otherwise.

A key question for Greens then is how to deal with the potential tension between a decentralised, small state on the one hand, and the pursuit of internationalist principles of solidarity, human rights protection and self-determination for oppressed groups around the world on the other. Reduced state capacity and, as noted above, greater economic self-sufficiency, might necessarily leave a Green state in a more isolationist position, lacking the ability to act on its internationalist and humanitarianist instincts, or even to discipline perpetrators of human rights violations. If there is reduced international trade, neither economic sanctions nor coercive means are a viable tool, and participation in collective security and humanitarian efforts would be significantly reduced. Overall then, less interventionism and the pursuit of less exploitative and extractivist policies towards other countries might reduce some of the sources of war and conflict, but the means to extend global protection to vulnerable citizens around the world would also be diminished. For Green security to gain wider support, further political work is required to wrestle with and resolve some of these tensions.

Notes

1 https://rethinkingsecurity.org.uk/
2 This quote is often attributed to Mahatma Gandhi. Others suggest the epigram is a twist on a famous Biblical injunction in the Book of Exodus [21:24]: 'An eye-for-eye and tooth-for-tooth would lead to a world of the blind and toothless'.
3 McDonald (2002: 287) observes that the 'idea of the changing structural context of international power is the basis for most calls to review definitions and practices of security that non-traditional issues are able to be included now that the power structures of the Cold War no longer require a narrow conception of what constitutes security'.
4 www.otago.ac.nz/ncpacs/otago638243.html
5 For example, Marc Levy et al. suggest in relation to intrastate conflict that 'severe, prolonged droughts are the strongest indicator of high-intensity conflict' (conflicts involving more than a thousand battle deaths). CIESIN www.ciesin.org/levy.html.
6 https://en.wikiquote.org/wiki/Robert_Oppenheimer
7 Taken from *Young India*, 27 February 1930.
8 http://teachingamericanhistory.org/library/document/the-power-of-non-violence/

4

Green Economy

The test of our progress is not whether we add more to the abundance of those who have much, it is whether we provide enough for those who have little.

(Franklin D. Roosevelt 20 January 1937)[1]

Arun Gandhi, grandson of Mahatma Gandhi, recalls an incident from his childhood which is revealing of how Greens think about the economy. Walking back from school one day in 1945 in rural India, Arun, who was eleven years old at the time, threw his pencil nub in the bushes. It had become too short to use. As night fell he was sent back with a torch to search for the pencil: the boy's grandfather had refused him a new writing implement and insisted he find the old one, which took the boy two hours. Arun picks up the story:

When I finally found the pencil and brought it to him, my grandfather said: 'Now I want you to learn two very important lessons. The first is that in the making of a simple thing like a pencil, we use a lot of the world's natural resources and throwing them away is violence against nature. The second lesson is that because we overconsume all these things, we are depriving people elsewhere of these resources and they have to live in poverty, and that is violence against humanity.[2]

This sense of the interconnections and interdependency between social inequality, uneven development and ecological degradation underpins a lot of Green thinking. It also speaks to the notions of ecological responsibility that Green thinking calls for from richer citizens of the world who overuse their share of the global commons.

In academic writing from Green perspectives, work on the economy is perhaps the most well developed. This is understandable given that the economy constitutes the metabolism between human society and the wider ecosystem of which it is a part in terms of materials, resources, energy and waste (Barry 2008). Much of this work draws on strands of political economy and political ecology to understand and critique capitalism's relation to nature. This includes work on socio-ecological relations and from world ecology perspectives (Moore 2015), as well as specific work on the metabolic rift and social metabolism of capitalism (Bellamy Foster et al. 2010). The Marxian concept of 'social metabolism' argues that production involves an exchange of resources and waste between human societies and the broader biosphere, revealing an unsustainable rate of metabolic exchange in which the impact of production exceeds the capacity of the biosphere to recycle and replenish – what Bellamy Foster terms a 'metabolic rift' (Bellamy Foster et al. 2010).

Work on global political ecology, meanwhile, shows how specific sites and instances of environmental degradation and social exclusion are intimately bound up with global economic processes and structures that serve to replicate and consolidate relations of power along the lines of race, class and gender (Newell 2005; Newell and Bumpus 2012). This view builds on perspectives from social ecology outlined in Chapter 2. Ecological political economy (Gale and M'Gonigle 2000) and Green political economy (Barry 1999), as well as *international* political economy perspectives on ecological questions (Helleiner 1996; Laferrière and Stoett 1999; Newell 2012; Katz-Rosene and Paterson 2018; Clapp and Dauvergne 2011; Newell and Lane 2018), offer further insights into the relationship between the organisation of the global political economy and the patterns of ecological degradation we observe today. Many of these perspectives reject the 'nature–society dualism', and instead propose that societies and the biosphere develop in co-constitutive processes as captured in concepts such as the 'anthropocene' and 'social' or socio-natures (Castree and Braun 2001). Since my purpose here is develop a political contribution from Green politics to global politics, rather than to articulate alternative theoretical understandings, I will refer only selectively to these works. It is worth noting that the contribution of this large body of literature is to relate the 'symptoms' of ecological crises, such as global warming or biodiversity loss, to the underlying unsustainable dynamics in socio-ecological relations from which they arise that have clear economic dimensions.

The critique of the contemporary global political economy, and articulation of alternatives which I develop below, also relates closely to Green views on development, the role of the state and global governance discussed elsewhere in this book. Let us hone in first on the critiques that Greens provide of the contemporary economy before considering alternative visions of a Green economy, as well as thinking about how to get from one to the other. Hence, I shall first outline Green critiques of today's global economy, in particular its ecological unsustainability and commitment to infinite growth on a finite planet. We will then look at what a Green economy might look like and how this departs markedly from ideas that invoke the same label, propagated by institutions like the Organisation for

Economic Cooperation and Development (OECD) and the World Bank. Finally, we shall explore the range of strategies Greens employ and propose to build a Green economy.

Critique

Perhaps above all other areas considered in this book, Green perspectives on the economy depart most radically from most other theories, perspectives and politics. They do so because of their critique of 'industrialism' in general as a way of organising the economy and of exponential growth as a legitimate, viable and sustainable goal. In International Relations, this challenges both Liberal orthodoxies about the foundations of peace through expanding commerce and Realist assumptions about growth and resource acquisition as means to survive in an anarchical international society, as touched upon in the last chapter. It also suggests that the problem with the economy is not just one of concentration in elite hands, of a particular class, or merely of more equitable distribution of wealth (as many critical and neo-Marxists accounts would emphasise) but rather the model of wealth generation itself that is premised on a problematic assumption of an abundant, disposable and infinite nature. As well as setting Green thinking apart from many other worldviews, it also raises strategic challenges about who the Greens can work with around a common vision for change. We will explore this in the section on strategy.

Greens are deeply critical of the globalised economy and its ecological irrationalities (Trainer 1996; Douthwaite 1996; Newell 2012). These include the prevailing orthodoxies and dominant practices around trade liberalisation, de-regulated finance and the internationalisation of production. The critique extends to the Bretton Woods' institutions and their role in propping up this system and perpetuating its social and environmental injustices (Goldman 2005; Park 2011).

One source of critique on which Greens draw seeks to historicise and contextualise the contemporary fetishisation of economic growth, showing that obsession with it is a relatively recent phenomena and not a permanent, given or timeless goal of human society (Dale 2012). While economic growth is often presented as an unquestionable given, an uncontestable and pre-political goal of human endeavour, Greens seek to demystify and denaturalise it as a modern project (Barry 2018). According to Dale (2012): 'The growth paradigm ... refers to the proposition that economic growth is *good*, *imperative*, essentially *limitless*, and the *principal remedy* for a litany of social problems. The growth paradigm appears ubiquitous, even natural, but it is uniquely modern ... For millennia no sense of "an economy" as something separate from the totality of social relations existed, nor was there a compulsion to growth.'

Importantly for Green thinking, we can trace the move to blur the distinction between 'needs' and 'wants' that Greens hold dear. Dale (2012) shows:

Linked to the flourishing of competitive consumption was a redefinition of human needs and desire. Against older traditions that associated luxury with excess and greed, writers such as David Hume and Adam Smith reconceived need and desire as 'conceptually indistinguishable', deeming it impossible 'to separate, morally or conceptually, needs and luxuries'. Needs were no longer regarded as natural, but as historical, and hence potentially insatiable. Desire was seen to stimulate demand, and in turn trade and the creation of wealth, further exciting the proliferation of desires. In parallel with this virtuous circle ran another, more potent one, according to which trade encourages the development of the division of labour, enabling specialisation that yields productivity gains and market expansion.

This move is ecologically significant in that a division of labour and emergent ideas of comparative advantage are premised on the construction of resource-intensive, export-orientated specialisation that, globally and historically, has precipitated the adoption of environmentally destructive models of development and the prioritisation of serving external demand over domestic need.

Contrary to myths about the natural outward expansion of markets through growing demand, the pace of innovation and the nature of technological progress, the construction of economies built along these lines coincides with, and presupposes, the use of force. Such use of force for acquisition of resources, both overseas and internally through dispossession to feed growth and against domestic populations resisting the intensification of labour exploitation or the acquisition of their land and resources for the profit of others, is a phenomenon we observe in relation to green grabs (Fairhead et al. 2012) and broader patterns of accumulation by dispossession (Harvey 2004). In geopolitics then, combined with capitalist competition (Desai 2013) – the characteristic feature of which is that it has no limit – we see the first articulations of military-industrial complexes as state strategies place greater emphasis upon the centrality of military power to national economic growth.

The first four decades of the twentieth century saw a shift in the growth paradigm amid a growing conviction that promoting growth is a matter of national priority (Barry 2018). In economics, the 1930s was the decade of Keynes and also of national accounting. In 1932 the US Congress commissioned the economist Simon Kuznets to devise a means to measure the nation's output. Gross Domestic Product (GDP) was the result. In essence, GDP presents a survey of economic activity from the perspective of legally transacted exchange value. It focuses on flows, to the exclusion of assets; it excludes illegal transactions and those in which no money changes hands – housework, DIY and voluntary work. GDP treats the sale of natural resources as income, without making any commensurate subtraction for resource depletion or depreciation. As economists such as Pigou and Coasce famously observed, it takes no account of 'externalities' – the costs that firms impose upon others but for which they are not charged, such as environmental degradation, noise pollution or congestion – except insofar as producing or countering them entails market transactions; in such cases these appear as additions to GDP. As ecological economists have frequently noted, what other economists often choose to forget is Kuznet's warning not to use GDP as a an indicator of growth, as opposed to a crude national accounting system. Andrew Simms, in discussing growth-based national accounting, shows how it came 'with a very big health warning attached ... One of the indicator's key architects, the economist Simon Kuznets, was explicit about its limitations. Growth did not measure quality of life, he made clear, and it excluded vast and important parts of the economy where exchanges were not monetary' (Simms 2013: 36–7). The latter includes the 'core economy' of family, care and community work, or what Greens and others often refer to as the 'care economy' that sustains all others.

For Dale (2012), the fact that GDP came to be regarded as a proxy for human well-being can only be explained in terms of power and ideology: in capitalist society the general interest becomes subsumed under the interests of those engaged in market transactions. Beyond its material functions and sources, there is an ideological dimension to the growth project. He argues that 'the growth paradigm – the idea that continuous economic growth is society's central and overriding goal – provides ideological cover for what is the true goal of capitalist production: the self-expansion of capital ... The ideology of growth ... obfuscates the exploitative process of accumulation, presenting it instead as something of general interest – growth'. Instead, Redclift claims: 'the concentration on "Growth" has served to obscure the fact that resource depletion and unsustainable development are a direct consequence of growth itself' (Redclift 1987: 56), a growth that is the imperative of fossil capitalism (Altvater 2006; Huber 2009; Malm 2016). This ideological project was backed with institutional power, exercised by the OECD in particular, in promoting its global adoption as *the* benchmark of economic performance (Schmelzer 2015, 2016).

From 1950 to 1973 capitalism experienced its golden age, and in the industrialised world the growth paradigm achieved its complete form. By producing 'avalanches of consumer goods' that 'progressively raise the standard of life of the masses', the economist Joseph Schumpeter promised, capitalist growth, if sustained, would abolish poverty. In the end, the reverse was true. The necessity for ever-increasing spending on consumer goods that people could not afford nor, in many ways, needed meant extending credit and, thereby, extending levels of indebtedness among the poor, while creating ever-longer 'shadows of consumption' (Dauvergne 2008; Lawson 2009). As we saw in Chapter 2, growth scepticism then emerged in the 1970s over concerns about rising pollution and diminishing supplies of non-renewable resources. The same decade saw the birth of ecological economics as well as a plethora of moral critiques of industrial civilisation in the years preceding the *Limits to Growth* report (discussed below) that formed the basis of Greens' critique of the unsustainability of growth.

According to many Greens and environmental commentators, the modern era of growth will inevitably draw to an end. For Andrew Dobson: 'Growth, the unexamined assumption that underpins our current political settlement, is nearing its sell-by date' (2014: 8). He notes, 'The past 250 years have been an era of exception, rather than normality and we believe that this era of exception is coming to an end, with potentially calamitous consequences, but also potentially liberating implications'. Speaking to arguments about the need to historicise the contemporary obsession with growth, he suggests: 'We have come to think of the industrial era of Promethean expectation and performance as normality, whereas it is in fact a world historical era of exception' (2014: 25). For some, this will occur as limits are placed upon the use of fossil fuels or because of the impacts of climate change causing negative growth, such that more and more state and private investment will be required to prop up existing infrastructures, to pay for emergencies and losses through health and 'natural' disasters. We will, in other words, be running to stand still economically. Forward projections of growth spell out the challenge of sustaining growth. When politicians aim to deliver annual growth rates of over two per cent per year (much more in many contexts), this implies an expansion of the economy by a factor of ten every hundred years or that in two hundred years the economy will be a hundred times bigger than it is now.

Limits to Growth

The origins of this critique date back to the 1970s. A central tenet of Green critiques of conventional economics and the organisation of the contemporary economy is the idea that there are 'limits to growth': the limits set by the resources available to us on planet Earth mean that growth cannot be infinite on a finite planet. These ideas took root in Green politics in the wake of the famous *Limits to Growth report* of the Club of Rome published in 1972. The report argued:

If the present growth trends in world population, industrialisation, pollution, food production, and resource depletion continue unchanged, the limits to growth on this planet will be reached sometime within the next hundred years. The most probable result will be a rather sudden and uncontrollable decline in both population and industrial capacity.

(Meadows et al. 1974: 23)

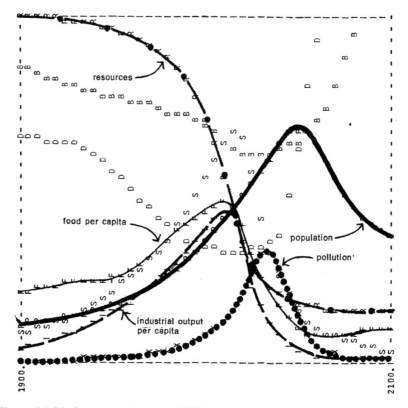

Figure 4.1 Limits to growth report 1972.
Source: Meadows et al., 1972, used with permission

Here is a graphic from the report showing how and why resource demands would outstrip supply (Figure 4.1).

Optimistically as it turned out, the report's authors claimed: 'We are convinced that the realization of the quantitative restraints of the world environment and of the tragic consequences of an overshoot is essential to the initiation of new forms of thinking that will lead to a fundamental revision of human behaviour and, by implication, of the entire fabric of present day society' (Meadows et al. 1974: 190). Subsequent reports by, *Beyond the Limits* (Meadows et al. 1992) and *Limits to Growth: The 30 Year Update* (Meadows et al. 2004) provide further and updated evidence of planetary overshoot and the likelihood this will continue unless our economic trajectory is fundamentally changed. As the authors write: 'Once the limits to growth were far in the future. Now they are widely in evidence. Once the concept of collapse was unthinkable. Now it has begun to enter into the public discourse' (2004: xxii).

Ecological limits constitute what ecological Marxists refer to as the second contradiction of capitalism (O'Connor 1991). If the first is that by exploiting labour and driving down wages, capitalists undermine the ability of workers to spend their wages in buying the products of capitalists, the second is that capitalism undermines the very conditions for its reproduction. That is: its expansionist logic ultimately undermines its ability to sustain itself over the long term by depleting the 'conditions of production' needed to support the endless accumulation of capital such as soil, water, and energy (O'Connor 1991). As Marx noted in *Capital*: 'the original sources of all wealth' are ultimately 'the soil and the labourer' (1974: 475). By depleting water tables, over-exploiting forests and land, capitalists diminish their own 'natural capital'.

Fixes for the Limits to Growth

The hunger and need of global capitalists to bring more and more areas of the commons into the private realm is identified by many Greens as a primary reason for the unsustainability of contemporary economies (The Ecologist 1993). Opening up areas of the world to 'the market', or market rule, privatising land and separating communities from their means of subsistence forces people to sell their labour to capitalists and begins the process of lengthening the chains of production and consumption. What could be exchanged or bartered locally now would have to be bought from the private owner or imported from elsewhere. It raises questions about who has the right to own and control land and its associated resources, which many have seen as 'common wealth'. Today's globalised economy is merely an extreme extension of this logic, such that price and narrow definitions of 'efficiency' determine *where* something is produced and for *how much* and *by* and *for whom* without reference to place, limits or need. These processes and structures obscure the value and work (from human labour and ecological services) that go into production for market.

This separation is essential to processes of *distancing*: where consumers are disconnected from an awareness or understanding of the social and environmental conditions in which the products they buy are produced. By virtue of greater purchasing power, they do not have to live with or witness the consequences of those consumption choices in the market, enabling reckless and unsustainable extraction to proceed out of sight for the world's wealthy consumers. This is in spite of campaigns aimed at raising consumer awareness about the destructive effect of everyday consumer goods linked to palm oil production or illegal logging, for example. Since communities are then denied alternative means of subsistence, they then have no option but to be complicit in forms of degradation that they know will produce further forms of (intergenerational and inter-societal) injustice as risks and burdens are borne by poorer communities or future generations that inherit the waste and a depleted resource base. The feminist writer Val Plumwood

(2002) describes this phenomenon in terms of 'remoteness', whereby privileged classes remain spatially, temporarily, epistemologically and technologically remote from the ecological consequences of their decisions in ways that perpetuate ecological irrationality and environmental injustice.

In making sense of this process, David Harvey's (2003, 2005) work on spatial and temporal fixes highlights the ways in which capital is able to displace responsibility for environmental problems and circumvent calls for regulation (which represent limits to capital) by paying others to reduce pollution. This reverses the logic of 'polluter pays' by allowing principal polluters to pay others to reduce pollution on their behalf – a process likened by activists to the 'new indulgences' whereby, in the Middle Ages, wealthy individuals could pay poorer people to go to prison on their behalf (Smith 2007). It also helps to explain phenomena such as the export of resource-intensive forms of production to the global South. These forms of 'ecologically uneven exchange' mean that the responsibility for pollution, as well as the pollution itself, is redistributed globally such that: '(e)missions are increasing sharply in developing countries as wealthy countries "offshore" the energy and resource intensive stages of production' (Roberts and Parks 2008: 169). It also accounts for the export of toxic and hazardous wastes to poor countries so that richer countries are not faced with the consequences of their consumption (Clapp 2001). Such strategies both feed upon and reproduce global inequalities, even if they clearly bring tangible benefits to elites within host countries. While moving things around makes sense for richer countries or social groups able to do so, and finds support from economists who view it as a more cost-effective route to pollution control, from an ecological perspective it serves simply to disperse rather than resolve environmental problems. In this regard, environmental justice literatures lend weight to Greens' concerns about this spiral of social and ecological degradation that flows from distancing and the long shadows cast by unsustainable models of global consumption (Sikor and Newell 2014; Dauvergne 2008).

For all of these reasons, Greens reject claims about the possibility of 'Green growth' and a 'Green economy' as articulated by the OECD, World Bank, UNEP (2011) and many governments and corporations. In a meeting with the OECD I was reminded that following the preface 'Green' with anything other than 'growth' was not an option for OECD members. It was 'no coincidence', I was told, that the accent was on growth rather than 'economy' or 'development'. Growth first, last and always. The level of 'taboo' around growth or discussions about quantitative reductions in production and consumption is borne out by what government negotiators refer to as 'no-go' areas that are off-limits, indicating the degree of commitment to growth at all costs (Søby 2018).

Advocates of growth have fought back. Critics of the Green position come from a range of positions. Some question the idea of limits to growth – on the grounds of the modelling on which the initial report was based, or its neglect or pessimism about the role of technology and innovation (Cole and Freeman 1973; Martell 1994; Asafu-Adjaye et al. 2015). In this regard, a famous bet took place between Paul Ehrlich, author of the book *Population Bomb* (1975) coming from a neo-Malthusian perspective, and the economist Julian Simon. Ehrlich feared that a growth in population would deplete natural resources. Simon counterintuitively argued that population growth would actually make resources more abundant because of long-term changes in income, as well as the impact that technology and human ingenuity would have on the availability of resources. In September of 1980, Simon challenged Ehrlich to a bet on resource depletion. Simon told Ehrlich he could choose a group of raw materials that he thought would become less abundant over the next decade. If the real prices of those materials increased over that time, then Ehrlich would win the bet. In the period between September 1980 and September 1990, population rose by 873 million people, and all five commodities that Ehrlich selected declined in real price, with an average drop of 57.6 per cent (Robbins et al. 2010: 29). The debate did not, of course, end there. Indeed, the *Factor Four* report presented to the Club of Rome suggested that wealth would likely double if resource use could be halved (von Weizsacker et al. 1997). Great emphasis is placed in critiques of the limits to growth on the role of technology and innovation as means to decouple growth from increased pollution in spite of Green critiques that efficiency savings often enable even greater consumption. For Greens, the fatal fallacy of the notion of Green growth is that while vast productivity increases do indeed incentivise a more efficient use of resources, they raise demand at the same time – thereby running counter to the goal of saving resources (Santarius 2012).

In another important strand of critique of the Green position, it is suggested that, contrary to the idea of a 'treadmill of production' where more growth always results in more pollution, a process of 'ecological modernisation' (Mol 2003; Weale 1992; Young 2000) is underway whereby environmental values and goals come to permeate institutions, markets and cultural values such that the apparent contradiction between growth and sustainability is overcome. This position is critiqued by Greens on the grounds that while efficiencies can be made, resource throughputs reduced, and production, technology and finance undoubtedly mobilised towards greener ends, the direction of travel, as captured in trends towards the overshoot of planetary boundaries (see Figure 8.1), suggest not only that the pace and depth of change is not fast enough but that these shifts fail to deal with the basic contradictions of the fantasy of infinite growth on a finite planet.

Growth-oriented economies cannot go on using finite resources. Technological innovations cannot solve the problems indefinitely, although appropriate small-scale technologies are seen as one aspect of the solution. Technological advances can only postpone the problems.

(Vincent 1993: 232)

The so-called Jevon's paradox looms large here. Writing about coal nearly 150 years ago Jevons showed how efficiency savings have the ironic and unfortunate effect of encouraging further energy use with the money saved (Jevons 1865). The phenomena whereby efficiency gains in a growth economy are often redirected towards overall increases in consumption highlights many of the limits of green economy thinking. For example, the development of more fuel- efficient cars has not led to reduced car use. Rather, people can drive them further or more frequently without paying more. Hence incremental efficiency gains are more than overshot by increased resource use in a growth-orientated economy.

Others critiques suggested that far from it being a structural or functional imperative of the state, as some Marxist and Green accounts suggest (Vlachou 2004), the treadmill of production persists in capitalist society because of the an enduring social consensus on the need for economic growth (Schnaiberg 1980). This brings us back to the relationship between accumulation and legitimation in capitalist society (Habermas 1973; Paterson 2010) and the ways in which an ideology of growth plays an important part in sustaining and reproducing the value systems and beliefs which protect this central political project from wider scrutiny, tying, as it does, the fate of labouring classes and subalterns to the fate of dominant elites. In this sense, the ideology and dogma of growth has to be understood more broadly in relation to enlightenment and liberal ideas about *homo economicus*, self-interested rational actors, human exceptionalism, the sanctity of property rights and confidence in the possibility of the boundless mastery of nature through never-ending scientific and technological progress (what I described earlier as cornucopian thinking). As Eckersley suggests, while 'These views might have made some sense in the seventeenth and eighteenth centuries, when it seemed more reasonable to suppose that everything about the world was potentially (and soon to be) knowable, available and rationally controllable' (2004: 108), it is clearly the case they no longer do. They do, nevertheless, hold sway in some accounts of ecological modernisation that succumb to the 'alluring momentum of material progress and the belief in the rational, technological mastery of nature in ways that uphold economic freedoms while ruling out more critical deliberation over the ultimate purpose and character of the modernization process' (2004: 108).

The Politics of Measuring Growth

Beyond the generic critique of growth, Greens are critical of how growth is counted: the indices and metrics employed to measure growth. 'Growth scepticism' about the disconnect between economic growth and social well-being, leads Greens to propose alternative indicators of well-being. Yardsticks such as the UN Human Development Index (HDI), the Genuine Progress Indicator (GPI) and the

Happy Planet Index have been developed to estimate well-being, as alternatives to GDP. These are gaining some traction in mainstream circles. The EU's Climate Commissioner Connie Hedegaard suggested, for example, that unless 'a more intelligent growth model' is adopted, involving a shift from GDP to broader measures of well-being, 'the world will face future severe crises' (cited in Dale 2012). The call then is for a more 'differentiated development' to discriminate between those sectors you want to grow and those you do not, as well as differentiating within GDP. As Cato observes:

GDP is an inappropriate measure of a green economy, since it is focused on activity, whether positive or negative in terms of well-being; because it measures flows rather than stocks; because it takes no account of equity; and because its unit of measurement is in incidental monetary terms. Government should have regard in particular to measures of material flows through the economy, minimizing the throughput of non-renewable resources and substituting renewable for non-renewable resources wherever possible.

(Cato n.d.)

As Robert Kennedy put it more bluntly, growth measures everything except 'that which makes life worthwhile' (cited in Simms 2005: 37). Building on this argument, Ekins (1986: 7) suggests: 'A large proportion of the outcome of the production process expressed each year in GNP does not represent any benefit to the quality of life and of the environment'. Indeed, quite the reverse. The blind pursuit of growth intensifies many of the economic problems it claims to address. It confuses means with ends, where growth is but one possible way of enhancing human welfare. It fails to ask questions about growth for whom, what is growing and with what consequences. As Ekins suggests,

It is only by showing that the growth has taken place through the production of goods and services that are inherently valuable and beneficial; demonstrating that these goods and services have been distributed widely throughout society; and proving that these benefits outweigh any detrimental effects of the growth process on other parts of society, that one can arrive at any sort of assessment as to whether a particular instance of economic growth is in fact a good or a bad thing. (1986)

Given, as noted above, the roots of Green politics in feminism, it is unsurprising that Greens are also critical of the way mainstream economies and economists undervalue labour, work and the informal as well as 'care' economy. That which appears 'cheap' in conventional economics is only so because labour and ecology have not been valued and represented (Patel and Moore 2018) and all negative costs duly 'externalised', i.e. on to society and the environment in the pursuit of profit. As Molly Scott Cato states: 'From the perspective of a green economist, the formal economy is embedded within a system of social and environmental structures: formal economic activity is only one aspect of economic activity. This contrasts sharply with the prevailing view of the predominance of markets as the ideal mechanism for the distribution of goods and resources' (Cato n.d.). The notion of the socially and ecologically embedded nature of the economy is central to Green critiques of the ways in which economies are currently organised.

Critique of Political Economy

Greens' concerns about the viability and desirability of today's economic system extend to a critique of *political* economy. Growth fetishism means state managers are reliant on business – or capital – for their electoral success. This affords capital enormous structural power and leads to attempts by corporations to infiltrate state decision-making in ways which lead to corruption and to threats to democracy where democracy is 'for sale' as Woodin and Lucas (2004) put it in their book *Green Alternatives to Globalisation*. The corporate penetration of key national and global institutions has been documented by numerous scholars and activists (Monbiot 2000; Lee et al. 1997; Karliner 1997; Levy and Newell 2005). Eckersley writes, 'The owners and controllers of capital have, for the most part, been more successful than any subsequent social movement in forging the basic constitutional structure and rationality of the liberal democratic state. Moreover, by virtue of their wealth and privilege, such classes continue to have a significant influence in the policy-making process, both nationally and transnationally' (2004: 106). Against neo-liberal forms of participation where the terms and nature of debate are set at the outset by the imperatives of protecting particular accumulation strategies (Newell 2010), the challenge is to question and expand the nature and scope of political participation and representation to include areas of economic decision-making that are currently off-limits.

Given the close relationship between growth and statehood and the maintenance of elite power, sensitivity around these issues is unsurprising. We have seen many deliberate attempts to suffocate debate about growth and its limits. Tim Jackson in his book (2017) *Prosperity without Growth* recalls the scandal caused by the publication of a report from the former Sustainable Development Commission in the UK posing questions about the link between growth and prosperity. This is not a phenomenon exclusive to capitalist societies. In China, for example, Goron (2017) shows where there are a few dissonant voices, they are often repressed. For instance, Bo Hechuan's *China on the Edge: The Crisis of Ecology and Development*, published in Hong Kong in 1991, which attributed environmental problems to what he judged misguided expansionary economic policies, was almost immediately banned in mainland China. Over 400,000 copies of the book were printed and read by China's top leaders before they banned it. Bo Hechuan went into exile. Ideological censorship prevented the linking of industrial pollution with capitalism, a notion that was deemed inapplicable to China. As in other political fields, it was impossible to reconcile the economic policies and practices of government institutions with the official doctrine of the party–state. The remarks of a Marxist scholar highlight this difficulty:

In the past, we thought environmental pollution and ecological crisis were maladies exclusively associated with capitalism. China as a socialist country would be unlikely to have such problems. However, in the past thirty years of reform and opening-up, China's resource and ecological problems have grown in proportion to the economic growth, whose level of severity even is no less deplorable than in the primitive accumulation stage of capitalism.

(Zhihe Wang, He, and Fan 2014 cited in Goron 2017)

As we shall see below, this critique of current political economies forms the basis of arguments for ecological and economic democracy, deepening and strengthening checks on the power of capital over the state and the hijacking of public institutions for private ends through party funding, revolving doors and privileged access to decision-making.

Social Limits to Growth

Greens increasingly also pair their concern about the ecological unsustainability of the global economy with evidence about its poor performance socially, and even on its own terms, economically (Hirsch 1976). Trickle-down economics: the assumption that concentration of wealth in the global elite eventually trickles down to the poor, has long been discredited. More recent arguments about the so-called 'spirit level' show that after a certain point growth is sustainable neither socially nor environmentally (Wilkinson and Pickett 2009). As Serge Latouche (2009: 22) concisely argues: 'If growth automatically generated well-being, we would now be living in paradise.' The relationship between GDP per head and well-being is limited, and such correlation between them as does exist tends to decline after a certain point: as a rule of thumb, when per capita GDP exceeds \$15,000. Beyond a certain level of growth that satisfies basic material needs, a rising proportion of incomes goes to 'positional goods', aimed at signifying social status (through property, expensive cars, etc.), the desire for which economic growth can never satisfy (Kallis 2015). Material wealth can be an important determinant of living conditions and the quality of life, but the relationship is contingent (Dale 2012). *The Spirit Level's* principal thesis is simple: as national income increases beyond a certain level, it ceases to translate into improvements in health or happiness (see Figure 4.2). Instead, the critical variable is the degree of equality.

Deploying an impressive body of evidence, *The Spirit Level* demonstrates that income inequality varies inversely with levels of trust, life expectancy, children's

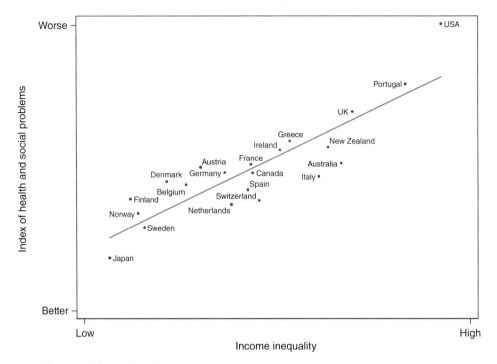

Figure 4.2 Spirit level.
Source: Wilkinson and Pickett, 2009, used with permission

educational performance and social mobility, and directly with rates of homicide, imprisonment, mental illness, alcohol addiction, infant mortality, obesity and length of working hours. The level of these social ills is much higher in unequal societies than in more equal ones. Equality is the key to social cohesion as societies with the highest levels of inequality perform worse over a bewildering range of social indicators, from physical and mental health to drug addiction, crime and violence. In other words, inequality undermines the social fabric of societies. Interestingly from a Green point of view, 'It is fortunate', Wilkinson and Pickett (2009: 215) conclude, that 'just when the human species discovers that the environment cannot absorb further increases in emissions, we also learn that further economic growth in the developed world no longer improves health, happiness or well-being'.

These inequalities in wealth are, nevertheless, endemic to contemporary capitalism according to the French economist Thomas Piketty (2014). Capitalism, in short, automatically creates levels of inequality that are unsustainable. The rising wealth of the 1 per cent is neither a blip, nor rhetoric. There is a fundamental tendency towards inequality that is unleashed wherever demographics or low taxation or weak labour organisation allow it. In this analysis, the long, mid-twentieth-century period of rising equality was actually the blip, produced by war, the power of organised labour (now much diminished), the need for high taxation, and by demographics and technical innovation. In this account, wealth will tend to concentrate to levels incompatible with democracy, let alone social justice, echoing Green arguments that the period of growth that lasted for large parts of the twentieth century is historically exceptional and not sustainable (Dobson 2014). 'Historically, growth and inequality have been partners in a macabre dance of reciprocal legitimation. Inequality is regarded as necessary for growth (if people are equal why would anyone bother to work?) and growth is used to quieten the voices of those asking for more equality by holding out the promise of an ever bigger cake' (Dobson 2014: 15).

Social Control of Science and Technology

Technological innovation is seen as key driver of growth in capitalist economies as waves of creative destruction bring about the rise of one set of technologies and a wave of growth, and signal the demise of incumbent ones (Schumpeter 1942). The role of innovation and entrepreneurship is essential to disturb this equilibrium and is the prime cause of economic development to avoid an economy falling into what economists would fear: a stationary state. Greens, on the other hand, are often caricatured as being luddites opposed to modern technology. In reality, Greens are not critical of technology per se but the means to which it is put and by whom and on whose behalf. The issue is social control and purpose and who decides that. Indeed, as Adams (1995: 98) points out, there is a confusion in Green thinking whereby environmentalism 'combines modern-ism and anti-modernism, a call for better science with a critique of the rationality of science'. Their critique is of science and technology as neutral drivers of progress and development and as an end in themselves, without regard to social need or social and environmental impacts. As Daly suggests (1977: 107–14), 'There is a limit beyond which the extra costs of surrendering control over one's environs and activities to the experts becomes greater than the extra benefits. This is not anti-science, it is merely a warning against the idolatry of science by some of its zealous fanatics who are consecrated to redoubling their efforts while forgetting their purposes'.

Greens are certainly wary of techno-fixes to social problems and economic ills. As the *Limits to Growth* report noted: 'We cannot expect technological solutions alone to get us out of this vicious cycle' (Meadows et al. 1974: 192). Greens are often opposed to large-scale technologies, such as genetic engineering, geoengi-neering and nuclear energy, as well as scientific practices such as vivisection that transgress ethical boundaries and responsibilities to other sentient beings. As we saw in the last chapter, concerns about arms races, militarism and the entrenched nature of the military-industrial complex in many societies that distort social priorities and progressive use of sources, are central to Green thinking. While welcoming of technologies that reduce resource throughput and create eco-efficiencies and are produced in socially useful and appropriate ways, they also point to the likelihood that progress made will be overwhelmed by overall resource consumption because of the Jevon's paradox in a growth-orientated society, as discussed above. A further concern is that some technological developments provide a way of 'exiting' resource limits on planet Earth rather than seeking to live sustainably within them. The race for the control of space and the pursuit of alternative habitable planets to meet the insatiable resource demands of the human population once planet Earth has been fully depleted, might be seen as an exit strategy from having to live sustainably on planet Earth. The fact that the National Aeronautics and Space Administration (NASA)'s budget dwarfs that of the National Science Foundation perhaps hints at where priorities currently lie.

There is a broader issue here that is about the role of expertise in decision-making and whose knowledge counts. Greens often emphasise the need to 'open up' assumptions about pathways and pluralise what counts as valid, authoritative and legitimate knowledge and expertise (Stirling 2011). This draws on work on 'citizen science' (Fischer 2002) and many practices adopted by environmental justice movements and local activists seeking to document and contest the deterioration and contamination of their local environments (Cole and Foster 2001; Newell 2005). It is also informed by a Green emphasis on the value of localised, indigenous, experiential and non-'scientific' (conventionally defined) knowledge (Shiva 2011). Which risks get assessed and by whom has enormous political consequences.

As noted in Chapter 1 in the discussion of 'deep ecology' in particular, Green thinking often also calls for humility, respect for the natural world and restraint and control when it comes to scientific and technological endeavour. We noted the rejection and critique of 'Newtonian atomism', and cornucopian assumptions that the planet is there only for the purposes of human experimentation, enjoyment and plunder. Knowledge production has often been undertaken in the service of visibilising the value of nature but with the (mostly unintended) effect of making it exploitable through its legibility. This charge is levelled at environmental economists in debates about pricing nature, for example (Costanza et al. 2014), but, as Escobar notes, 'Environmental sciences participate in reinscribing nature into the law of value; the lack of epistemological vigilance has resulted in a certain disciplining of environmental themes which has precluded the creation of concepts useful for the formulation of alternative ecological and economic rationalities' (Escobar 1995: 202). Where local and indigenous knowledge has been drawn upon, such as in relation to biodiversity protection, or more insidiously 'bio-prospecting', it is often exploited and abused (Shiva and Moser 1995). 'By bringing them into the politics of science, local forms of knowledge are recodified by modern science in utilitarian ways' (Escobar 1995: 204). For example, in public consultations around the design of National Biosafety Frameworks by which governments regulate risks associated with the introduction of genetically modified organisms (GMOs) into the environment as part of Cartagena Protocol on Biosafety, ethical, moral and religious concerns regarding GMOs brought to the discussion by indigenous groups and social movements were screened out of debates in an effort to keep public inputs narrowly focused on their potential impacts on biodiversity (Newell 2010).

In Commoner's (1970: 3) book *Science and Survival*, he asks the loaded question 'Is science getting out of hand?', suggesting that 'The age of innocent faith in science and technology may be over'. Writing about radioactivity (written in the shadow of the atomic bomb), pesticides and chemicals, the impact of the combustion engine and presciently about climate change, he also offered up a critique of dependence on large-scale interconnected infrastructures and technologies over which humans exercise diminishing control (cybernetics and the like). In part, this is the 'Frankenstein fantasy' of machines outsmarting humans (Commoner refers to the 'sorcerer's apprentice', making their labour redundant). It resonates strongly with contemporary anxieties over artificial intelligence and automation and broader fears about science and technology outpacing our ability to control them. As the back cover of the book *Science and Survival* reads, 'Science has unleashed vast forces without knowledge of what the long-term effects on the environment will be. Only by recognising this and the fact that everything is interrelated can we safeguard a future for mankind' [sic]. The point, as Commoner suggests, is not 'to declare a moratorium on the progress of science' (1970: 28). Rather: 'The obligation which our technological society forces upon us all, scientist and citizen alike, is to discover how humanity can survive the new power which science has given it' (1970: 156). The question is not *whether* to make use of this knowledge, but *how*. What are acceptable risks to take, who bears them and who makes the decision? Issues are thereby raised about access to and freedom of information, knowledge about risks and proper processes of prior and informed consent. Commoner (1970: 58) suggests: 'Knowledge about specific applications of scientific knowledge has long been restricted by military or commercial secrecy. But now even basic scientific work is often controlled by military and profit incentives that impose secrecy on the dissemination of fundamental results.' These concerns continue today around the murky links between civilian and military nuclear programmes (Cox et al. 2016), the problems of accessing public research behind private paywalls of commercial publishing or the reliance on businesses to conduct risk assessments of their own products in the biotechnology and pharmaceutical sectors, for example (Newell 2003).

Normative Vision

Greens have articulated as a response to the critiques above what they refer to as the 'new economics', after which the *New Economics Foundation* was named. Ekins (1986: 132) sums it up in the following way. The new economics is 'rooted in the recognition that human life and economic activity are an interdependent part of the wider ecological process that sustain life on earth and will either operate sustainably within those parameters or bring about their own demise'. The focus then is on satisfaction of human needs, social justice, equitable sharing and valuing of work, greater economic self-reliance at all levels and sustainable use of resources.

   Echoing Trainer's idea of a 'conserver society' (Trainer 1995), the UK Green Party (1989) put in their 1989 manifesto:

The key to a conserver economy is to take and use only what we really need: green politics is about 'enough', not about 'more and more' … In a green conserver economy, wellbeing would be measured not merely in terms of the amount we spend … It would be measured in terms of good health, clear air, pure water, un-poisoned food, stimulating education, cultural diversity, safe and friendly neighbourhoods, the variety of plants and animals sharing our environment. In a conserver society, values change too. A 'developed country' would no longer be one that can dominate world markets, but one which has the ability to house and feed its population properly … It would measure its success in terms of a healthy environment, its ability to care for people and share its wealth, and its capacity to guarantee the wellbeing of yet unborn generations.

The submission by the Greenhouse think-tank to the Environmental Audit Committee hearing on a Green Economy spelled out the following central tenets of green thinking about the economy.

A 'green economy' is not a globalised market economy producing a slightly different range of products; a green economy would be an economy whose design was compatible with the primary constraint on human life: that we live within ecological limits. The central change that a green economy requires is from considering the economy, environment and society as intersecting but separate to recognizing that the economy is located within society, which is in turn embedded within the environment.

(Cato n.d.)

This notion is fundamental to Green critiques of mainstream economics and forms the basis of Green economics: that the economy is merely a subset of society and the biosphere which sustains all life on Earth. To design and seek to expand an economic system that depletes the latter is to undermine the very basis of the existence of the former. Molly Scott Cato's submission to the Green economy enquiry of the UK's Environmental Audit Committee is again useful in summarising the alternative vision of the economy of many Greens:

A green approach to the economy would seek to move the target of our economy away from economic growth and towards flourishing, convivial human communities which do not threaten other species or the planet itself. In place of economic growth we should move towards a steady-state economy. As demonstrated by the report *Prosperity without Growth* by the Sustainable Development Commission, we reject the idea that 'business as usual' can lead to a sustainable future. The sorts of increases in energy and materials efficiency required to ensure our current level of consumption at a sustainable rate of resource use are simply not feasible. In a green economy businesses will need to learn from the ways of nature, hence the importance of closed-loop production systems and biomimicry. A green economy is likely to be dominated by co-operative businesses, guided by humane and respectful principles and values, rather than corporations, legally constrained to maximize value for shareholders. A green economy would not rely on lengthy supply chains for the provision of basic goods and resources, but rather would be based around a system of self-reliant local economies. A green economy is likely to focus more on livelihoods than simply on the labour-market, and opportunities should be made available for citizens to meet their own needs, especially by opening up access to land.

(Cato n.d)

Further:

A green economy cannot have the achievement of growth as its central guiding principle. Excessive growth creates feedback systems that undermine the quality of life that we were seeking to enhance and is hence self-defeating. There may be some scope for growth that does not rely on increased use of energy or raw materials and transport, and has a neutral impact on waste production and pollution, and in building the infrastructure we need for a sustainable society, but even during the transition to a green economy we need to limit energy and materials use. The design principle for a green economy should be circular rather than linear. Renewable resources should not be used at a faster rate than they can be replaced, while non-renewable resources should be recycled.

(Cato n.d)

The essence of Green thinking can perhaps be summed up by the phrase 'better instead of more'. There are strong preferences for shortening the circuits of production and consumption (Douthwaite 1996) to focus on needs, reduce the transport of goods and waste and the need for packaging. This policy implies supporting local economies through delinking and autarky and, in some versions, localising the money supply. Again, the distinction many Greens draw between 'needs' and 'wants' or 'greed' are important here, and there are strong echoes of Gandhian and Buddhist economics, expressed in the quote frequently attributed to Gandhi that 'the world has enough resources to meet everyone's need but not everyone's greed'. Efficiency in Buddhist economics is about reducing resource use rather than the dominant notion of the efficient deployment of capital to maximise returns. Experiments of communities organised along Gandhian lines around 'an economy of permanence' are often cited approvingly by Greens, such as the statement that: 'The Gandhian approach to economic development, based around self-reliant and close-knit villages, has also provided inspiration, and still offers sustainable livelihoods for many in India' (Cato n.d.).

Though criticised by those on the political Left for being 'small-capitalists', many Green views of the economy share more in common with recent contemporary ideas, such as 'Buen vivir' (Vanhulst and Beling 2014) or Ubuntu in South Africa. Gudynas (2017: 1) suggests, for example, '*Buen Vivir* as a radical critique of development points to alternatives that are at the same time post-capitalist and post-socialist, alternatives in which the recognition of the intrinsic value of the non-human is a core component'.

Steady-State Economy

The academic and economist (and former employee of the World Bank no less) Herman Daly has articulated most clearly what Greens refer to as a 'steady-state' economy as their alternative to ecologically blind growth fetishism (Daly 1996). This position is partly informed by the laws of thermodynamics – the law of conservation of matter-energy that states that: 'we do not produce or consume anything, we merely rearrange it' and the law of increasing entropy – that there is a continual reduction in potential for further use within the system as a whole. Even with recycling, some fraction of useful materials is irrevocably lost during each cycle of use. Daly (1977: 108) suggests: 'The effect of the entropy law is as immediate and concrete as the facts that you can't burn the same tank of gasoline twice, that organisms cannot live in a medium of their own waste products and that efficiencies cannot reach, much less exceed, 100 per cent.' Too much input impairs the capacity of the biosphere to assimilate waste. Yet our current economic institutions are designed to maximise throughput rather than minimise it, while 'Our national income accounts treat consumption of geological capital as current income'. Daly continues: 'Man [sic] is the only member of the biosphere who has broken this evolutionary budget constraint. It is only natural that this unique expansionary behaviour should cause repercussions and feedbacks from the rest of the system in the unhappy form of pollution and breakdown of local life-support systems.'

In this sense, the steady-state alternative 'is characterised by constant stocks of people and physical wealth maintained at some chosen desirable level by a low rate of throughput. Throughput flow begins with depletion (followed by production and consumption) and ends with an equal amount of waste effluent or pollution' (Daly 1977: 107–14). Though steady, this structure is not fixed in time. Daly suggests:

As values and technology evolve, different levels might become both possible and desirable. But the growth (or decline) required to get to the new level would be seen as a temporary adjustment process, not a norm ... In the steady state, technological and moral evolution would be autonomous rather than growth-induced. They would precede and pull growth in the most desirable direction rather than being pushed down the path of least resistance by the pressure of autonomous growth. Growth (positive or negative) would always be seen as a temporary passage from one steady state to another.

For Greens, the very goals and purpose of economic activity need to be reconsidered in the interests of building a sustainable society. Drawing on Buddhist economics (Schumacher 1974), so-called because of the 'right livelihood' requirement of Buddha's path, Greens emphasise that standards of living and quality of life are not best judged or valued in terms of levels of consumption. Local production for local use is the norm and default option since resource use has to reflect imperatives of long-term sustainability as well as short-term profit. As well as abandoning the idea of affluence at all costs, this implies the re-purposing of production around socially useful forms (Trainer 1985).

This approach also advances a different philosophy of work in the economy and how to value it, including of course care work and the informal economy. Greens are often assumed by trade unions and others of being insufficiently attentive to labour issues in spite of recent interest in 'just transitions' (Swilling and Annecke 2012; Newell and Mulvaney 2013). Barca (2017: 1), for example, highlights the place of labour, arguing that 'degrowth should aim for a truly democratic, workers' controlled production system, where alienation is actively countered by a collective re-appropriation of the products of labor and by a truly democratic decision-making process over the use of the surplus'. There is certainly common ground around the need for energy democracy,[3] for example, and the need for public control over key infrastructures, even if Greens and labour organisations may disagree about the level of decentralisation that should then ensue.

In conventional approaches to labour and work specialisation and the 'unitisation' of tasks, breaking down work into minute functions (as with Taylorism and Fordism) is aimed at reducing and rationalising production costs. This is along the lines of the 'pin' factory described in Smith's *Wealth of Nations* (Smith 2014). Work in Buddhist economics, on the other hand, is about enhancing faculties, realising potential, engaging in common and collective tasks and the provision of goods needed for a common existence. Work and leisure are seen as complementary parts of the same process. Beyond attachment to wealth 'since consumption is merely a means to human well-being, the aim should be to obtain the maximum of well-being with the minimum of consumption' (Schumacher 1974). This attitude is in contrast to the focus in conventional economics on consumption as the purpose of economic activity, with land, labour and capital the means.

Likewise, satisfying human wants from faraway places rather than local sources would signify failure rather than success for Greens.

Greens address the politics of redistribution that flow from this vision through proposals, discussed below, for a basic income scheme, ecological taxation and the like. As Daly (1977: 107–14) suggests: 'The usual objection to limiting growth, made in the name of the poor . . . Defends growth as an alternative to sharing which is unrealistic if not inconceivable.' Controversially, for some Greens such as Daly, sharing has to be combined with population control. He suggests: 'Without population control, sharing will simply make everyone equally poor. Without sharing, population control will at best reduce the number of the poor, but will not eliminate poverty.'

The politics of scale are also important to Greens for political and ecological imperatives. Many Greens argue for bioregions or communes as we saw in Chapter 2. For bio-regionalist Greens, modernisation has resulted in a demise of community and a 'disengagement of people from a specific land base and rural way of life or modes' (Barry 1999: 81). The model of development that has brought about this condition (the intensification and industrialisation of the food system) is the target for an alternative vision, particularly around agriculture. While we might aim for a post-industrial society, it is impossible to imagine a post-agricultural society (Barry 1999). In deep-ecology versions, the vision is clearly about a 'return to the land' (or 'dwellers in the land' to echo Kirkpatrck Sale's phrase (1985: 224)) as the proper place of human flourishing and fulfilment and the only pathway to rebalancing humans and nature. The vision is of a patchwork of self-sufficient, small-scale, autarkic, ecologically harmonious communities organised according to their own normative standards. This is about dramatically shortening circuits of production, exchange and consumption to live within limits that globalised patterns of trade have surpassed. This argument, however, raises questions both about the fate of resource-poor communities when exchange with resource-rich communities is discouraged and about global (re)distributions of resources to those parts of the world living in extreme poverty. There are also no guarantees that bioregional communities would be any more democratic or just (Dobson 1990). Barry (1999: 87) puts it nicely: 'small is not always beautiful and small scale, although an important consideration, is not a panacea for all social and ecological ills'. Indeed, such communities could be prone to parochialism, conservatism, intolerance and violence in the absence of higher law enforcement bodies. This is to say nothing of the implications for advancing international cooperation around public goods and the regulation of environmental (and other) harms discussed further in Chapter 6.

Many Greens advocate for re-embedding the economy within tighter frameworks of social control and for improved and heightened levels of regulation of economies at the national and international levels. Such policies might take the form of 'new protectionism' (Lang and Hines 1993), measures to protect local and infant industries from global competitors adopting lower social and environmental standards, for example, as well as treaties on corporate accountability discussed further in Chapter 6. For those Greens wary of an expanded or key role for the state, certain dilemmas are presented in so far as they require an extension of state authority, whereas others may view a strong state as a necessary buffer and protector of its citizens against global market power in the transition to a sustainable society. For example, Die Grünen in Germany state:

In our economic model, a strong state is responsible for education, environmental quality, the delivery of general interest services, a modern infrastructure, including the communications infrastructure, and a well-performing system of social security… the state will lead the way in assisting innovative, 'green' products and technologies to make the breakthrough, and has an assumed central place as the unnamed agent that strengthens economic freedom and self-determination by promoting fair market access, limiting market power and boosting competition. It also aims to unbundle ownership in networked economies by breaking up monopolies in sectors such as the railways or electricity production and to abolish excessive red tape and environmentally harmful long-term subsidies.[4]

One way that Greens might advance their proposals is through ideas about economic democracy (Johanisova and Wolf 2012), broadening the range of legitimate participants in debates about the economy, as well opening up more spaces for citizen engagement with, and input into, the design and purposing of the economy, as well as the policies which the state should pursue. Val Plumwood (1996) makes the argument that while liberal democracy permits a certain degree of political democracy, it severely restricts citizen participation in precisely those areas that really count in terms of generating ecological problems, such as decisions about consumption, investment, production and technology. As noted in the critique of the capitalist industrial state in Chapter 5, the state is not impartial or neutral in the ways it prioritises certain freedoms over others. Proposals to widen citizen engagement with the economy help to check against a state being captive to anti-ecological interests.

Appropriate Technology

As well as purpose and social use, scale is important to Greens in relation to technology, often captured in E. F. Schumacher's phrase 'small is beautiful', although as Dobson (1991: 112) reminds us, 'Schumacher didn't actually think that 'small is beautiful'. It is rather that 'because giantism is presently so much the rage that the virtues of smallness need to be stressed so strongly'. The preference is not always for 'small'. As Schumacher puts it: 'when it comes to the question of size:

there is no single answer. For his different purposes man [sic] needs many different structures, both small ones and large ones, some exclusive and some comprehensive'. Schumacher argued for 'intermediate technology' (Schumacher 1974) – technologies appropriate to human scale and needs driven and labour-intensive. 'Let us now approach our subject from another angle and ask what is actually needed.' This goes against a lot of conventional economic thinking focused on 'economies of scale', the idea 'that with industries and firms, just as with nations, there is an irresistible trend, dictated by modern technology, for units to become ever bigger' (Schumacher 1974: 53). Specifying a particular size a priori is less important than adapting the technology to the use to which it will be put: 'We cannot directly calculate what is right; but we jolly well know what is wrong!' (Schumacher 1974: 55).

In determining appropriate scale and social use Greens often advocate democratising technology (Chapman 2007). They claim that greater citizen engagement in technology needs assessment, evaluation and priority setting around research and development might help to steer science, technology and innovation in more sustainable directions. It would do this by encouraging consideration of a broad range of social concerns or, at the very least, making them less subject to capture by private and vested interests. Direct citizen engagement in innovation is part of the Green vision. A volume on 'Citizen-led innovation for a new economy' provides many such examples of community-owned enterprises, social innovation and efforts to construct a 'conservation economy' around issues of land, energy, health and housing (Mathie and Gaventa 2015).

Part of this would include Green industrial policy and research and development for a sustainable society. Whereas there are now many technology and innovation hubs ostensibly aimed at driving green innovation, many of these are aimed at bringing new technologies to market without addressing the need to reduce demand for more resources. In other words, they add to the mix of available technologies but do little to shift resource trajectories if business-as- usual demands continue to rise and nothing is done to discontinue existing incumbent technologies. As Molly Scott Cato puts it:

Because of the unfeasible nature of the increased efficiencies required (as demonstrated by the SDC's *Prosperity without Growth* report) and the nature of rebound effects associated with technological improvements, we believe that the reliance on technological solutions, especially seeking to decouple economic growth and production from CO_2 emissions, is an example of psychological denial. Structural change in the nature of our economic model, and major shifts in consumption patterns and the way we define 'a good life' are fundamental requirements of a green economy.

(Cato n.d.)

For Greens, there is a tricky normative path to tread between being less laissez-faire and more normative in their approach to technology development both in terms of its goals (sustainability) and processes (inclusive and participatory) while avoiding the traps of 'picking winners' whereby government planners determine which technologies to back. Though there would not be support for this from all Greens, there is a role for a 'green entrepreneurial state' here (Mazzucato 2015) (as explored in Chapter 5). The emphasis might move towards more bottom-up planning and needs assessment as well as a rebalancing of the respective roles of state and market actors. This would mean addressing the allocation of direct and indirect subsidies from the state to capital: how to move beyond public subsidies and risk-taking for technologies and innovations that the private sector then develops for commercial and exclusive ends and not the 'common good'. Where a Green position might differ from others would be in not reducing the definition and pursuit of the common good to the state as the only arbiter of this. Scope would be expanded for more decentralised, plural and democratic input into priority-setting, technology needs assessment and evaluation. Commoner (1970: 127) suggests: 'the notion that scientists have some special aptitude for the judgement of social issues – even of those which are due to the progress of science – runs a grave risk of damaging the integrity of science and public confidence in it'.

This argument implies the need to move beyond the aim of improving scientific literacy towards a re-evaluation of the terms of engagement between science and citizens (Leach et al. 2005), to include direct public participation and engagement and consultation over issues where more information is requested: what do you want to know rather what do 'experts' think you need to know. It would also imply giving social direction to science and constructing stronger and clearer ethical frameworks for its applications in relation to areas like genetics, animal testing and weapons development, given the Green critiques of these matters touched on throughout this book. Groups such as Scientists for Global Responsibility often ally with Greens in raising these issues and using their voice to promote science that is not in the service of the military industrial complex.

Strategy

In the near term, there has been an understandable attempt by parts of the Green movement to demonstrate the growth-enhancing benefits of the policies and programmes they would like to see adopted. Whether it be the Green New Deal, first articulated by Green thinkers in the United Kingdom in 2008 in the wake of the financial crisis and now being proposed both in the UK and in the United States by progressive Democrats in 2019, and the opportunity to use the stimulus of

public investment to promote Green jobs and investment in Green technologies (as
a form of Green Keynesianism), or the promise of the bio-economy or the new
climate economy (NCE 2018), there have been many clarion calls aimed at
persuading governments that investing in a Green economy is in their (enlightened) self-interest (Pearce et al. 1989). These proposals may make sense on their
own terms, or as a transitioning strategy, given that even some more radical Greens
recognise the continued and entrenched political unpalatability of tackling the
growth mantra head on and calling for zero-growth. The Green party in the United
Kingdom has found seemingly radical environmental organisations closed to the
idea of coming out in favour of no-growth or degrowth for fear of losing political
traction and credibility. The concern is that without growth, there is no traction
with policy elites, echoed in the earlier anecdote about my meeting with the
OECD. More controversially still, for others, 'going with the grain' has involved
an embrace of payments for ecosystem services (PES) (Juniper 2013) and mechanisms to price nature: 'selling nature to save it' (McAfee 1999).

   The question of how to promote, facilitate and manage the transition to a post-
growth world suggests the need for some of the following strategies.

Prosperity without Growth

Discursively and politically, the challenge is to sever the assumed connection
between growth and well-being and insist on the notion that growth is a means
to an end and not an end in itself. If unfettered growth produces ever-widening
inequalities, deleterious social consequences and environmental impacts, it can no
longer be said to be fit for purpose. A near-term strategy then is about reframing
the debate as being one about quality of growth and prosperity and well-being
without growth. This is perhaps preferable to the degrowth (D'Alisa et al. 2014;
Kallis 2018) or *décroissance* framing used by André Gorz (1983) that defines the
political demand negatively with reference to a dominant given. This is important
because beyond the critique of growth, 'de-growth signifies also a desired direction, one in which societies will use fewer natural resources and will organize
and live differently than today. Sharing, simplicity, conviviality, care and the
commons are primary significations of what this society might look like' (Kallis
et al. 2014: 3). Importantly then, degrowth is not the same as negative GDP
growth, even if the outcome of Green strategies to pursue the good life would
reduce GDP as currently calculated.

   Getting there will be no simple task. Decolonising the growth imaginary by
severing the association between 'more' and 'better' presents a gargantuan challenge. Ekins (1986: 8–9) notes: 'Most current economic policy, indeed the very
orientation of economic theory, boils down to the pursuit of economic growth, as

indicated by an increasing GNP ... The assumption is that growth is good and more is better. It is extraordinary that an entire social science, and the dominant discipline in today's world at that, can effectively have come to be based on such a simplistic assumption.' The discussion earlier about the historical and ideological foundations of the growth fetishism gives some clues as to how and why this is the case.

We have seen how the questioning of the received wisdom about the relationship between growth and increased welfare is becoming more mainstream. Happiness indicators such as the Happy Planet Index developed by the New Economics Foundation to 'measure what matters: sustainable wellbeing for all', which tells us how well nations are doing at achieving long, happy, sustainable lives[5] (NEF 2016) or measures of Gross National Happiness as adopted by Bhutan are indicative of approaches that Greens could adopt. Further challenges to orthodox neoclassical economics come from this heterodox and 'post-autistic' or 'real world' economics,[6] and the calls for economic reformation[7] that many Greens are part of. These ideas relate to broader arguments, outlined above, about the need to historicise, politicise and denaturalise the project of economic growth.

Globally, entry points for advancing this agenda include proposals such as 'contraction and convergence' discussed later in this book, that build an equity-based framework for ensuring per-capita entitlements to remaining carbon budgets, requiring richer countries to contract emissions to allow for poorer countries to converge upwards towards the agreed entitlement. It could be extended to other areas where remaining ecological space has to be equitably allocated. Likewise, a more radical reading of the Sustainable Development Goals (SDGs) would suggest that for developing countries to expand levels of production and consumption to achieve these goals will require that richer countries need to free up ecological space for growth in the global South.

Managing the Transition to Degrowth

This brings us to the question of how Greens will manage the politics of deliberate degrowth, given the social dislocation produced by lack of growth in a capitalist economy. As Dale (2012) puts it:

If the global growth rate projected by the World Bank continues unabated world gross domestic product (GDP) will have risen almost tenfold by 2100 and catastrophe is all but assured for humankind and the planet. At the same time, regions of the world that have experienced low or negative growth have seen appalling suffering. Worldwide, in the 15 years that followed the end of the Cold War some 270 million individuals died prematurely from poverty-related causes. This is larger than the death toll from all the wars, civil wars, genocides and other government repressions of the entire 20th century combined. These statistics, and the human experiences that they summarise, worsen during economic crisis. As sales decline, capitalists throttle their investment, growth slows and tax revenues fall, prompting governments to cut spending; incomes fall and a vicious circle of contraction ensues. The current crisis serves as a reminder of the indecent consequences of zero or negative growth in a capitalist framework.

(Dale 2012)

The argument also speaks to the issues raised by Dobson (2014) and others about the imperative of addressing 'the elephant in the room' now, so that a process of managed decline can be put in place rather than experience the disruption of a series of more destructive shocks as economies start to unravel. Slower by design and not disaster as Victor (2008) puts it. We have repeatedly seen this with regard to the demise of the coal industry and the effects of unmanaged but rapid deindustrialisation (Caldecott et al. 2017).

In this regard Molly Scott Cato notes:

economic growth is only possible in the short term as part of a transition strategy to move us towards an economy that is in a steady state. The infrastructure of our current economy reflects the era of cheap fossil fuel energy: replacing this infrastructure with one that enables self-reliant economies will be the major source of growth over the period up to 2050. Beyond that date we should aim to stabilize the economy within our national resource limits.

(Cato n.d.)

Greens also need to deal with arguments such as that of the economic historian Benjamin Friedman who, in his book *The Moral Consequences of Economic Growth* (2006), considers the historical relationship between economic growth and social values and identified a clear pattern. During periods of rising economic prosperity, people tend to be more tolerant, optimistic and egalitarian. Periods of stagnation and recession, by contrast, have been characterised by pessimism, nostalgia, xenophobia and violence. During times of scarcity, people are more likely to look for scapegoats than to pull together, more prone to zero-sum thinking and more susceptible to the appeals of populists and demagogues. The social costs of degrowth and how these would be handled as part of a 'just transition' will be discussed later and have received increasing attention (Asara et al. 2015; Barca 2017). The fact that simply contracting economies plunges societies into disarray (Latouche 2009) suggests the critical need for managed degrowth. 'The question for us is whether the inevitable transition to a post-growth world will be unplanned or planned, catastrophic or benign' (Dobson 2014: 9). Delays in preparing for degrowth 'make it less likely that the transition will be benign and more likely that it will be catastrophic'. Worse still, 'We have to get used to the idea of having a finite amount of time left to get the political preconditions in place for planned degrowth' (Dobson 2014: 12).

This also brings us to controversial arguments that we will discuss further in Chapter 5, where it is argued populations will resist the imposition of limits and not accept them voluntarily and that, therefore, democracy may be incompatible (Ophuls 1973; Hardin 1968) with, or severely tested, in a post-growth world. As Read, Makoff and Hutchinson suggest, because actors within the economic system will be pushing against the limits 'constant regulation and proliferation of rules and enforcement' will be required 'to militate against this' (cited in Dobson 2014: 16). Dobson's (2014: 14) retort is that 'sustainability may be compatible with both democratic and authoritarian regimes, but a *just* post-growth society is only compatible with the former'. If autonomy is to be circumscribed, citizens understandably want a say in shaping the rules of conduct. That said, Greens often also look to constitutional lock-in and principles of an 'untouchable character' (Dobson 2014: 14) that might include an 'Office of Environmental Defenders' charged with representing and defending public environmental interests including non-human species and future generations (Eckersley 2004) or 'Guardians of the Future' (Read 2012). This proposal could build on or strengthen bodies such as the UK Climate Change Committee, which is meant to hold the government to account for its climate change obligations and check and report on progress in meeting those. A more powerful body, however, would require the power of veto over policies and proposals inconsistent with these commitments.

Discursively and politically, the notion of 'limits' is problematic. The limits are not to be imposed on human freedoms, nor the collective imagination, but rather over-use of the commons. Nevertheless, it comes with strongly anti-Utopian connotations. Dobson (2014: 10) seeks to square this by claiming that 'We argue that there are (more or less) fixed limits to production, consumption and waste, but we have a utopian sense of what is possible within those limits.' He continues: 'Ecologism is the ideological embodiment of the idea that freedom is the recognition of necessity.' His view suggests the need to reframe how we think about scarcity: 'We have come to think of scarcity as the gap between what people want and what they have. This needs to be rethought. For the sake of equity and a more pacified relationship with the nonhuman natural world that sustains us, we should think of scarcity as the gap between what people need and what the world can sustainably provide for us' (Dobson 2014: 23).

Re-embedding and Re-balancing the Economy

Realising Green political visions would require both re-embedding the economy within frameworks of social and ecological norms and values, as well as a re-balancing of the economy away from a reliance on high finance towards a more socially useful and environmentally sustainable productive base, a shift towards recommoning and public control over private realms and the revaluing of the informal and care economy.

There are a variety of ways by which this might be achieved. The starting point would be organising the economy around the provision of basic needs for food, housing, energy, water, sanitation and work rather than wants, luxury acquisitions and levels of consumption and consumerism that are unjust in terms of using up resources poorer groups need and that are ecologically unsustainable. Reducing consumption and improving welfare would be pursued through policies that enable people to work less and job share, such as the four-day working week that many Green parties have proposed to help people rebalance work and care priorities. Likewise, many Greens advocate a basic-income scheme to reward carers and those working in the informal economy whose work is unpaid and undervalued but which makes a huge contribution to social cohesion and well-being and effectively hugely cross-subsidises the formal economy by absorbing costs that employers do not have to bear. The distribution of work in all its forms (i.e. not just formally paid 'employment' but also unwaged and informal/community or domestic work, including gendered reproductive labour, or political work in being an active citizen) is a central concern for Green politics (Barry 2016).

The phrase 'taking back control' now carries with it a series of negative connotations for progressives following its co-optation by nationalist and anti-European forces at the time of the Brexit referendum in the United Kingdom in 2016. But the slogan does capture a serious Green strategy to both localise the global economy and take back control of the provision of key services and infrastructures from health and education to transport from the private to the public. For example, prominent Greens, such as UK Green MP Caroline Lucas, have backed calls for the renationalisation of privatised services such as rail and the postal services. The next logical step from a Green point of view might be to decentralise or break up some of the monopolies that operate in those sectors to allow for greater downwards accountability and local ownership.

Economic independence is important to the Green economic project. To avoid the lock-in and the disciplinary power exercised by global institutions and market actors, Greens are keen on preserving policy autonomy and space to pursue their preferred developmental strategies (discussed further in Chapter 7). Protecting economic diversity (as long as this is consistent with the achievement of a sustainable society) is an important aim for Greens, who often oppose homogenisation. They are keen to preserve cultural, linguistic diversity and social and ethnic identities, contesting what Les Verts in France also called the 'McDonalds/Coca Cola civilisation' (Les Verts 1994) in reference to the 'McDonalization of society' (Ritzer 1993). These views include addressing concentrations of economic power by large companies, what in the retail sector Simms (2007) refers to as

'Tescopoly', to describe the powerful retailers' market domination at the expense of local suppliers.

To enable and accelerate this shift, combinations of regulation and new protectionism would be required as ways of localising and embedding the social economy. Concrete measures might include preferential business rates for local businesses as many Greens have proposed, as well as community reinvestment schemes such as have been adopted in the United States. The Community Reinvestment Act, adopted in 1977, for example, is designed to encourage commercial banks and savings associations to help meet the needs of borrowers in all segments of their communities, including low- and moderate-income neighbourhoods.

Socially Useful Production

Greens would argue strongly that another model of production is both possible and necessary. There are many precedents for organising and accelerating these shifts historically and in contemporary settings, including the repurposing of factories for socially useful production (Simms and Newell 2017). Both as an approach to re-embedding the economy within a framework of social values, as well as a means of redistributing wealth more equitably, Greens promote alternative (yet already existing) models of economic organisation. These involve greater focus on sharing the value of production between producer and consumer, as is typical in mutual organisations and cooperatives. Strong support for social enterprises, cooperatives and community-owned enterprise features prominently in Green thinking about building a steady-state economy.

New models of ownership and profit-sharing are envisaged, including re-commoning through public and community ownership and social and solidarity economies (Amin 2009). The case of Denmark indicates clearly the extraordinary investment that can be achieved through collaborative efforts between government and local cooperatives. This collaboration orientates organisations towards mutual, communal or general interests underpinned by principles of democratic inclusion, providing the space for the reduction and transformation (including democratisation) of both the state and capitalist spheres of economic production, distribution and consumption (Barry 2012). Guided by different principles and modes of organisation, self-organised and worker managed, they are inherently less expansionary than capitalist firms. The aim of what Barry (2016) describes as a 'green republican economy' is to have more people working less, rather than fewer people working more.

The flip side of redirecting production and aligning it with the imperatives of sustainability is the need to bring down levels of consumption and consumerism to sustainable levels. This objective is often accompanied with scepticism about a narrower focus on eco-consumer(ism). In this, Greens find allies with anti-consumerism groups such as Enough! that organise international 'buy nothing day' and the Canadian-based group Adbusters. Reducing demand also implies limiting the use of advertising to create desire for goods and services. Greens could point to bold moves by some municipalities to reduce or ban advertising in public spaces.

To combat what they called the visual pollution of excessive advertising, in 2007 Brazil's biggest city, São Paulo, led by the city's conservative mayor, Gilberto Kassab, introduced the Clean City Law. The result was a near-total ban affecting billboards, digital signs and advertising on buses. Several US states strongly control public advertising too, and in Paris, recent rules reduce advertising on the city's streets by 30 per cent and cap the size of hoardings. No adverts are allowed within 50 metres of school gates. The Indian city of Chennai banned billboard advertising, and Grenoble in France recently banned commercial advertising in public places in the city's streets, to enhance opportunities for non-commercial expression. Several hundred advertising signs were replaced by tree planting and community noticeboards.

(Simms and Newell 2007: 17)

Ultimately, reshaping productive sectors of the economy in line with the impera-tives of sustainability means, as well as providing access to finance and credit and favourable tax regimes for smaller and community-owned businesses (see below), being willing to revoke the licences of companies flouting environmental regula-tions. When the pursuit of wealth comes at the cost of society and the environment, the licence to operate in the interests of society has surely been compromised. This move has to be combined with changes to company law and corporate governance to increase accountability for the environmental impacts of a firm's activities and to increase worker representation on the boards of firms.

Finance for the Common Good

Finance is of course the lubricant of the global economy. The historically powerful role that finance has played in this period of history (Perez 2002) explains why much activist attention is directed towards divestment and shareholder activism as well as the redeployment of that finance in Greener and more socially just direc-tions (Newell 2015). Indeed, there has been growing attention from the inter-national community to a reform of the global financial architecture (UNEP 2015). A key strategic challenge for Greens will be how to handle capital flight and the prospect of delivering 'ecologism in one country' if larger firms threatened by Green proposals to deliver a sustainable society redeploy their capital or relocate their operations elsewhere.

In terms of public finance and the redistribution of wealth and opportunity, the basic-income scheme has gained support from a range of political quarters in recent years (Andersson 2009; Standing 2008; Raventos 2005). Often described as 'the flagship of Green economic policy' (Dobson 1991: 152), its ambition is to enable a permanent rather than temporary exit from poverty and social exclusion. It implies an overhaul of the current benefits system whereby every woman, man and child would receive a weekly payment as of right, non-means-tested and sufficient to cover basic needs. There are many versions of this, but in essence a Citizen's Basic Income is an unconditional, automatic and non-withdrawable payment to each individual as a right of citizenship (CIT 2017; Torry 2013; van Parijs 2004). As Ekins states (1986: 225–32): 'A basic income scheme would aim to guarantee each man, woman and child the unconditional right to an independent income sufficient to meet basic living costs. Its main purpose would be the prevention of poverty, as opposed to mere poverty relief.' It is aimed at encouraging flexible working patterns (across forms of paid, unpaid, voluntary and domestic work), providing financial independence and reducing poverty and unemployment. Although wealthier citizens would be entitled to the scheme, they would pay more into it in the first place through tax. It would also help to reduce the personal indebtedness that unscrupulous financial actors, such as pay-day loan companies and sub-prime lenders, thrive on.

The regulation of finance is important in terms of ensuring that financing of new infrastructures and policies is consistent with increasingly ambitious environmental targets. There may be a role here for environmental audit committees, as well as greater screening of export credit agencies and the use of state money to support private investment. To 'take back control' of the monetary system Greens often support local currencies such as Local exchange schemes (LETS), time banks, barter market currencies and convertible local currencies (North 1996, 2007; Glover 1999; Dittmer 2015). Regarding the latter, Molly Scott Cato suggests:

The flourishing of local currencies across the world represents a different type of liquidity, but one that has suffered from lack of credibility and from an absence of political support. Local authorities could generate truly 'effective demand' in their communities by introducing local currencies into their fiscal administration on a staged basis, beginning with local services, as partial payment of local tax, and eventually for the payment of staff. Examples from Japan's lost decade demonstrate how local currencies can help to replace the national currency and soften the blow of jobs losses and the inability to pay for local services.

(Cato 2012: 2)

In terms of monetary policy, Greens are often also supportive of 'peoples' quantitative easing' to create money to fill the Green investment gap. Quantitative easing could be used strategically to provide finance for Green infrastructure. Directly created money is presented as an alternative to private interest-bearing finance.

This is partly about the social control of finance. As feminist ecologist Mary Mellor explains: 'imposition of interest means that financial debt grows exponentially, creating future demand for goods and services which can only be produced from a limited store of natural resources. This link between the monetary system and the ecological crisis has been repeated by green economists in recent years, leading them to argue for an essential linkage between a stable money system and a sustainable economy' (Mellor 2015; Hutchinson et al. 2002). In one of the most successful enclosures of the commons in our time, commercial finance institutions have captured the power to create most new money through their discretionary lending. This power has become so normalised and pervasive that hardly anyone acknowledges the startling fact that commercial lending accounts for more than 95 per cent of 'new money' created. Government has in effect surrendered its enormous power to use its money-creating authority for the public good (Bollier 2016). Greens seek to challenge the hold that the private finance system has over the public sector. Mellor (2015) argues that the obvious answer to taxpayer bailouts and subsidies to private banks is to harness the democratic right to create money and use it to serve public purposes.

Social control of finance for the common good implies shifts in the purposes and timeframes within which finance operates, implying a greater role for 'patient capital' that secures a return over a longer time frame. There are proposals for a Green Investment Bank and Green investment bonds going beyond the limited versions of these that have existed to date. Though some iterations of these can be devoid of more radical intent, 'Local authorities might also be able to create green investments bonds, specifically for local energy developments, where they themselves are the planning authority. These bonds could be limited geographically to the citizens who are part of the local authority's area, adding greater accountability to balance the greater risk' (Cato and Essex n.d.). This builds on support for local banks, nationally owned and citizen governed.

Greens would need to identify new ways of raising finance consistent with their vision of a Green society. Taxation is important here. Ecological taxation follows the logic of taxing more what you want less of (pollution) and taxing less what you want more of (labour). In many cases this would imply higher levels of corporate taxation but also preferential tax rates for local businesses and social enterprises as noted above. Many Greens have argued for land taxes, as well as reallocating the staggering amounts of finance currently offered to environmentally damaging intensive agriculture, fossil fuel production and consumption, for example. Micro-credit schemes and other forms of affordable finance for micro and small-scale enterprise are other elements that Greens envision in building a sustainable economy.

As well as generating new streams of tax revenue, Greens have shown strong support for closing tax havens, tax loops and adopting common global measures for country-by-country reporting and collecting tax to address evasion and avoidance. According to the Tax Justice Network, tax havens are estimated to shelter $12 or $13 trillion in private deposits, depriving governments of $250 billion a year in revenues. Measures must also be included to address transfer pricing that cause developing countries to lose $160 billion in tax revenues each year (Jenkins and Newell 2013), as well support for 'publish what you pay' initiatives, such as the Extractive Industries Transparency Initiative, which encourage the full disclosure of profits made from resource exploitation.

Finance for the common good also includes Green lending along the lines of proposals for a Green New Deal advanced by Greens in 2008 (GND 2008) in light of the financial crisis, and given new life in 2019 in the United States where it is enjoying support among elements of the Democrat Party, as well as among progressives in the United Kingdom. In the wake of nationalisations of banks in all but name following the financial crisis and support from leading economists such as Joseph Stiglitz, this idea has come of age (Woodin and Lucas 2004). As originally conceived, this had two main components. First, it outlines a structural transformation of the regulation of national and international financial systems, and major changes to taxation systems. And, second, it calls for a sustained programme to invest in and deploy energy conservation and renewable energies, coupled with effective demand management (GND 2008). The UN secretary-general, the then Executive Director of the United Nations Environment Programme (UNEP) Achim Steiner and a further twenty-one UN organisations have also recently endorsed this call. To further tame global finance, Greens have often expressed support for capital controls and financial transaction taxes such as the Robin Hood and Tobin taxes (Woodin and Lucas 2004). At a UN meeting in 2004 over a hundred countries signed up in support of a transaction tax resolution, but resistance from bankers, the IMF and powerful governments such as the United States has thwarted further progress to date.

As with all other areas of the normative project of building a Green economy, the social and the ecological need to be addressed simultaneously. Building on the idea of 'planetary boundaries' outlined earlier, Kate Raworth (2017) proposes 'doughnut economics' as a way of describing the safe social operating space for humanity (see Chapter 7). Where the current economic model produces negative consequences, it is down to a failure of economic design, and new economic systems, such as the circular economy, must be embedded into the wider network of dynamic and complex natural systems on which human society depends. A new economic model needs to address the 'doughnut', with a 'hole' of critical human deprivation in the middle below a social foundation representing the minimum amount of well-being for humanity, an ecological ceiling in an outer ring representing planetary resource limits: between both of these remains a safe and just space for humanity. These are the 'simple ways' she suggests that economics can be brought back into the service of human needs. The politics of realising this vision remain anything but simple, however, given the interests stacked against change and the power of incumbent beneficiaries of the status quo of unsustainability.

Conclusions

We have seen then that there is a huge difference between the 'green economy' and the Green economy. The former constitutes an attempt, once again, to reconcile the contradictions between growth in a capitalist economy and the need to address resource depletion through pricing, internalisation of environmental costs, improved technology and renewed industrial strategy. The latter, on the other hand, questions the very premise that economic growth is compatible with the achievement of sustainability, and seeks to build an economy orientated to local needs, socially useful production and able to value labour and the environment properly.

A Green economy recognises that the 'real wealth of nations' resides in the environment which sustains us. As Dobson (2014: 23) notes: 'There is nothing outside the planet to which we have meaningful access in terms of sustaining life. This is why post-growth politics is on its way, whether we like it or not. The question is whether we plunge into it unplanned or descend into it gradually, with all the promise this holds of a more fulfilling life for us all … The politics of enough … is possibly the toughest nut of all to crack, as everything is geared to persuading us that we never have enough of anything, ever.' Cultural and value shifts are clearly a key, some might say prior, component of greening the economy, but there is clearly also a key role for the state, to which we turn our attention next.

Notes

1 www.fdrfourfreedomspark.org/blog/2015/2/17/fdrs-second-inaugural-address-january-20-1937
2 Vicky Power (2017) 'He saw my anger as fuel for change', interview with Arun Gandhi, *The Guardian* 30 September 2017, pp.4 5.
3 http://unionsforenergydemocracy.org/
4 www.gruene-bundestag.de/service-navigation/english/economic.html
5 http://happyplanetindex.org/. This assesses four dimensions: (i) Wellbeing: how satisfied the residents of each country feel with life overall; (ii) Life expectancy: the average number of years a person is expected to live in each country, based on data collected by the United Nations; (iii) Inequality of outcomes: the inequalities between people within a country in terms of how long they live, and how happy they feel, based on the distribution in each country's life expectancy and wellbeing data; (iv) Ecological footprint: the average impact that each resident of a country places on the environment, based on data prepared by the Global Footprint Network (NEF 2016).
6 See, for example, the Post-Autistic Economics Network www.paecon.net/HistoryPAE.htm
7 www.newweather.org/wp-content/uploads/2017/12/33-Theses-for-an-Economics-Reformation .pdf

5

Green State

The state figures centrally in Green debates about the prospects and possibilities of a transition towards a Green society. This is true across the spectrum of Green political thought from Anarchist traditions (Bahro 1994; Bookchin 1980; Kropotkin 1955) that advocate stateless self-governing communities, to emphasis on de-centralisation and subsidiarity, through to the multi-level or transnational eco or Green state (Eckersley 2004; Barry 1999; Meadowcroft 2004; Death 2016; Bäckstrand and Kronsell 2015).

The state is viewed, variously, as too large, too small, too captured and compromised by incumbent actors, elites and classes; too exploitative, violent or hierarchical and bureaucratic, depending on which version of Green politics is drawn upon (see Chapter 2). For some, it represents too large and distant an institution to build an ecological society, especially one that, for Greens, would have to have grassroots democracy at its heart. Yet for others, it is too small a unit to deal with ecological challenges (Ophuls 1973). This concern lies behind proposals for a transnational ecological state (Eckersley 2004), as well as calls for a World Environment Organisation (WEO) to match the power and authority of global economic institutions to strengthen Earth Systems Governance (Biermann 2001). In sum, Green politics provides neither a consensual nor clear guide to practical action around engagements with the state. This is reflected in the comment by the Italian Green Alexander Langer who saw the state as: 'both too big and too small. They are too big to allow real participatory democracy, to respect the requirements and the powers of local communities . . . And they are too small to be able to deal effectively with some of the contemporary problems such as the environment, or peace and disarmament' (cited in Bomberg 1998: 63). This resonates with Eckersley's (2004: 4) reflection that 'if a green posture toward the nation-state can be discerned from the broad tradition of green political thought, it is that the nation-state plays, at best, a contradictory role in environmental management in facilitating both environmental destruction and environmental protection and, <u>at worst, it is fundamentally ecocidal'</u>. Yet some strands and positions within Green thinking are more dominant than others. Barry's refers to 'the almost complete monopolization of the green political imagination by an anarchist vision of the society greens would like to create' (1999: 77), echoing Goodin's assertion that 'greens are basically libertarians-cum-anarchists' (1992: 152).

The notion that a <u>Green state is an oxymoron</u> is perhaps unsurprising, given that, historically speaking, <u>core state imperatives include the defence</u> of state territory, <u>the pursuit of national security</u> through military means and <u>the exploitation</u> of <u>economic resources for development</u>, defined narrowly as <u>economic growth</u> as we saw in the last chapter. <u>The state, in this rendition, is a cause</u> of, and barrier to, the <u>achievement of a sustainable society</u>. It is seen as the embodiment of 'materialism, institutionalized violence, centralization, hierarchy' (Porritt 1989: 216–17), values and practices that, as Barry suggests, are 'antithetical to the green perspective' (1999: 78). Historically speaking, as Conca notes: 'The emergence of the central-ising, industrialising, national state, with its capacity to centralise decision-making, concentrate capital, strip local communities of their historical property rights in nature, supply coercive power and protect elite interests, has been a key social innovation along the road to global planetary peril' (2005: 181). Against claims about the reformability of the state, he also argues that the deep structure of world politics, organised around sovereignty, capitalism and modernity, shows few signs of transformation despite the incursions of nearly fifty years of international environmental politics.

Moreover, political borders, organised along sovereign lines, make little sense ecologically, and provide a poor starting point for envisaging forms of political community that best respond to the needs of global publics and the global common good. There are, nevertheless, Greens willing to counter this view in seeking to defend the exercise of sovereignty as a force for good. Eckersley suggests, for example, that:

the territorial dimension of sovereignty might be made to work *for* the environment insofar as it might enable political communities to resist certain aspects of economic globalization or to censure and possibly halt practices in other states that threaten to undermine domestic ecosystem integrity. In these circumstances at least, territorial sovereignty – including self-determination and the associated principle of non-intervention – can serve as a bulwark against anti-ecological practices that encroach upon the territory and policy-making powers of particular nation-states.

(Eckersley 2004: 232–3)

Beyond these questions of scale and the design of the state, to some extent the question is whether the problem of unsustainability is one of lack of state capacity and resources, as opposed to more structural constraints or political will and interest in securing a more secure and ecologically sustainable future. This raises the question not only of whether the state alone has the power, authority and resources to bring about the transitions so urgently required but also whether it has the autonomy of action and political interest in pursuing and accelerating deeper transformations towards sustainability and away from an economy organised in ways which often enrich state elites.

There is also a question of which state we are talking about. The European focus in many studies of environmental policy and socio-technical transitions makes assumptions about a well-resourced, functioning, autonomous state able to act independently of private or foreign actors (Johnstone and Newell 2017). This is not a description that adequately accounts for the reality faced by many states in the global South where any greening of the state, perhaps more so than in other areas of the world, would have to be supported, or at least tolerated, by a range of other actors upon which it is dependent for political and/or financial support (Power et al. 2016). States are embedded within a wide variety of political economies and models of more or less state-based capitalism such that there is significant variation in the extent to which different models of political economy are likely, or even able, to be Green.

This is crucial to both critiques of contemporary (and historical) forms of statehood and state practices and alternative envisionings of a Green state. What is fixed, universal and given about the characteristics and functioning of states and what can be reversed, reformed and done away with in other historical, regional, political and economic circumstances? Looked at this way, we can repose the question as one about state form and forms of statehood rather than in terms of the characteristics we attach to a supposedly monolithic and universal state form.

Critique

For many of the reasons already noted, many Greens question whether the liberal democratic state is up to the task of steering the economy and society along a genuinely ecologically sustainable path. Greens often fear both the omnipotence of the state and its deep penetration of society and surveillance over the lives of its citizens but also its impotence in the face of the scale and complexity of the ecological problems it has to address. Impulses from the peace movement seek to disassemble state functions associated with violence, war and conquest, while some feminist thinking might look to preserve or even expand those state functions concerned with welfare, protection and redistribution – to administer a basic income scheme, for example, and to enforce the rights of workers, women and other unrepresented or systematically exploited groups.

Here I divide Green critiques of the state into three key areas (i) the undemocratic nature of centralised states; (ii) the problem of the unsustainable industrial capitalist state and (iii) concern with state violence and coercion.

Critique of the Centralising Undemocratic State

Understandably, there has been significant academic interest in 'ecological democracy' and its relationship to, as well as differences with, liberal democracy over the past four decades. Questions of democracy were the focus of a spectrum of Green thinking in the 1980s and 1990s (Dryzek 1992; Eckersley 2004; Goodin 1992; Doherty and de Geus 1996). More recently, the advent of the anthropocene epoch has reposed the question of whether the concept and practice of ecological democracy needs to be recast around ecological democracy on a planetary scale, a point to which we return in Chapter 6.

Despite scholarly interest in the emergence of a 'Green', 'environmental' or 'ecological' state, the feasibility of attaining such a state remains in doubt. Notwithstanding some advances in implementing democratic innovations for environmental protection (Mol and Spaargaren 2000), prospects for ecological democracy have become mired in broader concerns about whether democratic institutions can be sustained in the face of populism and authoritarianism and the pressures on the conduct of political debate generated by the reach, immediacy and popularity of social media campaigns that fill the political vacuum, encouraging short-term reactive gestures as opposed to deliberation over long-term issues.

The first area of critique then is of the administrative state, one that is incapable of systematically responding to the challenge of sustainability because of the concentration of political power, disembeddedness from social life and distance from the everyday lives of citizens. Functions uniquely performed by states include taxation, administration and coercive control (Skocpol 1979). That is the: 'coercive, highly centralized and bureaucratic centres of power with a set of security, disciplinary, surveillance and/or administrative imperatives that are fundamentally at odds with the green vision of participatory democracy and the ideal of the green public sphere' (Eckersley 2004: 86). Many critiques focus on the state as an embodiment and crystallisation of hierarchies and social exclusions along multiple social axes. Barry cites (1999: 80) the social ecologist Kossoff (1992) as saying: 'The state consolidates and protects the family of hierarchies [class, gender, race, age, mind-body] becoming a hierarchy in its own right.' This interpretation resonates with the work of other social ecologists such as Bookchin (see Chapter 2), as well Marxist theorists of the state such as Poulzantas (2014), who see the state as an expression of and vehicle for institutionalising particular alignments of class forces.

For Greens though, generic concerns with whom the state serves are often combined with a concern that liberal democracy performs particularly poorly in protecting long-range public environmental interests. This is especially the case with regard to safeguarding the interests of future generations, where today's decision-makers often engage in 'intergenerational discounting', passing costs and risks of today's decisions onto generations yet unborn. This results from a preoccupation with short-term election cycles, ties to interest groups such as corporations or trade unions with a stake in sustaining an unsustainable economy and the existence of multiple veto points and political opportunity structures that systematically allow for privileged access for well-resourced groups to the exclusion of the majority of citizens. The potential for elite capture in such systems is high because of a combination of party funding by wealthy interest groups, concentrations of ownership in the media and narrow class dominance of institutions of the state, the judiciary and police and military (Jones 2015).

This situation often means that elites and the 1 per cent of the wealthiest members of society can legally siphon off wealth from society, free-riding on state infrastructures where corporations have access to a healthy and educated workforce and vast subsidies, and then adopt tax avoidance and evasion strategies to avoid paying their share back to the state. The state is thereby deprived of much needed resources for welfare and other purposes, with particularly serious consequences for resource-poorer developing countries (Jenkins and Newell 2013). Large bodies of work on the resource curse also show that states heavily reliant on revenues from resources such as oil are less responsive to the needs of their citizens because the social contract based on 'no representation without taxation' breaks down (Watts 2009; Ross 2012). Governments less reliant on taxation, which is dwarfed by the revenues they receive from oil exploitation, for example, are harder to hold to account for their (inactions) since citizens cannot claim that it is 'their' money that the state is misallocating. Elite insulation from such pressures confers upon them the possibility of keeping consumption above ecologically sustainable levels long after crisis has struck poorer members of society.

What results in practice are 'low-intensity democracies' (Gills and Rocamora 1992), where fragile institutional constructs are bypassed and undermined by patronage and clientelist networks. In part, the lack of space for meaningful public engagement and representation is a function of the fact that some social goals and strategies for acquiring them are non-negotiable, and so many fundamental questions about political visions for the achievement of the 'good life' are placed off-limits by prior commitments to industrialism and growth at all costs. As Torgerson suggests: 'modernity appears flawed and incomplete because by its own standard of rationality the irresistible momentum of progress rules out rational deliberation over its purpose and direction' (1999: 145).

Indeed, decision-making is loaded in favour of industrial interests at the expense of communities affected by the impacts of industrialism by the privileging of growth as a meta-goal of policy, combined with channels of representation that are more accessible to those with wealth and elite social connections (Kenner 2019). This is something highlighted clearly by the literature on and the practice of environmental justice struggles, showing how procedural injustices leave those most affected excluded from consultation and decision-making and, therefore, most exposed to uneven and unjust distributional outcomes (Cole and Foster 2001; Newell 2007). Barriers to citizen participation, high requirements for legal and scientific expertise and the resolution of conflicts in arenas in which powerful actors dominate load the dice in favour of corporate actors (Newell 2001b). Moreover, states often intervene to override local decisions that oppose environmentally destructive initiatives – such as fracking in Lancashire in the United Kingdom where the local council had voted to oppose a proposed fracking development but had this decision overturned by central government. Many states in the global South have also invoked colonial legislation, such as India's *Land Acquisition Act* that allows the central state to acquire land in the 'public interest' – that the government alone gets to determine – and so can be used to undermine local opposition to destructive industrial development projects (Newell 2005).

This critique should not lead to a rejection of democracy but rather of the corrupted form which prevails in many parts of the world today, where the state is often captive to corporate interests (Monbiot 2000). Democracy is key in terms of providing a response channel, an early-warning system of non-functioning policy, and a means of articulating accountability between states and their citizens. This point echoes Sen's (1999) argument about 'Development as Freedom': that there are fewer famines in democracies; that, in theory, democracies require governments to satisfy the needs of the majority of their citizens in order to get re-elected. As a consequence, this view creates an incentive to distribute wealth across society, although in practice, as seen above, this does not always follow.

Greens need also to be wary of the ways in which the urgency of tackling the ecological crisis can be invoked for anti-democratic ends and pursued through non-democratic means. The demand for rapidity can give rise to claims about the need to suspend democratic politics as usual. This can take the form of overriding planning decisions (such as that of Lancashire council in the United Kingdom around fracking noted above) or speeding them up (to accelerate the adoption of nuclear power, invoking the urgency of transitioning to a low-carbon economy, for example), given the need to accelerate the adoption of technologies labelled low carbon by policy elites. This is one of the concerns behind the call for a 'slow race' around science and technological innovation (Leach and Scoones 2006). Urgency can be used to trump and supersede political conflict – what has been referred to as 'post-politics' (Swyngedouw 2010) – and accelerate the diffusion of controversial technologies (such as geo-engineering, genetic engineering, negative emission technologies) or to suspend forms of political engagement that are incompatible with business-as-usual politics and economics to 'go with the grain' of existing actors and institutions. As Stirling puts it (2015): 'urgency compels obedience. Democracy is increasingly dubbed a "failure" or a "luxury" that cannot be afforded, or even queried as an "enemy of nature". The iconically influential environmentalist Jim Lovelock insists that "democracy must be put on hold for a while"'.

Related to this is the real danger that an emphasis on urgency and, by definition, crisis management frames responses in terms of top-down interventions from elite actors, i.e. those with the power, resources and control over finance, production, infrastructures, or that can call upon the coercive powers of the state. Urgency diminishes the scope for more plural, bottom-up, inclusive and deliberative pathways to sustainability, where transformations are cultured and follow an ethic of 'care' rather than 'control' (Stirling 2011, 2014). 'The paths taken by scientific and technological progress are far from inevitable. Deliberately or blindly, the direction of progress is inherently a matter of social choice. A move towards plural, conditional advice would help avoid erroneous "one-track", "race to the future" visions of progress' Stirling suggests (2010: 1031). This builds on critiques of techno-managerial solutions to social and political crises as well as 'scientisation' and deference to the expertise of epistemic communities (Haas 1990), that were discussed in the previous chapter in relation to social control of science and technology. Those concerns might be magnified if combined with calls for 'eco-Leviathanism' (Duit et al. 2016) in which a Green state would enforce the recommendations of its leading scientists without scope for reflection and debate about the essentially contested nature of knowledge and expertise. Calls for stronger forms of (top-down) Earth systems governance (Biermann 2014) and planet politics (Burke et al. 2016) have been critiqued on these grounds (Chandler et al. 2017).

The concern with expanding state power for ecological ends comes not only from democratic theorists or more anarchist traditions within Green politics but also, of course, from market liberals and those on the political Right who prefer 'market rule' to any notion in which the state determines the public interest. The freedom of the consumer to choose is often invoked by market liberals in arguing against measures that Greens might be in favour of, such as moratoria (on GMOs), bans on certain goods and products (factory-farmed meat or diesel cars), and reference is often made, correctly, to liberal trading rules enforced by the World Trade Organisation (WTO) that prohibit interventions in the market considered to be incompatible with the rules that the global trade body espouses. The primacy of consumer choice: to purchase products that, however destructive in social or environmental terms they might be, are traded legally amounts to a significant barrier to progress towards a sustainable society.

Likewise, for those Greens who advocate state-led population control, the pushback from the liberal state would be equally strong in defence of the primacy of civil liberties and individual freedoms. Marcel Wissenburg in the book (1998) *Green Liberalism: The Free and Green Society* argues that liberal democracy is incompatible with any legal restrictions that seek to alter or dictate or restrict peoples' preferences, whether around birth control, consumption choices or life-style. The preference is always for softer modes of information-sharing among notionally free agents in a liberal market through education, labelling and the like.

Many Greens would be critical of this notion of the laissez-faire state, given the extent to which the liberal state is imbricated in upholding and protecting an unsustainable industrial order, parading as neutral arbiter while loading the dice in favour of capitalist interests. Not only does this deny our fundamental dependence on the natural world of which we are part but it naturalises and excludes from scrutiny systems of wealth generation and exploitation and their associated property rights regimes that systematically socialise social and ecological costs while privatising profits and gains. Whereas for Greens, ecosystem integrity is a precondition for individual and collective well-being. This is a theme to which we turn next, but it reveals a tension among Greens between anti-statism and an appreciation of the deeply embedded nature of the state in ecologically destructive social and economic relations on the one hand, and the rejection of liberal insistence on laissez-faire combined with frequent calls for a more interventionist and protectionist state on the other. In the latter regard, Greens are often willing to countenance restrictions on freedom of investment, production, consumption and property such that the task of 'laying down sustainability parameters' is one that should fall to the state (Eckersley 2004: 95).

Green politics can thus be viewed as 'post' not 'anti-liberal'. Important in this regard is separating free market capitalism as the dominant political mode of organising the economy – to which Greens are opposed – from liberalism as representative democratic governance in the creation of a sustainable society. In short, Greens ask: 'How do we maintain and sustain liberty in a post-liberal political, post-capitalist economic and post-carbon, sustainable order?' (Barry 2008: 4).

Critique of the Industrial Capitalist State

The second area of critique of the state for Greens is of its organisation along industrial capitalist lines. The starting point here is the problematic, compromised

Figure 5.1 Adbusters.
Source: Adbusters, used with permission

and complicit role of the state in the very processes of accumulation that are degrading the planet (Newell 2008b). As Michael Saward asks: 'Could it be that the contemporary state is simply not the type of entity which is capable of systematically prioritizing the achievement of sustainability?' (1998: 345). In one sense, this situation derives from a key set of contradictions and functional interdependencies between the capitalist state and the capitalist economy to secure the conditions of accumulation which serve both, and the 'grow-or-die' rationality of capitalism. As we saw above, this is what eco-Marxist writers refer to as the second contradiction of capitalism: that it systematically undermines the conditions for its own reproduction by diminishing the resource base upon which the economy depends for survival, such that the costs of production increase over time (O'Connor 1991). Capitalism can only contract or expand but not 'stand still' for any protracted period of time.

This condition also reflects the historical character and nature of statehood, organised around the defence and expansion of state territory though military means and the exploitation of natural resources in the pursuit of national economic development – understood as 'overriding imperatives of all states and constitutive of the state's very form' (Eckersley 2004: 19). Besides the problematic and arbitrary nature of sovereign borders from an ecological view, formed as they are through violence and political settlement (Tilly 1993), it is also the division of the world into sovereign entities that affords transnational capital in particular structural power over states keen to attract increasingly mobile capital to invest in their territories (Gill and Law 1988). States increasingly resemble 'competition states' more attuned to the needs of global investors than their own citizens (Cerny 1995). 'Neoliberalism is transforming states from being protective buffers between external economic forces and the domestic economy into agencies for adapting domestic economies to the exigencies of the global economy' (Cox 1995: 39). It is, after all, states that sign trade and investment agreements that remove protection, that chose not to regulate finance and that issue licences to operate to companies to produce in ways which knowingly destroy the environment. The reliance of states on capital for investment, jobs and tax has distorted the purpose and rationale of government and, as we saw in Chapter 4, can lead to competitive deregulation and lowering or freezing of standards of protection in some sectors and regions of the world. The overall effect of this and the evidence for a 'race to the bottom' is contested, but there is no question that policy-makers take very seriously the threats of firms and business associations to relocate their operations in the face of proposals to tighten environmental regulations (Newell 2012). 'Disciplinary neo-liberalism', where the granting of aid, investment or market access is offered or denied to countries according to their ability to adopt neo-liberal reforms, has been applied to check progressive policy moves by states and to assert the preferences of a transnational capitalist class (Gill 1995). This has the effect of restricting the 'policy autonomy' and 'developmental space' of states to pursue their preferred development pathways. Globally this manifests itself as the 'new constitutionalism' and is observable in provisions in regional and global trade and investment agreements and investor dispute tribunals that protect the rights of capital (Newell 2012). Fear of capital flight and investment strikes are among the strategies used to impede the introduction of higher social and environment standards and presents a challenge for Greens wanting to, or facing the prospect of, pursuing 'ecologism in one country'.

Even if globalised forms of capitalism intensify these challenges, for Greens extractivism and unsustainability is not exclusive to capitalism, since the state's role in industrialism is what is important regardless of the owners of the means of production and the recipients of the fruits of that production. The state is not then a neutral actor with regard to the actors and processes that produce environmental harm (Saurin 2001; Paterson 2001). Indeed, it is possible to question the very division of state and market. Vlachou expresses it in the following way: 'state policies towards nature and the ecological changes initiated in capitalism are not "external or artificial" barriers to capital. They are the outcome of internal processes and also constitutive elements of capital as a social relation' (2004: 928). Political elites often have major interests in key economic sectors that exact significant environmental damage, including commercial logging, mineral and oil exploitation and plantation cropping (Dauvergne 1997; Evans et al. 2002). We find evidence here of Marx's contention that the capitalist state is 'based on the contradiction between public and private life, on the contradiction between general interests and private interests' (1975: 46). Its role is to maintain market discipline and mediate between the contradictions of general and particular interests within capital, such that competing fractions of capital seek to present their interests as consistent with those of capital-in-general in environmental as in other issue areas (Newell and Paterson 1998).

Indeed, states assume many of the key functions of coercion, regulation and enforcement required to reproduce the conditions for the expansion of capital, public and private. Legal rules cannot be divorced from the material conditions in which they are produced and seek to preserve. As we saw earlier and will see below, this can be through violent acts of dispossession, as well as by constructing laws that protect and safeguard the interests of businesses, discipline citizen protest and labour agitation, as well as by interventions in social and cultural spheres aimed at legitimising and reinforcing state power and visions of 'development'. Hence the complicity of the industrial state in ecological destruction, even in ways which undermine the ability of the economy to reproduce itself. This behaviour amounts to what Ulrich Beck referred to as 'organised ecological irresponsibility', or simply organised crime, as depicted in Figure 5.1. For Dryzek, however, it is the *combination* of capitalism, liberal democracy and the administrative state that compound ecological problems where the former 'imprisons' the state by constraining policy freedom and applying punishments to those states that step out of line (Dryzek 1992).

Some such accounts of the state have been criticised for generalising too much, ascribing timeless, ahistorical and universal characteristics and immovable logics to states as reified structures and thus downplaying or undermining possibilities for their reform (Mol 2000). The question is how far these constraints upon the state constitute a structural imperative or rather reflect a prevailing, but changeable, consensus around the desirability and necessity for growth. This point speaks to the issues raised in Chapter 4, demonstrating that the project of growth politically, and as a set of specific metrics which afford a way to measure growth, are recent phenomena in broader historical terms (Dale 2012). Moreover, the tension in capitalist states between accumulation and legitimation (Habermas 1973) creates contradictory pressures that create openings for Green strategies to delegitimise destructive accumulation strategies, potentially creating space to separate 'the state' from a particular understanding of and pursuit of growth.

Critique of State Coercion and Violence

The third source of Green critique of the state relates to its ties to militarism and the coevolution of the state with war, violence and dispossession of its own and other citizens. As Charles Tilly (1993) famously noted, 'war made the state and the state made war'. Classic understandings of the state often refer to the monopoly on the legitimate use of physical force within a given territory (Weber 1978). What counts as a legitimate use of force, as well as how to put limits on the exercise of force beyond a 'given territory', are key preoccupations for Greens. At the heart of this is a concern with the state-military-industrial complex (the term 'prison' is sometimes also added), which serves as a vehicle for the systematic exploitation of society as a whole at home and abroad in pursuit of control and profit.

On the one hand, there is the internal everyday violence that industrialism requires and generates in its wake resulting from its extractivist orientation and growth obsession that demands what Harvey refers to as 'accumulation by dispossession' (2004). The extraction of resources such as oil and minerals, often against the wishes of host communities who rarely benefit from the revenues from it, necessitates acts of dispossession against excluded groups such as indigenous peoples. It produces a deliberate neglect or blindness regarding the 'slow violence' (Nixon 2011) and everyday environmental injustices visited upon poorer groups in society by wealthier groups with the state's endorsement, complicity or active involvement (Garvey and Newell 2005). In this regard, especially in eco-anarchist and social ecology traditions, the state is viewed as a vehicle for mobilising violence for the preservation of hierarchies and social order, based on extracting wealth from poor to rich, South to North and rural to urban areas (Bookchin 1982).

On a more individual level, anarchist traditions meanwhile are alert to the encroachment of the state upon civil liberties or community autonomy. Indeed, many Greens have expressed opposition to the extension of EU power in the wake of the Maastricht Treaty around issues of justice and 'home affairs', and to the use of identification cards, and were active in campaigns against legislation such as the Criminal Justice Bill in the United Kingdom, as well as other more recent attempts to criminalise the protest around fracking, for example (Brock et al. 2018).

At the same time, Greens seek to defend and, on occasion, expand the protective powers of the state. The preoccupation with diversity, for example, raises difficult questions about the role of the state in promoting and defending difference. As Bomberg suggests (1998: 64): 'peaceful coexistence among and between societies is only possible with mutual tolerance of ethnic, social, political and sexual minority groups' – a path to guaranteeing human rights and protection from state encroachment on liberties and a powerful check on the development of nationalism. Respect for individual freedom and democratic self-determination are key to this; unity in diversity. Yet state power in the form of law and detention is often called upon to address those individuals and organisations that express racism, misogyny, intolerance and abuse. Greens often invoke the state to promote and protect diversity to ensure, as Die Grünen put it: 'the recognition and promotion of the cultural diversity of the different nationalities and historical regions of Europe' (1984: 39). Some feminists might argue along similar lines: rather than there being *too much* state, it is the state's absence and acts of omission through a reluctance to intervene in the 'private' sphere of the family that enables domestic violence to exist.

The question for Greens is whether the enforcement and coercive powers of the state can be used for the achievement of a sustainability society, eliciting punishments, fines and imprisonment for unsustainable behaviour by corporations and individuals, suspending freedoms and civil liberties where 'freedoms to' (travel, trade) have an impact on 'freedoms from' (environmental degradation, ill-health, poverty) for others. As Dobson explains: 'The post-growth state is necessary not just as a promoter of decentralism but also as a defender of social, economic and cultural equality' (2014: 22).

In reality, it is when these elements of the state that Greens critique combine that diminish the prospects of reform. This reflects Dryzek's claim, noted above, that it is when capitalism, liberal democracy and the administrative state work together that environmental crises are compounded. Indeed, there is often a mismatch between the level at which ecological contradictions are generated (based on the growth imperative of globalized capital accumulation) and the level at which political responsibility and crisis management is allocated (the liberal democratic state). In this school of thought then:

without a transformation in the role and functions of the liberal capitalist state and capitalist society, the contradictory requirements of legitimation and accumulation cannot be solved (as distinct from politically managed) by changes in the policy tools, policy setting, and even the hierarchy of policy goals. It is the character of the system (the mutual dependencies of the capitalist economy and the liberal capitalist state) that set limits to the effectiveness of such state interventions.

(Eckersley 2004: 81)

Greens have to engage with the multi-functionality of states and their deep embeddedness in broader structures of social power if they are to articulate theories of change and pursue strategies that will bring about lasting change. To this end, they require a more nuanced account of and engagement with states, recognising their plurality in form and the very different contexts in which they function. We turn now to their visions of what a Green state might look like.

Normative Vision

We have noted a general tendency in Green political theory for scepticism towards the state and a strong preference for bottom-up theories of change through social movements and citizen mobilisation. What might ecologically responsible state-hood look like? There is a growing recognition of scope for the Greening of the state (Eckersley 2004; Barry and Eckersley 2005). Scholars have looked at differ-ent dimensions of the Green state. Christoff, for example, develops categorisations of eco-fascist, neoliberal and welfare environmental states (Christoff 2005), while others have sought to explore what types of legal, constitutional and institutional innovations we might expect to see in a *greening* state or in a fully-fledged 'green state' (Barry 2008; Barry and Eckersley 2005).

More optimistically, accounts of the Green state show how there has been a growing entrenchment and institutionalisation of environmental policy as a key rationale and component of state policy and regulatory authority (Meadowcroft 2004). Assuming a broader range of responsibilities for resource management, protection and conservation and steering transitions in the ways pointed to by work on transition management (Kemp et al. 2007), this argument finds strong resonance in claims of ecological modernisation, for example, regarding the ability of states to adapt their core functions to ecological imperatives (Mol 2000). In other words, as Eckersley (2004: 14) states: 'it is too hasty too assume that the social structures of international anarchy, global capitalism and the liberal democratic state are necessarily anti-ecological and mutually reinforcing or that they foreclose the possibility of any progressive transformations of states as governance structures'. For her, in a Green state, 'securing private capital accumulation would no longer be the defining feature or primary raison d'être of the state. The state would be more reflexive and market activity would be disciplined, and in some cases curtailed, by social and ecological norms' (2004: 83).

For Eckersley, a reinvention of the state is in order – a broadening and deepening of the notion of ecological stewardship and boundaries of the political community which the state serves and can held accountable to. Hence the 'new' role of the state is as 'ecological steward and facilitator of transboundary democracy' (Eckersley 2004: 3), grounded in new forms of ecological citizenship. In this reading, 'the anti-ecological behavioural dynamics that are generated by the social structures of international anarchy, global capitalism and administrative hierarchy can be reversed' (Eckersley 2004: 15). They can be reversed in her view through a combination of more ambitious environmental multilateralism, eco-logical modernisation and (transnational) environmental advocacy. The former builds on the development of principles of precaution and 'polluter pays', 'common heritage' and 'common but differentiated responsibilities' that appear in treaties covering issues such as climate change, acid rain and the protection of Antarctica. Principle 21 of the Stockholm declaration, for example, places upon states 'the responsibility to ensure that activities within their jurisdiction or control do not cause damage to the environment of other States or of areas beyond the limits of national jurisdiction'. The challenge being that we have arguably seen each of these in abundance over the last twenty to thirty years but have yet to buck the trends towards environmental collapse – begging the question: is this enough? Critiques both of ecological modernisation (Bailey et al. 2011), the limits of even accelerated forms of Earth systems governance (Stirling 2015) and of environmental advocacy (Dauvergne 2016) point to the limits of these strategies. It is also the case that for every progressive principle in international environmental laws, commercial trade and investment law, which is frequently afforded greater protection and enforcement powers, provides a counterweight and often decisive influence, raising the question once again of 'whose rules rule' (Newell 2012).

Clear criteria about what constitutes a Green state are elusive, therefore. For many, Green principles of post-sovereign governance, deepening democracy and non-militarism would have to be at the heart of configuring a Green state. At the most general level, it might be thought to be about using state power domestically and globally in defence of the environment. The mere expansion in the growth and volume and reach of environmental legislation should not be taken as a proxy, however, for greening, given significant non-implementation and non-enforcement and the offsetting and undermining effect of business-as-usual non- or anti-environmental policy in areas such as trade, energy and industrial policy (Newell 2008b).

'Environmental', 'eco' and 'ecological' prefixes to the state are often used interchangeably. For Christoff, '*Green states*, were they to exist, would be characterized by the predominance of types of state activity aimed at strong ecological modernization' (Christoff 2005: 41) or where ecological considerations are at the core of state activities (Meadowcroft 2004). Eckersley (2004) argues that Scandinavian and Nordic states most closely resemble the Green state, while others (Dryzek et al. 2003) suggest Germany is most likely to fulfil this potential. These examples raise questions about the ways in which wealth is accumulated in unsustainable ways to finance them (oil wealth in Norway or destruction of forests in Sweden, for example), or of 'outsourcing' transitions: undertaking them by importing required food and energy from neighbouring states (such as in the case of Germany banning nuclear energy at home but importing electricity derived from nuclear energy from other countries). These actions feed suspicions on the part of former colonies about the accumulated ecological debts and privileged disposition of post-industrial states built on histories of environmental destruction at home and abroad (Acción Ecológica 1999). For others, a Green state would also have to be an eco-socialist state (O'Connor 1998; Weston 1986), although the details of how this would emerge and function are underdeveloped in the literature (Eckersley 2004). In such a case, many Greens would have concerns, articulated above, about the persistence of a centralised administrative state and whether the socialist principles underpinning it would end up being locked into a defence of industrialism as a project of radical redistribution.

In anarchist visions, left to themselves people will naturally and instinctively organise themselves into self-governing communities underpinned by principles of mutual aid and sociality (O'Riordan 1981). The anarchist Kropotkin expresses it in the following way: 'No ruling authorities, then. No government of man by man; no crystallisation and immobility, but a continual evolution – such as we see in nature. Free play for the individual, for the full development of his [sic] intellectual gifts' (1955: 59). Some accounts of the 'commons' project celebrate the virtues and viability of this vision as one that accurately describes many communities around the world that have yet to be enclosed by the state or the market. In this account, the commons and public goods, order and environmental protection are secured on the basis of necessity that derives from mutual interdependence and accountability for actions, where exit from the community and escape from the consequences of actions taken is not a possibility (The Ecologist 1993). As Susan George suggests: 'This doesn't mean the commons dwellers are more noble or worthier than the rest of us – they simply realize they're going to remain a member of their group for the foreseeable future' (2010: 265). This thinking unites, in many ways, both deep ecologists such as Naess and social ecologists such as Bookchin who advocate the abolition of the state (see Chapter 2). The bioregionalism, discussed in Chapter 4, proposes a 'commune of communes'.

Shallower versions of 'ecological democracy' in a more liberal vein imagine the state as 'public ecological trustee', the embodiment of the collective will and protector of the public good, as well as good ecological citizen globally (Eckersley 2004). Important here is the notion of a Green 'public sphere' in the Habermasian sense. It rests on 'deepening the democratic accountability and responsiveness of states to their citizens' environmental concerns, while also extending democratic accountability to the environmental concerns of transnational civil society, international organizations and the society of states in general' (Eckersley 2004: 14–15). This view resonates with concerns to extend and deepen notions of transnational environmental harm for which states and other transnational actors can be held to account (Mason 2005). This policy would be accompanied by the promotion and embedding of deeper forms of ecological citizenship as part of a new social and ecological contract between states and their citizens (Dobson 2003). This new 'ecological social contract' requires that citizens gain increased decision-making power over the design and shape of the economy, society and politics but within (ecological) limits set by the state and perhaps enshrined in a constitution (Dobson 2014).

In this regard, as noted above, Green politics is described not so much as anti-liberal, but post-liberal (Doherty and de Geus 1996; Eckersley 2004). It is post-liberal in the sense that 'it emerges from an immanent (ecological) critique, rather than from an outright rejection, of liberal democracy' (Eckersley 2004: 2). 'Ecological freedom for all can only be realised under a form of governance that enables and enforces ecological responsibility' (Eckersley 2004: 107). Critics of Green politics often focus on what they perceive to be a neo-Malthusian interpretation of scarcity that justifies the imposition of limits on freedom (Barry 2008). In actual fact, the freedoms most Greens are wanting to restrict are freedoms to exploit others – but extending that protection to non-humans and future generations.

Constitutional innovations are important to Greens, nevertheless. For Barry (2008: 4), 'green constitutionalism' offers a way of 'conjoining a green commitment to human rights, procedural democratic rights and rights of participation, community right to know laws with protection of the environment and the political regulation of the economy for social and environmental and not just economic objectives such as profit-making'. Steering a course between eco-modernists who place their faith in the reformability of liberal capitalism and the related role of the state, and the outright rejection of a role for the state by many eco-anarchists, Barry makes a strong case for foundational legal contracts to enshrine duties and responsibilities on states and citizens alike. Indeed, he also suggests such ideas would find favour among social ecologists and those of a more anarchist persuasion, such as Murray Bookchin. He quotes the latter as saying:

I believe in law, and the future society I envision, would also have a constitution. Of course, the constitution would have to be the product of careful consideration, by the empowered people. It would be democratically discussed and voted upon. But once the people have ratified it, it would be binding on everyone. It is not accidental that historically, oppressed people who were victims of the arbitrary behavior of the ruling classes ... demanded constitutions and just laws as a remedy.

(quoted in Barry 2008: 4)

Constitutionalism potentially provides the means to institutionalise environmental rights, confer legal standing upon non-human interests (rights for nature) and the institutionalisation of the precautionary principle. This would help to consolidate the essential aims of environmental protection as being a matter of public interest rather than a partisan cause (Hayward 2005). Importantly, constitutional-level political changes can alter and redistribute political and economic power within and between societies, especially with regard to 'setting and changing the terms on which the economy and its agents operates' (Barry 2008: 5). This point is vital, since much as Greens may wish to re-embed the economy within ecological systems, as well as resist the idea that the two can in any case be separated, for this ecological re-embedding to be achieved, the economy must be politically re-embedded within society and social norms and attuned to non-economic institutions and objectives (Polanyi 1980 [1944]). This challenges the reification of the 'market' as a space separate from the polity, society and ecology, all of which bring it into being, and sustains and imbues places of exchange with their values and culture. Taken to its logical conclusion, therefore, a Green republican perspective, as Barry describes it, would endorse and promote the political – including constitutional and legal – regulation of the economy 'to ensure that it does not grow and develop in a manner which undermines its own ecological foundations' (Barry 2008: 8).

Many features of Green politics make it compatible with republican visions of the state from Aristotle and Rousseau onwards, including ideas about active citizenship as a form of ecological stewardship (Dobson 2003), in which duties as well as rights are central. A democratised and decentralised state is seen as a necessary institution to promote the common good of sustainability and a sense of justice and connection between past, present and future generations (Read 2012). Green republicanism focuses on (public, political) citizen (and not private, economic) consumer identities and practices as is commonplace in neo-liberalism (Barry 2008; Toke 2000). Barry (2016) goes as far as to suggest that debt-based consumer capitalism (and especially its more recent neo-liberal incarnation), is simply incompatible with a version of democratic politics and associated norms and practices of citizenship required for the transition away from unsustainable development. This is because of consumer capitalism's passive and clientelistic nature, its capture by elite and private interests and the lack of space for meaningful engagement with the conduct of politics. Moving away from such understandings and practices of citizenship towards more active and politically engaged ones is critical for advocates of Green republicanism.

Many Greens also share the importance that Republicans attach to valuing 'contestation over consensus'. This can mean expanded spaces and scope for deliberation over plural pathways to sustainability and the use of deliberative and inclusive policy-making processes, such as standing panels of citizens, regular polling, multi-criteria mapping and citizen assemblies and juries. To really deepen democracy and open up the state would mean including issues of core state interest that are currently off-limits for debate and not only what are dismissively termed 'low-political' issues. Social movements have played a key part in opening up such spaces around trade policy in Latin America, for example (Newell 2007), that have traditionally been closed to meaningful citizen engagement. This helps to break down the division between more open and participatory spaces for 'softer' issues and closed and expert-only venues for discussion of 'harder' 'high political' issues of security and economy.

Optimistically, in a post-capitalist context it might be possible to imagine that the state would no longer operate as the 'managing committee for the affairs of the bourgeoisie', as Marx and Engels put it (1998 [1848]), or the servant of capital, if it ceases to assume as one of its main tasks the reproduction of capitalist social life. Some accounts of a post-capitalist Green state suggest 'securing private capital accumulation would no longer be the defining feature or primary raison d'être of the state. The state would be more reflexive and market activity would be disciplined, and in some cases curtailed, by social and ecological norms' (Eckersley 2004: 83). More anarchist versions of Green thinking would suggest that the need for a centralised redistribution through the state would be diminished since more localised and autarkic communities would have their own incentives and mechanisms for ensuring redistribution, grounded in a shared sense of collective fate and patterns of reciprocity and mutual aid.

The key question in many ways is: how would a Green state sustain itself in a post-growth economy? Where will the wealth come from that will be taxed and redistributed? It is certainly the case that some drains on public expenditure might fall away. Fewer resources would be required to support the military if visions of Green security were to be pursued (see Chapter 3). There would be fewer public subsidies to the private sector through Private Finance Initiatives (PFIs) and other schemes, and immense savings on reigning in wasteful subsidies for fossil fuel production and consumption that currently stand at USD 10 million per minute according to the IMF (2015), for example. Some Greens might advocate 'progressive austerity' in this regard, where curtailing of some areas of state expenditure can be a positive measure if combined with policies and programmes that, for example, tackle the root causes of ill-health and economic insecurity rather than merely its symptoms. It again comes back to Dobson's (1990) telescope analogy whereby some areas of state power might be extended, while others are contracted.

Withdrawal of support for neo-liberal multilateral institutions such as the World Bank and IMF, for example, would also save huge amounts of state funds. Preserving policy space and autonomy to pursue a Green vision in the face of probable capital flight will present a huge challenge, but some of the disciplinary straightjackets around fiscal expenditure might be removed. The structural power of capital is only powerful if you are highly dependent on mobile capital. A more self-sufficient, or autarkic society, would be less so. History does not provide many precedents for 'ecologism in one country' as those socialist and left-leaning regimes that have gone it alone have funded their visions through highly centralised, industrialised and extractivist economies. Think of Hugo Chávez's Venezuela or Evo Morales's Bolivia, or the legacy of environmental devastation left by many former Communist countries in Central and Eastern Europe, to say nothing of the ecological legacy of China's breakneck growth under the guise of 'capitalism with Chinese characteristics'. Perhaps the nearest positive parallel would be some of the innovation in self-sufficiency, organic food production and an 'energy revolution' that took place in Cuba in the wake of the country's imposed isolation by the United States (Simms 2013).

Related to the issue of the resourcing of a Green state, is the issue of order and the monopoly on the use of violence, especially where the coercive functions of the state have been deliberately curtailed. Here, more anarchist or communalist lines of Green thought emphasise that, contrary to Hardin's 'Tragedy of the Commons' (1968), external coercion or force from above is not required to ensure that some form of order is preserved. In the commons it is claimed, 'Woods and streams feeding local irrigation schemes remained intact because anyone degrading them had to brave the wrath of neighbours deprived of their livelihood and no one was powerful enough to do so. Everyone was subject to everyone else's personal scrutiny and sanctions' (The Ecologist 1993: 5). Local accountability and mutual dependence serve as the societal disciplining mechanisms, or more insidiously, shaming, ridicule and ostra-cisation serve as the sanctioning mechanisms in stateless communities. 'When subsistence is at stake [communities] often improvise or reconstruct rough and ready commons regimes rather than pin their hopes on either the market economy or public institutions. For better or worse the commons is the social and political space where things get done and where people derive a sense of belonging and have an element of control over their lives' (The Ecologist 1993: 6). Rather than an exceptional state of affairs, it is suggested that 'for the vast majority of humanity the commons is an everyday reality' and 'new commons are constantly being born, even among what might seem the most fragmented communities' (The Ecologist 1993: 7). The commons is, nevertheless, hard to define, as even its proponents concede.

It provides sustenance, security and independence and yet typically does not produce commodities. Unlike most things in modern industrial society, moreover, it is neither private nor public: neither commercial farm nor communist collective, neither business firm nor state utility, neither jealously guarded private plot nor national or city park. Nor is it usually open to all. The relevant community typically decided who uses it and how.

(The Ecologist 1993: 7–8)

It is particularly hard for conventional economists to understand the nature and functioning of the commons. As Escobar notes (1995: 198): 'economics cannot understand the language of the commons because the commons have no individuality and do not follow the rules of scarcity and efficiency'. Yet as Visvanathan suggests, 'What one needs is not a common future but the future as commons' (1991: 383).

Strategy

Whatever the ultimate vision or preference for the role of the state in a Green society, its existence and continuation in the short term represent a reality most

Greens will have to deal with, either as a force for good, providing protection and regulation for the common good, or as a vehicle of oppression and the centralisation of control and resources. In reality, they will have to deal with both aspects of state power, benign and malign. Eckersley puts it the following way:

> one can expect states to persist as major sites of social and political power for at least the foreseeable future and that any green transformations of the present order will, short of revolution, necessarily be state-dependent ... And if states are so implicated in ecological destruction, then an inquiry into the potential for their transformation or even their modest reform into something that is at least more conducive to ecological sustainability would seem compelling.
>
> *(2004: 5)*

We need to keep in mind here Hedley Bull's caution about engaging in a 'counsel of despair' by demanding the abolition of the state as a pre-requisite for building an alternative society, rather than building upon what is there (1979: 112). Whichever way we look at it, the state will play a crucial, albeit contradictory, role in the politics of green transformations (Newell 2015; Mazzucato 2015; Johnstone and Newell 2017). From law maker to law enforcer, as the bearer of the monopoly on the use of force, as broker, convenor of key social and economic actors, as notional representative of the will of the people (in many contexts at least), the state is clearly vital to the prospects of a sustainable society.

Despite the political and ideological assault on the state and the marketisation of environmental governance (Newell 2008b), states are central even to market-led environmental transformations (Scoones et al. 2015) as rule makers and enforcers, delegators of authority, innovators and financers of projects and infrastructures that private actors will not support. Compromised by ties to the very actors implicated in environmental degradation, and in many cases exercising only limited policy autonomy to effect change, it remains the case that, as Eckersley notes (2004: 7), 'there are still few social institutions that can match the same degree of capacity and potential legitimacy that states have to redirect societies and economies along more ecologically sustainable lines'. It is for that reason that, despite the enduring resonance and appeal of anti-statism in Green political theory and practice, many in the environmental movement and engaged in Green politics orientate much of their campaigning towards better state regulation of the economic and social practices that generate environmental harm. The question we return to below is: in a Green society, which aspects of state power would we want to see less of and which more of? Such consideration perhaps moves us beyond seeing Green views of the state as either contradictory or the product of a necessary ambiguity (Paterson 1999).

In so far as states and corporations are the primary actors driving environmental degradation and the latter are only marginally and indirectly responsive to social pressure, states will remain key targets for Green strategies as actors in their own right, financing and fuelling destruction, and because of their power – should they chose to use it – to reign in corporate power (Korten 1995). States are 'more amenable to democratization than corporations' Eckersley suggests (2004: 8). It is also worth recalling that some states, in some places, at some times have played proactive, interventionist leadership roles in driving progressive change (Simms 2013). Greens are drawing on these experiences as a strategy to accelerate action in the here and now, arguing that state action has brought about radical, progressive, rapid and disruptive change in the past and can do so again today. Think of the New Deal in post–World War II America, a Green version of which is now enjoying a revival today, or strategies of wholesale industrial conversion in the United Kingdom or state-led 'energy revolutions' in Cuba (Simms and Newell 2017). Ideologies and ideas of what states can and should do, the degree of policy autonomy and developmental space they have been able to enjoy, are therefore not fixed. They are negotiated and contingent on the weight of historical forces at key moments. Hence, as noted above, after decades of onslaught on the efficiency and effectiveness of the state, the prevailing orthodoxy today is that states can and need to play a proactive part in leading transitions to sustainability.

Most Greens foresee a major role for national governments in creating the framework within which a Green economy can flourish, including the setting of suitable tax incentives and the control of industries that are contributing to environmental problems. Likewise, there are clear roles imagined for redistribution and planning. Again, the tension for Greens is that while many are in favour of an interventionist state in relation to regulation and taxation over other market-based mechanisms, for example, this assumes the existence of a powerful, well-resourced central state. Many Greens are in favour of ecological taxation, taxing pollution rather than labour as we saw in Chapter 4. Only the state has the power to rebalance the economy. For example, in their submission to the Environmental Audit Committee on the Green economy, Scott Cato et al. suggest (n.d.): 'We urgently need government to bring about the immediate cessation of activities that will plainly not be part of the green economy, like building new coal power stations, development of coal mines, major new road projects or runways, and the use of artificial fertilizers. Simultaneously we need governments to strongly encourage the development of key green economy sectors, especially renewable energy infrastructure'. Likewise, elsewhere it is suggested the governments should take a stronger role in controlling corporations whose activities are destructive to the environment, including removing their licences to trade.

Concretely, and with respect to promoting technological innovation and harnessing the levels of finance required to support transitions to a Green economy, for example, there is interest in a 'Green entrepreneurial state' (Mazzucato 2015) and stronger forms of Green industrial policy (Pegels 2014).

As Molly Scott Cato puts:

> we would propose the introduction of a number of Ecological Enterprise Zones, in areas where the resources necessary for a sustainable economy to succeed are present, but which have not thrived in the competition for financial investment. These EEZs would be supported by government grants to become hot-houses for the innovation of green technologies and sustainable lifestyles. In return, they would be expected to achieve significant cuts in carbon emissions, resource usage, and levels of waste production. Government should enable local authorities in such areas to experiment with policy tools, such as carbon taxation and import and export duties. The aim would be for the EEZ to become a prototype of the self-reliant local economy that a green economy requires.
>
> *(Cato n.d.)*

The problem is that states have failed to turn around the key trends towards overshooting planetary boundaries, such that short-lived victories for environmental campaigners, or even seemingly effective environmental treaties may have bought us time but have yet to buck the march towards environmental ruin. Pockets of decoupling and gains in efficiencies are too often dwarfed and overwhelmed by overall increases in resource use (Ward et al. 2016). We return, once again, to William Jevons and his paradox (1865) that implies the need for more fundamental shifts to reduce levels of production and consumption. These might include processes of enabling and overseeing political decentralisation and a reorientation of the global economy towards meeting local needs that require active state policy and intervention, including plans for national resilience.

As discussed in Chapter 6, Greens need to clarify how they square the demand for an internationalist, developmental, interventionist, and in many ways Keynesian state, able and willing to stand up to transnational capital and powerful financial actors with visions of a neutered, smaller and less well-resourced state. For example, in their opposition to austerity many Greens have also argued that frontline public services around health and education could be protected if corporate tax evasion were stamped out. Closing tax loops again requires a proactive state but also serves as a key way of resourcing the state.

Ironically, precisely because of the ecological crisis, the state will be called upon to deal with emergencies as environmental disasters continue to increase in frequency and magnitude. Depending on how it responds to these situations, the 'disaster state' may either enhance its power through the popular legitimacy it gains from acting decisively and effectively on behalf of its citizens, or be the target of blame for its failure to deal with a multitude of problems for which it will be held to account but over which in many cases it may only wield indirect control and responsibility.

States in a capitalist society will be wary of adopting the sorts of measures many Greens propose because of a fear of inflation, capital strikes and labour unrest in response to attempts to regulate capital more stringently, or to internalise the externalities that are currently routinely passed on to society and the environment. A Green state could well be isolated and would need to form alliances and solidarities with other sympathetic states.

Towards Ecological Democracy

Deepening democracy would go beyond the extension of democratic control over the economy for the common good. Eckersley suggests (2004: 242): 'Ecological democracy would differ from liberal democracy in enabling more concerted political questioning of traditional boundaries between what is public and private, domestic and international, intrinsically valuable and instrumentally valuable'. But what does this mean in practice? It would imply a range of constitutional innovations and charters that deal with issues such as rights, responsibilities, participation and consultation, as proposed in Green republican visions described above, but combined with liability and redress and public information to improve accountability and to ensure societies are living within ecological limits. Together these would amount to a fundamental reframing of the purpose of the state.

Strategies for democratising the state and improving downward accountability include the decentralisation of power towards regional and local decision-making bodies, consistent with Green principles around subsidiarity. As discussed in Chapter 6, this would be pursued as part of a broader reorganisation of decision-making power across governance units. Multi-level governance would include bodies such as the Committee of the Regions, as functions in the EU. Many Greens call for electoral reform including systems of proportional representation and lowering the voting age to sixteen. A reduction in the voting age would reflect the fact that younger people will bear many of the costs and consequences (as well as reap the benefits) of decisions made today about how to run the economy and in whose interests. Chapter 6 also notes recent innovations in parliaments in Wales, Hungary and Israel, for example, where commissioners for future generations have been appointed to help secure intergenerational justice.

These strategies will have to be targeted both at putting down limits and boundaries around the state in some spheres (new frontiers of exploitation, the police state), seeking to shape and promote a Greener state (willing and able to use regulation, taxation and redistribution to manage the transition to a Greener society) and articulating a vision of an alternative ecological state. Wishing away the state is probably neither practical nor desirable, and it is worth recalling Hedley Bull's (1979) reflection that violence, insecurity, injustice and ecological degradation pre-date the state system and would likely survive the demise of the state system whichever alternative structures may arise.

A challenge for Greens will be to draw a distinction between post-growth decentralisation and 'small-state fanaticism'. As Dobson suggests, 'Localism is often a cover for the take-over of public space by the rich and the powerful. This "hollowing out" of the state has the effect of driving all responsibility downwards, whether the levels at which this responsibility is then supposed to reside ... have the means of fulfilling their obligations or not' (Dobson 2014: 21). The latter is seen as 'a ruse by small-statists to achieve their objective: the dominance of our social life by the private and commercial sectors' (Dobson 2014: 21). We see this around the call by the political Right for a 'big society' based on charity and voluntarism to pick up the slack on the provision of welfare, health and education as state financing is withdrawn for these services.

Besides downwards decentralisation and disassembling those parts of the state considered to be problematic from an ecological point of view, many near-term strategies focus on the deepening and appropriate use of existing policy instruments and norms around precaution and harm and prior informed consent, for example. The precautionary principle could be used and constitutionally protected, as Eckersley suggests, not only 'to regulate the use (by preventing the abuse) of nature but also provide a risk-adverse decision-making framework that is able to protect nature for its own sake' (2004: 103). The precautionary principle makes a presumption against taking decisions with irreversible consequences or risks. It amounts to a reversal of the burden of proof and a move away from the 'polluter pays' for damage done to preventing damage from occurring in the first place through fuller and more inclusive deliberation on the scale and nature of the risks that societies and communities of the affected are willing to accept (Baber and Bartlett 2005).

There are strong elements of accountability and redress here around the idea of democracy *for* the affected. As Eckersley puts it: 'all those potentially affected by a risk should have some meaningful opportunity to participate or otherwise be represented in the making of the policies or decisions that generate the risk' (2004: 111). This requires 'a reconceptualization of the demos as no longer fixed in terms of people and territory' (Eckersley 2004: 113) where those not necessarily capable of reciprocal recognition are included. In Chapter 4 we saw how, in practice, this could be pursued through ideas about addressing environmental harm through corporate accountability measures in international law, transnational environmental litigation and the like as a means to avoid the unfair distribution and concentration of burden and risk on poorer communities, often in the global South (Newell 2001b).

In terms of temporal and intergenerational justice there is scope to adopt some of forms of proxy representation for future generations and non-human species described above, as well as tribunes for non-citizens and an independent environmental defenders office (Eckersley 2004; Dobson 1996). These could play a key role in preventing the discounting of costs and risks of decisions taken today that will be predominantly borne by future generations. Representation would obviously and necessarily be indirect and would require a degree of internalising and projecting what the interests of groups without voice and direct participation would be. This is, in many ways, a second-best solution but, as Goodin (1996) argues, this is preferable to their interests not being considered at all. As well as facilitating a degree of inter-generational empathy and justice, decision-making informed by such an approach requires current decision-makers not to close off alternative pathways and options by pursuing policies that are non-reversible or which are characterised by high degrees of lock-in that deny choices to future generations. Reversibility and reflexivity in this way help to pluralise decision-making in the here and now with the requirement to avoid mutually exclusive pathways.

Democracy would be deepened through deliberation moving beyond 'power trading among self-interested actors' and in favour of 'unconstrained egalitarian deliberation over questions of value and common purpose in the public sphere' (Eckersley 2004: 115). Optimistically, it is conceived of as the means and process by which we learn and can act upon an appreciation of mutual dependence and dependence upon the environment, enabling better collective decision-making about longer-range problems. There may be limits to the notion that the 'force of the better argument' wins through amid stark social and resource and therefore power inequalities, as well as the deeply engrained belief systems around growth and progress that are intrinsic to industrialism that Greens would like to scrutinise. An assumed openness to change opinions perhaps also implies that participants do not have a (material) stake in the outcome, or indeed in preserving the status quo, such that privileging general over private and vested interests is easier called for than enacted. This is the basis of critiques of deliberation – for its assumptions about the possibility of dispassionate and rational exchange as well as being very Eurocentric in the models from which it draws inspiration.

As discussed in Chapter 4, deliberation can provide an important check on the 'scientisation' of politics and the narrow forms of 'neo-liberal participation' I have described elsewhere (Newell 2010) and assumptions that power and authority best reside with experts who have the appropriate knowledge to adjudicate on the correct pathways to sustainability. On the contrary, citizen science (Fischer 2002), indigenous knowledge and vernacular understandings of environmental change and how to address it need to be brought to bear to ensure that a diversity of knowledges inform policy and planning. It is always critical to ask 'whose reality counts' (Chambers 1997) and who speaks for whom.

The onus on Greens is to expand, extend and deepen democratic arenas of decision-making, while being alert to the power dynamics which may frustrate the ambitions and practice of deliberative democracy. Hence it is the processes by which decision-making is organised and institutionalised; the extent to which law and science are the mediums of exchange and the means by which competing claims are evaluated, for example, as well as the question of who is represented, that matter. Greens would seek to build on bodies of law and regulation that articulate principles around procedural and distributional rights. These might include rights of access to information, participation and representation (such as the Aarhus Convention)[1] or around Prior Informed Consent that are covered in treaties on waste, chemicals and human rights, as well as instruments that provide access to justice (Newell 2001b).

Conclusions

In sum, a Green state would be a very different type of state. It would inevitably, in some regards, be a smaller state, if military functions are reduced and greater control passed to local authorities and regions. However, as principle and practice suggest, there may be a scope for a more activist and interventionist state, not afraid to stand up to incumbent actors and interests (made possible by severing some of the financial ties and party donations that compromise the independence and integrity of political parties today), and willing to construct visions and plans for a sustainable society but held to account for these through stronger mechanisms of citizen engagement and oversight. A Green state would be willing to drive socially useful and ecological sustainable forms of technology and investment in new infrastructures, and willing to redistribute through a basic income scheme and to tax corporations and pollution to redirect resources to where they are most needed.

It would be post-liberal in the sense that decisions about investment, production and consumption would not be assumed to be private. They would be subject to political oversight in relation to collectively agreed ecological and social boundaries and how to live within them. It would recognise that social and economic structures always shape which freedoms can be exercised and by whom. As Eckersley puts it: 'When the liberal democratic state permits social actors to displace ecological costs on to others, it restricts the ability of environmental victims (both inside and outside the borders of the nation-state) to enjoy the full range of freedoms that liberalism supposedly upholds, including the freedom to participate or otherwise be represented in the making of decisions that bear upon their own lives' (2004: 242).

Holding these disparate (and at times competing) functions in play simultaneously will pose serious challenges. It will require a state whose functions and roles can expand in some areas where necessary but also shrink and retract in others where its presence is no longer desirable or required. Here, the state can extend and contract depending on function (retract around surveillance, control and dispossession, and extend in terms of regulation and distribution). The same may be true across levels of governance. Bookchin, for example, suggests '"the state" can be less pronounced as a constellation of institutions at the municipal level, and more pronounced at the provincial or regional level and most pronounced at the national level' (Bookchin 1992: 137).

The concrete politics of building such a state require further thought: in particular, how to unsettle the relations of power which bind the state, military and industrial sectors together so closely, and which will be united in their fierce (and possibly violent) resistance to attempts to take power away from them. This can only be done through exposing the darker side of the state (without reinforcing right-wing and neo-liberal caricatures of state incompetence and corruption aimed at rolling back only the protective and welfare functions of the state but not its role in sustaining industrial and military society) and building mass movements and support for political parties whose explicit agenda is a very different type of politics with a transformed notion of the role of the state and whom it should serve.

Greens need to take on board then the relational nature of the state and its embeddedness within society and the economy. Strategy has to reflect that and not treat the state as an aspatial and universal, homogenous governance structure abstracted from social and economic relations. In reality, the messy and everyday politics of green transformation will necessarily be a function of the interplay between competing pathways and their associated ideologies, visions, networks and institutions, between more state-led, citizen-led and market-led pathways (Scoones et al. 2015). How they interact and pan out will be a function of the nature and capacity of the state, the role of political culture and where countries are located in the global economy (the degree of autonomy they have from donors and private capital etc.) such that the Greening of the state, or moves towards a Green state, will be an uneven globally differentiated process. Greens' strategies will need to reflect these considerations if they are to succeed. It is a process, rather than a clear endpoint regarding the form and character of a Green state. It will be a protracted and conflictual struggle and, as Eckersley notes, 'the project of building the green state can never be finalized' (2004: 16). This is especially true given the shifting nature of demands on the state from human and non-human sources in the face of ever shifting challenges.

Note

1 The Aarhus Convention was adopted in 1998 and entered into force in 2001. Overseen by the UN Economic Commission for Europe, it establishes rights to environmental information, public participation and access to justice on the part of all citizens of states party to the Convention. Eckersley describes it as 'a significant step towards transnationalizing ecological citizenship' (2004: 194).

6

Green Global Governance

Global governance is a particularly challenging area of global politics in which to assess and develop Green contributions because the nature of global governance reform that Greens would like to see is far less clear than for Green visions regarding related areas such as the economy, the state or security, for example. So what insights can be derived from Green politics and political thought for debates about reforming and rethinking global governance? I argue there is a clear need for a Green account of global governance, one which uniquely assesses the project and practice of global governance as a whole from the point of view of its ability to create a sustainable society rather than its ability to preserve order as an end in itself. Where it does exist, Green thinking about global governance is divided, inconsistent and at times somewhat contradictory. Nevertheless, I want to suggest that it contains within it useful contributions to critique, normative visions and discussions of strategy that I shall try to draw out here.

This chapter first outlines Green critiques of prevailing global governance arrangements focusing on their democratic deficits and poor levels of accountability, the concentration of power in global neo-liberal institutions such as the World Trade Organisation, World Bank and IMF and their failure to advance a more sustainable model of development. Second, it proposes a vision for Green global governance in which there is a rebalancing and repurposing of global governance institutions around the need to move towards a sustainable society. It also shows why some of the problems and crises that global governance institutions have to address today might be less relevant in a sustainable society. Third, it evaluates strategies for achieving Green global governance. These include overhauling the mandates of some institutions while revising the mandates of others; using international law and regulation to articulate, protect and advance new norms and responsibilities towards the environment and poorer groups, as well as pursuing a more peaceful denuclearised world; and seeking to deepen democracy in the international system through better participation, representation and accountability, including of course the interests of future generations and greater collective control over decisions about resource use through re-commoning. It concludes with reflections on Green contributions to understanding and engaging with the practice of global governance, as well as some of the dilemmas and challenges Greens need to address for these views and strategies to gain traction.

Although there is now considerable literature on transnational environmental advocacy and Earth Systems Governance (Biermann 2014), perspectives from Green political thought and the practice of Green politics have not been sufficiently brought to bear on the question of how to 'ecologise' global governance. In part, this situation reflects the fact that scholars writing from more critical Green positions are often sceptical about the achievements and political projects associated with global governance. This attitude manifests itself, first, as a 'social ecology' critique of the overriding focus of liberal institutionalism on explaining international cooperation rather than dominant social and economic hierarchies. This is done by emphasising the marginal importance of 'regimes' and international (environmental) institutions for understanding the processes that routinely generate environmental harm (Saurin 1996) and a scepticism, therefore, about the likelihood that international institutions have either the willingness or ability to address the causes of environmental degradation. There is a corresponding analytical preference to look to underlying structures and relations of power for explanatory traction (Paterson 2001; Newell 2008b), often combined with a resistance to the power of global economic institutions, whose role in ameliorating the ecological crisis is ambivalent at best, and actively destructive at worst (Goldman 2005; Young 2002). There is an antipathy towards many of the global institutions currently charged with managing the global economy such as the World Bank, IMF and WTO who play such a powerful role in organising it along unsustainable lines (Rich 1994).

Second, the neglect of global governance by Greens also relates to strong tendencies towards anti-statism in Green political thought (Barry 1999), despite calls for transnational ecological states in some quarters (Eckersley 2004), and strong ideological preferences for decentralisation and local control, combined with foundational critiques of (techno) managerialism by global elites and institutions (The Ecologist 1993). This view is reflected in the popular mantra 'think global, act local' and in calls for the decentralisation of power and radical subsidiarity. In explaining this conscious neglect of global governance, Katz-Rosene and Paterson conclude their book on *Thinking Ecologically about the Global Political Economy* by noting:

we are led back to questions about global governance. It may seem strange that we have left out a discussion of this, or at least mentioned it only tangentially until now. This is not an accident. It is not that the various institutions of global economic governance . . . are for us irrelevant. It is more that we wanted explicitly to foreground the questions of politics in our analysis – that is questions of who gets what, the competing visions, interests, and the struggles for power and authority, that are central to thinking ecologically about the global political economy. Literature that starts with governance often gets drawn too quickly into more managerial questions about which rules should be made, how competing governance organisations should interact, and whether global governance is, or is not, effective. Entailed in this tends to be a presumption that there is some meaningful sense a global 'we', a universal humanity on whose behalf global governance is presumed to act. In political economy terms, global governance always contains a hegemonic moment – the presentation of specific interests as universal ones.

(2018: 134)

Their argument reflects a resistance to reducing global politics to questions of 'governance' and institutional design, together with a scepticism about universalising political projects articulated by and for elites.

Though Greens are often considered to be internationalists by virtue of their commitment to ecology, peace and feminism (Spretnak and Capra 1984), the necessarily global nature of those struggles that provide the fulcrum from which Green ideas have developed and the intrinsically post-national/sovereign project in which many Greens are engaged (Eckersley 2004), they have not often articulated a clear version of an alternative system of global governance or world order. Opposition to neo-liberal economic institutions and the forms of unsustainable development they finance and promote, from the World Bank to the WTO and IMF can be taken as given, and will be explored further in the section below. Likewise, there is considerable evidence of solidarity with global peace movements, struggles for workers and indigenous peoples' human rights, and for stronger multilateral environmental treaties.

Yet the now urgent need for radical transformations in the economy and society in order to keep within planetary boundaries, which Greens strongly emphasise, implies a potentially key role for the state and more proactive forms of global governance, albeit overseen by institutions with very different mandates and modes of operation. This new terrain poses important challenges and dilemmas for Greens that will be noted throughout this chapter and returned to in the conclusions. Is there a broader Green view of global governance in critique and normative vision that yields a set of strategies for moving from the status quo to an alternative? If not, what might one look like?

Critique

There can be little doubt that most Greens are highly critical of the way in which the world is currently organised. The highly unsustainable, unequal and conflictual world we currently inhabit is about as far away from most Greens' idea of the

'good life' as possible. Many Greens are deeply critical of existing global governance arrangements and sceptical both about the role of the state and more technocratic versions of Earth System Governance (Stirling 2014). This attitude is often
informed by scepticism and resistance to new forms of global managerialism that
are seen as attempts to consolidate and extend forms of control over new resource
frontiers and imply a technocratic vision, deference to elite expertise and reasser-
tion of corporate power (The Ecologist 1993). These critiques were first clearly
articulated in a literature on 'global ecology' that emerged in the wake of the Rio
Earth summit in 1992 (Sachs 1993; Hildyard 1993; Chatterjee and Finger 1994).
From driving us beyond planetary boundaries, to deepening inequalities and
proliferating violence, Greens would also share much in common with more recent
activist academic critiques of the global order, such as those articulated by Susan
George (2010) in her book *Whose Crisis, Whose Future?* Such critiques are often
grounded in concerns about the neo-liberal orientation of more powerful global
governance institutions, the growth of private governance and privatisation of the
UN (Lee et al. 1997) and the weak forms of democratic inclusion, representation
and deliberation that they permit. So let us start by considering Green critiques of
existing global governance. Here I divide the critique into three main areas: the
critique of the (increasingly) neo-liberal character of global governance; the
critique of the undemocratic nature of global governance; and the critique of its
unsustainability.

Critique of Neo-Liberal Global Governance

As former United Nations Secretary General Ban Ki-moon declared at the opening
of the General Assembly in September 2014: 'we are living in an era of an
unprecedented level of crises' (Borger 2014). Greens would regard many of the
crises engulfing the world today around poverty and inequality, war and conflict
and environmental degradation as both interrelated and resulting from a dysfunc-
tional economic system over which the key institutions of global governance
preside. It is an economic system that, as history has repeatedly shown, is prone
to cyclical crises and deepening inequalities of a structural nature (Piketty 2014).
They would point to the need to deal with these issues in tandem, as manifestations
of common problems and interrelated crises (finance-food-energy-water-conflict)
that need to be addressed at source by fundamental changes to the economic
system that is driving them, rather than treating each crisis in isolation to be
resolved through combinations of 'spatial' and 'temporal' fixes that displace crises
to poorer parts of the world or into the future (Harvey 1981). For example,
conflicts over land and access to water are often tied to land and green grabs in
the global South by investors looking for profitable outlets for their capital as crises

of under-consumption take hold in the global North. In turn, the acquisition of land to accommodate the expansion of biofuels as a response to the energy crisis is provoked by reduced access to fossil fuels and the political costs of extracting them in conflict zones. Solutions to one problem cause crises elsewhere. Crises get moved around rather than resolved.

This exploitation of global inequalities and patterns of uneven development through a range of strategies to move problems around reflects capitalism's inability to solve the underlying contradictions that they represent. Examples would include the World Bank's promotion of crop insurance to poorer farmers to 'protect' them against the impacts of climate change (to which they have contributed very little) on their crops (Isakson 2015), or the UN's promotion of carbon trading that enables richer polluters to buy permits generated from projects in poorer parts of the world rather than reduce their own emissions at source (Lohmann 2006). Hence the ineffectiveness of current systems of global governance would be regarded by Greens as a result of their misdiagnosis of the problems they ostensibly seek to address, and their inability to address them with the solutions they propose and those they are unwilling to consider.

Rather than assume that global governance systems seek to effectively manage and 'tame' global capitalism, many Greens would see global economic institutions in particular as handmaidens of the global economic system: managing it on behalf of powerful economic actors and seeking to contain popular resistance to the social and economic turmoil and ecological degradation that results from its operations. In their critique of neo-liberal forms of global governance, Greens' views are in many ways aligned with, and can draw on, critiques on political economy regarding *who* governs globally (Avant et al. 2010) and on *whose behalf*. They ask the key political questions of any governance arrangement: who wins, who loses, how and why? (Newell 2008b). Such questions allow us to query the distribution of wealth and who gets to decide this; who benefits from trade liberalisation, for example, and who bears the cost; and whose resources are being negotiated on whose behalf. They also point to the procedural inequities that generate such skewed outcomes in which the losers of globalisation are largely excluded from decision-making about global economic management. For Greens, an important part of this story would be the ecologically uneven exchange that characterises global patterns of extraction and trade (Roberts and Parks 2008), drawing on dependency thinking discussed in Chapter 2.

While perhaps framing the issue more in terms of global managerialism and elite politics than around the operations and power of a global managerial *class*, as those on the traditional left might do (Cox 1981), Green critiques of existing global governance would share much in common with critical traditions of international political economy. Many Greens were part of the 'Occupy' movements targeted at

Wall Street and the City of London and refer in public discourse to the 1 per cent of the world's wealthiest citizens who control large swathes of its wealth (Kenner 2015, 2019). Susan George refers more specifically to the 'Davos class' as a group of powerful and determined people, suggesting that 'together they have class interests, they profit mightily from the status quo, they know each other, they stick together – and they don't want anything fundamentally changed' (2010: 6). This argument builds on work on bodies such as the Trilateral Commission and the World Economic Forum that serve as closed agenda-setting bodies for global ruling elites, protected from global public scrutiny (Gill 1991).

Greens' concern about the ways in which global governance institutions work to accommodate and resist more radical ecological agendas resonates with neo-Gramscian perspectives on global governance in IR (Cox 1987; Gill 1995). These have been applied to point to the ways in which incumbent power and resistance to moves towards a Greener society is maintained through forms of discursive, institutional and material power that are mobilised to protect, privilege and project the preferred solutions of global elites (Levy and Newell 2002). Attempts to evacuate the potentially radical content of thinking behind the Green economy and replace it with proposals for new rounds of accumulation organised along marginally Greener lines are indicative of this (Wanner 2015; Brand 2012). Greens would be sympathetic to the suggestion that 'common sense' ideas around growth, and its achievement through 'open' markets and 'free' trade, are realised through their embodiment and institutionalisation in the mandates and work of bodies such as the World Bank and WTO, as well as regional economic institutions and banks. These preferences and ideological expressions derive from the globalising production and investment strategies of different elements of transnational capital (van Appeldoorn and de Graaf 2015) that are supported by state strategies (Sell 2003).

Although, as noted below, many Greens are passionate defenders of the United Nations, these literatures would suggest that there has been a shift in the functioning and normative vision underpinning contemporary global governance. The shift is from a Bretton Woods system that was about managing and stabilising the global economy to the growing acceptance and use of more predatory sets of institutional interventions, aimed at expanding global capitalism and removing remaining barriers to the expansion of capital (Helleiner 1994; Panitch and Gindin 2012). In this reading, global governance serves as a vehicle for locking in forms of disciplinary neo-liberalism and global imperialism that provide a legitimating cover for western interests (van der Pijl 2014). Critiques from Green theory, and the practice of Green parties, of NATO and many western-led military ventures suggest some affinity with this view.

Specifically, Greens are often opposed to what critical IPE (International Political Economy) scholars would call the 'new constitutionalism', whereby corporations are afforded legal rights and protection through law (Gill 1995) in regional trade agreements such as NAFTA whose investor protection chapters allow corporations to sue governments (Newell 2007). We have also seen the creation of closed investment arbitration panels overseen by the World Bank that adjudicate on cases where corporations claim governments have impeded their ability to make profits. Greens were active in anti-globalisation protests to shut down the World Trade Organization (WTO) and in campaigns and transnational, trans-movement alliances such as the Hemispheric Social Alliance that campaigned against the proposed Free Trade Area of the Americas (FTAA) (Icaza et al. 2010). These are seen as part of an attempt by global institutions to use their power to bring more areas of public social and economic life under market rule. This is done, for example, by insisting that private companies can tender for the provision of public services; that public providers are afforded no extra privileges even if serving broader public needs. For this reason, Greens were actively involved in campaigns against the Transatlantic Trade and Investment Partnership (TTIP) and previously the GATS (General Agreement on Trade in Services) agreement (Weber 2005), seeking in different ways and through the adoption of an array of strategies of protest, participation in citizen plebiscites, research on environmental impacts and trade literacy work to 'democratise' and 'ecologise' trade politics (Newell 2007).

Greens have often also been very critical of the lending practices of the World Bank and regional development banks (Park 2011; Rich 1994; Goldman 2005) and were involved in the '50 years is enough' campaign to mark the fiftieth anniversary of the founding of the World Bank. The critique would extend to the ways in which transnational public–private governance and private regulation, which have proliferated through delegation and outsourcing of public functions and oversight to private entities (Cutler et al. 1999; Green 2017), have served to deepen and embed global neo-liberalism. For many Greens, these strategies need to be understood as part of longer historical processes of deepening market rule – what ecologists sometimes refer to as the 'new enclosures' (Goldmann 1998) in reference to earlier attempts to dispossess people of their land in the transition from feudalism to capitalism to force them into selling their wage labour (Wood 2002).

Critique of Undemocratic Global Governance

Consistent with their desire to deepen democracy and strengthen civic engagement, Greens would also be critical of the procedural aspects of global governance: how decisions are taken, according to which processes and whose priorities. Accountability gaps persist across institutions of global governance, meaning that it is often not clear who is held to account for what and by whom (Held and Koenig-Archibugi 2005; Scholte 2011). There are patterns of institutional and wider political exclusion, failures of representation (and hence democratic deficits) and shortcomings in accountability mechanisms between those who govern and those who are governed. This critique operates on a number of levels.

First, Greens would share the critical stance many NGOs and commentators adopt towards the outdated set of structures and voting arrangements that characterise the UN Security Council that reflect a post Second World War world order and not a world in which India, China, Brazil and South Africa are more powerful, for example, as well as the 'money for votes' systems operated by the World Bank and IMF which lock in donor veto power. In the case of bodies such as the WTO, the issue is not formal voting rights but the reality of decision-making through 'green room decision-making' among powerful states that set and steer the agendas that other states are then invited to adopt. Civil society groups such as Civicus and One World Trust, the Bretton Woods Project, the Institute for Policy Studies, Global Justice Now and many others have campaigned for decades on these issues with limited success, at least in relation to substantive procedural reforms, although their demands continue to feature in broad-based civil society calls for reform. The active exclusion of ecosystems and non-human species has provided another source of critique, again suggesting common ground with a Green critique. Burke et al. argue: 'Diplomacy is carried out by official representatives of states and transnational institutions also created by states. Corporations have lobbied, bought, and bribed themselves into the game. Everyone else is an NGO, or worse, a person, a nothing. And non-human species, oceans, ecosystems – the very living complexity of the planet – have no status at all' (2016: 507).

Second, Greens have concerns about the level of decision-making, especially where global institutions and agreements increasingly exercise direct and indirect control over key resources such as water and forests and energy and sectors such as agriculture, health and education (as noted above in relation to the GATS agreement and many bilateral trade and investment agreements). What is at stake here is the concentration of power, and remoteness and insulation from democratic scrutiny. Or, as the German Greens put it: 'The existing decision-making structures are completely inappropriate as a means of solving . . . international problems in a way that accords with the principles of ecology and grassroots democracy' (Die Grünen 1984: 9). The assumption here is that a new 'global order' cannot be prescribed or enacted from above but has to emerge from below. Hence, there is concern about concentration and reinforcement of power among global elites (building on the 'global ecology' critique noted above), as well as around which groups are excluded from global decision-making, especially where such groups are not only victims of unsustainable development, but potentially the strongest advocates for more effective policies, including environmental defenders such as indigenous and grassroots groups (Global Witness 2017). Despite these suspicions and voices of caution, calls for world federalism and world government can be found in different strands of Green thinking from Falk (1971) or Ophuls (1977: 214), who claims 'some form of planetary government' is a pre-requisite for survival, to more recent advocates of 'world government' but with direct citizen participation (Younis 2015).

Rather like Green views of the state, to some extent these tensions can be explained by invoking the telescope analogy that Dobson (1990) applies to thinking about the state: there are some areas of global governance that Greens would want to extend (around human rights, the environment and gender) and others where they would rather retract, where they would prefer much greater de-centralisation of power and stronger forms of social control to protect sovereignty. This would not be about protecting sovereignty in a territorial sense but as an expression of autonomy, independence and democratic control over systems such as food, energy and water that should be 're-commoned' and protected from private control by regional and global institutions. Indeed, the call for 'world government' among some Greens expresses the need to reign in the power of market actors and to increase citizens' voices in global decision-making. This does not undermine the very real practical and political concerns about how to occupy those spaces effectively in a world of such extreme resource inequities and poorly distributed political opportunity structures, where 'higher' levels of decision-making end up privileging wealthier and well-connected groups that can afford to participate directly in global forums, lobby for their interests and network with policy elites. These are not just challenges confronting more meaningful citizen participation. Majority world states are often systematically excluded from global deliberations by the same resource constraints and lack of scientific or legal capacity to engage and shape discussions on their terms. This suggests that Greens need to think through what calls to democratise global governance mean in practice, a point returned to below.

Third, Greens would raise issues about who frames participation and on what terms. Where it does exist, participation in global processes is often limited to discussion but rarely the shaping of decisions about the limits of what is up for discussion. Mechanisms are available for those that engage 'constructively' (meaning on terms set by the institution) but not those who pose more difficult challenges about overall ends and trajectories (Wilkinson 2002). Earlier work of mine revealed these dynamics at play around trade liberalisation (Newell 2007), the global governance of biotechnology (Newell 2010) and consultations about the effectiveness of UN carbon market mechanisms (Newell 2014). Forms of 'neo-liberal participation' prevailed whereby the 'limited forms of meaningful participation and deliberation observed reflect a neo-liberal model of public participation in which citizens are encouraged to engage in policy in their role as consumers of products rather than as social agents with a right and a capacity to contribute towards new forms of social regulation' (Newell 2010: 472). Embedded in such exclusions, and their justification by global governance institutions, are problematic assumptions about whose knowledge counts and has value, often resulting in the privileging of the input of scientists, lawyers and economists as the preferred architects and builders of international law and policy. These biases and hierarchies often entrench the resource exclusions noted above.

Bringing many of these critiques together Burke et al. suggest:

> This system is still based on consensus and delay, allowing spoilers enormous influence; it still keeps the voices of scientists, civil society and indigenous peoples on the margins; it fails to integrate environmental, security, and economic governance, or harmonise them in normative terms; and it has no effective mechanisms to admit the claims of the nonhuman. And beyond the problem of climate, a coordinated, accountable, and democratic global machinery to protect crucial ecosystems, restore oceans, end deforestation, and ensure breathable air remains far off – fractured between states, corporate lobbies, and weak and fragmented international organisations kept separate from the 'real business' of global economic and security governance.
>
> *(2016: 509)*

For Greens, though, it is not just the process, practice and organisation of global governance that is problematic. It is the content and ideological orientation of the policies, programmes and interventions that powerful bodies oversee, often in their view, to the detriment of society and the environment. Although the ends and means of global governance are connected – hence the need to both 'democratise' and 'ecologise' – effectiveness has to be ultimate goal. Indeed, the UN climate negotiations are among those most open to active civil society participation and representation. Yet as Burke et al. note: 'the UN-based system has presided over an alarming increase in emissions in the three decades since the gravity of the climate crisis was comprehensively identified; emissions that may lock in devastating changes to the biosphere that will be difficult to avoid' (Burke et al. 2016: 509). Or, as Tom Princen (2005) claims, the world has become a whole lot more cooperative, and a whole lot more efficient, but at the same time a whole lot more unsustainable. Hence, notwithstanding the obvious need to open up global economic governance to a plurality of actors and voices, in the absence of changed mandates and goals, and low levels of political will or appetite to engage more seriously with the pursuit of a sustainable society, no amount of opening up and democratising global governance would satisfy many Greens, even if the latter might provide one route to achieving the former.

Critique of Unsustainable Global Governance

For many Greens, the system of global governance we currently have was not designed to tackle the sustainability crisis, and it shows. Despite increasing warnings over the last thirty years, and a strong consensus among expert scientific communities about the gravity of our ecological predicament, most institutions proceed as if there is no crisis that warrants a fundamental change of direction and certainly no limits to growth. Indeed, an a priori commitment to growth at any cost, taking their cue (and funding) from the world's more powerful states, places global institutions in a weak position regarding their ability or inclination to address the causes of unsustainability with which they are often intimately implicated, or to promote solutions that will do anything other than exacerbate the crisis.

For many Greens then, the fragmented, incoherent and ineffective system of global governance we currently have, at least from the point of view of delivering social and environmental justice, needs to be overhauled (Woodin and Lucas 2004). Those institutions with the most power and the greatest sanctions (WTO and the World Bank and the IMF) are those whose actions are most complicit in driving and accelerating unsustainable development. Many institutions protect those actors that bear most responsibility for the generation of environmental harm (states and corporations), afford weak protection for its victims (the poor and future generations), furnish and legitimise false solutions to social, economic and environmental problems (market mechanisms and techno-fixes) and promote an ideology of growth without end that Greens know to be an oxymoron on a finite planet. In many ways this is unsurprising given how those institutions are funded and the role of powerful industrial nations in setting and policing their mandates. It is, nevertheless, deeply problematic in terms of building global institutions able to play a role in protecting the global commons rather than accelerating their enclosure and decline.

Greens could point to any number of examples to support their view that global institutions fail to tackle the causes of social and environmental problems and are weak in facing up to the power of states and corporations. Take the case of business regulation. The question of the regulation of multinational companies (MNCs) has a history that stretches back to at least the 1970s when demands were made for an international code of conduct to regulate the activities of MNCs. The United Nations Centre for Transnational Corporations was set up in 1973 to draft a code, but after two decades of failed negotiations, the Centre was closed in 1993 and replaced by the Division on Transnational Corporations and Investment located within UNCTAD (United Nations Conference on Trade and Development), and now formally known as the Division on Investment and Enterprise. The issue of regulating the environmental impact of TNCs was dropped from the

United Nations Conference on Environment and Development (UNCED) in 1992 and the World Summit on Sustainable Development (WSSD) in 2002 despite civil society efforts to elaborate the terms of a UN-led Corporate Accountability Convention. The preference instead has been to articulate the responsibilities of firms in general terms through voluntary instruments such as the Global Compact. So there is a clear case and need for legally binding and stringent international regulation, a strategy Greens have pursued through the UN as we shall see below.

The issue is not just one of weak regulation, however. It is the power imbalances between institutions charged with managing and expanding the global economy on the one hand, and those charged with protecting society and the environment on the other. In relation to trade, it is a case of 'whose rules rule' (Newell and MacKenzie 2004), where trade rules are often allowed to trump other social and environmental considerations where there are conflicts, in ways Greens vocally oppose (Woodin and Lucas 2004). Overshadowing all of these individual critiques is the ideology of growth, which operates as a given for institutions of global governance and which Greens find problematic and dangerous, given the centrality of ideas about the 'limits to growth' in Green thinking (Meadows et al. 1972) as we saw in Chapter 4.

Normative Vision

Green global governance can be articulated either as a desirable end state, or as the process of ecologising (and democratising) global governance – as a near-term project of reforming global governance systems according to different priorities and worldviews. The process of contesting and opening up existing institutions and processes in order to 'ecologise' them requires the democratization of global governance. 'Ecologise' here means to read, think and act ecologically about the function, practice and purpose of global governance: the nature of the relationships between the different components of the global governance ecosystem (or complex) including states, international and regional organisations, private and non-state actors and whether or not it leads to balance, equilibrium and stability from the point of view of sustainability. It implies evaluating global governance in terms of its effectiveness in moving towards a sustainable society and not merely providing a greater degree of order and cooperation in the world than would otherwise be the case. Earlier critiques of mainstream scholarship on international regimes tended to view success in terms of whether agreements arise from bargaining between states rather than whether the resulting treaty actually does anything to reverse environmental decline (Kütting 2000). This latter tendency reflects the central defining preoccupation of the discipline of IR in terms of how to ensure order and stability and minimise (inter-state) conflict in an anarchical society (Bull 1977) as noted in Chapter 1.

Green views also suggest the importance of understanding the system of global governance in relation to the socio-ecologies that it embodies and of which it is part, that it represents and shapes. This approach is not only about the systemic properties of the international order in terms of resilience, balance and sustainability, as noted above, but its grounding in particular ecologies of production and the materialities that underpin and constitute contemporary global governance. International institutions and the growing array of state and non-state, private, city-based and civil society actors with whom they collaborate and cooperate in the pursuit of collective goals do not sit above or outside of the ecologies they seek to govern and control. They are a product of a particular historical moment and mode of production and the implied social relations and distributions of power and (natural and financial) resources (Rupert 1995). Many Greens would argue that contemporary global economic institutions in particular operate as the vanguards of a 'petro-market civilisation' (Di Muzio 2015) by enabling, funding and protecting extractivist strategies in a fossil-fuel dependent era. As we can see, across global governance arenas from trade and investment to climate change and fossil fuel subsidies, enormous political work is required to protect the current model of global extractivism from facing up to its contradictions. It is vital to accommodate threats to its everyday functioning and legitimacy from a range of environmental, labour, rights activists and indigenous social movements. These circumstances highlight again the importance of appreciating and then challenging the sources of discursive, institutional and material power that keep these global structures in place.

In many ways, the normative vision for an alternative system of global governance flows from the critiques above. The project of managing the international system needs to be driven by principles and values other than those derived from neo-liberalism and the need to service an unsustainable global political economy. In a world of growing inequality, and that is rapidly bypassing planetary boundaries, alternative world views and attitudes towards law, regulation, responsibility to other nations and the natural world are essential. In turn, ensuring that the interests of excluded groups and future generations are taken into account, for example, requires significant reform of global governance institutions to improve levels of direct and indirect representation, participation and accountability – hence the need to 'democratise' in a deep sense as a pre-requisite to 'ecologising' global governance. Global solutions cannot be imposed from above on the terms of global elites and the beneficiaries of prevailing arrangements but have to be built and negotiated in more open and inclusive ways. The assumption is that this would make it more likely, in due course, that a system of global governance would emerge, able to respond to the imperatives of supporting and pursuing a sustainable society.

Moreover, Greens might argue that some of the need for more and stronger global governance might dissipate in a world in which economies are necessarily and by design more locally orientated; in which international trade flows are reduced; in which finance is subject to tighter social and national control; and in which the sources of many of the world's environmental problems and drivers of poverty, inequality and underdevelopment have been more seriously addressed through managed shifts in production and consumption and the re-distribution and ceding of control over resources to wider society. Likewise, put bluntly, there would be less need for arms treaty discussions if there were far fewer arms in circulation. In other words, domestic and bottom-up transitions and transformations embodying Green values might do away with some of the need for the top-down interventions required of today's system, even if global institutions and international law would still have a vital role to play in some domains as implied by the telescope analogy discussed above.

Hence, as well as managing and responding to crisis, it is worth considering whether the multiple crises facing the international system also create opportunities to remake and reorder global politics in more progressive and ecological ways. In other words, is it possible that 'shock doctrines' (Klein 2007) and moments of crisis could create openings to move towards a more sustainable society overseen by a system of Green global governance? Growing recognition of the sources and scale of the crisis now facing human society as a result of the anthropocene shift, as we saw in Chapter 1, may enable reflection and a re-evaluation of whether the current system of global governance is fit for purpose. Key shifts would be required to bring the mandates and powers of institutions in line with the new planetary reality. For example, the WTO could take on a stronger mandate to pursue sustainable development, allowing exemptions from normal trading rules for policies and measures aimed at tackling climate change (consistent in aim at least with World Bank calls for a new 'energy round') or a range of other environmental threats, or be redesigned along the lines proposed by Molly Scott Cato and others for a body on International Trade and Sustainable Development (LeQuesne 1996; Cato n.d.). Fundamental reform of the IMF and World Bank would also be required, if not the disbandment of those institutions, given the narrow ideologies and policy proscriptions they advocate that are incompatible with designing economies for a more sustainable world. If the former, these institutions that have invested so heavily in fossil-fuel infrastructures to date could play a central role in financing, for example, the transition to a low carbon economy through taxes on fossil fuels and the redistribution of fossil-fuel subsidies alongside the Green Climate Fund and Adaptation Fund.

In the climate change negotiations, the need to forge a new global settlement could take the form of the adoption of the principle of 'contraction and convergence' promoted by the Global Commons Institute and supported by a wide range of developing countries. This initiative models globally which countries are entitled to 'converge' their emissions up to an agreed per capita entitlement and which have to 'contract' them to equitably share remaining carbon space compatible with tackling climate change (GCI 2018). Because it incorporates historical responsibility and therefore reflects the Green notion of 'ecological debt', it has garnered support among many Greens. Other approaches to placing equity centrally include the Greenhouse Development Rights framework (GDR 2018) that seeks to tie obligations to reduce emissions to levels of development across society and is not calculated on the basis of nation-states which tends to obscure who consumes and produces the most greenhouse gas emissions. There might also be potential for alliances within countries and globally between beneficiaries and winners from action on climate change (coalitions of the 'willing and the winning') and the many victims of climate change impacts, driving more ambitious global action mobilised under the banner of climate justice. A key driver here would be that as countries fail to deliver on mitigation, the costs of adaptation rise significantly (Stern 2007). These pressures would be amplified by the growing chorus of demands for 'loss and damage' compensation and waves of human rights' claims and climate change litigation (Humphrey 2009).

Such policies could be accompanied by non-proliferation treaties for oil and coal, organised along the lines of existing nuclear non-proliferation treaties with proper mechanisms for mutual monitoring and reporting of compliance (Simms and Newell 2018; Newell and Simms 2019). A clearer role might also be envisaged for the UN Security Council in condemning, and coordinating action against, state actions that violate climate norms, boundaries and targets. There is also a need for the articulation of clear principles of transnational harm and liability for environmental negligence beyond state borders (Mason 2005; Eckersley 2004), including strengthened corporate liability regimes, taking in Foreign Direct Liability, in order to hold companies to account for common and universal social, human rights and environmental responsibilities when operating abroad (Ward 2002).

More fundamentally, it would require an overhaul of the priorities that currently govern global politics. Susan George in her book *Whose Crisis, Whose Future?* proposes reversing the current spheres of priorities in today's financialised world of global politics to one which looks like the following:

Our beautiful finite planet and its biosphere ought to be the outermost sphere because the state of the earth ultimately encompasses and determines the state of all other spheres within. Next should be human society, which must respect the laws and the limits of the biosphere but should otherwise be free to choose democratically the social organization that best suits the needs of its members. The third sphere, the economy, would figure merely as one aspect of social life, providing for the production and distribution of the concrete means of society's existence; it should be subservient to, and chosen by, society so as to serve its needs. Finally, and least important would come the fourth and innermost sphere of finance, only one among many tools at the service of the economy.

(2010: 3)

George's view has some resonance of course with Kate Raworth's (2017) ideas about 'doughnut economics', discussed in Chapter 4, where a safe social operating space for humanity as well as planetary boundaries needs to be accommodated. The concept of the 'doughnut' describes a 'hole' of critical human deprivation in the middle below a social foundation representing the minimum amount of well-being for humanity, and an ecological ceiling in an outer ring representing planetary resource limits. Between both of these is a safe and just space for humanity. This analogy might suggest some basic design principles for Green global governance.

For Greens there is the need to reconsider *what* global governance is for. What are the appropriate values and ethics required for a system of global governance able to respond to today's challenges? Advocates of Planet Politics suggest: 'it is crucial and urgent to realise that extinction is a matter of *global ethics*. It is not simply an issue of management or security, or even of particular visions of the good life. Instead, it is about staking a claim as to the goodness of *life itself*' (Burke et al. 2016: 517). While Planet Politics is founded upon 'the spectre of a coming catastrophe' (Burke et al. 2016: 519) and runs the risk of constructing political responses in that mould, (a point we return to below), they issue an 'urgent call for a profound restructuring of international politics and order that can assure the planet's survival, written from a time when its devastation can be seen with an awful clarity' (Burke et al. 2016: 522). They further insist that 'as governance it is struggling to be born. Planet Politics must be very different from the elitist and state-centric global governance that is today's handmaiden of extinction' (Burke et al. 2016: 507), where 'extinction is treated as a problem of scientific management and biopolitical control aimed at securing existing human lifestyles' (Burke et al. 2016: 517).

In sum, for the Greens 'a new global order is needed to deal with cross-national concerns of peace, social welfare and the environment' (Bomberg 1998: 62). Most generally, as the editors of the *Green European Journal* suggest in their special issue on Green foreign policy:

when one asks the Greens what foreign policy actually means to them, invariably the answer revolves around the same preoccupation: dealing with conflict, or the conditions of the use of force ... In fact, the green vision is in essence so transnational and global that it seems 'conflict' would be the only thing 'foreign' to them. Development cooperation and a global trade regime that is fair and sustainable are cornerstones of what might be called a green foreign policy. Opposing the evils of globalised capitalism and its worst externalities (global financial markets, unregulated free-trade, global resource race etc.) is not opposing globalisation in essence. Globalisation is also global interconnectedness and interdependency ... Greens are the one political family to comprehensively understand this concept and build their political approach on it: think global act local. They strive for a sustainable globalisation, whose ultimate goal would be a kind of world government with direct global citizens' participation. Global governance would not mean then end of 'conflict'. But it would be the end of 'foreign' policy.

(GEJ 2015)

One way of delivering this vision and of protecting and enforcing planetary boundaries is through a fundamental reform of existing institutions and their mandates and a conscious and deliberate rebalancing of power and authority between them. At the same time, as well as seeking to strengthen provisions within existing spaces of global governance, or even calling for some form of 'world government' as above, there is often a strong critique of managerialism and a questioning over whose common future is at stake when it is being negotiated by global elites that would at the very least strike a note of caution about any such project (The Ecologist 1993; George 2010). We saw above how this attitude found expression in the critical literature on 'global ecology' that emerged in the wake of the Rio summit in 1992 (Sachs 1993; Hildyard 1993; Chatterjee and Finger 1994). This literature drew attention to the ways in which wealthier states and corporations had managed to co-opt the agenda of sustainable development by placing themselves and their preferred vision of (capitalist) development as central to efforts to protect the environment. More recent critiques of 'cockpitism', as Hajer et al. (2015) put it, where a small elite of experts and technocrats is given the responsibility of steering the planet onto a safer and more sustainable footing, are consistent with broader Green and other critiques of 'control' over 'care' as an underlying ethos (Stirling 2014). It resonates with a general scepticism in Green thought towards techno-fixes, and solving structural crises with institutional reforms and bureaucratic fiat, equated by Williams (1996) to trying to fix a structural haemorrhage with an institutional sticking plaster.

Indeed, the push to democratise global governance extends to consciously delimiting the powers of global institutions: preventing incursions on resources by global institutions under the guise of trade and investment treaties which aim to open up new resource frontiers for exploitation. Greens are supportive of attempts to conserve and expand the space of 'sovereign' control over resources, advocating reclaiming control over land, water and energy and key sectors of the economy such as health and education as part of a defence of the commons. The group Re: Common, for example, argues: 'only through "commoning" we can all together grant a right to life to everyone, fight for justice and practice a deep transformation of our societies'. Strategically, this means 'to expose power, by holding public institutions and corporations to account, unsettling existing power relations and opening space for change; and to disperse power, by rethinking civil society action and new democratic institutions based on commoning' (Re:Common 2018).

Concrete ways, for example, in which this policy has been pursued include greater citizen and parliamentary oversight of the negotiation and implementation of trade treaties to ensure fuller accountability and citizen engagement about the terms of such deals (Icaza et al. 2010), as well working with and through movements such as *Via Campesina* in their backing for food, energy or water 'sovereignty'. Struggles to achieve these are also observable in efforts to protect water rights (RTA 2019). To clarify the meaning of sovereignty in this context, as George suggests (in relation to food sovereignty): 'Sovereignty does not mean autarky and isolation or control over every detail of the food chain, with no exchange or trade. It does mean having a choice, particularly the political choice of deciding which spheres of national life must remain free from vulnerability and dependency on the choices of outsiders' (2010: 134–5). Likewise, with water the argument is that water capture, management and distribution should be 'under democratic control that includes robust and enforceable price mechanisms' (George 2010: 141). This is because the properties of water are so attractive to private investors: the market for the good is permanent; demand for it will increase regularly (if not exponentially); price increases will follow; consumers can be charged virtually anything for it 'because life itself is at stake' (George 2010: 140). As Polanyi suggested, limits to market rule have to be laid down to avoid the annihilation of the commons. He noted:

To allow the market mechanism to be sole director of the fate of human beings and their natural environment ... would result in the demolition of society ... Nature would be reduced to its elements, neighbourhoods and landscapes defiled, rivers polluted, military safety jeopardized, the power to produce food and raw materials destroyed ... the commodity fiction disregarded the fact that leaving the fate of soil and people to the market would be tantamount to annihilating them.

(1980[1944]: 73)

In the short term, however, and less in the vein of normative vision and more of a future warning, Greens might also point to the ways in which the ecological collapse and the surpassing of planetary boundaries will place extra strains and pressures on the existing system of global governance. Climate change will draw attention to itself both through spectacular disasters such as droughts, floods and extreme weather events, as well as the slower moving but equally lethal, disruption and destruction of the water, land and atmospheric systems that sustain life on Earth (Nixon 2011). These will require major international responses involving unprecedented cooperation and resource demands, as well as causing potentially heightened conflict and insecurity induced by tensions over affected resources, or as a result of population displacement in politically volatile regions. An almost permanent crisis mode can be expected to become the norm for the institutions of global governance. As governments face increasing demands on their resources and tests of their legitimacy and ability to protect their citizens as a result, it is far from guaranteed that responses will be guided by a new ethic of humanitarianism, as opposed to a lifeboat ethic where richer populations protect themselves at the expense of others (Hardin 1968). We know from bitter experience that disasters and catastrophes are as likely to be used as opportunities to advance and entrench socially regressive forms of politics and unsustainable trajectories – as Naomi Klein's (2007) book *Shock Doctrine* shows so clearly – as inspire forms of 'disaster collectivism', where acts of community and solidarity flourish.

The development sector would be centre stage in such a scenario of permanent crisis, called upon by global governance institutions to work in the wake of these 'natural' disasters. In a more dystopian vision, there could be scope for renewed militarism in moments of crisis and emergency and demands for ever increasing 'states of exception' that validate military responses to contain threats to security that bypass public political discussion and potential contestation in favour of 'high politics' (Newell and Lane 2018). Indeed, there is growing interest from the military establishment in the threat posed by environmental factors to national and international security through a variety of direct and indirect means, such as flows of refugees from flooded areas, intensification of conflicts over oil and water, health security pandemics caused by environmental factors (malaria, spread of disease), disruptions to infrastructures (stresses upon transport systems), disruption to food supplies and the ensuing potential for civil unrest (as we saw in Chapter 3). Addressing these issues is potentially attractive to military actors keen to find new roles for themselves, utilising the financial resources these would imply as protectors of supplies of water and land around the world: the 'green beret' phenomena described by Eckersley (2004) and Elliott (2004). It is precisely interest on the part of the military establishment that Greens are generally both suspicious and critical of.

Hence Green politics offers up a mix of utopian projects for the reform of global governance, even extending to calls for world government from some quarters but more often than not seeking a rebalancing of the power of global governance institutions or more radical overhauls of the mandates of many of them in line with a safe social and ecological operating space for humanity. However, it also projects fears of dystopian global governance through control, fear, securitisation and militarisation, whereby powerful incumbent actors exploit moments of crisis to entrench and extend their power rather than engage in progressive reform. The complex relationship between the desire to 'ecologise' global governance and to 'democratise' it produces interesting and productive tensions about how best to Green global governance. This takes us directly to the question of strategy.

Strategy

Praxis 1

The challenge for many Greens is that the fact that their diagnosis of the causes of many problems confronting international society, is often incisive, holistic and correct, does not do away with the need to articulate and adopt positions on how best to react to crisis in the here and now. The refrain that 'we wouldn't start from here' does not cut much ice, nor provide clear roadmaps for navigating complex policy dilemmas. Engaging with the messy politics of individual situations becomes inevitable. An article in the *Green European Journal* reflecting on a range of contemporary crises and conflicts comments: 'These examples raise fundamental questions with regards to the attitude of the Greens when the time for analysing the roots of a conflict is over and real actions are needed to stop a war and mend the peace' (GEJ 2015). Cutting across different areas of global governance, the following section discusses and elaborates common strategies for Green global governance that can be derived from the theory and practice of Green politics.

Alliance Building for Joined-Up Global Governance

Global governance institutions often fail to act in coordinated ways where bureaucratic silos and competition for funding means more holistic approaches to tackling global problems are frustrated or overlooked because of their implied critique of the current system. In response, Greens have sought to highlight and mobilise around the common thread and connections that link seemingly distinct aspects of a common global malaise, building on the critiques outlined above. One way of articulating that common thread and mobilising around agreed solutions has been to form alliances with elements of civil society, as well as on occasion making strategic 'progressive alliances' between Green and political parties on the Left (Wall 2017). Part of the value of such alliances or coalitions, beside their awareness-raising function, and especially when they stand in elections, is to put pressure on mainstream political parties to clarify their own positions on these global issues, where often they are silent or vacuous in content.

Inevitably, such alliances paper over ideological and strategic differences of opinion, and politically stop short of naming capitalism or industrialism as the culprit, and its propensity to crisis and structural inability to deal with many of these problems at source, as purely Green critiques would require. However, they do serve to show how economic, social and environmental problems are deeply entwined in their sources and potential solutions. Indeed, in the United Kingdom at the turn of the century, leading Greens such as Sara Parkin were instrumental in allying with a range of twenty-five civil society organisations working on issues of development, poverty and social exclusion, peace, health, community action and sustainability to form a Real World Coalition to outline a manifesto of action *From here to sustainability*. Emphasis was placed on 'joined-up' policy – exploring 'the causal links between, and therefore the solutions to achieving environmental sustainability; social justice; eradication of poverty; peace and security; democratic renewal' (TRWC 2001). It proposed 'a radical agenda of reform in national and international politics and economic policy . . . a coherent strategy for reversing the current trends and regaining quality of life and a shared sense of purpose to our lives and societies'. It notes:

The problems are rooted in the deeper paradox: that much of the 'business as usual' which has created better living standards for hundreds of millions of people and made possible rapid technological and commercial growth is itself a source of our greatest dangers . . . The model of economic and social development that has swept all before it for 50 years is in danger of becoming once again, as in the 1930s, its own worst enemy as it accentuates divisions between the richest and poorest and generates levels of resource depletion, waste and inequality that undermine the environmental services and social capital on which the system depends.

(TRWC 2001)

To tackle this, a 'global new deal' is called for, including the reform of global economic governance and the trade system in particular; reductions in consumption in richer countries; reductions in arms production and greater regula-tion of the arms trade; debt cancellation and a refocussing of aid and new international rules for corporate accountability. In a way that seems somewhat dated now, 'sustainable development' is wheeled out as 'the robust framework for radical and coherent "joined-up" policy-making that recognises not only the connections between policy domains, but also between economic development and quality of life; between the developed world and the poorer countries; between technological potential and environmental risk; between the interests of the present generation and those of our children and grandchildren' (TRWC 2001: 192). Although sustainable development and its three pillars (economic, social and environmental) captures these connections, the concept has been largely eclipsed by the more recent focus on the Green economy, and more specifically and un-coincidentally, on Green growth (see Chapter 3).

Less proactively, there is also scope for issue-specific alliances with other groups in civil society seeking to resist destructive global governance initiatives. Visions for regional alternatives have been articulated for Europe around the idea that 'Another Europe is Possible' and in the Americas, by groups like the

Hemispheric Social Alliance, for example (Icaza et al. 2010), that represent a 'social' vision of agreements and institutions for the 'people' rather than for private corporations. Their basis in multi-movements, which in one sense constitutes their strength, also means that ecological visions are often diluted or compromised when presented as an extra set of concerns and critiques alongside those presented by labour, women's, human rights and indigenous peoples' organisations. In other words, these movements are united more by their opposition to neo-liberal economic integration than by a shared vision of what would take its place, and as a result the explicitly ecological components of such a vision are often harder to discern.

Progressive Regionalism?

Where goes regionalism fit in Green thinking about global governance? The debate about Europe and Brexit in the United Kingdom is quite revealing of the dilemmas Greens face in navigating the space between internationalism on the one hand and localism on the other. Most Greens in the United Kingdom found themselves arguing to remain in the EU but to work for a stronger social (rather than neo-liberal) Europe. As the Green MP Caroline Lucas, MEP Molly Scott Cato and many others explained, being in Europe is a prerequisite to making sure Britain's voice is heard in shaping a better future. Greens argued to keep strong safeguards and checks on national governments regarding workers' rights and human and animal rights and gender discrimination, for example, while resisting the drive towards further embedding neo-liberalism within Europe and exporting it around the world through trade and investment agreements and the use of aid. Indeed, unless deeper and more expansive forms of neo-liberalism are kept in check, downward pressures on labour and human rights and the environment are likely to proliferate, exacerbating the problems and the condition of the very people Greens want to protect by being part of Europe.

At the same time, Greens might approve of reclaiming the 'leave' campaign slogan 'Take back control' – except for a Green political project. This would be a post-Brexit project of 'taking back control' through land, food and energy sovereignty, for example, charting a Greener course (Cunningham 2017) and re-asserting control of the economy by and for society and for 'the common good', the slogan adopted by the UK Green Party. Powerful allies would be needed to realise this ambition, given the more powerful and better-resourced visions and narratives about a post-Brexit political and economic landscape with which Green visions are competing. Critics of the EU, of which there are many across the Green movement (Porritt 1989), raise questions, however, about whether such an ambition is realistic and tenable in a community set up to pursue market integration and which by most accounts serves liberal elites and transnational capital very well (Bieler 2000), often at the expense of social cohesion and environmental sustainability (Balanyá et al. 2000; Hutter et al. 1995).

For this reason, many Green parties in the 1980s and 1990s adopted positions critical of the (then) EC. The Swedish Greens stood on a position of opposition to EU membership and scepticism was widespread. According to the British Greens (Green Party 1994: 17): 'the EC project is being shaped exclusively for the benefit of large corporations and the banking systems: the needs and concerns of ordinary people are being sold short', while *Les Verts* in France denounced a 'Europe of merchants' (1994: 4–5). Examples of wasteful subsidies associated in particular with the Common Agricultural Policy (CAP), windfall profits for large polluters as part of emissions-trading schemes, investments in large infrastructural projects such as roads and the imposition of fiscal discipline and restrictive monetary policy would support a position of scepticism. The intensive chemical- and industrial-based farming system that the CAP promotes comes in for particular fire. Die Grünen in Germany stated, 'After 30 years of CAP the results are disastrous ... The use of nitrogen fertilizers has increased fivefold and the use of pesticides threefold ... [it] destroys ecologically sound ways of farming, decentralised distribution systems and healthy food' (1989: 8–9). In a similar vein, the UK's Ecology Party described the EU in its 1984 manifesto as: 'a profoundly un-ecological body. It promotes an agricultural system that relies on the heavy use of fossil fuels and artificial fertilisers; a system which is damaging the long-term fertility of the soil and steadily destroying the countryside.'

Likewise in Germany, Frankland and Schoonmaker (1992: 11) note of the (then) EC: 'The Greens have reacted negatively to its technocratic apparatus, its ineffective parliamentary institution and its inherent bias toward monopolistic capitalism.' They continue, 'Rather than advocating a Europe of the Twelve, the Greens have advocated a Europe of the Regions. Rather than envisaging Europe as a superpower in world affairs, they have envisaged Europe as a very loose confederation that does not threaten or exploit anyone at home or abroad.' Reticence about state power is reflected in Green concerns that it is 'inevitably used for economic competition, large scale exploitation and massive wars' (Spretnak and Capra 1984: 48). Core elements of a Green programme for Europe to deliver on these lofty ambitions include: decentralisation, ecological sustainability, community/grassroots democracy and diversity. As early as 1979 Petra Kelly, co-founder of the German Green party, articulated the case for regionalism and federalism in Europe. The preference is for loose confederations and not a European super-state. The British Green Party, for example, stated in its 1994 manifesto: 'Our objective is a European confederation of culturally diverse and economically self-reliant regions' (Green Party 1994: 3). This view builds on Green traditions centred on the desirability of 'communitarian decentralisation' (Bahro 1986).

Theirs is a vision which involves recasting the very purpose and modus operandi of the EU, given explicit calls for economic growth to take a back seat to the goal of ecological sustainability (Green Party 1989; Simon 2016). Critical of inflated bureaucracy and lack of democratic control, an alternative is sought to an 'EC of bureaucracies, bombs and butter mountains' (Die Grünen 1984: 38). Greens favour devolution of power not to the national level but to regional and local levels. These would operate as a confederation of regions that are 'culturally defined, historically developed, self-determined but intertwined' as Die Grünen (1984: 38) put it. This is Petra Kelly's vision of a 'Europe from below' – an ecological, decentralised, non-military Europe of the regions (Kelly 1994), one that challenges the arbitrary imposition of nation-state borders.

What many Greens fall back on then are ideas about multi-level governance and subsidiarity that would be applied within Europe and to other regions of the world, such as Asia, Africa and Latin America, where projects of regional economic integration are less well advanced. This is not to rule out the critical role of national and regional institutions but to introduce a working principle that, wherever possible and practicable, decisions should be made at the lowest level. 'Subsidiarity is important here: while some policies can only be effective at the global level (for example, strict limits on CO_2 emissions), the principle of NIMBYism can be used to defend local environments against economic expansion if power is genuinely devolved to local people and their democratically elected representatives' (Cato n.d.).

This point is important, not just as a check and balance on regional power but also on national governments that at times currently use their power to override local governments, as happened recently in Lancashire UK, for example, after the local council rejected the siting of fracking in their area. In the European context, Greens are often supportive of a committee of the regions brought into being by the Maastricht Treaty that consists of 350 representatives from local and regional government (CoR 2018). The committee is able to present proposals for directives to the Commission and requires that the committee be consulted on relevant proposals for legislation. Its powers are only advisory, and fall far short, therefore, of Green visions of a more decentralised Europe. There is clearly much more thinking to do about the form of, and strategy for achieving, an alternative Europe – about the true nature of a 'Europe of the regions', for example.

How to engage with this 'missing middle' between the global and the local has been a challenge for Greens. Despite these commonalities around subsidiarity within systems of multi-level governance, 'a general ambivalence and lack of agreement among the Greens in European policy has precluded the formulation of a coherent "green" Euro-political alternative' (Bomberg 1998: 56), despite the work of groups like the Green European Foundation. Writing in the late 1990s Bomberg noted: 'Because the EU is neither global nor local, it is often neglected as a forum for the pursuit of green objectives' (Bomberg 1998: 64). Notwithstanding some of the critiques above about its neo-liberal character, today regional institutions often serve as a fall back for Greens as a way to navigate between internationalism and commitments to post-sovereign and post-national politics and agendas of localism, and the European Parliament at least provides a space where Greens have greater voice and representation than in their own national parliaments. As the editors of the *Green European Journal* argue:

Living in an increasingly post-Western and post-imperial world – where a modern state is losing its pre-eminence – should vindicate the green vision of the world. Instead it seems to bring a set of new, difficult questions and uncertainties to the debate. When it comes to global nuclear security, combating climate change, assuming responsibility for global development, and engaging with the Maghreb or with the rapidly rising centre of new power, namely South East Asia, the European Union is the favoured level of action for greens in matters of foreign policy.

(GEJ 2015)

Yet as they also note:

the EU does not resolve all contradictions. First, talking the talk is not enough. Turning the rhetoric into actions remains so far a privilege of established nation-states. The EU often lacks the actual means and legitimacy to rise above the interests of its member-states jealous of the symbols of their sovereignty represented by foreign policy. Secondly, the EU can allow itself to be easily confused with the broader West, defending the limited particular interests of one perspective rather than those of humanity and global peace. This can be particularly visible when it fails to put human rights ahead of rights of businesses or when it fails to uphold coherence and consistency between its various external policies.

In sum, most Greens are in favour of regionalism with strong elements of de-centralisation and in a form quite distinct from the system that presides in Europe today.

Reforming and Strengthening (Some) Aspects of Global Governance

On one level, many Greens would support and have sympathy with the proposals to reform global governance coming from liberal and cosmopolitan positions (Held 1995; Linklater 1998). There is not much that most Greens would disagree with in the report of The Commission on Global Governance, *Our Global Neighbourhood* (CGG 1995), for example, with its emphasis on procedural and voting reforms, the need to embrace broader notions of security and greater attention to issues of poverty, social justice and sustainability. Their understanding, however, of the relationship between the issues and the underlying nature of global crises would depart from this more orthodox liberal analysis. As noted above, some Greens (Katz-Rosene and Paterson 2018) are also suspicious of the ways in which powerful states can invoke a abstract notion of a global public interest or common good to justify military interventions (even if ostensibly humanitarian in nature) or the imposition of economic sanctions against 'rogue' states and other actors not playing by 'the rules' (which they have largely set themselves).

Among many Greens, however, there remains strong support for the values and role of the UN. Die Grünen in Germany, for example, states: 'The United Nations plays an indispensable role in promoting peace, justice, freedom and sustainability worldwide. The immense challenges arising within the context of globalisation require a strong and effective UN.'[1] Mindful perhaps of Hedley Bull's (1977) 'counsel of despair' and political programmes whose point of departure is the need to do away with the existing institutions and structures of international society, Burke et al. acknowledge in their call for *Planet Politics*: 'In the near term, we will have to work with flawed institutions, but the gravity of this crisis means that it is right to demand more profound and systemic change, and to explore, in politics and in scholarship, what that change should be' (Burke et al. 2016: 510). 'In a century preoccupied by world war, genocide, civil war, and nuclear holocaust, the architecture and focus of the UN system made some sense, yet it is also possible to decry its failure to address those crises adequately in action, policy, or law' (Burke et al. 2016: 512).

Given what was said above, many Greens are in favour of a rebalancing of global governance institutions and might support initiatives for stronger protection of the environment and human and workers' rights. They would, however, argue for a diminished, curtailed or fundamentally reformed mandate for institutions such as the WTO and the World Bank so that their mandates and modus operandi are fully in tune with the requirements of moving towards a sustainable society: defined as a safe social and environmental operating space for humanity (Raworth 2017). This policy reflects a desire to ensure that those institutions and bodies dealing with what are dismissively referred to as 'low politics' issues (i.e. those which impact most majority world populations, lower-income groups and future generations), are given greater weight, authority and power.

In the case of the World Environment Organisation (WEO), which finds support among some (Biermann 2001) but not all Greens (Newell 2002), it is a question of a rebalancing of global institutions and their mandates so that economic issues do not take precedence. There is a long history of multilateral environmental treaties being negotiated in the 'shadow' of trade agreements (Conca 2000) whose principles and existence are often invoked to check the inclusion of measures that, while critical to protecting the environment, could be classified under WTO rules as trade-discriminating. Greens strongly believe that the imperatives of sustaining the planet should trump the prioritisation of trade rules above all others, often leading them to advocate for stronger protection of human and labour rights and environmental safeguards such that no trade agreement should be concluded without these conditions. This approach has been a source of distrust and antagonism in numerous trade negotiations between richer and poorer nations, with the latter fearful of a rising tide of eco-protectionism, and between NGOs and trade unions on the one hand and business groups on the other. It manifested itself in the famous 'battle of Seattle' in 1999 and the campaign against the Multilateral Agreement on Investment in 1997, and many times since.

Despite scepticism towards the state and top-down solutions to sustainability then, many Greens are attracted to the use of international law and to the international authority of the UN and its institutions as vehicles for promoting a safer and more sustainable world. Whether it is calls for Non-Proliferation Treaties (Newell and Simms 2019) or the adoption of the agreement to ban nuclear weapons; the development of a World Environment Organisation (WEO) to better represent and secure the status of environmental issues alongside equivalent bodies on trade, labour and social issues (Biermann 2001); or international laws and tribunals on 'ecocide' and the rights of nature (Higgins 2010), international law and diplomacy is viewed by some Greens as at least one more set of tools in the struggle for a sustainable society. There have also been calls for a 'world constitution for environmental and ecological justice', including a World Environment Council and a World Environment Court (Eckersley 2004). *Planet Politics* advocates suggest the creation of an 'Earth System Council' much like the current UN Security Council that would operate on the basis of majority voting with representation from Earth system scientists, major ecosystems, species groups and states (Burke 2016: 516). There is a clear commitment in many quarters, therefore, to an enhanced and bolder multilateralism regarding security, environment and issues of social justice.

Likewise, Green internationalists are supportive of the work of the International Criminal Court and have spoken in favour of debt write-offs, financial transaction taxes, corporate regulation and other similar demands that have existed in various forms since the advent of the New International Economic Order in the 1970s (Williams 1994). Greens have often echoed calls for stronger mechanisms of oversight and accountability of states, international organisations, and corporations, such as a legally binding UN treaty on corporate accountability. In this regard in 2014 a victory was celebrated at the United Nations Human Rights Council: the adoption of Resolution 26/9 that established a new Intergovernmental Working Group (IGWG) to develop an international legally binding instrument to regulate transnational corporations and other companies with respect to human rights.

In 2016, the UN started negotiations on a draft text with elements for the treaty at the third session of the IGWG. Lucia Ortiz of Friends of the Earth said: 'It is a time for a legally binding instrument to control transnational corporations ... A treaty that also gives victims of corporate abuses access to justice where there is none and challenges the economic and political power of TNCs' (Friends of the Earth 2016). Environmentalists have also actively participated in non-legal accountability processes, such as Permanent Peoples' Tribunals on the conduct of TNCs in general, as well as around specific issues such as water (Newell 2001b). Indeed, proponents of Planet Politics suggest more broadly: 'Planet Politics aims to open new discussions on corporate accountability, animal rights, environmental justice, international law, and ecological security' (Burke et al. 2016: 515).

As always, questions of sanctions and enforcement are pertinent for Greens to consider, especially for a weakened Green state engaged in less trade where economic sanctions may not constitute a serious threat. 'We need creative thinking about what rights could apply, what rights need to be recognised, and how we enforce and penalise violence – slow and fast – against nonhuman communities and ecologies' Burke et al. (2016: 516) suggest. These stances include 'crimes against biodiversity': to expand international human rights law to take in precious species and ecosystems, and to criminalise avoidable activities that do them grave harm. Some of these proposals may raise concerns with those who have documented the effect of 'war by conservation' strategies supported by wealthy global conservation NGOs and institutions that have actively sought to militarise local conservation efforts (Duffy 2016). Indeed, the malign and coercive correlates of Planet Politics draw fire from critics who suggest: 'Burke et al. spend no time considering what new violences are afforded and enabled in their call for new global governance bodies to enforce and penalise violence – slow and fast – against nonhuman communities and ecologies as they seek to legislate for securing the planet against errant humanity' (Chandler et al. 2017: 10).

Beyond a rebalancing of mandates and the content of international law, many have outlined proposals to address procedural and democratic deficits in the global system. These suggestions build on regional struggles for better citizen representation in panels considering cases where communities have been blighted by industrial pollution from investors subject to trade accords such as NAFTA (Newell 2007), as well as restrictions on the rights of transnational companies to sue governments in investor tribunals. The Chile–Canada Agreement on Environmental Cooperation, for example, negotiated in parallel to their bilateral free trade agreement, contains a provision that allows citizens and NGOs of the two parties to make submissions alleging a party's failure to effectively enforce its environmental laws (Matus and Rossi 2002). Greens have often been strong advocates of treaties such as the Aarhus Convention on Access to Information, Public Participation in

Decision-making and Access to Justice in Environmental Matters. Transparency, participation and accountability are crucial then to opening up global governance to progressive pressures for change.

Following from normative commitments to enhance procedural justice in global governance, a range of proposals can be located or derived from Green thinking. Some Greens and academics have sought to identify and promote greater direct and indirect representation of citizens in global decision-making though citizen assemblies and the like (Stevenson and Dryzek 2014). In terms of the questions of voice and representation, Greens have called for an ombudsperson for future generations (Read 2012) following recent moves to create representatives for future generations in parliaments as diverse as Wales, Israel and Hungary, discussed further in Chapter 8. Burke et al. (2016: 516), meanwhile, propose that 'It is time to consider whether major ecosystems – such as the Amazon basin, the Arctic and Antarctic, and the Pacific Ocean – should be given the status of nations in the UN General Assembly and other bodies, or new organisations established with the sole purpose of preserving their ecological integrity.'

As discussed in the previous section, Greens are not united in their view about the desirability of strengthened 'governance from above', however. Chandler et al. (2017: 7) critique Planet Politics proposals on the grounds that 'Instituting global governance in "firm and enforceable" ways, as if there were universal solutions that could be imposed from above, is a recipe for authoritarianism and new hierarchies and exclusions'. Moreover, they suggest the notion of 'planet politics' 'reflects a top-down, universalist or "God's eye" perspective', a form of 'global or planetary rhetoric' which 'is more likely to reinforce international hierarchies of power than to challenge them' (Chandler et al. 2017: 8). Reflecting Green anxieties about the politics behind universalising claims, they critique attempts to impose limits on human freedom on the basis of what 'the planet' is 'telling us' (2017: 8) without clarifying how 'the planet' coveys that message and who is 'us'. They caution: 'Singular humanity is a dangerous trope when there is the aspiration for a political project that "will necessarily involve agonism and conflict" and "new forms of cooperation and ongoing contestation"' (2017: 10).

There are the familiar dangers here of the post-politics of control and in Ophul's version, of authoritarianism. Indeed, Planet politics is critiqued by Chandler et al. (2017) on the grounds that it is 'dangerously authoritarian and deeply depoliticising' (2017: 1) in relation to its 'advocacy of managerialism rather than transformation; the top-down coercive approach of international law; and use of abstract modernist political categories', resorting to abstract, high-flown and idealist notions, such as 'global ethics'. It is criticised for not being 'averse to totalising global claims of governance and intervention, including those of the "planetary boundaries" and "safe operating spaces" of Earth system science' (Chandler et al.

2017: 5). This view points to the dangers of eco-political interventions institution-alising new legal and political inequalities, which they see with calls for the Earth System Council functioning much like the UN Security Council. The assumption, they suggest, is that we need to 'suborn the human to the planetary governance of elites in the name of the Anthropocene' (Chandler et al. 2017: 15), underscoring the need to both 'democratise' as well as 'ecologise' global governance.

To be clear, the views of advocates of Planet Politics do not represent the view of most Greens, even if many might share their critique of the current system of global governance. Greens might be divided, however, between those advocating for stronger global governance institutions to protect the global common good, as echoed in calls for a WEO, and those from more critical, anti-statist or anarchist traditions who would want to radically decentralise power away from elite regional and global institutions, away from arenas where the power and resources of lobby-ists can be employed to such influential effect and instead closer to those affected by decisions made. They might be sceptical for instance about calls for 'Earth steward-ship' (Steffen et al. 2015b) and strengthened systems of Earth system governance (Biermann 2014). Governance here is undertaken by expert international institu-tions, through the conclusion of environmental treaties, and by seemingly objective economic mechanisms, such as the development of Green economies and Green growth. The political and ideological contestation over definitions, problem identi-fication, desired outcomes and proposed mechanisms to achieve these is replaced by techno-managerial planning and decision-making or what Hajer et al. (2015) refer to as 'cockpit-ism': the idea that top-down steering by governments and intergovern-mental organizations alone can address global problems.

The humility about the role of humans in global ecology that Greens call for is certainly absent in some visions of Green global governance. How Greens balance the simultaneous desires to 'ecologise' and 'democratise' global governance and determine which objective takes precedence, where questions of urgency and the perceived desirability of top-down solutions might be allowed to trump the preference to deepen democracy across all spheres of global politics, will define the terrain of discussion about desirable and feasible strategies for greening global governance for many years to come.

Conclusions

The need to formulate pragmatic responses to these developments pre-sents a serious challenge to the vision of peace, human rights and ecological justice espoused by Greens. A world ridden with conflicts is pushing the Greens out of their comfort zone and their certainties. How do you deal with a violent reality when most of your political practice is

rooted in the non-violent opposition to the system; when your message
of peace, tolerance, interdependence, and responsibility, both individual
and collective, constantly puts you at odds with the general perception of
the public? How do you implement ideals in the desert of the real?

(GEJ 2015)

As the quote above suggests, Green political thought and practice is stronger in its critique of the existing international order than in articulating clear visions about an alternative, particularly one that would have political purchase, less still in offering a blueprint for a differently constituted international order. Indeed, many Greens would be suspicious of the idea of articulating global blueprints. Perhaps this reflects the fact that Green politics, rather like Planet Politics, must be 'simultaneously a practice of governance and of subversion, of regulation and resistance, at multiple scales and locales' (Burke et al. 2016: 517). It seeks change within and beyond the system, combining engagement and reform with oppositional and revolutionary politics, depending among other things upon which strand of Green politics is being invoked, as well as broad-based tendencies towards 'fundi' or 'realo' politics (Doherty 1992), working within and without the system as protest movements and decision-makers.

Greens are often in favour of a post-sovereign world, no longer divided by meaningless sovereign borders. Yet they are stuck, for now at least, with a world structured along those lines. They want to see a system of global governance guided by the imperatives of stewarding and redistributing global resources, tailoring resource availability to resource needs, but this would imply oversight of who uses which resources and for what purposes. It raises questions about whether this can be done in an inclusive, democratic and non-authoritarian way. It takes us to the discussion about Greens' 'post-liberal' credentials (Doherty and de Geus 1996) when it comes to accepting the need to set boundaries and limits on human and economic activity and needing institutional actors to enforce those limits, while wanting to preserve the democratic space to debate, deliberate and pursue multiple pathways consistent with living within ecological limits.

Likewise, the discussion about reforms many Greens would like to see implies a potentially significant role for international institutions in regulating the arms trade, tackling trans-border environmental issues and promoting human rights, for example. For Greens, the strategic dilemmas arise from being internationalist but wanting to see a smaller state in many cases, as well as demilitarised forces and an economy that is increasingly autarkic or localised. What scope would there be then for multilateralism and diplomacy in a more autarkic world? What weight would a Green state wield in international affairs in such circumstances? It would gain more weight and legitimacy perhaps, but if Green states were to pull out of 'free' trade agreements, they would forego the right to shape and renegotiate them. If their military resources are greatly reduced, then it makes no sense to remain a member of military alliances such as NATO, and many Greens have consistently opposed membership of such military clubs in any case. So there would be a gain in autonomy and being free from some of the 'disciplinary' and other pressures that apply to states that compete in these forums but an inevitable loss in terms of influence and voice in the world.

Greens will also need to address concerns about how a more de-centralised society would be coordinated: how relations between and within communities would be universalised and regulated. As Laferrière and Stoett (1999: 158) suggest, social ecology 'reduces international relations to inter-municipal relations' with its call for post-state municipalities to 'join with other municipalities in integrating [their] resources into a regional confederal system' (Bookchin 1989: 194). Here, the global order is extrapolated from local schemes for sustainability. Laferrière and Stoett's comment mentioned in Chapter 1 that: 'Much of the ecological literature produced in this century reads as though it were written with a political system roughly the size of Thoreau's Walden Pond in mind' (1999: 2) is pertinent here. The appropriate boundaries, size and scale of community are disputed however. For deep ecologists and bio-regionalists (Sale 1985; Trainer 1996), the nature of the ecosystem determines the boundary of the political community. And there are no guarantees that decentralisation does not lend itself to elite capture and corruption (Blair 2000) or that, without oversight, local economies would not grow into capitalist markets reproducing inequality, exploitation and environmental degradation.

This aspect touches on a core tension in relation to the role of the state in particular, where protecting 'freedoms from' (exploitation, degradation, discrimination) implies an enabling role for the state and restrictions on 'freedoms to' do these things imply a state able to control and regulate actors and activities that do not serve the common good (who will revoke corporations' licences to operate, for example?). Who enforces, or more benignly, seeks to protect and defend, the 'good ecological society' in a fragmented, weakened and de-centralised system of governance? Dobson (1995: 25) expresses it slightly differently: 'how to have a conception of the Good Society that requires people behaving in a certain way, and yet advertise for diverse forms of behaviour'. The question again is one of the process for arriving at a consensus about what form that would take in a world where liberalism, and certainly ecologism, would compete with other philosophical, religious and value-based systems. How do Greens reach out to and engage those who do not share their vision – which form far and away the majority of the world's inhabitants at this moment in time – and how are they to overcome the inevitable and deeply entrenched resistance of well-resourced (and armed) incumbent and status-quo actors who profit hugely from unsustainable development?

These issues and challenges which face Green thinkers and activists (though clearly not just Green activists) do not diminish the validity of Green critiques of global governance, nor the desirability and legitimacy of systems of governance, global and below, organised around principles of democracy, equality and ecology for which they advocate. There is a clear and tangible need to re-balance contemporary global governance from a system which preserves the power of the wealthiest in global society to one which seeks to uphold shared and universal values around peace, human rights and sustainability. This means re-defining the role of key institutions of economic governance to deliver welfare and prosperity rather than growth at any cost. The goals of global governance would become peace, welfare enhancement, rights protection and sustainability, and all global governance agencies would have to ensure their activities contribute to the realisation of these ends. In other words, economic rules and principles should not trump legitimate attempts to improve welfare or protect vulnerable citizens or the environment as so often happens at present. In this regard, Greens sometimes refer to the 'new protectionism' (Lang and Hines 1993), where the scope for trade restrictive measures is enlarged when it can clearly be shown that a common social and environmental good is the subject of that protection. This might be akin to current calls for a 'social Europe' by Green parties: working with European institutions and within Europe to rebalance the goals of the EU towards social and environmental goals rather than purely economic ones. It implies a broader re-purposing of global governance around a new global ethic of care. Achieving this objective represents a still larger and more complex challenge than imagining and pursuing Green global governance.

Note

1 www.gruene-bundestag.de/service-navigation/english/globalisation.html

7

Green Development

Development is sometimes referred to as the central organising principle of our time (Cowen and Shenton 1995). So what can Green Politics offer to the understanding and practice of international development? Greens have traditionally had a lot to say about key aspects of development, including peace and security, poverty and social exclusion, gender and, of course, sustainability, in ways which reflect the involvement of peace, feminist and environmental movements in Green politics. The discourse and practice of 'sustainable development', in particular, is now omnipresent. So, on the face of it Green politics should be playing a central role in debates about international development. But critical Green insights about the causes of poverty and destitution and how these relate to the organisation of the global economy, the role of aid, trade and multinational corporations, as well as around what inclusive, just and Green solutions to these problems might look like, have often been overlooked. There is an urgent need to redress this oversight.

Greens often hold quite divided, even contradictory, ideas about development, but are Greens anti-development as is often claimed? If many Greens oppose development institutions such as the World Bank and are critical of conventional ideas about economic growth, surely they are anti-development. In reality, most greens are against *some* forms of development, including those pushed for by these institutions, but they are in favour of development which can be sustained to meet the needs of current and future generations – in other words improvements in the quality of life and well-being of all people and the ecosystems upon which we depend across generations. The distinction is between a model of development in which growth is an end it itself and one in which enhancing social and environmental well-being is the goal but requires a different approach to development to achieve it. In particular, this shift of emphasis builds on Green ideas about 'prosperity' and well-being, social and ecological (explored further in Chapter 4), as being more appropriate goals for 'development' than the dogged pursuit of economic growth at all costs (Jackson 2011).

172

It is worth first reflecting on the reasons for the deliberate neglect of Green perspectives on international development. Greens often ask the awkward questions about growth and globalisation, global militarism and the effect of donors' policies on the world's poorest people. In other words, they have an account of international development and its failings that powerful state and corporate elites and international economic institutions do not want to hear; nor, for that matter, do many of those involved in the development industry. This is because of the implication of these actors in the very problems they claim to be addressing, and because of their prior ideological commitments to growth at any cost. The development industry is notorious for faddism and looking at new ingredients to add to the development mix (add gender, governance, sustainability) without asking if the recipe is the right one. This also makes Greens unpopular with some international civil society organisations whose funding depends on the pursuit of conventional ideas of development.

Think of recent attempts to 'green' growth (OECD 2011) or promote 'climate compatible development' (Mitchell and Maxwell 2010), in which more growth is always presented as the answer, whatever the problem. Having failed to advance 'sustainable development', which was the watchword from the late 1980s in the wake of the Brundtland report in 1987 (WCED 1987), Green growth is the latest attempt to obscure the contradictions between infinite economic growth and the fact we inhabit a finite planet (Brand 2012). Green approaches shift the development gaze from the poor and what is failing in 'underdeveloped' societies to the overconsuming rich and unsustainable models of development in the North and the lifestyles enjoyed by the 1 per cent of the world's richest citizens (Kenner 2015, 2019). It is not popular to state that how those in the richer parts of the world produce and consume energy, food and water and how they meet their transport, heating and dietary requirements – all need to radically change. It is more comfortable to focus on market pricing, technology or incremental policy reform that can be accommodated within a business-as-usual trajectory, as well as on 'governance failures' in the global South, often attributed to current policy elites rather than longer colonial histories of dispossession and pillage. The Greens have an important message, but it does not present easy or politically convenient answers.

A great deal of contemporary development thinking from donors to civil society organisations also focuses on strengthening and enhancing state capacity (Green 2008). This can be accomplished by deepening democracies, strengthening state capacities to tax, regulate and enforce, as well as to compete in the global economy (Rodrik 1999). Much of this makes a great deal of sense and is urgently required, but again it raises difficult questions for Greens who are often at best agnostic about the state and often hostile to proposals to expand state power, as we saw in Chapter 5. I suggest below that some of these issues might be addressed by taking a more differentiated and context-specific view of the state. This view builds on the discussion in Chapter 5 and the potentially central role of the state in steering, financing and realising transitions to sustainability and managing opposition from powerful incumbent actors. Such an account needs to be squared with the emphasis Greens place on the need to contain the threats posed by a 'police' or 'surveillance' state, as well as the need to dismantle the military state. Although the development industry places a great deal of emphasis on conflict resolution and peace building, the actions of other aspects of donor states in selling weapons and military hardware frequently undermine the effects of those interventions.

Critique

The Development Project and the Causes of Poverty and Underdevelopment

In 2015 the UN Sustainable Development Goals (SDGs) were agreed, addressing a range of global development issues and sustainability challenges. Covering everything from access to water and energy to health, education and security, the seventeen goals chart a course for the international community over the coming decades in its elusive quest for development-for-all that 'leaves no one behind'. At the same time, the goals make no mention of the causes of poverty and unsustainability. Without critical attention to the ways in which the global economic model is implicated in exacerbating these issues, there is little prospect that the SDGs will be any more successful than the Millennium Developmental Goals (MDGs) that preceded them. Indeed, SDG 8 is premised on securing more economic growth.

Critical questions about why, in a world of unprecedented wealth, technological advancement and so-called progress, such levels of poverty and inequality remain so high, have not been seriously posed, let alone addressed by mainstream development actors. If the growth-based market-led model of development that has been accelerating over the last fifty years has been so successful, why do one in eight people go to sleep hungry every day (842 million hungry people worldwide) and why does a child die every minute from a water-related disease and one in nine people in the world lack access to safe water? Why do 1.6 billion of the world's inhabitants lack access to electricity? The shameful roll-call of failed development could go on. Something is not working. If increases in growth are a prerequisite for development, why is a developmental model founded on that principle so obviously failing to deliver for the mass of humanity? Periods of spectacular growth since the Second World War have not seen corresponding reductions in poverty but rather growing inequalities. As Ben Selwyn puts it on the cover of his book on

[handwritten marginal note: better than before?]

The Global Development Crisis, 'The central paradox of the contemporary world is the simultaneous presence of wealth on an unprecedented scale, and mass poverty' (2014). The neglect of these critical questions represents an important opportunity for critical thinking to make an important contribution to addressing this neglect and redefining the debate about what forms of development can be considered sustainable.

Green thinking can draw on several antecedents in making such a contribution. First, there is the academic literature on 'anti-developmentalism' (Escobar 1995; Sachs 1992; Crush 1995) that casts a critical eye on the Eurocentric, colonialist origins of the development project, calling it in Sachs's words 'a blunder of planetary proportions' (1992: 1). Themes in this literature include the infantilising gaze, paternalism and assumptions of the need to emulate European models of development without questioning their applicability or sustainability. They date back to the deployment of saviour narratives and 'white man's burden', often invoked by way of moral legitimation for colonialism (Tharoor 2016). It lives on in the language, tools and ideologies of the development industry today, i.e. through private-led 'Grow Africa' initiatives or German government-led 'Marshall Plans' for Africa.

This is about the construction of the 'third world' in the post-war world as a set of countries whose needs can only be served by the vision and generosity of states at the core of the global economy; whose future prospects depend on their capacity to emulate the 'success' of the richest countries. It embodies a project of ordering by which people come to understand themselves as developed or underdeveloped[1] in which there has been an evolution of clients of the development apparatus from peasants and women to the environment. The point here is that development discourses promote and legitimate interventions that have very real consequences for people and places (Crush 1995). They often do so in ways that obscure or deny the complicity of the development industry in perpetuating underdevelopment. Broad and Cavanagh open their book on *Development Redefined* with a quote from a farmer in the Philippines who asks: 'Why is that rich countries give aid, investments and trade that are supposed to help us, but that end up destroying us? If you really want to help us, go back to your country and figure out why the world works this way' (2009: 1).

Beneath these discursive constructions lie a series of material and economic interests for whom the project of development brings great benefits and opportunities for recycling surpluses, exporting technology, opening up markets and providing subsidies to domestic industries in donor countries. Multilateral Development Banks (MDBs) are key to this. As Escobar explains regarding the World Bank, an institution that 'as perhaps no other . . . embodies the development apparatus' (Escobar 1995: 167):

This is how the World Bank maintains intellectual and financial hegemony in development. It channels the largest amount of funds; it opens new regions to investment through transportation, electrification and telecommunications projects; it contributes to the spread of MNCs through contracts; it deepens dependence on international markets by insisting on production for exports; it refuses to lend to 'unfriendly countries'; it opposes protectionist measures of local industries; it fosters the loss of control of resources by local people by instating on large projects that benefit national elites and MNCs; it responds closely to the interests of international capitalism in general and US foreign policy in particular; and it collaborates with and helps to maintain in power corrupt and undemocratic regimes throughout the Third World.

(1995: 165)

In this tradition of work, the concept of development and of 'underdeveloped countries' dates back to addresses by US President Harry Truman, who claimed in his inaugural address as president in 1949: 'For the first time in human history humanity possesses the knowledge and the skill to relieve the suffering of those people [living in poverty] … What we envisage is a program of development based on the concepts of democratic fair dealing … Greater production is the key to prosperity and peace. And the key to greater production is a wider and more vigorous application of modern scientific and technical knowledge' (cited in Escobar 1995: 1).

This vision laid the foundations for modern development as we know it, with combinations of elite expertise, science and technology brought to bear to accelerate production. As Escobar (1995: 4) explains: 'capital, science and technology were the main ingredients that would make this massive revolution possible'. The scale of the ambition should not be underestimated, nor should the explicit aim of development as a project of restructuring and reordering the world to align it with capitalist imperatives. As the UN Department of Social and Economic Affairs asserted in 1951:

There is a sense in which rapid economic progress is impossible without painful adjustments. Ancient philosophies have to be scrapped; old social institutions have to disintegrate; bonds of cast, creed and race have to burst; and large numbers of persons who cannot keep up with progress have to have their expectations of a comfortable life frustrated. Very few communities are willing to pay the full price of economic progress.

(1951: 15 cited in Escobar 1995: 4)

The quote is uncannily reminiscent of Marx and Engels' claim in *The Communist Manifesto* that:

The bourgeoisie cannot exist without constantly revolutionizing the instruments of production, and thereby the relations of production, and with them the whole relations of society. Constant revolutionizing of production, uninterrupted disturbance of all social conditions, everlasting uncertainty and agitation, distinguish the bourgeois epoch from all earlier ones ... The bourgeoisie, by the rapid improvement of all instruments of production, by the immensely facilitated means of communication, draws all, even the most barbarian, nations into civilization. The cheap prices of its commodities are the heavy artillery with which it batters down all Chinese walls, with which it forces the barbarians' intensely obstinate hatred of foreigners to capitulate. It compels all nations, on pain of extinction, to adopt the bourgeois mode of production; it compels them to introduce what it calls civilization into their midst, i.e., to become bourgeois themselves. In one word, it creates a world after its own image.

(1998[1848])

Second, there is a more political critical and activist literature (Hancock 1989) that views the development industry (or 'machine' as Ferguson [1990] refers to it) as a vehicle for enhancing dependency, promoting market access for their companies and locking in unsustainable development. What is particularly significant from a Green position, is its role in exporting an unsustainable growth model throughout the world. For instance, the failings of the nuclear industry and the shunning of the coal industry in large parts of Europe, North America and Asia lead those industries to relocate to African countries where they anticipate (often wrongly) that they will meet less resistance.

There is a little doubt about the historical and contemporary use of aid and the activities of key MDBs and global governance institutions such as the IMF in embedding neo-liberalism (Green 2003; Tellam 2000). These institutions promote and enable many of those aspects of industrial society that Greens critique, regarding extractivism, commodification and financialisation to be globalised as the model of development to be aspired to. As we have seen in other chapters, these have been secured through a mix of spatial and temporal fixes, including outsourcing (labour), displacement (waste), trading (carbon), accounting tricks and discounting the future (cost-benefit analysis) and dispossession (Green grabs). In regard to the last, as Jacques Diouf, director-general of the FAP warned: 'The race by food importing countries to secure farmland overseas to improve their food security risks creating a neo-colonial system' (quoted in George 2010: 121).

More broadly in their critique of the reproduction of uneven development global inequalities via the day-to-day functioning of the global economy, Greens could draw on rich strands of academic scholarship on dependency and world systems theory (Gunder Frank 1966; Amin 1976; Wallerstein 1979) and more activist scholarship on extractivism (Galeano 1997), debt (George 1992), trade (Madelely 2000) and aid (Hayter 1989). What is particularly important is how this work shows, both historically and contemporarily, that Northern affluence is a product of, and continues to rely on, extraction of wealth and resources from poorer countries. This practice is no longer (necessarily) achieved through the use of force and the exercise of imperialism, and categories of core and periphery may be harder to clearly identify than in the 1960s and 1970s when some of these ideas

were developed. The practice now occurs through trade and investment agreements, aid and international markets that are designed to structurally disadvantage
poorer countries. As we saw in Chapter 4, Green readings of this unequal distribution and accumulation of wealth also emphasise ecologically uneven exchange
(Roberts and Parks 2008), ecological debt (Simms 2005) and the overexploitation
of the commons (The Ecologist 1993).

What is interesting and important from a Green point of view is that despite all
the fads and 'add and stir' phenomena in development (add gender, participation,
governance, micro-credit, sustainability) in the ongoing search for the magic
formula for overcoming ongoing underdevelopment and social exclusion, there
is a deliberate neglect of the very economic model being promoted as a possible
culprit. Export-led, private-led, capitalist industrial development is the answer to
whichever way you pose the development question. As Crush notes, 'development
is always the cure, never the cause' (1995: 10). It is a given of the development
industry, and questioning of it is off-limits. As a World Bank official told me off
the record, despite increasing attention to ideas about post-growth, de-growth or
prosperity without growth, there is no space to raise or take on the significance of
these issues in the neo-liberal institution whose funding comes from the world's
richest capitalist countries. It is almost as if modernisation theory and ideas about
'stages of development' never went out of fashion (Rostow 1960).

Normative Vision

In a future Green society it might be expected that there would be less need for the
development industry and overseas aid, for example, since the causes of underdevelopment would be reduced. Greens would argue that this would be the case if
commons were protected, communities were allowed to reclaim control over
resources to sustain their livelihoods and tougher environmental safeguards were
in place; if land were directed towards production for domestic rather than overseas
markets; if conflict were to be reduced and there were fewer arms in circulation; if
foreign investors were better regulated; if services were provided by and for the
people; if debts were written off and so on.

Nevertheless, as discussed in Chapter 6, shifts to the global economy that
favoured the global periphery would have to be overseen by multilateral institutions – a consequence that would give rise to many of the dilemmas raised in the
next section. An important role for global institutions, albeit with new or renewed
mandates to promote sustainable development, would be to provide and protect
policy autonomy and development space for poorer countries in the face of
pressures from other countries or global capital (Gallagher 2005). Such institutions
in a Green vision would also be expected to mobilise, coordinate and support the

financing of sustainable transitions across the world, as well as deal with collective action problems and coordination challenges, such as closing tax loops, overseeing financial transaction taxes and coordinating actions to reduce subsidies on fossil fuels. In a globalised economy in which capital flight can be used to punish countries taking bold and progressive action, and capital can relocate to regulatory havens or pollution havens, coordinated international action by institutions with a mandate to promote and protect Greener forms of development could have a vital role to play in reducing the possibility that global capital can play off different sovereign jurisdictions against one another for its own advantage. Proposals from broad-based civil society coalitions in which development NGOs are well represented, such as the Real World Coalition (2001), discussed further below, suggest there would be some support for proposals along these lines.

While deeply critical of framings around the 'white man's burden', Greens are also supportive of the idea that former colonial powers bear a significant responsibility to reverse the extractivist model that they oversaw and which forms the basis for a great deal of the wealth they enjoy today. Molly Scott Cato, the Green MEP suggests, for example: 'We also argue that the UK's history leaves the country with a special responsibility to assist the poorer countries of the world to expand domestic production for their own needs' (Cato n.d.). Taking responsibility might take the form of aid, debt relief, preferential trading arrangements or, more radically, reparations. In this regard, Greens might advocate for a more ecological version of the New International Economic Order (Williams 1994), replete with calls for fairer terms of trade, debt relief and regulation of TNCs, only this time it would be a New International *Sustainable* Economic Order. Some semblance of a development industry would be expected to continue in a Green society to address these needs and responsibilities, many of which are historically constituted, even in a world in which fewer development needs would be generated by an economy organised along more socially just and ecological lines.

Some writers have sought, nonetheless, to articulate the contours of an alternative Green development model, one which resonates with some of the features of a Green economy described in Chapter 4. Friberg and Hettne (1985) (cited in Adams 1995: 94) call for a model that challenges the industrial, bureaucratic, market, techno-scientific and military-industrial complex. It would a strategy of 'de-modernisation', a new 'non-modern, non-capitalist development project' with strong elements of self-reliance, social justice and ecological balance. This model resonates with many of the calls for a 'commune of communes', the bioregionalism and recommoning described in Chapters 2 and 4, as well as the support Greens express for the ideas and practices behind 'sufficiency' and 'solidarity' economies (Amin 2009). Promoters of this vision, they claim, would include traditional communities of tribes, kinship groups, peasants and those involved in the informal economy, groups marginalised and disenfranchised by the existing development model and those who hold post-material values in the environmental movement. The strategies by which such a vision might be realised are discussed further in the next section.

Strategy

The universal and interrelated nature of the SDGs in many ways provides an opportunity to advance Green perspectives on development, since in theory economic and human development goals can no longer be pursued at the expense of social and environmental ones, nor addressed by displacing problems and responsibility elsewhere, since the goals are universal and apply equally to richer countries. Because the goals are universal, the scope for spatial fixes and displacing responsibility and burdens elsewhere in the economy *should* come to an end. In other words, delivering on goals around energy poverty and security, for example, cannot be at the expense of other countries by buying up land for biofuels for export[2] or for securing future supplies of water, for example. Greens would point to the obvious fact that for these goals to be achieved simultaneously and globally requires that some countries give up some ecological space for others that have not yet used up their share of the commons, and to face up to some of the inherent contradictions and conflicts between goals around climate, protecting life on land, improving access to water and energy as well as promoting industry and growth as usual.

Thinking more holistically and ecologically, to take a 360° view of development policy interventions will be crucial to ensuring that the pursuit of one goal is not at the expense of another. This objective requires going beyond imaginaries of 'win-win' or 'triple-win', which the development and business community is so fond of, and the pursuit of multiple synergies that, while desirable and useful in building alliances, often end up being dishonest. Many development interventions seek to obscure or fudge these contradictions, as for example, with 'Climate Smart Agriculture', which seeks to reconcile industrial agriculture with responding to the threat of climate change by identifying 'triple wins' around poverty alleviation, and climate mitigation and adaptation. The problem is that it does this by ignoring the role of industrialised and intensive forms of agriculture in contributing to climate change, as well as using the climate crisis to advance a series of technologies and techniques to which many Greens would be opposed, such as genetic engineering, biochar, biofuels and increased fertiliser use (Newell and Taylor 2018). The problem, as we have seen above, is that a prior commitment to unfettered growth and industrialism precludes a meaningful search for more effective responses and means of dealing with the root causes of underdevelopment.

Given what has been said previously, it is perhaps particularly true that for Greens 'development starts at home'. This is because of the long ecological and historical shadows that development in the core of the global economy cast over its periphery, such that patterns of development and underdevelopment are deeply intertwined through ecologically uneven exchange and extractivist models of economic development within and between states. Hence shifts towards a Green economy and state, adopting many of the strategies outlined in Chapters 4 and 5, would form the basis of strategies for promoting Green development by freeing poorer countries from existing exploitative ties, as well as providing ecological space to expand where necessary to meet their developmental needs.

It also means countering neo-classical development economics as the dominant worldview that underpins and legitimates the actions of the development industry. There have been attempts by Greens to infiltrate and reform it, most notoriously through the Green economist Herman Daly's attempt to bring about reform from within the World Bank where he worked in the environment department for six years. Whether Washington or post-Washington consensus (the so-called new developmentalism) and its more balanced view of how to achieve neo-liberalism (armed with an appreciation of institutions, governance and the role of civil society and social capital), the destination is not in doubt and the ecological costs of getting there, largely ignored.

It is also about opening up processes to meaningful participation and account-ability from excluded groups that are the stated beneficiaries of development interventions. Harnessing the 'voices of the poor', as has been attempted by the World Bank previously, for example, is clearly not enough (Narayan et al. 2000). It is about constructing genuinely open spaces for dialogue and envisaging differ-ent development pathways, including those which radically depart from prevailing development orthodoxies. These might include Herman Daly's recommendation to the World Bank in his leaving speech to: 'Move away from the ideology of global economic integration by free trade, free capital mobility and export led growth-and toward a more nationalist orientation that seeks to develop domestic production for internal markets as the first option, having recourse to international trade only when clearly much more efficient' (Daly 1994).

Democratising development and shifting patterns of ownership and control would be central to Green development. This undertaking is about more than participating in institutions and decision-making processes on terms set by other more powerful actors. It would imply support for 'intermediate technologies' that are labour-generating, appropriate to local contexts and needs and sustainable over high-tech alternatives promoted by businesses and donors (Schumacher 1974). Access to key technologies, without having to navigate intellectual property rights regimes, and forms of innovation developed by and for citizens, will be crucial.

Where private actors are involved, as they must, their participation would be on terms set by public actors responding to collective needs and priorities.

Strategically and normatively, many Greens would identify with the struggles and aims of many grassroots organisations and calls for 'counter modernist' alternatives to development (Manzo 1995), drawing on the anti-development critiques discussed above as well as traditions of 'liberation ecology' (Peet and Watts 2004). As well as solidarities with local groups contesting the effects of 'development' and at the frontlines of the extractivist economy involving oil, mining and coal extraction for example, Greens often express sympathies with transnational social movements around land (Via Campesina) and food, water and gender and human rights. In many ways these movements are engaging in the construction of everyday development alternatives. By resisting encroachment, enclosure and extraction, they force governments and corporations to explore alternatives. They are the 'environmental defenders' as Global Witness refers to them (2017), putting their lives on the line to say 'enough is enough'.

Many of these movements also articulate alternative visions themselves around food, energy and water sovereignty, reclaiming control over land or bringing the provision of water and energy back into the public domain (Gottlieb and Joshi 2010; Balanyá et al. 2005). Again, these are not only struggles in and from the global South. Campaigns in the global North around renationalising the railways and the 'land is ours', for example, express similar visions of an economic system that puts people before profit, just as initiatives to promote a circular economy, reduce food waste, repair and free-cycle embody a vision of the conserver society (Trainer 1995). Greens have often been vocal supporters of these movements. Where some might depart from others on the left demanding renationalisation of key sectors of the economy, is in ultimately seeking greater local and community-level control of these assets. As Broad and Cavanagh state: 'In essence many of these groups are proposing a paradigm shift that would replace the consumption-oriented, high-growth model with a low-carbon, low-growth economy where a more equitable income distribution would allow for a rise in the living standards of the poor' (2009: 104). In Green visions of development, the legitimate means of wealth and value creation will be publicly agreed in the interests of the common good rather than private gain.

There are a series of dilemmas that Greens face, nevertheless, around how to approach international development. There are the dilemmas about de-linking from the global economy, shortening the circuits between production and consumption, which many Greens advocate but which development economists argue would have a hugely detrimental impact on the livelihoods of the world's poorest people, many of whom are locked into export-orientated production of commodities. This issue came to the fore in debates about reducing food miles by encouraging

De-linking would cause harm, too, because many poor people locked into that system.

consumers to buy more local rather than imported food. Development groups such as the Overseas Development Institute (ODI) responded with calls for a 'good for development' label to recognise the many millions of poorer workers and farmers locked into these export-led markets whose livelihoods are dependent on these products. The issue then is one of managed disengagement and a transition away from such a model towards one in which shorter circuits of production and consumption are enabled and become the norm in a way that minimises disruption for poorer groups and actively builds alternative livelihood options for them, preferably around their own control of the means of production. This plan might also benefit consumers in the global North who, through the business models of leading supermarkets, are exposed to vulnerability by design: a reliance on just-in-time production from faraway places that require shipping and aviation and intensive forms of export production. The latter are vulnerable to a mix of financial instability (shifts in commodity and fuel prices), crop failures (due to disease) and climate disruption (to growing conditions and export channels). Strengthening localism would be one way of building resilience against these types of shock.

localism

Longer term, it is certainly possible to argue that making peoples' livelihoods dependent on the fickle consumption patterns of wealthy consumers and fluctuating prices for commodities (whose production is also increasingly effected by environmental problems such as climate change), does nothing to improve a precarious existence. Recognition of this problem does not do away the real short-term dilemmas and trade-offs about how to transition to a Greener economy that Greens need to address. The growing popularity of the idea of 'just transitions' captures this (Swilling and Annecke 2012; Newell and Mulvaney 2013) to describe the social compacts that will be required within and between societies as they move from environmentally destructive models of development to more benign ones to ensure that poorer groups who might lose out receive adequate compensation, retraining and the like.

While this is undoubtedly true at the level of a general claim, there is need for caution about the way these claims are sometimes invoked to stall shifts towards alternatives and where double standards are rampant. Hence, while the coal industry argues that any reduction in output should come with full consideration of compensation and retraining for those who might lose their jobs on grounds of tackling climate change, that industry and many others like it, routinely uproot their operations and move to other locations in pursuit of higher profits or less demanding standards without a second thought for those who have lost their jobs or the social dislocation they leave in their wake. Therefore, those who have profited most from historical patterns of resource extraction, whether corporations or states, should assume primary responsibility for managing this dislocation.

It is also the case that Greens are often also ambiguous, or even suspicious, about the role of the state and international institutions, making strong arguments in favour of decentralisation and subsidiarity to avoid concentrations of wealth and political power in few hands. Yet Green New Deals and versions of Green Keynesianism and just transitions, critical to a global transition to a lower global carbon economy, all require a strong, well-resourced and interventionist Green state. As discussed in Chapter 5, this presents difficult dilemmas for Green thinkers and activists.

Getting to the roots of underdevelopment is where Green politics can make a real contribution to development policy and debates: probing and addressing the causes of the world's development problems to advance meaningful and effective solutions to them. I am reminded of the comment by the Brazilian Catholic archbishop and liberation theologist Hélder Câmara who famously said: 'When I give food to the poor, they call me a saint. When I ask why they are poor, they call me a communist.' It is a critical time to ask why, in a world of such wealth and opulence, do we still need sustainable development goals in 2019?

This is not to cast doubt on the fact that carefully targeted aid associated with international development has improved the livelihoods of many of the world's poorest people: providing greater access to water and sanitation, to energy and basic health services than would otherwise have been the case, despite the appalling gaps in the provision of each of these. They are important and praiseworthy achievements, but the export, growth-obsessed and neo-liberal doctrines that have underpinned development policy since the era of structural adjustment have also brought great social dislocation and environmental devastation in their wake. The blurring of the security and economic interests of the world's most powerful countries with their 'development' interventions is an increasing source of concern as the causes of poverty come to be identified as opposition to western foreign policy (hostile religious or state socialist 'ideologies') or barriers to private investment (by intervening or 'populist' states).

There are obvious contradictions between acknowledging that war is 'development in reverse' and recognising the role of conflict and insecurity as key drivers of increasing poverty on the one hand, and on the other, the way in which the global North continues to support the export of arms to some of the poorest countries in the world, financing repressive regimes and strengthening their ability to repress internal dissent (Stavrianakis 2010). Greens address this issue directly by calling for tougher regulation of the arms trade.

From the point of view of global sustainability, the export of a resource-intensive and wasteful model of development to the majority world through pressure to intensify exports to western markets, privatise state assets and to make a 'fortune' for business by targeting the poorest consumers at the 'bottom of the pyramid' (Prahalad 2005) goes against the desire of most marginalised groups to have greater control over their land and to acquire the means to secure their own water, food and energy, rather than be subject to the vagaries of the global market. This view is increasingly expressed in the language of food, water and energy sovereignty expressed by movements and some governments, as well as around defence of the commons.

Of course, the needs of the poor are frequently invoked precisely to justify development-as-usual. You may have noticed recent attempts by oil multinationals such as Exxon to proclaim their concern for the world's energy poor, one which unsurprisingly leads them to the conclusion that we need to extract and burn even more fossil fuels to meet the needs of the poor. 'Coal has a fundamental role in providing access to base load electricity and is a critical building block for development' the World Coal Institute claims (WCI 2018). Given the low levels of purchasing power of the poor, the fact many live off-grid and where they can access a grid they cannot pay for the connection charges or bills that follow – to say nothing of the increased exposure of the poor to the effects of climate change – this is wishful thinking at best, invoking the needs of the poor to justify business-as-usual.

[margin annotation: coals' concern for the energy poor leads to more extraction]

Articulating a post-growth politics that is able to deal honestly and openly with the trade-offs that come from efforts to put welfare over output and actively encourage a slowdown in conventional economic activity without further immiserating the poor will be a huge challenge. The Cambridge economist Joan Robinson once famously said that: 'The misery of being exploited by capitalists is nothing compared to the misery of not being exploited at all' (2006: 45). The quote captures the 'catch 22' dilemma that many poor and marginalised groups find themselves in, especially in the global South, but also the insidious logic that not being exploited is somehow not permissible.

[margin annotation: catch 22 of critique]

Addressing these issues globally will require striking deals on resource use that recognise the rights and needs of poorer groups to use a greater share of remaining ecological space to service their pressing development needs, while ensuring that richer countries accept the greatest burden to drastically reduce their own demands upon finite global resources given the historical responsibility they bear for our collective predicament to date. Domestically, it will require a major re-balancing of the economy away from financialisation, militarisation and globalisation and towards a recentring of the economy towards productive, worthwhile, welfare-enhancing, employment-creating forms of work and exchange that serve the common good.

[margin annotation: dev.]

This is a critical time for international development. The SDGS provide the basis of the vision for development that will bind the world for the rest of this century. They commit the international community to reducing poverty and inequality; addressing gender inequalities; promoting food security and improving access to energy. We need to bring some critical Green thinking to bear on this vision. Without it, a set of hackneyed solutions revolving around trickle-down growth, the primacy of private solutions to public problems and calls for further waves of neo-liberal reforms will triumph. Greens have argued, for example, for a full-scale overhaul of EU development aid such that it contributes to ecologically sustainable development and is less orientated towards economic restructuring in order to service the needs of the global market (Bomberg 1998). They also call for a renegotiation of trade agreements to promote ecological sustainability, social justice and self-reliant local economies (Woodin and Lucas 2004).

The debate does not end there. The relationship between Green politics and international development is not an easy one. Progressive internationalism is a cornerstone of Green politics. As the manifesto of the UK Green Party (2010) for the 2010 election states: 'Green Party international policy is aimed at reducing global inequalities, in the name of fairness, sustainability and peace, and in the context of an interdependent world'. Arms control and disarmament, stronger international environmental regulation, a 'Robin Hood' tax on financial transactions and radical reform of global institutions such as the IMF, World Bank and WTO are among the policies advocated by Green parties as we saw in Chapter 6. So far, so good. We need strong global governance to better regulate a global economy dominated by powerful corporate and financial actors, to ensure a fairer trading system and to protect human rights. Yet Greens also favour the radical decentralisation of power away from the state and international institutions. Who then will have the power to drive change in these global bodies?

To take another example: Greens routinely support calls, such as those made at the Copenhagen climate summit, to drastically increase levels of climate aid for mitigation and adaptation, but therein lays another dilemma. Such increases in aid to pay off ecological or carbon debts to the developing world require increases in economic activity that, in a system as tied to fossil fuels as the current global economy, implies further emissions of greenhouse gases to tackle the problem of climate change! It is rather like existing proposals to fund adaptation to the effects of climate change through a levy on air travel. Not a bad idea on the face of it, until you realise you are tying the access of the world's poorest people to adaptation money to increased flying by the world's rich. Such are the contradictions of modern capitalist life: the solutions offered often intensify and worsen the problems they are meant to address because they fail to address the source of the problems.

One aspect of international development policy that divides Greens is how much emphasis to place on population control. The problematic relationship with population has a long history, dating particularly to the interventions of thinkers like Paul Ehrlich in his (1975) book *Population Bomb*. This thinking is drawn on by Green authors such as David Icke who, writing about the 'baby boom' quotes approvingly from David Bellamy who argues: 'though I know we can solve the problems of poverty, starvation and environmental misuse, there is no future unless the population bomb is diffused now' (Icke 1990: 82). For others, the focus on population serves as a distraction, displacing focus on western consumption and often used to validate deeply problematic interventions such as forced sterilisations of poorer and vulnerable women as has happened in the past. Although such interventions are often combined by arguing that population control and restraint in the richer or overdeveloped part of the world is the priority in ecological terms, given the likely environmental footprint of a child born in the global North compared with a child in the South, and the need for access to family planning in poorer countries, the issue continues to divide Greens.

Conclusions

Where does this leave a Green view of international development? Green party manifestos contain a series of positive progressive policies aimed at addressing inequality, promoting peace and stability and tackling global environmental problems that exacerbate poverty. Meeting all of these goals simultaneously means being open and honest about real trade-offs, conflicts and dilemmas, such as those I mention here, in order to establish key priorities for change.

For me, one of the most important contributions of Green politics is to challenge the way in which a resource-intensive and wasteful model of economic development is promoted so uncritically by the international institutions and governments that have such influence over the world's poorest nations because of tied aid, debt repayments and economic restructuring. Standing up for the rights of countries to pursue their own development paths and to resist those which lock them into an unequal position in the global economy is an important first step. Demonstrating the viability and desirability of an alternative development path in the richer parts of the world is ultimately the surest way of moving towards a sustainable development path that others may want to emulate. This is where Green Party domestic policy is also the source of its international development policy: doing as we do, not as we say, dealing with our own development dilemmas among richer populations in the global North rather than making demands of poorer groups in the global South.

What Greens can also bring to this debate is the idea that moving towards a more sustainable society is not just imperative for social and environmental reasons. It is also a moral responsibility. In an ecologically and economically interdependent world, the patterns of development in the richer part have direct implications for the ability of the world's poorest people to access the land, water and energy resources necessary for their survival. As is often said in the context of climate change, we in the North have to live differently in order that others can merely live. This is a developmentalism that starts at home by reducing impact abroad through foreign-policy decisions, military interventions and kicking away the development ladder of the majority world through circumscribing policy space. This should result in less need for aid and charity. This does not mean, however, an abandonment of humanitarianism and solidarity. It is about freeing up ecological space for others to develop.

The questions are whether global solidarities and an ethic of care and responsibility can be expressed outside of conventional development frameworks, and whether ideas of development can be constructed that are not automatically conflated with growth. This approach means not abandoning critical projects aimed at delivering education and improving health or protecting rights but at the same time probing the underlying causes of social dislocation, inequalities and exclusions and the power relations that hold them in place, within and beyond the contexts in which they manifest themselves.

While the sorts of critiques outlined at the start of the chapter make clear that development as it is commonly understood and practiced today is a product of the rise of the West and the globalisation of a particular type of capitalist global political economy, the onus is on Greens and their allies to demonstrate that other ways of engaging, working with and for communities in other parts of the world are possible – ones that aim to promote peace, justice and sustainability rather than seeking to recreate and extend unsustainable models of development. The point, as E. P. Thompson suggests, is to fight 'not against development, but about it'.

Notes

1 It relates closely to the famous work by Said on orientalism (1979) that he describes as 'a western style for dominating, restructuring and having authority over the Orient' (1979: 6).
2 Rising support for and investments in biofuels has been directly attributed to rising food prices. The head of the Trade and Agriculture Department at the OECD stated: 'As a large part of the [land] use expansion was due to biofuels, there cannot be any doubt that biofuels were a significant element in the rise of food prices ... biofuel support policies have contributed greatly to the rise in global food prices' (quoted in George 2010: 123).

8

Green Sustainability

Why deal with sustainability last in a book about Green politics which has as its premise the need to place sustainability at the heart of global politics? The answer lies in the question. If the global economy, global security, development, the state and global governance had the achievement of sustainability as one of their overriding rationales and objectives, then a separate set of policies, institutions and initiatives to undo, contain and offset the excesses of industrial society would not be necessary. There would be no need, in other words, for global environmental policies and regimes. The fact that they exist is an indictment of a system and a society living beyond its means and in unsustainable ways.

Critique

Unsustainable Development as Business-as-Usual

Empirically, it is hard to dispute that we are living through a series of deepening environmental crises, a situation some describe as 'living through the end of nature' (Wapner 2010). Climate change is perhaps the greatest 'meta' environmental threat we face, although loss of biodiversity is certainly close in terms of gravity and irreversibility, tied as it is to mass extinctions, ocean depletion, pollution and overfishing. Many threats are non-spectacular and slow moving but nevertheless bring devastating consequences in their wake.

That real progress and gains have been made in some areas with respect to controls on some types of chemical, air, and water pollution, for example, does not outweigh the significance of our collective overshoot of key planetary boundaries that have given rise to our current predicament (see Figure 8.1).

What is particularly telling from a Green point of view is the seeming correlation between huge expansions in growth and exponential increases in environmental degradation, including, for example, the 'great acceleration' in the post-war

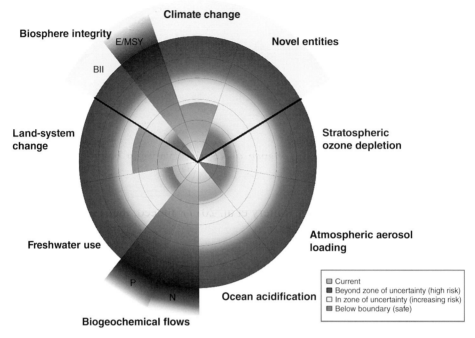

Figure 8.1 Planetary boundaries.
Source: Steffen et al. (2015b), used with permission

years, as well as in the wake of the industrial revolution (Steffen et al. 2015a). Likewise, unsurprisingly, carbon emissions dropped in the wake of the financial crisis of 2007–8 when levels of production and consumption fell. In other words, global economic slowdown achieved in a few years what decades of environmental policy and negotiations failed to achieve. The challenge, to which we return below, is how to manage economic decline and minimise the disruption and negative impacts, upon poorer groups in particular, as we seek to realign the global economic system with what our ecosystem can bear.

The gulf is vast between the scale and urgency of action required to contain and reverse these trends and the adequacy of policy responses to date from states, corporations and international institutions. For example, there is a gaping chasm between government policies proposed thus far and the types of action that science suggests are necessary to keep global warming below dangerous levels. In the wake of the adoption of the much feted 2015 Paris Agreement, it has become clear that the Nationally Determined Contributions that governments have put on the table currently leave us on course for warming of up to 3.4°C (UNEP 2018), and that's assuming they are all implemented! Reaching these temperature rises would be to commit ourselves to a world of sea-level rise, increasing intensity of extreme weather events, droughts and reduced rainfall for those areas of the world most dependent on agriculture. Runaway climate change is set in train once 'positive' feedbacks kick in as methane is released from melting ice; oceans warm and acidify; and forest fires become more common, releasing further CO_2 into the atmosphere and thus accelerating the cycle of decline. It is clear the world over that we are already living with climate change, even if some, mainly those least responsible for causing the problem, are feeling its effects most acutely.

The obligations contained in the Paris Agreement on climate change mean that rapid transitions offer the only chance of keeping warming below 1.5°C or 2°C (Anderson 2015), with one recent report suggesting we now have only a 5 per cent chance of keeping warming below this critical threshold unless transformational interventions are forthcoming (Raftery et al. 2017). Indeed, the IPCC SR15 report on 1.5°C in unusually unguarded terms calls for 'transformative systemic change' (IPCC 2018). The report further notes that:

> While transitions are underway in various countries, limiting warming to 1.5°C will require a greater scale and pace of change to transform energy, land, urban and industrial systems globally ... There is an urgent need for more rapid and deeper transitions to limit warming to 1.5°C. Such transitions have been observed in the past within specific sectors and technologies. But the geographical and economic scales at which the required rates of change in the energy, land, urban, infrastructure and industrial systems would now need to take place, are larger and have no documented historic precedent.

This situation has led to a series of local governments in the United Kingdom and elsewhere declaring a 'Climate emergency' and has galvanised global 'Youth 4 climate' strikes by children and young adults. They are demanding an immediate realignment of priorities in line with the reality of now having less than eleven years to prevent 1.5°C warming and to avoid the catastrophic consequences of temperature increases spiralling out of control.

What Greens tend to highlight is not only the manifestations of environmental problems, although they do that too, but their (common) roots in everyday processes of production, commodification, consumption and exchange. Rather than address those causes, however, strategies of displacement, blame, and a series of techno, spatial and temporal fixes have provided the most common forms of response by state and corporate elites and many international institutions, offering short-term palliatives to deep structural problems, which Williams (1996) described as analogous to applying an 'institutional bandage' to a 'structural haemorrhage'. Blaming forest degradation on poor forest dwellers (Fairhead and Leach 1998), paying the poor to pollute less to enable the rich to pollute more through carbon markets (Bachram 2004) or promoting projects of technological control in relation to food (genetic engineering), energy (nuclear) and climate (geo-engineering) are among strategies that have featured prominently in recent decades. Many of the ambitions of the 2015 UNFCCC Paris agreement about net-zero emissions, for example, imply the widespread use of NETs (negative emission technologies), the most commonly proposed form of which are BECCS (Biomass Energy with Carbon Capture and Storage), utilised in more than 80 per cent of IPCC pathway projections. BECCS involves the mass plantation of trees to absorb carbon dioxide from the atmosphere. Even in spite of the technological issues involved, for these to work at the scale necessary, plantations three times the size of India, consuming one third of the planet's arable land, would need to be created (Anderson 2015; Anderson and Peters 2016). The lengths to which global elites will go to avoid necessary structural changes to the economic system are extraordinary.

Greens highlight the fact that proposed solutions often make things worse, because they fail to deal with the causes of environmental degradation or unsettle the power relations that produce those problems, resulting in unevenly distributed, persistent and socially regressive measures, moving problems around through 'spatial' and 'temporal' fixes (as Harvey 1981 puts it) rather than resolving them. Examples include 'Green grabs' of land for the purposes of carbon offsets, or 'accumulation by conservation' (Büscher and Fletcher 2015) and restoration (Huff and Brock 2017). Responses have to be consistent with growth at all costs. Whether it be the marketisation of environmental governance (Newell 2008b) and the preference for market-based over so-called command and control (regulatory) solutions; the rise of payments for ecosystem services approaches to conservation (whereby communities are financially compensated for their protection of natural resources); or the commodification of water, forests and carbon as responses to environmental problems (where attempts are made to price their value), the dominant responses serve to entrench capitalism, rather than attend to the need for structural reform in advanced capitalist economies that environmental crises demand.

Problems generated by overconsumption of resources, such as fossil fuels, become an investment opportunity for entrepreneurs to buy and sell 'offscts'. These allow companies and individuals to purchase emissions reduction opportunities in the developing world and claim them as part of their own emissions reductions efforts, all the while keeping existing structures of production and consumption intact. Meanwhile, water scarcity is presented as a problem produced by inefficient state institutions and a failure to incentivise conservation by allocating property rights, such that privatisation becomes the obvious solution (Bakker 2010). Institutions such as the World Bank play an important role in preparing the ideological grounds for such interventions. The World Bank's 2003 World Development Report on 'Sustainable Development in a Dynamic Economy' advances the idea that the spectacular failure to tackle poverty and environmental degradation over the last decade is due to a failure of governance, 'poor implementation and not poor vision'. The report (World Bank 2003) notes: 'Those [poverty and environmental problems] that can be coordinated through markets have typically done well; those that have not fared well include many for which the market could be made to work as a coordinator.' The challenge for governments is therefore to be more welcoming of private actors through, among other things, 'a smooth evolution of property rights from communal to private' (World Bank 2003: 3.22). Those who have been on the receiving end of processes to move from communal to private regimes would be unlikely to describe them as 'smooth', but rather as coercive, alienating, disruptive and often violent.

In a similar vein, the problems generated by the unsustainability of the global system of food and agriculture have become an opportunity for advancing 'climate smart agriculture', repositioning the biotechnology, meat and livestock industries as climate saviours, obscuring the significant climate impact of their sectors. As one NGO coalition explains: 'Agribusiness corporations that promote synthetic fertilisers, industrial meat production and large-scale industrial agriculture – all of which are widely recognised as contributing to climate change and undermining the resilience of farming systems – can and do call themselves "Climate Smart"' (Climate Smart Agriculture Concerns 2015). As Newell and Taylor suggest in their analysis of climate smart agriculture:

Thus, an emphasis on emissions trading has displaced a focus on emissions reduction; an emphasis on control through technology has predominated over access to technology and radical innovation; consolidation of land rather than redistribution; and reinforcement of property rights rather than sharing of technologies central to climate-resilient agricultural practices. CSA has become a site for the attempted resolution of the need for finance to find something to invest in, extending their control over land; for governments and neo-liberal global institutions to shore up flagging carbon markets by expanding into agriculture; for biotechnology firms to re-invent GMOs as 'climate-smart'; and for global agricultural institutions to raise their profile and diversify their funding streams by taking on mandates for tackling and responding to climate change.

(2018: 18)

Most insidious of all is the move to make the poor pay for the over-consumption of the global North and the world's wealthy: through land to produce 'cheap' energy in the form of biofuels; through money as crop insurance against failed yields because of climate change to which they have contributed almost nothing (Isakson 2015); through labour to maintain forest sinks for continued fossil-fuel growth in the North and through giving up livelihoods and lives to make way for mega-development projects of benefit to urban elites and global ruling classes.

Perhaps unsurprising, therefore, strategies of global environmental management pursued by elites with close ties to and material interests in the very processes causing environmental degradation, serve to narrow the terrain of debate to solutions and proscriptions consistent with minor amendments to the status quo. Bernstein (2001) refers to this as the 'compromise of liberal environmentalism' whereby progress in advancing sustainable development is rendered contingent and dependent on the maintenance of an open liberal market (capitalist) order. For example, the Brundtland report *Our Common Future* had to address the contradictions raised by the *Limits to Growth* report (discussed in Chapter 4) to establish, once more, that growth is a prerequisite to environmental protection. From limits to growth to 'growth of the limits' as Sachs (1988) suggests. As Escobar maintains: 'By adopting the concept of sustainable development, two old enemies, growth and environment, are reconciled' (1995: 195). Laferrière and Stoett (1999: 37) wisely infer that 'Sustainable development simply extends the ecological threshold of no-return and keeps alive the liberal argument that technological innovation and wise use will respect the carrying capacity of the planet'.

It is growth that has to be sustained, and since growth is thought to be both synonymous with, and a prerequisite to development, questions about whose development and what type of growth are bracketed. In this rendition, poverty is a driver of environmental degradation (not overconsumption and affluence) and, therefore, more growth is the always answer. Escobar suggests 'The epistemological and political reconciliation of economy and ecology proposed by sustainable development is intended to create the impression that only minor adjustments to the market system are needed to launch an era of environmentally sound development, hiding the fact that the economic framework itself cannot hope to accommodate environmental considerations without substantial reform' (1995: 197).

In the wake of the Rio Earth Summit in 1992, an emphasis on eco-efficiency has continued, promoted by business bodies such as the World Business Council on Sustainable Development (Schmidheiny 1992; Holliday et al. 2002) and the growth of ideas about the greening of business (Prakash 2000), albeit deriving in many ways from the Brundtland report's call to 'produce more with less' (1987: 15). As noted in Chapter 4, the issue from the point of view Greens is not relative efficiency savings, but absolute reductions in resource use. Otherwise, resource efficiencies get overwhelmed by the ecological impact of overall increases in output, as we saw in the discussion about Jevon's paradox in Chapter 4. Greens would be critical of more technocentric readings of ecology that draw on ideas of rational utilisation, 'maximum sustainable yields', 'carrying capacity' and 'wise use' etc. (Adams 1995) whereby the pursuit of sustainable development is about maximising human benefits without incurring significant environmental costs and without threatening economic growth. Brundtland, in this sense, made the argument for 'environmentally sustainable growth within a Keynesian-managed world economy' (Adams 1995: 89). This approach shares and advances the central tenets of both developmentalism and industrialism based on competitive individualism, growth, efficiency, specialisation and centralisation on a large scale. Hence 'there are no ideological conflicts with the dominant capitalist industrialising model, only debates about methods and priorities' (Adams 1995: 90).

So much of global environmental governance wilfully and deliberately neglects, ignores, discredits or dilutes the key issues, tools and evidence that could lead to more effective responses: anything that conflicts with particular ideas and ideologies of trade liberalisation, growth, or that invokes market regulation. The compromise of liberal environmentalism, so aptly described by Bernstein, has run its course. We need a new social and ecological contract.

Whose Common Future?

As well as accommodating environmental threats to business-as-usual capitalism, uneven social power is key to locating causation and understanding the uneven impacts of environmental change. Hence, although these are global problems, for which collective responses are required, Greens are quick to highlight the unevenly distributed responsibility for causing them and the uneven exposure to their effects. They often refer to unevenly shared historical responsibility for problems such as climate change and biodiversity loss or ocean depletion, acknowledged formally in principle in multilateral environmental agreements such as 'common but differentiated responsibility'. It is also captured in ideas of 'ecological debt' developed by Green economists such as Andrew Simms (2005), but questions of responsibility for environmental harm, as well as uneven exposure to its effects, can also be socially differentiated by class, gender and race as analysis of global environmental inequality has proposed (Newell 2005). The extensive body of work on environmental justice (Bullard 2005; Cole and Foster 2001; Sikor and Newell 2014) lends weight to Greens' claims about the social injustice deriving from the fact that those exposed to the worst effects of environmental degradation are often least responsible for causing it. This resonates with the discussion, introduced in Chapter 1, about whether the anthropocene condition should more precisely be labelled the 'capitalocene', as Jason Moore (2013) and others have suggested, to reflect the overwhelming role of capital in producing the current crisis.

This forms part of a broader Green critique of global techno-managerialism, or what Escobar calls 'ecocracy' (Escobar 1995). The debate is thus moved beyond questions of how the environment should be 'managed' to *who* will manage it and in whose interest (The Ecologist 1993). The 'global ecology' (Sachs 1993; The Ecologist 1993; Chatterjee and Finger 1994) literature that analysed the failure to address environmental issues contributes to this line of thought. What was 'unsaid' at UNCED (Thomas 1996), according to Greens: attention to the role of debt, militarism and consumption – with President Bush stating at the time that the 'The American way of life is not up for negotiation' – is as important and telling as what was agreed. As The Ecologist (1993: vi) asked pertinently: 'if, as Maurice Strong, Secretary-General of UNCED, claimed "there was a groundswell of support from the grassroots for the objectives of the Earth Summit", why were the issues which have been central to the work of grassroots groups – in particular the right of local communities to determine their own future – excluded from the agenda?' Moreover, UNCED provided 'a convention on biodiversity, but not on free trade; on forests but not on logging; on climate but not on automobiles'. Agenda 21 featured clauses on 'enabling the poor to achieve sustainable livelihoods but none on enabling the rich to do so; a section on women but none on men. By such deliberate evasion of the central issues which economic expansion poses for human societies, UNCED condemned itself to irrelevance even before the first participatory meeting got under way' (The Ecologist 1993: 1–2).

The explanation lies in part with who assumed responsibility for the summit of 'ecology as spectacle' (Doran 1993): the actors were many of the world's largest corporations whose business strategies brought about the need for such a summit. For Hildyard, this left the 'foxes in charge of the chickens' (Hildyard 1993). 'The corporate sector, which throughout the UNCED process enjoyed special access to the secretariat, was confirmed as the key actor "in the battle to save the planet"' (The Ecologist 1993: 1). 'Unwilling to question the desirability of economic growth, the market economy or the development process itself, UNCED never had a chance of addressing the real problems of "environment and development"' (The Ecologist 1993: 1). Things have not improved with time. The first Conference of the Parties to the climate regime since the release of the alarming IPCC special report on 1.5°C in October 2018 was sponsored by the coal industry! (Farand 2018).

In this sense, Greens are often sceptical of calls for common humanity and one worldism that, rather like the anthropocene concept, erase socially differentiated responsibility and an account of causation and fail to ask: 'Whose common future is to be sustained?' The Ecologist (1993: 2) argued: communities' struggle 'is not to win greater power for the market or state, but to reinstate their communities as sources of social and political authority'. As with the Rio + 20 Summit, The United Nations Conference on Sustainable Development (UNCSD) in 2012 that produced the document 'The Future We Want', the key question here is who the 'we' is. Its content made very clear that only those versions of the future fully aligned with the expansion and deepening of neo-liberal capitalism were up for discussion. As Escobar observes: 'the global is defined according to a perception of the world shared by those who rule it' (1995: 195).

As part of this critique of techno-managerialism, whose knowledge frames problem definitions and proposed solutions is also a concern for Greens. This critique of science and rationality comes from various points of view (feminist and other) (Plumwood 1993), as we saw in Chapter 2, amid calls for respect for diversity of knowledges about the environment – local, indigenous and experiential. This objective involves ways of integrating every day and lay knowledge (such as 'barefoot epidemiology') (Merrifield 1993) and engaging with 'citizen science' (Fischer 2002) produced by and for those often living on the frontline of environmental contamination. Concretely, these concerns manifest themselves, for example, in debates about the values to be attached to biodiversity and whether benefits and innovations can be monetarised and individualised, a notion alien to many cultures and cosmologies (Shiva and Moser 1995). It also relates to concerns, discussed in Chapter 5, about the state in relation to ecological democracy and the importance of more deliberative and inclusive decision-making processes around risk, uncertainty and different pathways that might be pursued (Stirling 2014).

Potentially problematically for Greens, many of whom embrace the concept and modelling of planetary boundaries as a reference point for their critiques of the contemporary global economy, some of these critiques apply to that very framing, asking questions about who sets the boundaries and on whose behalf (Leach 2014). Cries of impending catastrophe and disaster can legitimate top-down power grabs, undermining democracy and social justice, including deference to technocratic elites invoking critiques of 'cosmologies of control' Stirling (2015), or a 'cockpit mentality' as Hajer et al. (2015) have termed it.

As Stirling suggests:

Whether it be in Paul Crutzen's foundational Anthropocene idea of humanity 'taking control of Nature's realm', or John Schellnhuber's vision of 'a self-conscious control force that has conquered the planet' or Johan Rockström's own framing (with other colleagues) of Anthropocene planetary boundaries as 'control variables' – this is clearly mainly about control. And associated work by Johan and others also gives a pretty clear sense of what style of control this is – variously described as 'non-negotiable', with 'absolutely no uncertainty' brooking 'no compromise' ... What 'planetary management' requires, extends far beyond governance of merely human affairs (in all their intractable unruliness). It encompasses aspirationally determining power over the even more recalcitrant 'Earth System' itself.

(2015)

This type of control, in Stirling's view, clears the path for geo-engineering and other forms of 'planetary management'. The danger is that this path takes us back to foundational Baconian views of science about 'dominion over creation' that Greens often rebut so strongly (see Chapter 2). Importantly for emancipatory politics, Stirling (2015) declares: 'This is a discourse of fear, not of hope. It is about subordination, not emancipation. It substitutes imagined certainties of control, for the experienced ambiguities of care.' The challenge for Greens in many ways is to make use of the modelling of planetary boundaries, seeking to anticipate and avoid key tipping points in the Earth system, incorporating many aspects of the core ideas (as well as limitations) of limits-to-growth approaches without encouraging a politics of global control and managerialism proscribed from above. A more differentiated picture emerges when the dimension of social boundaries, as proposed by Kate Raworth's 'doughnut economics' discussed below, is introduced.

Normative Vision

Normatively, as noted at the start of this chapter, the ultimate aim of most Greens is to live in a world where the environment does not need protecting, where special, separate policies are not required to deal with the after effects of industrialism as if the environment did not matter. A Green agenda would be properly mainstreamed into all other areas rather than isolated as a separate policy concern or treated as an after thought. Ecology would be woven into all decision-making as a core underlying and organising principle, deriving either from enlightened self-interest that there can be no economy, no development and no security without a habitable planet, or from more eco-centric values that express some humility and respect towards the global ecosystems of which, as humans, we are a part.

Institutions, at all levels, consistent with ideas about multi-level governance and subsidiarity (see Chapter 6) would exercise their authority and use their power in pursuit of the goals of sustainability. Policy would be designed around living within planetary (ecological and social) boundaries but pursued through means and strategies negotiated with, and agreed upon, by broader publics in an ecological public sphere (Eckersley 2004) such that the boundaries provide parameters but not maps about how to arrive at an agreed destination. Such an approach would imply significant 're-commoning' and de-centralisation of control over resources as a move away from global managerialism and towards local democratic control over livelihoods, a Polanyian re-embedding of the market within frameworks of social control supportive of sustainability.

This is not, therefore, a call for an urgency-driven, authoritarian form of global environmental governance by edict or control. It is about the creation and enforcement of rights-based frameworks, space, control and autonomy for communities over the stewardship of common resources, in part as a defence against the incursions of global capital. Living within planetary boundaries as a first step means leaving large swathes of resources in the ground. Mobilisation and resistance can make this happen, putting down limits, questioning the social licence to operate and adding costs to business-as-usual. But it also requires a rebalancing of the rules, institutions and power relations away from a global system dominated by militarism and growth towards one that recognises the centrality of ecological and social well-being as overriding societal aims where law and regulation undoubtedly have a role to play. To take one example, advocacy of a Fossil Fuel Non-Proliferation Treaty (Newell and Simms 2019) that captures and generalises commitments some governments are already making to keep fossil fuels in the ground, would be informed by a calculation based on available science and models of the percentage of fossil fuels that we can afford to use to stay below 1.5°C. The social momentum behind it, and the protection it would afford, resides in networks of resistance and communities at the frontiers of the fossil-fuel economy.

The Green view of a sustainable society is in many ways an accumulation of all of the normative commitments described in previous chapters around the pursuit of Green security, a Green economy, Green development, a Green state and system of global governance. These commitments would be key to addressing the causes of environmental crises by moving beyond industrialism and fantasies of infinite production and consumption; by challenging violence and war (by pacifying the state and pursuing peaceful cooperation with other states and regions); by providing other countries and regions with the autonomy and policy space to pursue development alternatives appropriate to their needs (as part of a revised approach to development, aid and trade) and constructing national and global systems of governance that support and enable the pursuit of a sustainable society rather than constrain and prohibit it as currently occurs through the IMF and WTO, for example.

Much of the normative position would depart from the idea that industrialism is the problem and, therefore, unlikely to provide the framework for addressing sustainability. Yet, as Leff claims: 'There does not exist yet a sufficiently worked out theory of sustainable development based on an ecological rationality' (cited in Escobar 1995: 205). As we saw previously, Green political theory and philosophy is not short of (sometimes competing) ideas of the ecological good life, and some consensus can be gleaned around principles of non-violence, radical democracy, feminism and sustainability. Indeed, in their report *A Wealth of Possibilities: Alternatives to Growth*, the Green European Foundation describes many policy initiatives featured in this book, from basic income schemes and ecological taxation, to job guarantees, community-based currencies and solidarity economies (Cattaneo and Vansintjan 2016; Seyfang and Longhurst 2013). In reality, emergent practice, trial and error and sharing of positive practice through learning and exchange provide a more practical and desirable pathway to change, informed by the key underlying principles that inform Green politics.

Later, we will look at concrete policies and strategies that are being adopted and have been proposed to move towards a Green society. There are, of course, tensions between overarching and underpinning principles, derived from Green philosophy and thought, and the practical politics of negotiating and delivering near-term change. They raise dilemmas around the role of the state, of coercion and the appropriate mix of top-down and bottom-up strategies and measures.

Strategy

As noted above, the theory and practice of Green politics with which we have become familiar over the course of this book, suggests a myriad of pathways to change and indeed a plethora of theories of change. So what are the strategies Greens use or would adopt to achieve such a vision? As before, in relation to the pursuit of a sustainable society, in many ways they amount to a combination of all the strategies suggested above in pursuit of a Green state, global order and practices of security, economy and development. Nevertheless, areas of common ground and shared theories of change can be discerned.

Change within and beyond the State

Many short-term struggles are, and will continue to be, fought over deepening democracy through subsidiarity and decentralisation of power: a move away from elite eco-managerialism that was subject to critical interrogation in the first section of this chapter. Although the state may be the target of these struggles, the ultimate aim is to extend democratic control over the economy (production, finance and technology), for example, as well as the conduct of politics in formal institutional settings. There will be demands for greater deliberation and democracy over pathways and environmental futures but cognisant of the need for these to work within and aligned to the boundaries set by key ecological thresholds that have to be socially agreed. Thus for Greens, deliberation over preferred pathways has to respect ecological parameters, even if the ways of achieving them and the nature of intra- and inter-societal choices that will have to be made are to be negotiated and agreed.

In a short- and near-term sense, it would be about greening the state through various means (Craig 2018). These include improved coordination across policy areas and greater policy coherence. This might be the type of 'joined up' policy advocated for by the Real World Coalition (2001) that goes beyond siloed thinking and seeing 'the environment' as a stand-alone area of policy. As Cato and Essex (n.d.) stated in their submission to the Environmental Audit Committee on Green finance: 'We suggest that the discussion of "green finance" is not limited to areas of government investment currently labelled as "green" by the government, such as the Green Deal and Green Investment Bank. Rather, we would propose that green investment must constitute an overall shift and prioritisation of treasury, fiscal and monetary investment priorities so that all government investments are viewed through a green lens.' As noted at the start of this chapter, future energy, transport, agricultural and foreign policy would have to be aligned with the imperative of moving rapidly towards a more ecological society, implying a fundamental reorientation of traditional policy goals.

Elevating the status of ecological thinking would be achieved in part by constitutionally enshrining principles such as the precautionary and polluter pays principles, (as discussed in Chapter 5) as well as obligations to consider implications for future generations pursued through ideas explored below in terms of representatives for future generations. Greens would want to see greater weight and enforcement power given to the pursuit of sustainability at all levels of governance, from cities and regions to the state and institutions of global governance. They would also want to see greater powers of oversight and ultimately veto vested in independent oversight bodies such as Climate Change Committees and broader Environment Agencies or Sustainable Development Commissions (see below) that can assess, challenge and block policy proposals that are inconsistent with agreed environmental targets, budgets and thresholds.

More ambitiously still, together with indigenous groups, Greens have been seeking rights protection for natural resources where some recent cases suggest interesting precedents. Initiatives are increasingly taking root – from the United States to India, and Ecuador to Bolivia, Turkey and Nepal – that give rights to nature. In February 2019 voters in Toledo, Ohio approved a ballot to give Lake Erie rights normally associated with a person, while in March 2017 the New Zealand government passed legislation recognising the Whanganui River as holding rights and responsibilities equivalent to a person. The river – or those acting for it – will now be able to sue for its own protection under the law (RTA 2019).

As we saw in Chapter 6, most Greens recognise the need to reform, confront and engage global institutions. Consistent with the argument in this chapter, this is ironically less about working with global environmental institutions such as UNEP, or the Global Environment Facility and others (though Greens would need to do that too), and more about critical overhaul of the mandates and ways of working of the central global economic institutions of the world. This is because these institutions, most obviously the World Bank, IMF and WTO, play such a powerful role in propagating and accelerating unsustainable models of development, while at the same time constraining the space for progressive and ambitious Green policies (Newell 2012; Woodin and Lucas 2004).

Greens of different shades have given considerable thought to the types of global governance innovation that might be required to enshrine sustainability as a guiding political principle or project, or to protect it from the political fray (Stevenson and Dryzek 2014; Eckersley 2004; Paehlke 2004; Baber and Bartlett 2005). Though this could have problematic implications, such as ring fencing certain ideas from critical scrutiny and engagement and handing them to global managers (incurring many of the critiques rehearsed above), concrete proposals include the following. The Intergenerational Foundation lobbied for the UN to create a new, independent office to oversee and monitor its work, and the work of member states, from the perspective of the long-term interests of future generations. Efforts by campaigners such as Future Justice or the World Future Council, the Foundation for Democracy and Sustainable Development and the Alliance for Future Generations to see this included in *The Future We Want* document at the Rio+20 summit were frustrated, despite the inclusion in a draft zero of the document stating: 'We agree to further consider the establishment of an Ombudsperson, or High Commissioner for Future Generations, to promote sustainable development.'[1]

Adopting a similar approach, the World Future Council argues: 'To create our common future, we need to have our voices heard through NGOs, the media and politicians. What is missing is a voice with legal authority; a voice with the force of the law to protect our environment and our future.' This vision led to a call for 'Ombudspersons for Future Generations at all governance levels, international, national and local, to provide an official champion and watchdog for sustainable development' (World Future Council 2012).[2] The basis for this proposal is that 'Public participation and equity are at the core of sustainable development and need to be strengthened. Young people are underrepresented and future generations almost entirely omitted in domestic and international decision-making processes.' The hope is that Ombudspersons for future generations will help turn sustainability goals into a reality, and balance short- and long-term interests more effectively, holding decision-makers to account, connecting citizens and their political representatives. In practical terms, the institution of an Ombudsperson is designed to be a 'representative'. This individual is an official, usually appointed by the government or by parliament, who is charged with representing the interests of the public. Usually, she or he does this by investigating and addressing complaints reported by individual citizens. Some mandates foresee independent initiatives by the Ombudsperson and their office as well. Figure 8.2 graphically illustrates the rationale and functioning of this role.

In Green academic and activist Rupert Read's (2012) 'guardians of the future' idea the 'Guardians' would have the power to veto legislation and even have the authority to initiate new laws and to work on studies about the needs of future

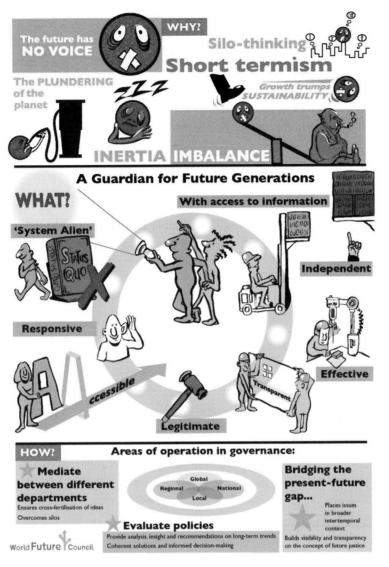

Figure 8.2 World Future Council.
Source: World Future Council, used with permission

generations. This group would be selected in a similar way to those doing jury service – they would be ordinary people selected by lot. This method of random selection (or 'sortition') originated at the start of democracy 2,500 years ago when ordinary Athenian citizens chose their democratic representatives and more recently has been proposed as a method for overcoming policy stalemate about issues such as Brexit in the United Kingdom. Such individuals, once chosen, would be trained and then empowered to represent the interests of future generations. Such groups would embody Edmund Burke's view that society is 'a partnership not only between those who are living, but between those who are living, those who are dead, and those who are to be born' 1899: 359). The challenge here, as Caney (2013) identifies, is that an ombudspersons for future generations would only be as good as the laws that they were charged to uphold: 'If they are no good then these sorts of mechanisms are toothless.'

Responsibilities to future generations can be institutionalised, however. Constitutional references to future generations exist in countries as diverse as France, Norway, Poland, Ecuador, Argentina, Chile, Iran, South Africa, Tunisia, Kenya, Malawi, Australia and Japan. In Hungary, where there is a Commissioner for Future Generations, 'Even if a decision can be interpreted to be true to the letter of the law, the Parliamentary Commissioner can challenge the constitutional "spirit" of the law in question and suggest that it violates, say, the rights of future generations to a healthy environment' suggests Sándor Fülöp, former Parliamentary Commissioner for Future Generations. These interventions have included preventing the building of a large power plant in a UNESCO World Heritage landscape, helping to 'green' the national budget (allowing it to address long-term environmental challenges), assisting in saving the state's public seed research institute, crucial for preserving genetic heritage and the nation's agriculture adaptability, as well as saving green belts around several large cities (World Future Council 2012).

Other countries that have created specific posts or committees to focus on future generations include Wales, Israel, Finland and Scotland. Wales has a Commissioner for Future Generations established under the Well-being of Future Generations Act in 2015, while Israel has a Commission for Future Generations. Possible proposals for reform could include changing voting rights to lower the voting age or giving extra votes to parents depending on the number of children they have; having specific representatives in the legislature for future generations; or changing the tenure of the legislature. Further options include (re)creating Sustainable Development Commissions (such as that which was abolished under the UK's coalition government). Newly elected governments could, after one year, be required to issue a statement on what they were doing about long-term problems, with a select committee to evaluate the statement and hold the government to account. The aim of all these proposals is to tackle the causes of myopia: out of sight, out of mind; temptation and weakness of will and to create a standing accountability mechanism. Any global institutions created to focus on future generations would need to be very ambitious in their aims. 'It would have to be something that plays a role at G7, at the World Bank, at COP negotiations, not something that is free floating. It has got to be something locked into the policy process' Caney (2013) suggests.

Rebel for Life

Given the need to engage not just in institution building and working via the state, and that Greens have always had a reluctant or sceptical attitude towards change through government (as we saw in Chapter 2, often describing themselves as 'movements in power' when holding office), the pursuit of a Green society also implies ongoing strategies for defending the commons; alignments with environmental organisations and direct action movements and those engaged in resistance, such as the Extinction Rebellion movement that started in the United Kingdom from whom the slogan 'Rebel for Life' originates. Vital to realising Green visions of sustainability is giving support to environmental defenders against mining, oil extraction, logging and bioprospecting to safeguard livelihoods in what is sometimes called the 'environmentalism of the poor' (Martinez-Alier 2002). Greens also stand with those opposed to fracking and nuclear power, and in richer parts of world are challenging the 'environmentalism of the rich' (Dauvergne 2016). This is about putting down markers and limits about the unacceptability and unsustainability of business-as-usual. For example, arguments about 'unburnable carbon'[3] (McGlade and Ekins 2015) and the need to keep the 'coal in the hole' and the 'oil in the soil' underpin support for indigenous movements opposing new oil pipelines, such as the Keystone XL and Dakota Access pipelines. As Martinez-Alier (2012: 56) puts it, 'The EJOs [Environmental Justice Organisations] of the South defend local identities and territories, however their growth is explained not only by the strength of identity politics, but also by the conflicts erupting from the social metabolism of the world economy now reaching the last frontiers. The EJOs and their networks are, then, a main force working to make the world economy less unsustainable.'

Beyond reactive resistance politics, Green visions of sustainability are also being pursued through the construction of bottom-up projects such as Transition Towns, community energy, food cooperatives and struggles for re-commoning (Douthwaite 1996; van Gelder 2017), or what Mathie and Gaventa (2015) call 'Citizen-led innovation for a new economy'. These are not just site-specific struggles but draw from, and have implications for, global movements for ecological justice around land, food, water and energy, for example, with whom transnational alliances are often formed (Sikor and Newell 2014). Even local initiatives are increasingly globally connected and networked. The speed with which the Transition Town movement grew over ten years bears testimony to the potential pace of change. From its birth in Totnes Devon in 2006, by May 2010 there were over 400 community initiatives recognised as official Transition towns and by September 2013, there were 1,130 initiatives registered in 43 countries from Chile to New Zealand, to Italy, Canada and the United Kingdom.

From alternative currencies, to repair cafes, food and energy cooperatives, car sharing schemes, carbon rationing clubs, waste reduction schemes to alternative intentional communities, resistance is fertile. Greens are seeking to reclaim spaces for public use, re-commoning and actively reversing processes of privatisation, commodification and individualisation.

(Transitions Network 2017)

Reconciling Equity and Ecology

Squaring ecology and equity will be key to the success of Green visions of sustainability. Globally, many Greens lend their support to the idea of 'contraction and convergence' to tackle climate change, first proposed by the Global Commons Institute as part of a move towards per-capita entitlements. The idea acknowledges both unevenly shared historical responsibility and the need for poorer regions of the world to converge up to an agreed level of per-capita CO_2 consumption, and the corresponding obligation upon richer countries to contract their emissions down to that level (GCI 2018).

Others advocate Greenhouse Development Rights that seek to protect the 'right to development' in a carbon-constrained world, initially designed to hold warming below 2°C. Led by the Stockholm Environment Institute, the NGO Christian Aid and the Heinrich Böll foundation, targets are calculated by the number of people above a development threshold ($20 a day): the 'global consuming class' (GDR 2018). It combines responsibility and capacity indicators where responsibility equals GDP and population and cumulative emissions and capacity is calculated according to income available after meeting basic needs. Similar principles might be applied to other areas where equitable access to remaining ecological space in the global commons needs to be negotiated.

Kate Raworth's 'doughnut' offers another approach to squaring the pursuit of the Sustainable Development Goals with life within planetary boundaries (see Figure 8.3). As Raworth puts it,

The environmental ceiling consists of nine planetary boundaries ... beyond which lie unacceptable environmental degradation and potential tipping points in Earth systems. The twelve dimensions of the social foundation are derived from internationally agreed minimum social standards, as identified by the world's governments in the Sustainable Development Goals in 2015. Between social and planetary boundaries lies an environmentally safe and socially just space in which humanity can thrive.

(2017a)

The idea has quickly gained traction, from the UN General Assembly and the Global Green Growth Forum to the protest movement 'Occupy'. A dramatic shift is implied in the way we approach and measure 'development': (i) from monitoring *monetised* goods and services, to goods and services provided *outside* the monetary economy, too – such as ecosystem services and work performed in the unpaid care economy;

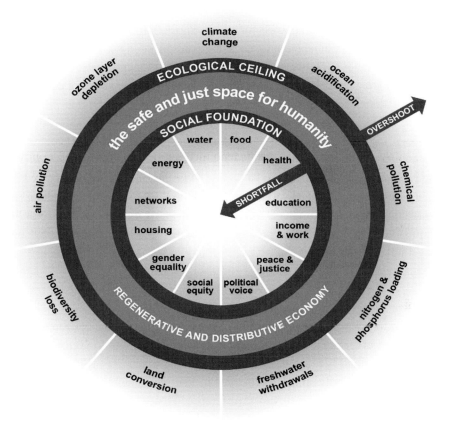

Figure 8.3 The safe and just space for humanity.
Source: Kate Raworth (2017), used with permission

(ii) from a focus on the *flow* of goods and services to studying *changes in the level* of wealth, too – including human, natural, social, physical and financial forms of capital and (iii) From a focus *on aggregate or average* measures in the economy to placing far more importance on the *distribution* of economic benefits across households (Raworth 2017a). Less so than most Greens, Raworth is agnostic about whether living within the 'doughnut' implies de-growth. She asks: 'Would this kind of "doughnut economics" necessarily be post-growth economics? Not by definition: GDP could grow, so long as it remained compatible with staying within social and planetary boundaries. Whether or not this can be achieved in practice is another question: history doesn't bode well, but economic possibilities may go far beyond our economic experience' (2017a).

International Law

If the strategies above aim to address deficits in representation, participation and accountability, other strategies would seek remedy through new international laws, improved enforcement and sanctions and strengthened multilateralism, as we saw in Chapter 6 and in the context of calls for a new 'Planet Politics' (Burke et al. 2016). As well as support for the ratcheting up of protections afforded by Multilateral Environmental Agreements (MEAs), many Greens would be sympathetic to ideas about making 'ecocide' an actionable crime in law, imposing a legal duty of care on states and corporations to prevent climate and ecological ecocide (Higgins 2010). More specifically, ecocide is defined by the group Earth Justice in a draft model law as 'loss or damage to, or destruction of ecosystem(s) of a given territory(ies), such that peaceful enjoyment by the inhabitants has been or will be severely diminished'. Although gaining traction in activist circles more recently, over twenty years ago ecocide crime was at the eleventh hour excluded from the Rome Statute as an international crime and from the UN State Responsibility crimes (Earth Justice 2017).

Many Greens also supported proposals to regulate TNCs through a UN Corporate Accountability treaty as was proposed (but rejected) at the 2002 World Summit on Sustainable Development. These proposals have received renewed attention since 2014 when the United Nations Human Rights Council adopted a resolution (26/9) that established a new Intergovernmental Working Group (IGWG) to develop an international legally binding instrument to regulate transnational corporations and other companies with respect to human rights. In October 2017 the UN started negotiations of a draft text.

Greens have strongly supported treaties in line with planetary boundaries (such as proposals for a Fossil-Fuel Non-Proliferation Treaty (Newell and Simms 2019) and the protection of groups and individuals that Global Witness refers to as 'Earth defenders' (indigenous communities). There might be some sympathy with the 'Planet Politics' agenda discussed above, and with proposals for a World Environment Organisation (Biermann 2001; Whalley and Zissimos 2001) perhaps, but many would have concerns about the effectiveness of such an organisation and whose interests it would serve, depending on the model proposed (Newell 2002). The approach of Greens to the global governance of the environment, as with global governance in general, is that the role and powers of some elements of that system might be curtailed or fundamentally redesigned (as would the case for the WTO, World Bank and IMF), while others expanded, rather like the telescope analogy used by de Geus (1996) and Dobson (1990) in relation to the state. A Green position would therefore move beyond a generic disengagement from international commitments to a more strategic, issue-by-issue, set of engagements with global bodies sympathetic to the pursuit of sustainability.

Eco-socialists would be sceptical about the autonomy and willingness of capitalist states to address the root causes of environmental problems, and would fully expect that international law would be written and interpreted in ways that uphold and reinforce accumulation regimes based on private property and thus a particular form of class power (Cutler 2002). And anarchists would be suspicious of any manoeuvre that granted new powers to institutions beyond and including the state. However, these ideas would find support among more 'realo' factions of Green parties and even some radical environmentalists, including those coming from environmental justice struggles, who have mobilised the law to useful effect in defence of poorer communities and the commons. This is notwithstanding the considerable challenges of navigating and reforming legal systems that are often costly, slow and exclusionary in the forms of knowledge and representation they consider valid for claim-making (Newell 2001b). It speaks to a generic challenge of avoiding the trap identified by Murray Bookchin whereby 'Power is gained at the cost of losing the only power we really have that can change this insane society – our moral integrity, our ideals and our principles' (1980: 82). His fear is of an ecology movement 'institutionalised into a mere appendage of the very system whose structure and methods it professes to oppose' (1980: 83).

Conclusions

Recognition of the unsustainability of the current system and the need for drastic short-term action to reverse the pathway we are on leads Greens to propose a myriad of strategies for realising their vision of sustainability. From grassroots innovation and community-building to new international treaties and innovations in international law, a plethora of, at times contradictory, approaches are suggested, reflecting the diversity of the Green movement. They seek to square an acknowledgement of urgency with concerns to deepen democracy; to see environmental limits respected but in ways that are equitable to current and future generations, while recognising uneven historical responsibilities. They seek to reform the state but are distrustful of relying on the state. Many seek to use the market but also want to rein in the dominance of market society over social life and the environment. Holding all these concerns in play results in the plural pathways Greens are understandably and rightfully pursuing. To return to the point made at the start of this chapter, a separate domain of environmental policy should not, and would not, be required in a society that had sustainability as a core vision and value. Ecologising the economy, security, the state, development and global govern-ance should do away with the need for environment policy as the imperatives of sustainability would already be woven into the very fabric of a Green society.

Notes

1 www.if.org.uk/2012/09/19/after-rio20-pressing-for-an-ombudsperson-for-future-generations/
2 www.futurejustice.org/our-work/ombudspersons-for-future-generations/
3 Carbon Tracker (2013) suggests that as much as 80 per cent of coal, oil and gas reserves are now unburnable from a climate point of view.

Ecologise

Conclusions

Global Politics for the Common Good

'*It Doesn't Have to Be Like This.*' This was the title of a book written in 1990 outlining the contours of Green politics (Icke 1990): a critical starting point for an alternative envisaging of global politics, to establish that what we take as given is not fixed; that what seems permanent, is transitory; that structures, institutions and power relations that hold incumbents in place, eventually fade away;[1] that things have been radically different before and could be so again; that this is not a natural order of things. As human beings with immense wisdom, skills, compassion and ingenuity, we can turn our collective creative abilities to the goal of building a world fit to live in, one that works in harmony with the natural world that sustains it rather than accelerates its destruction.

In the face of increasingly alarming evidence of the narrow and closing window available to get a grip on threats such as climate change, keeping the possibility of change alive and tangible is challenging. Some elements of the Green movement from the Dark Mountain Project (2017), the UK-based Extinction Rebellion group, and advocates of 'deep adaptation' appear to have all but abandoned the project of transformation of this economy and society given the inevitability, as they see it, of near-term social and ecological collapse (Bendell 2018). Instead, they set their sights on the design of post-apocalyptic worlds and 'hope beyond hope' in the 'unknown worlds' ahead of us (The Dark Mountain Project 2017).

While honesty about the severity of our situation is a must, there is a case for generating hope in the present and not just in some indeterminate future existing beyond this civilisation. 'To be truly radical', Raymond Williams wrote, 'is to make hope possible rather than despair convincing' (Williams 1989: 118). Visions, strategies and new narratives (Monbiot 2017; Kemp and Wall 1990; Wall 1990) are required that are not grounded in naive optimism or a failure to face up to the gravity of our predicament, or based on the desire to sell false hope. As intertwined social, economic and ecological crises deepen and accelerate, those who have attractive, appealing and grounded ideas that resonate with deeply held values find that people

210

will turn to them for an alternative. As Milton Friedman (2009: 14), someone I rarely quote approvingly, argued: 'Only a crisis – actual or perceived – produces real change. When that crisis occurs, the actions that are taken depend on the ideas that are lying around. That, I believe, is our basic function: to develop alternatives to existing policies, to keep them alive and available until the politically impossible becomes the politically inevitable.' Or, as someone I am more comfortable quoting, E. F. Schumacher (1974: 30), suggests: 'Perhaps we cannot raise the winds. But each of us can put up the sail, so that when the wind comes we can catch it.'

We are at a key juncture in global politics and global ecological politics. In many ways it is analogous to what Gramsci (1971) described in the *Prison Notebooks* as an 'interregnum' where many 'morbid symptoms' are evident. 'The crisis consists precisely in the fact that the old is dying and the new cannot be born; in this interregnum a great variety of morbid symptoms appear.' Whether we are now in an interregnum or not could be a point for debate, but we appear to be surrounded by many 'morbid symptoms' and forces on all sides of the political spectrum are searching around for alternatives. The challenge we are faced with is how we learn to build and make new worlds in the shell of the old.

Rethinking Global Politics as If the Earth Mattered

In this book I have sought to demonstrate the value, insights and applications that can be derived from developing and applying Green thinking to key areas of global politics. Whereas I have not developed the argument that Green politics per se provides a 'new theory' of the states' system or the international order, I have suggested it provides a rich set of resources for the critique of contemporary global politics, powerful and necessary narratives and imaginaries for how they could be otherwise organised, and nearly fifty years of political practice and experience to draw on in considering strategies for bringing about a more just and sustainable global system.

Earlier in the book we discussed the views of those arguing for a *Planet Politics*. In their case:

We are thus challenging IR to reorganise its very foundations around the complex system of processes and interactions that bind society and nature so terribly together and are producing such world-shaking results, rather than around the anthropocentric drama of human cooperation and conflict. ... the dominant intellectual and institutional architecture of international society fails both to see the Anthropocene as the reality and threat that it is, and fails to address its ecological, moral, and industrial challenges in any way adequately. IR can still explain the world of states and power politics, it can still make and do things, but only by treating the shuddering ecological tectonics of the planet like a shadowy ghost in that human picture, rather than as a brute ontic fact that threatens to overwhelm everything that 'man' has made.

(Burke et al. 2016: 520)

Many of these challenges are well taken, but there is also a case for caution regarding 'nature determinism', ecological base and superstructure arguments where ecology trumps all, or that its commandments can be read and interpreted by experts as offering guidance that should prevail over all other social demands. At times too much deference to ecology as a science that politics can and should replicate is problematic. Pirages (1997: 57) suggests, for example, that: 'Using human populations and their biological and ecological circumstances as a starting point, a theoretical framework can be developed that grounds international relations theory in ecological realities.' What is balanced and by whom and which limits are set and by whom, are not politically neutral questions, nor should they be. This assertion implies the need to move beyond an obsession with causation where 'From an ecological perspective on international relations, interaction with microorganisms is simultaneously a causal factor in influencing state success and behavior' (Pirages 1997: 62). Even in more anarchistic renditions, bio-regionalism, for example, takes as its starting point that 'the natural world should determine the political, economic and social life of communities' (Dobson 1990: 41). I have argued against the problematic resort to 'natural laws' and reading politics from laws of nature, and physics (Ophuls 2011). Such approaches can be very anti-political or post-political or, worse still, lend credence to an authoritarian project organised around deference to managerial elites. Such approaches form the basis of the critiques described earlier of some accounts that have called for 'Earth systems governance' or for 'Planet politics' (Stirling 2014; Chandler et al. 2017).

The claim made here is that Green politics, and the reality of the issues and predicaments it responds to and seeks to address, unsettles conventional understandings and ways of thinking about and 'doing' security, organising the economy, practicing statehood, performing global governance and advancing development and sustainability. It suggests the need for a wider analytical gaze and a guiding principle of 'holism': recognising that the whole is always greater than the sum of the parts, beyond reductionism and abstractionism and promoting 'humility' and by so doing avoiding anthropos hubris.

It is, nevertheless, true that theories that proceed from the premise that the greatest threats to survival are the ones that states pose to one another, or that welfare can only be enhanced by exponential and infinite growth on a finite planet, both blind and mislead us as interpretations and representations of the current conjuncture. Theories of IR, including its more emancipatory and radical traditions that are ecologically blind are not fit for purpose, as they knowingly misrepresent a basic reality – that whatever else changes in terms of warfare, economic development and redistribution, or in the realm of knowledge and identity politics, or even fundamentally altered relations of power, the planet will not be habitable unless dramatic changes take place in the relationship between ecology, economy and society.

The analysis in this book has also suggested the potential, as well as the challenges, of globalising Green political theory. As noted at the outset, although often not described in those terms, many of the central concerns of Green political theory are intrinsically global. Yet explicit attention to foreign policy and global politics is often missing in Green politics thereby exacerbating the systematic neglect of Green perspectives in the study of global politics; something I have sought to partially remedy with this book. This perspective requires us to take up the challenge posed by Barry (1999) to adopt an 'immanent' rather than 'utopian' Green critique. As he suggests, 'Immanent critique here simply means a preference for working from within the existing conceptual or real-world situation towards an alternative understanding or position, as opposed to basing critique on a "view from nowhere"' (1999: 2). For Barry (1999), this means challenging, where necessary, many 'sacred cows' of Green thought around ecocentrism (in favour of ecological virtue as a check on the dominance of anthropocentric reasoning), anti-statism (as 'regulative' rather than 'constitutive'), anti-urbanism, post-materialism, hostility to market economic relations and the bias towards direct democracy.

Towards Global Green Politics

> withdrawal from the world is no solution.
>
> *(Bahro 1986: 104)*

> Radical ecology's role for the twenty-first century is as a condition for
> the possibility of its reformist cousin.
>
> *(Dobson 1990: 213)*

We have seen throughout the book that there is much that unites Greens in terms of their overall notion of the good life: a more communal society organised around the provision of needs rather than the accumulation of profits – where well-being and prosperity is not defined in economic terms only and its pursuit is consistent with living within planetary boundaries; where institutions are charged with the protection and defence of the commons, in which in most visions power is significantly redistributed downwards to strengthen democracy and in which societies promote values of pacifism and equality.

Important differences exist, however, around how to achieve this version of the good life. Writing in the early 1980s, Tim O'Riordan suggested four institutional pathways were open to Greens (i) a new global order, (ii) an authoritarian commune, (iii) centralised authoritarianism or (iv) the anarchist solution (O'Riordan 1981) – a full spectrum from radical decentralisation to world government. For many Greens today, none of these offer a particularly attractive way forward. As I have argued and

[handwritten margin notes:] 4 options — 1. New global order 2.)authoritarian commune 3. centralised authoritarianism 4) Anarchist solution

shown throughout the book, there is no *one* Green politics or Green global political project around which all elements of the Green movement can mobilise. Inevitably, we will see ongoing competition for different versions of Green; ones that demand a break from modernity as we know it to ones that, initially at least, seek to go with the grain as a means of bringing about broader transformations.

Depending on their views of the state, democracy and capitalism, Greens will pursue parallel, and at times competing, pathways to change. Indeed, as we have seen, there have been achievements on all fronts using a variety of strategies from multilateralism to localism, litigation to disobeying the law, campaigning through civil society organisations as well as forming alliances with business and labour movements, and from direct action and civil disobedience through to the more 'mundane' and compromised but vitally important environment of party politics and coalition government. Although it is naive to expect this outcome, it strikes me that this possibility underscores the need to avoid incessant infighting over the 'right road'. Without falling into the 'post-political' trap of suggesting there is no time for further division, debate and conflict, the protracted and inwardly focused discussions about purity of adherence to Green values, traditions and principles that often characterise discussions of theories of change are not helpful. Of course, let us reflect and debate on what works, when and for whom, but an appreciation of diversity in our theories of change, a respect for the choices and dilemmas others confront and the strategies they pursue would suggest a strategy of 'let all flowers bloom' has some merit. As Barry (1999: 99) suggests, a commitment to the possible and not merely the desirable implies a compromise in terms of radicalism, but in the end is all the more radical for positioning itself as a more likely contender and realisable alternative to the status quo.

This is not to deny that choices have to be made, or that the pursuit of one strategy might not undermine, sideline or de-legitimate others. Think of the conflict among Greens over how best to value nature: with ecological economists on one side wanting to price nature to protect it and raise its visibility in the one way capitalists recognise (Costanza et al. 2014; Juniper 2013), with many others wanting to argue that 'Our world is not for sale' and against the financialisation and commodification of nature (McAfee 1999; Lohmann 2006). The latter would argue that approaches based on payments for ecosystem services (PES) actively undermine their arguments for the necessity and requirement for state-led regulation or community ownership. Likewise, those pursuing more 'insider' strategies of research-based advocacy and lobbying, around genetically modified crops, for example, sometimes express frustration that those activists destroying field trial sites undermine public support and sympathy for the argument that genetic engineering is neither safe nor necessary.

Amid grounds for consensus and tolerance for multiple theories and practices of change, some tough choices have to be made, nevertheless. One is around how to engage the state. Without negating the validity of critiques of the state and the obvious need for a very different type of state – less orientated and organised around serving particular class interests, the interests of capital, industrial and military elites – imagining away the state, or assuming somehow that we can do away with the state seems naive at best, at least in the short to near term. This is particularly so in face of the equally pressing need for a state to stand up to powerful incumbent interests and to use all the (peaceful) tools at its disposal to create and enforce laws and regulations, to impose limits in the name of protecting the environment and to use distributive channels to manage equitably fraught and contentious processes of transformation. Articulations of what a Green state might do and look like and the strategies by which it might be brought about, as we saw in Chapter 5, are imperative.

Value shifts are also key. Since elite state actors claim to be responsive to electoral demands (when it suits them), demonstrating demand for more radical change through voting, behavioural change and citizen action, including disobedience, is vital. Although media and social media can communicate, disseminate and enable value shifts, the momentum has to come from within political and civil society. Corporate controlled media, dependent on advertising revenues from private companies are unlikely to be the cheerleaders for a new Green politics of sustainability and survival (Herman and Chomsky 1994). They are ultimately financially dependent on the current system of accumulation that is built upon and accelerates ecological destruction through growth, mass consumerism and waste. Remarkably, through the work of NGOs, citizen mobilisation, alternative and social media and growing awareness about the non-viability of global politics as usual, environmental values have (in differing ways and to differing degrees) nevertheless taken hold.

I have sought to engage with and build upon eco-centric and anarchistic tendencies in Green politics while recognising their limits as guides to action and effective strategy right now when we require all the resources, and need to mobilise all the positive dimensions, of state power towards the aim of building a sustainable society. And we need to build allies among non-Greens and broader publics for whom narrow or purist versions of eco-centrism are alien and work as a barrier to developing new coalitions around a vision of both a socially and environmentally sustainable world. Intention and motivation – why people join us – are less important than that they do so. If anthropocentric motivations are the guide to action, so be it if the end is a more sustainable society, in which it is more likely that eco-centric values and ethics can take hold. As Hayward (1994: 200) puts it: 'If ecological politics has to be radical to be ecological (versus environmentalism), it also has to be realistic (versus ecologism). The challenge for a green political theory is to avoid the fallacies of ecologism without lapsing back into the complacencies which are attendant on a reformist environmentalism.' In this sense, I agree wholeheartedly with Barry that ecological thought does not have 'a monopoly on defining the scope, principles or values of green politics' (1999: 5). And while a discussion of limits, boundaries and thresholds will inevitably underpin any Green political project, as Paehlke (1989: 55) suggests 'The Malthusian perspective is neither necessary nor helpful in engendering positive change'.

There is also a need to appreciate and be realistic about the extent, depth, persistence and embedded nature of incumbent power. As we saw in Chapter 5, the 'deep state' runs very deeply. Powerful state and corporate elites that have enriched themselves at the expense of the planet and the majority of the world's citizens are not about to give up their position of privilege and opulence without a fight. Incumbent resistance will be fierce and entrenched. The use of violence to quell protests by environmental defenders is a daily occurrence (Global Witness 2017). Unsustainable development is profitable and desirable for the world's most powerful actors, including large swathes of the population for whom a reorientation of the economy away from a narrow pursuit of growth at all costs would bring concerns about welfare, economic security and employment. Opposition to the mantra that growth is good and a prerequisite for the pursuit, let alone achievement, of any other social goal, means challenging a widely held given, an ideology and truism that runs deep and is continually reinforced in political and media discourse and by the relentless waves of advertising mass consumerism.

New narratives and imaginaries are urgently required that articulate in a variety of ways what alternatives might look like, that highlight the power we have to change the world, as we have done before and that give lie to the idea that there is no alternative. Strategies to unseat incumbents need to operate in the public, political, institutional, social and cultural realms since incumbents derive their power through control of public debate and the political terrain in these spaces. The full range of strategies reviewed in each of the chapters of this book will, therefore, be required to meet this challenge. There is no one strategy for creating a Greener world.

Concrete Utopias[2]

For the Common Good

> The world has enough resources for everyone's needs but not their greed.
>
> (Gandhi)

A key challenge for Greens is to nurture the seeds of an alternative Green society in the soil of society as it exists today. Whether it is food and energy cooperatives, the sharing of transport or repair workshops, solidarity economies and experiments in communal living, 'nowtopians' are not waiting for others to deliver structural change, nor willing to assume it would take a form consistent with their Green values. They are doing it for themselves, building concrete utopias in the present. Carlsson (2015: 182) suggests, 'When people take their time and technological know-how out of the market and decide for themselves how to dedicate their efforts, they are short-circuiting the logic of the market society that depends on incessant growth'. These are the 'revolutions where you live' that van Gelder (2017) describes.

One goal and priority around which most Greens, and many other fellow travellers could agree, is the need for 'recommoning'. This objective is true both as a long-term goal in terms of changing ownership and distribution of land and resources and reclaiming the land but also in an immediate sense in terms of resisting the further privatisation and acquisition of land through land grabs and an array of legal and illegal means. Resistance and direct action have a role to play here, as do changes to constitutions such as occurred in Uruguay to make access to water a human right. For example, between 2000 and 2015, there were 235 cases of water 'remunicipalisation' – the process by which a city, region or national government terminates or refuses to renew water concessions, leases or management contracts with private companies, in order to bring water back under public control. As a result of this rapidly spreading trend of re-municipalisation, 100 million people across 37 countries now benefit from water as a public good rather than as a private commodity (RTA 2019). Campaigns to redistribute land, meanwhile, have been led by the movement for the landless in Brazil (MST) and internationally by movements like Via Campesina, while 'back to the land' movements also often embody Greens values (Jacob 1997). As Green economist Molly Scott Cato (2014) recognises: 'The land is ours. If the law respected this, the land would be better cared for and used to provide for our needs rather than generate profits for the few.'

Equitable Transitions

If they are to be socially as well as ecologically sustainable, transitions and transformations to a Green economy and society will have to be just, and seen to be so (Scoones et al. 2015; Newell and Mulvaney 2013; Swilling and Annecke 2012; Evans 2010). This realisation requires open and honest public dialogues about different pathways, development models and trajectories and their associated and unevenly dispersed costs and benefits. There will be winners and losers and difficult and contested decisions to be made in the process of restructuring the economy and bringing about a different state. There is both a shorter- and longer-term politics of transition here.

The first involves the process of handling the de-commissioning and closure of industries and mines, for example, raising issues of compensation and retraining. For instance, dampening the impacts of fossil-fuel decline on workers and communities can be enacted by using a mix of safety nets, vouchers and cash transfers. It implies developing and negotiating explicit social contracts for sustainability transitions with losers as well as winners, including compensation and severance packages, as has occurred in Poland; or (re)training assistance, which is currently a contested terrain in China in the face of closures of coal plants (Whitley and van der Burg 2015). Also as a means of enacting a 'just transition', some governments have sought to impose social obligations on investors through, for example, Black Economic Empowerment criteria in South Africa's Renewable Energy Independent Power Producer Procurement Programme (Baker et al. 2014), or by developing regional economic development programmes (as has been done in Germany) to manage transitions away from fossil fuels in more equitable ways (Pegels and Lütkenhorst 2014). Both as a buffer against disruptive change, as a redistributor of wealth and resources and as an accelerator of the technologies, infrastructures, finance and institutions required to deliver a Greener economy, the state will have a vital role to play.

The long-term politics of transition are about rewiring the economy to ensure that it is both Green and fair.

> Given ... the need to end economic growth, it follows automatically that issues of equity will become of greater importance: if the pie cannot grow larger than it is more important to ensure that everybody has a fair share. Hence a green economy must have a much greater policy emphasis on equality, including higher levels of redistribution, broadening of asset ownership, and policies to reduce wage differentials.
>
> *(Cato n.d.)*

As we saw in Chapter 7, equitable transitions also have a global dimension and Greens are often in favour of proposals such as 'contraction and convergence' or a Development Rights Framework that seeks to establish fair entitlements to use the commons or atmospheric space based on a mixture of need, historical responsibility and capacity.

In many ways, Greens need to broaden the just transition debate away from a focus merely on managing decline to actually addressing the causes of social inequality. Barry (2008: 10) suggests: 'the green path to tackling inequality is premised on redistribution (of existing social wealth) without the commitment to unsustainable and undifferentiated economic growth, alongside a radical shift from money and commodity-based measurements of welfare to a focus on well-being, quality of life and above all else free time'.

Subsidiarity and Renewed Democracy

As part of the project of 'taking back control', (a slogan that was toxified in the Brexit discussions in the United Kingdom), Green politics needs to renew democracy at all levels, a policy critical to including and mobilising broader publics and those with a stake in a Green future as well as diffusing and diluting the concentration of power in actors who have little (short-term) interest in building a sustainable society. Deepening democracy may be accomplished through electoral reform, as well as more meaningful spaces for citizen engagement (such as participatory budgeting, use of referendums), controls on the concentration of media ownership and decentralisation of decision-making. Again this raises dilemmas for Greens when regions demand autonomy and populist politics take hold (as has happened in a referendum in Spain, for example) with often destabilising and violent consequences in the short term. There are dangers too that the decentralisation of power reinforces local elite control and is less subject to democratic scrutiny (Blair 2000).

Globally, democratic renewal and subsidiarity would imply greater citizen input and oversight of the mandates and activities of global institutions. It would also imply strengthening the downward accountability of global, regional and national institutions. The model discussed in Chapter 6 of the committee of the regions perhaps offers one model. There is scope here too, however, for fragmentation and lack of clarity regarding the lines of authority in a neo-medieval system that might result. As discussed in Chapter 5, the tension lies in the simultaneous need, demand and expectation that the state will play proactive roles on behalf of society in addressing incumbent power and laying down the basis for a transition to a Greener society.

Economic democracy, meanwhile, means reclaiming democratic control over institutions, production processes, finance and technology so that they can be repurposed for the common good (Cumbers 2012), possibly encompassing workplace representation of workers on boards of companies, publicly accountable Green investment banks, participatory needs assessments for technology and local, regional and national recovery plans along the lines of the Green New Deal now being advocated for in the United States and the United Kingdom. At the global level, as discussed in Chapter 6, this plan would imply root and branch reform of global institutions in terms of their mandates, ideology and operating principles. The rules that would rule would be those that secure sustainability, peace and social justice – and not conventional economic development at any cost.

Managing ecological transformations in a globalised capitalist economy raises the question of sequencing: who moves first and how can they avoid being isolated politically, or punished economically, for pursuing a Greener path at odds with prevailing capitalist ideology? As far as possible, simultaneous, coordinated, multi-level change across levels of governance is more desirable to avoid destructive competitive logics. Ecologism in one country would be difficult to sustain over time and of course in global terms would be wholly insufficient. That said, early movers who are able to showcase the multiple benefits of a Green society might well inspire others to adopt similar models.

New Alliances

Building a Green society cannot be done by the environmental movement alone. Attempts to recommon the economy and politics will need broad-based support and alliances with those disenfranchised and disillusioned with 'grey' politics, as well as those who might gain from working and living in a sustainable society. These are the 'coalitions of the willing and the winning', required to mount effective challenges to incumbent power. This brings with it a range of strategic dilemmas and complex coalition-building with former adversaries, groups with whom Greens have found themselves in conflict and opposition in the past, including trade unions and potentially some elements of the private sector.

Greens are sometimes dismissed by those on the left as being 'small capitalists' (Pepper 1995). Their objections are essentially about scale, rather than the commodification of labour per se (Martell 1994; Weston 1986) and the preference often for exchange through the market rather than centralised state control (Daly and Cobb 1989; Daly 1996). Greens are often critical of what they perceive to be the outdated ways of doing and thinking about politics on the left: trapped in old models of taking the state based on the October 1917 (Russian revolution) moment in which a vanguard elite determines the appropriate moment to storm the barricades. Likewise, they are critical of the elitism and sexism in the leadership of trade unions as well as in private business and an a priori and problematic from the point of view of Greens, commitment to industrialism. For example, in relation to trade unions in debates about just transitions, relations have not always been harmonious amid differences of opinion about their protest cultures, class politics and who they represent (whether mass member organisations or 'non-governmental individuals') (Obach 2004; Newell 2007; Icaza et al. 2010).

In relation to indigenous groups and 'environmental defenders' as Global Witness refers to them, there have been alliances around key frontiers of commodification, such as forest carbon projects for example (Leach and Scoones 2015), or frontiers of extraction such as destructive mining and oil (Collinson

1996; Evans et al. 2002) and infrastructural projects such as pipelines and dams (McCully 1996). There have also been regional-wide attempts to link across labour, indigenous and environmental movements, such as the Hemispheric Social Alliance in the Americas, to resist neo-liberal trade agreements and articulate 'People's regional agreements' based on solidarity and exchange, protection of workers' rights, defence of indigenous rights and the environment (Newell 2007). These attempts clearly fall short of cross-movement articulation of a Green alternative for global politics, but Greens would find themselves in agreement with much of the content of these initiatives and alternatives. In the case of Ecuador's embrace of *Buen Vivir* and writing the rights of mother nature into the constitution, there may be grounds for strategic links between Green parties and governments in other parts of the world. Yet such governments might be fickle and unpredictable allies at best. Evo Morales, for example, looks set to approve a series of hydroelectric dams in Bolivia to export energy to the Andean region at the expense of local communities who would be displaced and in spite of the vast ecological damage that would undoubtedly be incurred, while Ecuador has recently committed to opening up ecologically sensitive reserves to further oil exploration.

One interesting and significant initiative in the spirit of forging cross-movement coalitions was the construction of a 'Real World Coalition' in the United Kingdom, a cross-sector, civil-society-led[3] umbrella for the promotion of a 'joined-up' approach to sustainable development, to try, at minimum, to push the issue higher up the electoral and policy agenda. It proposed 'a radical agenda of reform in national and international politics and economic policy', 'a coherent strategy for reversing the current trends and regaining quality of life and a shared sense of purpose to our lives and societies'. Its point of departure is founded on a critique with which most Greens would have some empathy:

For more and more people, politics is increasingly divorced from the problems it should be addressing and solving. The evidence is all around us in food safety and other health scares, traffic congestion and decaying infrastructure, rural decline and urban squalor, natural disasters, loss of species and habitats and the threat of climate change to the very systems that support life itself.

(TRWC 2001: backcover)

Remaking the Future

Green global politics and the articulation of a vision for a Green society constitutes a break with liberal and state-based capitalism.

Globalising Green politics is about reclaiming, not only resources but our lives and communities and our planet: working less, sharing more and living with less but improving the quality of our lives as more equal societies are healthier, less stressful and have lower crime rates (Wilkinson and Pickett 2009). It is about revitalising communities drained by depravation and exploitation. Farmers markets, repair workshops, Local Exchange Trading Schemes (LETS) and transition towns all help to do this. It is a project of social, economic and community renewal. These elements have to be part of a positive and progressive narrative, and not merely grounded in the politics of sacrifice and austerity. Although sacrifice is seen as negative, we make sacrifices all the time for children, family, colleagues and tend to think of these as helping and caring – gaining something in the process rather than giving up and losing something (Maniates and Meyer 2010).

In part, we remake the future by being inspired by the past and the rapid and progressive transformations that have taken place previously, often in the face of adverse economic and social conditions (Simms and Newell 2017; Sovacool 2016). This is about calling out inaction with reference to evidence of positive practice elsewhere, what we in the Rapid Transition Alliance call 'evidence-based hope' (RTA 2019). The shift towards global Green politics implies a move beyond the politics of transition as a realignment of technologies, financial flows and institutions from one way of meeting capitalist growth imperatives to another, towards a politics of ecological transformation. It implies different means, goals and boundaries. It is a move beyond techno-fixes, incremental realignments and the project of growth as being non-negotiable. Ecological virtues and ethics serve as the guiding framework for such a shift but cannot be reducible only to justice for nature. Dilemmas, priorities and sacrifices have to be made with social justice and intra- and inter-generational justice in mind.

Unsettling incumbency and undoing unsustainability requires us to challenge each of the material, institutional and discursive, as well as ideological, pillars that together sustain the hegemony of the current system. Institutions and dominant ideas are built on and reflect and serve to secure the prevailing material conditions and needs of a growing capitalist economy (Cox 1987). They are sites of struggle in and of themselves but require shifts in social forces and control over production if they are to achieve transformational ends through change in the material base and the superstructures to which it gives rise. This is not a linear view of transformation and how it might be achieved. It does not obviate the short-term need to navigate and engage to secure the reform of actually existing capitalism, but it does underscore the need to change the material base of society.

Final Thoughts

Although environmental values and thinking have taken hold in many parts of global society over the last thirty years, the project of ecological modernisation has reached its limits. Amid the passing of key planetary thresholds and continuing evidence of environmental decline and gaping global social inequalities, bolder, more ambitious and transformative politics are required. I have argued here that Green politics fills that void with a set of critiques of the current conduct of global politics, radical but achievable normative visions, and critical thinking about strategies for realising those visions grounded in years of struggle. Campaigning is required through formal and informal political arenas of party politics, social movement mobilisation, direct action and building alternatives.

The time for Green politics has come – to go beyond 'business-as-usual environmentalism' or the 'environmentalism of the rich' (Dauvergne 2016) and the platitudes of sustainable development and Green growth. It's time to offer a coherent alternative that seeks to address the causes of our planetary predicament, and not just some of its most visible manifestations. Overlooked or deliberately neglected by mainstream media, academia and civil society, as well as corporate and state elites, Green politics offers to transcend the traditional politics of Left and Right, North and South to offer a platform and vision for social and ecological justice, including justice for nature.

First and foremost, we need an economy that seeks to expand the welfare and well-being of the greatest number of people within the limits imposed by planetary boundaries. This does not imply un-problematically reading politics and priorities off ecological thresholds; still less that action plans that follow from the need to align our economy with our ecology are imposed by an epistemic elite with the full backing of the state. Living within limits, however these are arrived at, necessarily means both contraction of rates of production and consumption in some parts of the world, and an expansion of them elsewhere to ensure that the SDGs are achieved equitably. Overconsumption and extreme inequality are intimately linked and need to be addressed together. How this situation will be addressed and by whom will have to be negotiated across sites of governance, as well as deriving from the spontaneous actions and momentum of transition movements and social movements mobilising for transformation. This objective means challenging the growth fetish and revealing clearly its social and environmental unsustainability. Articulating and fighting for viable alternatives, whether prosperity without growth, *buen vivir* or degrowth, is vital. The merits of producing and consuming locally, building smaller-scale and more resilient economies and building social capital in an uncertain and turbulent world need to be brought to the fore. Working less, sharing more, travelling less; an economy of care and solidarity rather than competition and breakneck growth will be at the heart of this.

We need a redefinition of growth, progress and with it, development, not as something that moves through stages, is measured through economic indicators and aspires only to swell GDP. It is about sustainable progress in well-being and welfare, human and non-human. The policy autonomy and developmental space of poorer countries needs to be expanded, defended and protected, meaning real bottom-up ownership of the development process, where it is clear that the benefits of any external interventions remain with local beneficiaries rather than extractivism under another guise. Some reversal of orthodox development thinking to validate the careful and selective use of the new protectionism will be needed: measures to support strategically important sectors, technologies and economies and to protect them from non-competitive behaviour by transnational businesses and global conglomerates. Rather than kicking away the ladder, we need to allow countries to build their own ladders out of their own materials in their own ways.

Greens need to adopt a more nuanced view of the state and a strategic engagement with it, consistent with the telescopic view of the state described in Chapter 5. There is a critical need for expanded regulatory functions to manage and lead transitions: to redirect finance, to redistribute, to stand up to incumbents and represent the Green state in global forums. This is not to be naive about the nature of the state, especially in a globalising capitalist economy, and the need for fundamental reform that involves severing the links that bind the military-industrial complex; democratisation and devolution; and introducing new constitutions that include stronger ecological components. Some of these proposals will imply a shrinking of some state functions, but ignoring or wishing away the state risks throwing the baby out with the bathwater. With the scale and severity and urgency of the problems we face, now is not the time, even if we had the choice, to abandon the state. Reigning in state power in some areas is vital, placing clearer moral and normative boundaries around its legitimate conduct, and dismantling and shrinking some functions. Even if their critiques of modern bureaucratic administrative states have enormous value, anarchistic visions of doing away with the state altogether seem misplaced, fanciful and even dangerous in the absence of other bodies with the capacity and resources to oversee, finance and direct the transformations so urgently now required.

We need fundamental reform of global governance: a system fit for purpose that adequately represents all nations and has planetary well-being as its overarching aim. All other initiatives, institutions and treaties will be subsumed within this overall broad aim. The rules that rule from now on will need to be those which protect life on the planet and not capitalism-as-usual. We need to secure a 'Green peace': treaties that accelerate the move towards global disarmament and a sustainable planet; arms reduction treaties and bans; agreements to leave fossil fuels in the ground and to protect biodiversity and to deindustrialise the global agrifood system. Cooperation on security, health, economy, development and the environment through global and regional institutions is vital, affirming again the importance of strong Green states.

We need to recognise that security starts at home – literally. By challenging everyday violence from the home outwards, value shifts and state power need to be used to guarantee the rights and protection of all individuals. Societies need to address violence as well as the causes of violence in culture, economic insecurity, alienation, dispossession, discrimination and the like. Controls on the arms trade, reductions in military expenditure and enhanced peaceful global cooperation are essential.

Theoretically, the study of global politics can no longer afford to take as its basic premise – a world of abundant resources, exploitable through infinite growth by an international system of sovereign, largely capitalist, states that have set us on a course to global self-destruction. Ecological dimensions of discussions about security, economy, development, sustainability and global governance have to be present, their implications taken seriously and spelled out for scholarly endeavour and practical global politics. We cannot afford for this blind spot to continue in IR, nor in any discipline that seeks in some way to improve the human and planetary condition. Our theories and research will lack plausibility in fundamental ways unless this myopia is addressed. We would also be doing a grave disservice to future generations of students if they go into the world without being cognisant of perhaps the greatest of all challenges facing the world.

This is of course a bold, ambitious and, some would say, unrealistic set of ideas and demands and there are obviously tensions among them. The section in each of the preceding chapters on strategies has laid out some of the ways in which progress towards them might be achieved in the short and near term. And, it goes without saying, they will require compromises, negotiation and deal brokering to come to fruition. There will be no imposition of a Green vision, nor should there be. To do so would go against the thrust of a lot of Green principles. Yet some of the ideas, I hope, give a flavour of the bold normative agenda that Green politics affords world politics and the type of imagination and ethical vision that the world is sorely lacking at the moment. As John Barry (2008) claims: 'Just as it is commonplace to declare that the 21st century will be China's century, equally the politics of the 21st century are and will be the politics of sustainability.' The question for all of us is whose politics and on whose terms?

Notes

1 Mahatma Gandhi, frequently cited by Green scholars and activists, wrote in his book *The Story of My Experiments with Truth*: 'Remember that all through history, there have been tyrants and murderers, and for a time, they seem invincible. But in the end, they always fall. Always.'
2 For further discussion of the origins of this term in ecological thought, see Hayward (1994: 210).

3 The groups that were members of the coalition included the following: Bassac, Black Environment
   Network, Campaign Against Arms Trade, Charter88, Christian Aid, Church Action on Poverty,
   Community Action Network, Electoral Reform Society, Forum for the Future, Friends of the
   Earth, IIED, The Iona Community, Medact, National Peace Council, Oxfam, Pesticide Action
   Network UK, Population Concern, Quaker Peace and Social Witness, Save the Children, Town
   and Country Planning Association, Transport 2000, UK Public Health Association, United Nations
   Association, The Wildlife Trusts, World Development Movement, WWF-UK.

References

Abbey, E. (1990) *The Monkey Wrench Gang*, Utah: Dream Garden Press.

Acción Ecológica (1999) 'No More Plunder, They Owe Us the Ecological Debt!', *Bulletin of Acción Ecológica* 78 (October), Acción Ecológica: Quito, Ecuador.

Adams, W. (1995) 'Green Development Theory? Environmentalism and Sustainable Development', in Crush, J. (ed.), *The Power of Development*, London: Routledge, 87–100.

Agathangelou, A. M. (2016) 'Bruno Latour and Ecology Politics: Poetics of Failure and Denial in IR', *Millennium: Journal of International Studies* 44, 3: 321–47.

Agyeman, J., Bullard, R. D. and Evans, B. (eds.) (2003) *Just Sustainabilities: Development in an Unequal World*, Cambridge, MA: MIT Press.

Altvater, E. (2006) 'The Social and Natural Environment of Fossil Capitalism', in Panitch, L. and Leys, C. (eds.) *Coming to Terms with Nature: Socialist Register 2007*, London: Merlin Press, 37–60.

Amin, A. (2009) *The Social Economy: International Perspectives on Economic Solidarity*, London: Zed Books.

Amin, S. (1976) *Unequal Development: An Essay on the Social Formations of Peripheral Capitalism*, New York: Monthly Review Press.

Anderson, K. (2015) 'Duality in Climate Science', *Nature Geoscience* 8: 898–900.

Anderson, K. and Peters, G. (2016) 'The Trouble with Negative Emissions', *Science* 354, 6309: 182–3.

Andersson, J. O. (2009) 'Basic Income from an Ecological Perspective', *Basic Income Studies* 4, 2: 1–8.

Aron, R. (1966) *Peace and War: A Theory of International Relations*, New York: Doubleday.

Asafu-Adjaye, J., Blomqvist, L., Brand, S., Brook, B. and Defries, R. (2015) *An Ecomodernist Manifesto*, www.ecomodernism.org/manifesto-english/.

Asara, V., Otero, I., Demaria, F. and Corbera, E. (2015) 'Socially Sustainable Degrowth as a Social–Ecological Transformation: Re-politicizing Sustainability', *Sustainability Science*, 10, 3: 375–84.

Atack I. (2001) 'From Pacifism to War Resistance', *Peace and Change* 26, 2: 177–86.

Atack, I. (2017) 'Pacifism and Perpetual Peace', *Critical Studies on Security*, 6, 2: 207–20.

Avant, D., Finnemore, M. and Sell, S. K. (eds.) (2010) *Who Governs the Globe?*, Cambridge: Cambridge University Press.

Baber, W. and Bartlett, R. (2005) *Deliberative Environmental Politics*, Cambridge, MA: MIT Press.

Bachram, H. (2004) 'Climate Fraud and Carbon Colonialism: The New Trade in Greenhouse Gases', *Capitalism, Nature, Socialism* 15, 4: 1–16.

Bäckstrand, K. and Kronsell, A. (eds.) (2015) *Rethinking the Green State. Environmental Governance towards Climate and Sustainability Transitions*, London and New York: Earthscan from Routledge.

Baer, H. (2018) *Democratic Ecosocialism as a Real Utopia: Transitioning to an Alternative World-System*, New York: Berghahn Books.

Bahro, R. (1986) *Building the Green Movement*, London: GMP Publishers.

Bahro, R. (1994) *Avoiding Social and Ecological Disaster: The Politics of World Transformation*, Bath: Gateway Books.

Bailey, I., Gouldson, A. and Newell, A. P. (2011) 'Ecological Modernisation and the Governance of Carbon: A Critical Analysis', *Antipode* 43, 3: 682–703.

Baker, L., Newell, P. and Phillips, J. (2014) 'The Political Economy of Energy Transitions: The Case of South Africa', *New Political Economy* 19, 6: 791–818.

Bakker, K. (2010) *Privatising Water: Governance Failure and the World's Urban Water Crisis*, Ithaca, NY: Cornell University Press.

Balanyá, B., Doherty, A., Hoedeman, O., Ma'anit, A. and Wesselius, E. (2000) *Europe Inc: Regional and Global Restructuring and the Rise of Corporate Power*, London: Pluto Press.

Balanyá, B., Bolwer-Ailloud, M. and Gelebart, K. (eds.) (2005) *Reclaiming Public Water: Achievements, Struggles and Visions from around the World*, Amsterdam: Transnational Institute and Corporate European Observatory.

Barbier, E. and Markandya, A. (2012) *A New Blueprint for a Green Economy*, London: Routledge.

Barca, S. (2017) 'The Labor(s) of Degrowth', *Capitalism Nature Socialism*, doi: 10.1080/10455752.2017.1373300.

Barnett, J. (2001) *The Meaning of Environmental Security: Ecological Politics and Policy in the New Security Era*, London: Zed Books.

Barry, J. (1994) 'The Limits of the Shallow and the Deep: Green Politics, Philosophy and Praxis', *Environmental Politics*, 3, 3: 369–94.

Barry, J. (1999) *Rethinking Green Politics*, London: Sage Publications.

Barry, J. (2008) 'Towards a Green Republicanism: Constitutionalism, Political Economy, and the Green State', *The Good Society: A PEGS Journal* 17, 2: 1–12.

Barry, J. (2012) *The Politics of Actually Existing Unsustainability: Human Flourishing in a Climate Changed, Carbon Constrained World*, Oxford: Oxford University Press.

Barry, J. (2016) 'Citizenship and (Un)Sustainability: A Green Republican Perspective', in Gardiner, S. M. and Thompson, A. (eds.), *The Oxford Handbook of Environmental Ethics*, New York: Oxford University Press.

Barry, J. (2018) 'A Genealogy of Economic Growth as Ideology and Cold War Core State Imperative', *New Political Economy*, doi: 10.1080/13563467.2018.1526268.

Barry, J. and Eckersley, R. (eds.) (2005) *The State and the Global Ecological Crisis*, Cambridge, MA: MIT Press.

Bartley, J. and Berry, S. (2018) 'Our Green Party Will Be Bold and Brave in Both Ideas and Actions', *The Guardian* www.theguardian.com/commentisfree/2018/sep/05/green-party-bold-brave-ideas-britain?CMP=share_btn_link.

Baxter, B. (1999) *Ecologism: An Introduction*, Edinburgh: Edinburgh University Press.

BBC News (2015) 'Jeremy Corbyn Row After "I'd Not Fire Nuclear Weapons" Comment' www.bbc.co.uk/news/uk-politics-34399565.

Beck, U. (1999) *World Risk Society*, Cambridge: Polity.

Begon, M., Townsend, C. R. and Harper, J. (2006) *Ecology*, Oxford: Blackwell.

Bell, D. (1973) *The Coming of Post-Industrial Society*, San Francisco: Basic Books.

Bell, K. (2016) 'Green Economy or Living Well? Assessing Divergent Paradigms for Equitable Eco-Social Transition in South Korea and Bolivia', *Journal of Political Ecology* 23: 71–92.

Bellamy Foster, J., Clark, B. and York, R. (2010) *The Ecological Rift: Capitalism's War on the Earth*, New York: Monthly Review Press.

Bendell, J. (2018) 'Deep Adaptation: A Map for Navigating Climate Tragedy' *IFLAS Occasional Paper* 2, www.iflas.info.

Bernazzoli, R. M. and Flint, C. (2010) 'Embodying the Garrison State? Everyday Geographies of Militarization in American Society', *Political Geography* 29, 3: 157–66.

Bernstein, S. (2001) *The Compromise of Liberal Environmentalism*, New York: Columbia University Press.

Bieler, A. (2000) *Globalisation and Enlargement of the European Union: Austrian and Swedish Social Forces in the Struggle over Membership*, London/New York: Routledge.

Biermann, F. (2001) 'The Emerging Debate on the Need for a World Environment Organisation: A Commentary', *Global Environmental Politics* 1, 1: 45–56.

Biermann, F. (2014) *Earth Systems Governance: World Politics in the Anthropocene*, Cambridge, MA: MIT Press.

Bishop, M. and Green, M. (2009) *Philanthrocapitalism: How Giving Can Save the World*, London: Bloomsbury.

Blaikie, P. (1985) *The Political Economy of Soil Erosion in Developing Countries*, London: Longman.

Blair, H. (2000) 'Participation and Accountability at the Periphery: Democratic Local Governance in Six Countries', *World Development* 28, 1: 21–39.

Blewitt, J. and Cunningham, R. (2014) *The Post-Growth Project*, London: GreenHouse Publishing.

Bollier, D. (2016) 'Mary Mellor's "Debt or Democracy": Why Not Quantitative Easing for People?' 31 March 2016, www.bollier.org/blog/mary-mellor's-"debt-or-democracy"-why-not-quantitative-easing-people.

Bomberg, E. (1998) *Green Parties and Politics in the European Union*, London: Routledge.

Bookchin, M. (1971) *Post-Scarcity Anarchism*, Berkeley: Ramparts.

Bookchin, M. (1980) *Toward an Ecological Society*, Montreal: Black Rose Books.

Bookchin, M. (1982) *The Ecology of Freedom: The Emergence and Dissolution of Hierarchy*, Palo Alto: Cheshire Books.

Bookchin, M. (1987) *The Rise of Urbanization and the Decline of Citizenship*, San Francisco: Sierra Club Books.

Bookchin, M. (1989) *Remaking Society: Pathways to a Green Future*, Montreal: Black Rose Books.

Bookchin, M. (1992) *Urbanization without Cities: The Rise and Decline of Citizenship*, Montreal: Black Rose Press.

Bookchin, M. (1994) *Which Way for the Ecology Movement?, Essays by Murray Bookchin*, Edinburgh: AK Press.

Booth, K. (1991) 'Security and Emancipation', *Review of International Studies* 17, 4: 313–26.

Borger, J. (2014) 'World Living in an Era of Unprecedented Level of Crises', *The Guardian* 21 September www.theguardian.com/world/2014/sep/21/ban-ki-moon-world-living-era-undprecedented-level-crises.

Boyle, D. and Simms, A. (2009) *The New Economics: A Bigger Picture*, Abingdon: Earthscan.

Brand, U. (2012) *Beautiful Green World: On the Myths of a Green Economy*, Berlin: Rosa Luxemburg Foundation.

Brand, U. and Wissen, M. (2013) 'Crisis and Continuity of Capitalist Society-Nature Relationships: The Imperial Mode of Living and the Limits to Environmental Governance', *Review of International Political Economy* 4: 687–711.

Brenton, T. (1994) *The Greening of Machiavelli*, London: RIIA/Earthscan.

Bretherton, C. (1998) 'Global Environmental Politics: Putting Gender on the Agenda? *Review of International Studies* 24, 1: 85–100.

Broad, R. and Cavanagh, J. (2009) *Development Redefined: How the Market Met Its Match*, Boulder: Paradigm Publishers.

Brock, A., Huff, A., Verweijen, J., Selby, J., Ockwell, D. and Newell, P. (2018) 'Fracking Democracy, Criminalising Dissent', *The Ecologist* https://theecologist.org/2018/oct/18/fracking-democracy-criminalising-dissent.

Brodie, B. (1946) 'War in the Atomic Age', in B. Brodie (ed.), *The Absolute Weapon: Atomic Power and World Order*, New York: Harcourt and Brace.

Brown, K. (2016) *Resilience, Development and Global Change*, Abingdon: Routledge.

Bull, H. (1977) *The Anarchical Society*, London: Macmillan.

Bull, H. (1979) 'The State's Positive Role in World Affairs', *Daedalus* 108: 111–23.

Bullard, R. D. (2005) *The Quest for Environmental Justice: Human Rights and the Politics of Pollution*, Berkeley, CA: University of California Press.

Burchell, J. (2002) *The Evolution of Green Politics: Development and Change within European Green Parties*, London: Earthscan.

Burke, A., Fishel, S., Mitchell, A., Dalby, S. and Levine, D. (2016) 'Planet Politics: A Manifesto from the End of IR', *Millennium: Journal of International Studies* 44, 3: 499–523.

Burke, E. (1899) '"Reflections on the Revolution in France," 1790', *The Works of the Right Honorable Edmund Burke*, vol. 3, Toronto: F. and C. Rivington.

Büscher, B. and Fletcher, R. (2015) 'Accumulation by Conservation', *New Political Economy* 20: 273–98.

Buxton, N. and Hayes, B. (2016) *The Secure and the Dispossessed: How the Military and Corporations Are Shaping a Climate-Changed, World*, London: Pluto Press.

Buzan, B. (1983) *Peoples, States and Fear*, London: Wheatsheaf.

Caldecott, B., Sartor, O. and Spencer, T. (2017) *Lessons from Previous 'Coal Transitions': High-level Summary for Decision-Makers*, IDDRI and Climate Strategies. www.iddri.org/en/publications-and-events/report/lessons-previous-coal-transitions.

Campbell, K. (ed.) (2008) *Climatic Cataclysm*, Washington, DC: Brookings Institute.

Caney, S. (2013) 'Governing for Future Generations: What Are Our Options?' www.oxfordmartin.ox.ac.uk/news/201311_SimonCaney.

Carbon Tracker Initiative (2013) *The Unburnable Carbon 2013: Wasted Capital Stranded Assets*, London: Carbon Tracker Initiative and Grantham Research Institute on Climate Change and the Environment.

Cardoso, F. H. and Faletto, E. (1979) *Dependency and Development in Latin America*, Berkeley, CA: University of California Press.

Carlsson, C. (2015) 'Nowtopians', in G. D'Alisa, F. Demaria and G. Kallis (eds.), *Degrowth: A Vocabulary For a New Era*, London: Routledge, 182–4.

Carr, E. H. (1946) *The Twenty Years' Crisis 1919–1939: An Introduction to the Study of International Relations, 2nd edition*, New York: St. Martin's Press.

Carruthers, D. (1996) 'Indigenous Ecology and the Politics of Linkage in Mexican Social Movements', *Third World Quarterly* 17, 5: 1007–28.

Carson, R. (1965) *Silent Spring*, Penguin: Harmondsworth.

Carter, A. (1999) *A Radical Green Political Theory*, London: Routledge.

Castree, N. (2003) 'Commodifying What Nature?' *Progress in Human Geography* 27, 3 273–97.

Castree, N. and Braun, B. (2001) *Social Nature: Theory Practice and Politics*, Oxford: Blackwell.

Cato, M. S. (2008) *Green Economics: An Introduction to Theory, Policy and Practice*, London: Routledge.

Cato, M. S. (2011) *Environment and Economy*, London: Routledge.

Cato, M. S. (2012) *The Bioregional Economy: Land, Liberty and the Pursuit of Happiness*, London: Earthscan.

Cato, M. S. (2014) 'This Land Is Our Land', editorial, *Green World,* 3 October.

Cato, M. S. (n.d.) Response from Green House, the environmental think tank. *Environmental Audit Committee Inquiry into the Green Economy*, www.greenhousethinktank.org/responses.html.

Cato, M. S. and Essex, J. (n.d.) Response from Green House, the Environmental Think Tank. *Environmental Audit Committee Inquiry into Green Finance*, www.greenhousethinktank.org/responses.html.

Cattaneo, C. and Vansintjan, A. (2016) *A Wealth of Possibilities: Alternatives to Growth*, Brussels: Green European Foundation.

Cerny, P. (1995) 'Globalization and the Changing Logic of Collective Action', *International Organization* 49, 4: 595–625.

CGG (The Commission on Global Governance) (1995) *Our Global Neighbourhood*, Oxford: Oxford University Press.

Chambers, R. (1997) *Whose Reality Counts? Putting the Last First*, Rugby: Practical Action.

Chandler, D., Cudworth, E. and Hobden, S. (2017) 'Anthropocene, Capitalocene and Liberal Cosmopolitan IR: A Response to Burke et al.'s "Planet Politics"', *Millennium: Journal of International Studies* 6, 2: 1–19.

Chapman, A. (2007) *Democratizing Technology: Risk, Responsibility and the Regulation of Chemicals*, London: Earthscan.

Chatterjee, P. and Finger, M. (1994) *The Earth Brokers: Power, Politics and World Development*, London: Routledge.

Chenoweth, E. and Stephan, M. (2011) *Why Civil Resistance Works: The Strategic Logic of Nonviolent Conflict*, New York: Columbia University Press.

Chew, S. (2001) *World Ecological Degradation: Accumulation, Urbanization, and Deforestation, 3000BC–AD2000*, Lanham, MD: AltaMira Press.

Christoff, P. (2005) 'Out of Chaos. A Shining Star? Toward a Typology of Green States', in J. Barry and R. Eckersley (eds.), *The State and the Global Ecological Crisis*, Cambridge, MA: MIT Press.

Christoff, P. and Eckersley, R. (2013) *Globalization and the Environment*, Plymouth: Rowman and Littlefield.

CIT (Citizen's Income Trust) (2017) *Citizen's Basic Income: A Brief Introduction*, London: Citizen's Income Trust.

Clapp, J. (2001) *Toxic Exports: The Transfer of Hazardous Wastes from Rich to Poor Countries*, Ithaca, NY: Cornell University Press.

Clapp, J. (2011) *Food*, Cambridge: Polity Press.

Clapp, J. and Dauvergne, P. (2011) *Paths to a Green World: The Political Economy of the Global Environment*, 2nd edition, Cambridge, MA: MIT Press.

Clapp, J. and Helleiner, E. (2012) 'International Political Economy and the Environment: Back to the Basics?' *International Affairs* 88, 3: 485–501.

Clark, N. (2014) 'Geo-Politics and the Disaster of the Anthropocene', *The Sociological Review* 62: 19–37.

Climate Smart Agriculture Concerns (2015) 'COP21 Statement: *Don't Be fooled! Civil society says NO to "Climate Smart Agriculture" and urges decision-makers to support agroecology*', www.climatesmartagconcerns.info/cop21-statement.html

Cole, H. and Freeman, C. (1973) *Models of Doom: A Critique of the Limits to Growth*, New York: Universe Publications.

Cole, L. and Foster, S. (2001) *From the Ground Up: Environmental Racism and the Rise of the Environmental Justice Movement*, New York: New York University Press.

Collard, A. and Contrucci, J. (1988) *Rape of the Wild*, London: Women's Press.

Collinson, H. (ed.) (1996) *Green Guerrillas: Environmental Conflicts and Initiatives in Latin America and the Caribbean*, London: Latin American Bureau.

Commoner, B. (1970) *Science and Survival*, New York: Ballentine Books.

Conca, K. (2000) 'The WTO and the Undermining of Global Environmental Governance', *Review of International Political Economy* 7, 3: 484–94.

Conca, K. (2005) 'Old States in New Bottles? The Hybridization of Authority in Global Environmental Governance', in J. Barry and R. Eckersley (eds.), *The State and the Global Ecological Crisis*, Cambridge, MA: MIT Press, 181–207.

CoR (Committee of the Regions) (2018) 'The EU's Assembly of Regional and Local Representatives', https://cor.europa.eu/en/members/Pages/National-delegations.aspx.

CorporateWatch (2015) 'Shareholder Activists Target Barclays AGM', https://corporatewatch.org/shareholder-activists-target-barclays-agm/ 24 April.

Corry, O. and Stevenson, H. (eds.) (2018) *Global Environmental Politics: International Relations of the Earth*, Oxon: Routledge/Earthscan.

Costanza, R. (ed.) (1991) *Ecological Economics: The Science and Management of Sustainability*, New York: Columbia University Press.

Costanza, R., de Groot, R., Sutton, P., van der Ploeg, S., Anderson, S. J., Kubiszewski, I., Farber, S. and Turner, R. K. (2014) 'Changes in the Global Value of Ecosystem Services', *Global Environmental Change* 26: 152–8.

Cowen, M. and Shenton, R. (1995) 'The Invention of Development', in J. Crush (ed.), *The Power of Development*, London: Routledge, 2744.

Cox, E., Johnstone, P. and Stirling, A. (2016) 'Understanding the Intensity of UK Policy Commitments to Nuclear Power', *SPRU* Working Paper, SWPS 2016–16. Brighton: Sussex Policy Research Unit.

Cox, R. (1981) 'Social Forces, States and World Orders: Beyond International Relations Theory', *Millennium* 10, 2: 126–55.

Cox, R. (1987) *Production, Power and World Order*, New York: Columbia University Press.

Cox, R. (1995) 'Critical Political Economy', in B. Hettne (ed.), *International Political Economy: Understanding Global Disorder*, Halifax: Fernwood Publishing, 31–45.

Craig, M. (2018) 'Greening the State for a Sustainable Political Economy', *New Political Economy*, doi: 10.1080/13563467.2018.1526266.

Crush, J. (ed.) (1995) *Power of Development*, London: Routledge.

Cudworth, E. and Hobden, S. (2011) *Posthuman International Relations: Complexity, Ecologism and Global Politics*, London: Zed Books.

Cumbers, A. (2012) *Reclaiming Public Ownership: Making Space for Economic Democracy*, London: Zed Books, 195, 197.

Cunningham, R. (2017) *The Potential Impact of Brexit on the Prospects of a Green Transition in Europe*, Brussels: Green European Foundation.

Curry, P. (2011) *Ecological Ethics*, Cambridge: Polity Press.

Cutler, C. (2002) 'Historical Materialism, Globalization and Law', in M. Rupert and H. Smith (eds.), *Historical Materialism and Globalization*, London: Routledge, 230–56.

Cutler, C., Haufler, V. and Porter, T. (eds.) (1999) *Private Authority and International Affairs*, Albany: State University of New York Press.

Dalby, S. (1994) 'The Politics of Environmental Security', in J. Kakonen (ed.), *Green Security or Militarized Environment*, Aldershot: Dartmouth, 25–53.

Dalby, S. (2009) *Security and Environmental Change*, Cambridge: Polity Press.

Dale, G. (2012) 'The Growth Paradigm: A Critique', *International Socialism* 134, http://isj.org.uk/the-growth-paradigm-a-critique/.

D'Alisa, G., Demaria, F. and Kallis, G. (2014) *Degrowth: A Vocabulary for a New Era*, London: Routledge.

Daly, H. (1977) 'The Steady-State Economy: What, Why and How?', in D. Pirages, (ed.), *The Sustainable Society: Implications for Limited Growth*, New York and London: Praeger.

Daly, H. (1994) Farewell Speech, www.whirledbank.org/ourwords/daly.html.

Daly, H. (1996) *Beyond Growth: The Economics of Sustainable Development*, Boston: Beacon Press.

Daly, H. and Cobb, J. (1989) *For the Common Good: Redirecting the Economy toward Community, the Environment and a Sustainable Future*, Boston: Beacon Press.

The Dark Mountain Project (2017) *Walking on Lava: Selected Works for Uncivilized Times*, Chelsea, VT: Chelsea Green Publishing.

Dauvergne, P. (1997) *Shadows in the Forest: Japan and the Political Economy of Deforestation in South East Asia*, Cambridge, MA: MIT Press.

Dauvergne, P. (2008) *The Shadows of Consumption: Consequences for the Global Environment*, Cambridge, MA: MIT Press.

Dauvergne, P. (2016) *The Environmentalism of the Rich*, Cambridge, MA: MIT Press.

Dauvergne, P. (2018) *Will Big Business Destroy Our Planet?*, Cambridge: Polity Press.

Dauvergne, P. and LeBaron, G. (2014) *Protest Inc: The Corporatization of Activism*, Cambridge: Polity Press.

Death, C. (2016) *The Green State in Africa*, New Haven, CT: Yale University Press.

De Geus, M. (1996) 'The Ecological Restructuring of the State', in B. Doherty and M. de Geus (eds.), *Democracy and Green Political Thought*, London and New York: Routledge, 188–211.

Desai, R. (2013) *Geopolitical Economy: After US Hegemony, Globalization and Empire*, London: Pluto Press.

Desombre, B. and Barkin, S. (2011) *Fish*, Cambridge: Polity Press.

Deudney, D. (1990) 'The Case against Linking Environmental Degradation and National Security', *Millennium* 19, 3: 461–76.

Devall, B. and Sessions, G. (1985) *Deep Ecology: Living as If Nature Mattered*, Salt Lake City, UT: Peregrine Smith.

Die Grünen (1984) *Common Statement of the Greens for the 1984 Election to the European Parliament*, Bonn: die Grünen.

Die Grünen (1989) *Platform der Grünen zur Europawahl '89*, Bonn: die Grünen.

Dillon, M. (1996) *Politics of Security*, London: Routledge.

Di Muzio, T. (2015) *Carbon Capitalism: Energy, Social Reproduction and World Order*, London: Rowman and Littlefield.

Dinar, S. (ed.) (2011) *Beyond Resource Wars*, Cambridge, MA: MIT Press.

Dittmer, K. (2015) 'Community Currencies', in G. D'Alisa (ed.), *Degrowth: A Vocabulary for a New Era*, London: Routledge, 149–51.

Dixon, R. (2011) *Slow Violence and the Environmentalism of the Poor*, Cambridge, MA: Harvard University Press.

234 *References*

Dobson, A. (1990) *Green Political Thought*, London: Routledge.
Dobson, A. (eds.) (1991) *The Green Reader*, London: Andre Deutsch.
Dobson, A. (1995) *Green Political Thought*, 2nd edition, London: Routledge.
Dobson, A. (1996) 'Representative Democracy and the Environment', in W. Lafferty and
    J. Meadowcroft (eds.), *Democracy and the Environment: Problems and Prospects*,
    Cheltenham: Edward Elgar, 124–39.
Dobson, A. (2003) *Citizenship and the Environment*, Oxford: Oxford University Press.
Dobson, A. (2007) *Green Political Thought*, 4th edition, Abingdon: Routledge.
Dobson, A. (2014) *The Politics of Post-Growth*, Dorset: Green House.
Doherty, B. (1992) 'The Fundi-Realo Controversy: An Analysis of Four European Green
    Parties', *Environmental Politics* 1, 1: 95–120.
Doherty, B. and de Geus, M. (eds.) (1996) *Democracy and Green Political Thought:
    Sustainability, Rights and Citizenship*, London: Routledge.
Doran, P. (1993) '"The Earth Summit" (UNCED) Ecology as Spectacle', *Global Society:
    Journal of Interdisciplinary International Relations* 7, 1: 55–65.
Douthwaite, R. (1996) *Short Circuits: Local Economies in an Unsustainable World
    Totnes*, Devon: Green Books.
Doward, J. (2018) 'Arms Industry Spending Millions to Promote Brands in Schools', *The
    Guardian*, www.theguardian.com/world/2018/sep/01/arms-industry-spending-mil
    lions-normalise-weapons-in-schools?CMP=Share_iOSApp_Other 1 September.
Doyle, M. (1986) 'Liberalism and World Politics', *American Political Science Review* 80,
    4: 1151–69.
Drengson, A. (1995) *The Deep Ecology Movement*, Berkeley, CA: North Atlantic Books.
Dryzek, J. (1992) 'Ecology and Discursive Democracy: Beyond Liberal Capitalism and the
    Administrative State', *Capitalism, Nature, Socialism* 3, 2: 18–42.
Dryzek, J., Downies, D., Hunold, C., Schlosberg, D. and Hernes, H. (2003) *Green States
    and Social Movements: Environmentalism in the United States, United Kingdom,
    Germany and Norway*, Oxford: Oxford University Press.
Duarte, S. (2009) 'Bringing Democracy to Disarmament', Keynote Address Delivered at the
    Conference Reaching Nuclear Disarmament – The Role of Civil Society in Strengthening
    the NPT, Stockholm: Swedish Network for Nuclear Disarmament, 6 November 2009.
Duffy, R. (2016) 'War, by Conservation', *Geoforum* 69: 238–48.
Duit, A., Feindt, P. H. and Meadowcroft, J. (2016) 'Greening Leviathan: The Rise of the
    Environmental State?', *Environmental Politics* 25, 1: 1–23.
Dyer, G. (2008). *Climate Wars*, London: Random House.
Earth Justice (2017) 'Eradicating Ecocide', http://eradicatingecocide.com/our-earth/earth-
    justice/.
Eckersley, R. (1992) *Environmentalism and Political Theory: Towards an Ecocentric
    Approach*, London: UCL Press.
Eckersley, R. (2004) *The Green State*, Cambridge, MA: MIT Press.
Eckersley, R. (2007) 'Ecological Intervention: Prospects and Limits', *Ethics and Inter-
    national Affairs* 21: 275–396.
Eckersley, R. (2010) 'Green Theory', in T. Dunne, M. Kurki and S. Smith (eds.), *International
    Relations Theories: Discipline and Diversity*, Oxford: Oxford University Press.
The Ecologist (1993) *Whose Common Future?*, London: Earthscan.
Ehrenfeld, D. (1978) *The Arrogance of Humanism*, New York: Oxford University Press.
Ehrlich, P. (1975) *The Population Bomb*, Minneapolis, MN: Rivercity Press.
EJOLT (2018) www.ejolt.org/.
Ekins, P. (ed.) (1986) *The Living Economy*, London: Routledge and Kegan Paul.
Elliott, L. (2004) *The Global Politics of the Environment*, Basingstoke: Macmillan.

Escobar, A. (1995) *Encountering Development: The Making and Unmaking of the Third World*, Princeton, NJ: Princeton University Press.

Escobar, A. (2015) 'Degrowth, Postdevelopment, and Transitions: A Preliminary Conversation', *Sustainability Science,* April DOI:10.1007/s11625-015-0297-5.

Evans, G. (2010) *A Just Transition to Sustainability in a Climate Change Hot-Spot: From Carbon Valley to a Future Beyond Coal*, Saarbrücken: VDM.

Evans, G., Goodman, J. and Lansbury, N. (2002) *Moving Mountains: Communities Confront Mining and Globalization*, London: Zed Books.

Fairhead, J. and Leach, M. (1998) *Reframing Deforestation: Global Analysis and Local Realities: Studies in West Africa*, London: Routledge.

Fairhead, J., Leach, M. and Scoones, I. (2012) 'Green Grabbing: A New Appropriation of Nature?' *Journal of Peasant Studies* 39, 2: 285–307.

Falk, R. (1971) *This Endangered Planet*, New York: Random House.

Falkner, R. (2008) *Business Power and Conflict in International Politics*, Basingstoke: Palgrave.

Farand, C. (2018) 'Polish Coal Company Announced as First Sponsor of UN Climate Talks in Katowice', 27 November Desmog, www.desmog.co.uk/2018/11/27/polish-coal-company-announced-first-sponsor-un-climate-talks-katowice.

Ferguson, J. (1990) *The Anti-politics Machine: 'Development', Depoliticisation and Bureaucratic Power in Lesotho*, Cambridge: Cambridge University Press.

Fischer, F. (2002) *Citizens, Experts, and the Environment: The Politics of Local Knowledge*, Durham, NC: Duke University Press.

Foreman, D. and Haywood, B. (eds.) (1989) *Ecodefense: A Field Guide to Monkeywrenching*, Tuscon, AZ: Ned Ludd Books.

Forsyth, T. (2003) *Critical Political Ecology: The Politics of Environmental Science*, London: Routledge.

Fox, W. (1990) *Toward a Transpersonal Ecology: Developing New Foundations for Environmentalism*, Boston: Shambhala.

Frankland, E. G. and Schoonmaker, D. (1992) *Between Protest and Power: The Green Party in Germany*, Oxford: Westview Press.

Freedman, L. (1994) *War*, Oxford: Oxford University Press.

Freire, P. (1996) *Pedagogy of the Oppressed*, London: Penguin.

Friedman, B. (2006) *The Moral Consequences of Economic Growth*, London: Vintage Press.

Friedman, M. (2009) *Capitalism and Freedom*, Fortieth Anniversary Edition, Chicago: University of Chicago Press.

Friends of the Earth (2016) 'The UN Treaty on Transnational Corporations and Human Rights', 17 October, www.foei.org/what-we-do/un-treaty-on-tncs.

Gaard, G. (1998) *Ecological Politics: Ecofeminists and the Greens*, Philadelphia: Temple University Press.

Gale, F. and M'Gonigle, M. (eds.) (2000) *Nature, Production and Power: Towards an Ecological Political Economy*, Cheltenham: Edward Elgar.

Galeano, E. (1997) *Open Veins of Latin America: Five Centuries of the Pillage of a Continent*, anniversary edition, New York: Monthly Review Press.

Gallagher, K. (ed.) (2005) *Putting Development First: The Importance of Policy Space in the WTO and International Financial Institutions*, London: Zed Books.

Garvey, N. and Newell, P. (2005) 'Corporate Accountability to the Poor? Assessing the Effectiveness of Community-Based Strategies', *Development in Practice* 15, 3–4: 389–405.

GCI (Global Commons Institute) (2018) 'Contraction and Convergence', http://gci.org.uk/.

GDR (2018) 'Greenhouse Development Rights', http://gdrights.org/.

GEF (Green European Foundation) (2016) *A Wealth of Possibilities: Alternatives to Growth*, Brussels: GEF.

GEJ (Green European Journal) (2015) 'Peace, Love and Intervention – Green Views on Foreign Policy' 10, March, www.greeneuropeanjournal.eu/peace-love-and-intervention-green-views-on-foreign-policy/

George, S. (1992) *The Debt Boomerang*, London: Pluto Press.

George, S. (2010) *Whose Crisis, Whose Future?*, Cambridge: Polity Press.

Gill, S. (1991) *American Hegemony and the Trilateral Commission*, Cambridge: Cambridge University Press.

Gill, S. (1995) 'Globalization, Market Civilisation and Disciplinary Neoliberalism', *Millennium: Journal of International Studies* 24, 3: 399–423.

Gill, S. and Law, D. (1988) *The Global Political Economy*, Hemel Hempstead: Harvester Wheatsheaf.

Gills, B. and Rocamora, J. (1992) 'Low Intensity Democracy', *Third World Quarterly* 13, 3: 501–23.

Global Witness (2017) *Defenders of the Earth*, London: Global Witness.

Glover, D. (1999) 'Defending Communities: Local Exchange Trading Systems from an Environmental Perspective, *IDS Bulletin* 30, 3: 75–81.

GND (2008) *A Green New Deal*, London: New Economics Foundation.

Goldman, M. (ed.) (1998) *Privatising Nature: Political Struggles for the Global Commons*, London: Pluto Press.

Goldman, M. (2005) *Imperial Nature: The World Bank and Struggles for Social Justice in an Age of Globalization*, New Haven, CT: Yale University Press.

Goldsmtih, E., Allen, R., Allaby, M., Davoll, J. and Lawrence, S. (1972) *A Blueprint for Survival*, Harmondsworth: Penguin.

Gómez-Baggethun, E. and Ruiz-Pérez, M. (2011) 'Economic Valuation and the Commodification of Ecosystem Services', *Progress in Physical Geography* 35, 5: 613–28.

Goron, C. (2017) 'Climate Revolution or Long March? The Politics of Low Carbon Transformation in China (1992–2015)', PhD thesis, University of Warwick.

Goodin, R. (1992) *Green Political Theory*, Cambridge: Polity Press.

Goodin, R. (1996) 'Enfranchising the Earth, and Its Alternatives', *Political Studies* 44: 835–49.

Gorz, A. (1983) *Ecology as Politics*, London: Pluto Press.

Gottlieb, R. and Joshi, A. (2010) *Food Justice*, Cambridge, MA: MIT Press.

Gramsci, A. (1971) *Selections from the Prison Notebooks*, edited and translated by Q. Hoare and G. Nowell Smith. New York: International Publishers.

Green, D. (2003) *Silent Revolution: The Rise and Crisis of Market Economics in Latin America*, New York: Monthly Review Press.

Green, D. (2008) *From Poverty to Power: How Active Citizens and Effective States Can Change the World*, Oxford: Oxfam International.

Green, J. (2017) 'Transnational Delegation in Global Environmental Governance: When Do Non-state Actors Govern? *Regulation & Governance* 12, 2: 263–76.

Green Party (1989) *Don't Let Your World Turn Grey. European Election Manifesto*, London: Green Party.

Green Party (1994) *European Election Manifesto 1994*, London: Green Party.

Green Party (2010) www.greenparty.org.uk/policies-2010/2010manifesto-contents.html.

Grin, J., Rotmans, J. and Schot, J. (2011) *Transitions to Sustainable Development: New Directions in the Study of Long Term Transformative Change*, London: Routledge.

Grubb, M., Hourcade, J. C. and Neuhoff, K. (2014) *Planetary Economics*, Abingdon and New York: Routledge.

Gudynas, F. (2015) 'Buen Vivir', in G. D'Alisa, F. Demaria and G. Kallis (eds.), *Degrowth: A Vocabulary for a New Era*, London: Routledge, 201–5.

Gudynas, E. (2017) 'Value, Growth, Development: South American Lessons for a New Ecopolitics', *Capitalism Nature Socialism*, doi: 10.1080/10455752.2017.1372502.

Gunder Frank, A. (1966) *The Development of Underdevelopment*, New York: Monthly Review Press.

Haas, P. (1990) 'Obtaining International Environmental Protection through Epistemic Consensus', *Millennium: Journal of International Studies* 19, 3: 347–63.

Habermas, J. (1973) *Legitimation Crisis*, Boston: Beacon Press.

Hajer, M., Nilsson, M., Raworth, K., Bakker, P., Berkhout, F., de Boer, Y., Rockstrom, J., Ludwig, K. and Kok, M. (2015) 'Beyond Cockpit-ism: Four Insights to Enhance the Transformative Potential of the Sustainable Development Goals', *Sustainability* 7: 1651–60.

Hancock, G. (1989) *Lords of Poverty*, New York: Atlantic Monthly Press.

Hardin, G. (1968) 'The Tragedy of the Commons' *Science* 162: 1243–8.

Harvey, D. (1981) 'The Spatial Fix: Hegel, von Thünen and Marx', *Antipode* 13, 3: 1–12.

Harvey, D. (2003) *The New Imperialism*, Oxford: Oxford University Press.

Harvey, D. (2004) 'The "New" Imperialism: Accumulation By Dispossession', *Socialist Register* 40: 63–87.

Harvey, D. (2005) *A Brief History of Neoliberalism*, Oxford: Oxford University Press.

Hayter, T. (1989) *Exploited Earth: Britain's Aid and the Environment*, London: Earthscan.

Hayward, T. (1994) *Ecological Thought: An Introduction*, Cambridge: Polity Press.

Hayward, T. (2005) *Constitutional Environmental Rights*, Oxford: Oxford University Press.

Held, D. (1995) *Democracy and the Global Order*, Cambridge: Polity Press.

Held, D. and Koenig-Archibugi, M. (eds.) (2005) *Global Governance and Public Accountability*, Oxford: Blackwell Publishing.

Helleiner, E. (1994) 'From Bretton Woods to Global Finance: A World Turned Upside Down', in G. Underhill and R. Stubbs (eds.), *Political Economy and the Changing Global Order*, Basingstoke: Macmillan, 163–75.

Helleiner, E. (1996) 'International Political Economy and the Greens', *New Political Economy* 1, 1: 59–77.

Herman, E. and Chomsky, N. (1994) *Manufacturing Consent: The Political Economy of the Mass Media*, London: Vintage.

Heynen, H., Perkins, H. and Roy, P. (2006) 'The Political Ecology of Uneven Urban Green Space', *Urban Affairs Review* 42, 1: 3–25.

Higgins, P. (2010) *Eradicating Ecocide*, London: Shepheard-Walwyn.

Hildyard (1993) 'Foxes in Charge of the Chickens', in W. Sachs (ed.), *Global Ecology: A New Arena of Political Conflict*, London: Zed Books, 22–35.

Hinchliffe, S. (2007) *Geographies of Nature*, London: Sage.

Hirsch, F. (1976) *Social Limits to Growth*, Cambridge, MA: Harvard University Press.

Holliday, C., Schmidheiny, S. and Watts, P. (2002) *Walking the Talk: The Business Case for Sustainable Development*, Sheffield: Greenleaf Publishing.

Homer-Dixon, T. (1991). 'On the Threshold: Environmental Changes as Causes of Acute Conflict', *International Security* 16: 76–116.

Homer-Dixon, T. (1999) *Environment, Scarcity, and Violence*, Princeton, NJ: Princeton University Press.

Hornborg, A. (1998) 'Towards an Ecological Theory of Unequal Exchange: Articulating World System Theory; An Ecological Economics', *Ecological economics* 25, 1: 127–36.

Hovden, Eivind (1999) 'As If Nature Doesn't Matter: Ecology, Regime Theory and International Relations', *Environmental Politics*, 8, 2: 50–74.

Huber, M. T. (2009) 'Energizing Historical Materialism: Fossil Fuels, Space and the Capitalist Mode of Production', *Geoforum* 40, 1: 105–15.

Huff, A. and Brock, A. (2017) 'Accumulation by Restoration: Degradation Neutrality and the Faustian Bargain of Conservation Finance', *Antipode*, https://antipodefoundation.org/2017/11/06/accumulation-by-restoration/.

Humphrey, S. (ed.) (2009) *Climate Change and Human Rights*, Cambridge: Cambridge University Press.

Hutchinson, F., Mellor, M. and Olsen, W. (2002) *The Politics of Money: Towards Sustainability and Economic Democracy*, London: Pluto Press.

Hutter, C., Keller, H., Ribbe, L. and Wohlers, R. (1995) *The Eco-twisters: Dossier on the European Environment*, London: Green Print.

Icaza, R., Newell, P. and Saguier, M. (2010) 'Citizenship and Trade Governance in the Americas', in J. Gaventa and R. Tandon (eds.), *Globalizing Citizens: New Dynamics of Inclusion and Exclusion*, London: Zed Books, 163–85.

Icke, D. (1990) *It Doesn't Have to Be Like This: Green Politics Explained*, London: Green Print.

IMF (International Monetary Fund) (2015) IMF Survey: Counting the Cost of Energy Subsidies, www.imf.org/external/pubs/ft/survey/so/2015/NEW070215A.htm.

Inglehart, R. (1990) *Culture Shift in Advanced Industrial Society*, Princeton, NJ: Princeton University Press.

IPCC (2018) *Global Warming of 1.5°C: An IPCC Special Report on the Impacts of Global Warming of 1.5°C above Pre-industrial Levels and Related Global Greenhouse Gas Emission Pathways* IPCC. www.ipcc.ch/sr15/.

Isakson, R. (2015) 'Derivatives for Development? Small-Farmer Vulnerability and the Financialization of Climate Risk Management', *Journal of Agrarian Change* 15, 4: 569–80.

Jackson, T. (2011) *Prosperity without Growth: Economics for a Finite Planet*, London: Earthscan.

Jackson, R. (2017) 'Pacifism: The Anatomy of a Subjugated Knowledge', *Critical Studies on Security*. doi: 10.1080/21624887.2017.1342750.

Jacob, J. (1997) *New Pioneers: The Back to the Land Movement and the Search for a Sustainable Future*, Philadelphia: Pennsylvania State University Press.

Jenkins, R. and Newell, P. (2013) 'CSR, Tax and Development', *Third World Quarterly* 33, 3: 378–96.

Jevons, W. S. (1865) 'The Coal Question: Can Britain Survive?', in A. W. Flux (ed.), *The Coal Question: An Inquiry Concerning the Progress of the Nation and the Probable Exhaustion of Our Coal Mines (1905)*, 3rd edition, New York: Augustus M. Kelley.

Johanisova, N. and Wolf, S. (2012) 'Economic Democracy: A Path for the Future?' *Futures* 44, 562–70.

Johnstone, P. and Newell, P. (2017) 'Sustainability Transitions and the State', *Environmental Innovation and Societal Transitions* 27: 72–82.

Jones, O. (2015) *The Establishment: And How They Get Away with It*, London: Penguin.

Juniper, T. (2013) *What Has Nature Ever Done for Us?: How Money Really Does Grow on Trees*, London: Profile Books.

Kaldor, M. (2012) *New Wars and Old Wars: Organized Violence in a Global Era*, Cambridge: Polity.

Kaldor, M., Lynn Karl, T. and Said, Y. (eds.) (2007) *Oil Wars*, London: Pluto Press.

Kallis, G. (2015) 'Social Limits of Growth', in G. D'Alisa, G. Kallis and F. Demaria (eds.), *Degrowth: A Vocabulary for a New Era*, London: Routledge, 137–40.

Kallis, G. (2018) *Degrowth*, New York: Columbia University Press.

Kallis, G., Demaria, F. and D'Alisa, G. (2014) 'Degrowth', in G. D'Alisa, G. Kallis and F. Demaria (eds.), *Degrowth: A Vocabulary for a New Era*, London: Routledge, 1–17.

Kant, I. (1983 [1795]) *Perpetual Peace: A Philosophical Sketch*, Indianapolis, IN: Hackett Publishing.

Karliner, J. (1997) *The Corporate Planet: Ecology and Politics in the Age of Globalization*, San Francisco, CA: Sierra Club Books.

Katz-Rosene, R. and Paterson, M. (2018) *Thinking Ecologically about the Global Political Economy*, Abingdon: Routledge.

Kelly, P. (1994) *Thinking Green! Essays on Environmentalism, Feminism and Non-Violence*, Berkeley, CA: Parallax Press.

Kemp, P. and D. Wall (1990) *Green Manifesto for the 1990s*, London: Penguin.

Kemp, R., Loorbach, D. and Rotmans, J. (2007) 'Transition Management as a Model for Managing Processes of Co-evolution towards Sustainable Development', *The International Journal of Sustainable Development and World Ecology* 14, 1: 78–91.

Kenner, D. (2015) *Inequality of Overconsumption: The Ecological Footprint of the Richest*, GSI Working Paper 2015/2, Cambridge: Global Sustainability Institute, Anglia Ruskin University.

Kenner, D. (2019) *Carbon Inequality: The Role of the Richest in Climate Change*, Abingdon: Routledge.

Keohane, R. (1977) *Power and Interdependence: World Politics in Transition*, Colchester: The Book Service.

Kingsnorth, P. (2017) *Confessions of a Recovering Environmentalist*, London: Faber and Faber.

Klein, N. (2007) *The Shock Doctrine*, London: Penguin.

Koistinen, P. (1980) *The Military-Industrial Complex: An Historical Perspective*, New York: Praeger.

Korten (1995) *When Corporations Rule the World*, West Hartford, CT: Kumarian Press.

Kovel, J. (2002) *The Enemy of Nature: The End of Capitalism or the End of the World*, London: Zed books.

Krasner, S. (ed.) (1983) *International Regimes*, Ithaca, NY: Cornell University Press.

Kropotkin, P. (1955) *Mutual Aid: A Factor of Evolution*, Boston: Horizons.

Kuehls, T. (1996) *Beyond Sovereign Territory: The Space of Ecopolitics*, Minneapolis: University of Minnesota Press.

Kütting, G. (2000) *Environment, Society and International Relations: Towards More Effective International Environmental Agreements*, London: Routledge.

Kütting, G. (2005) *Globalization and the Environment: Greening Global Political Economy*, Albany: State University of New York Press.

Kütting, G. (2014) 'Rethinking Global Environmental Governance: Coordinating Ecological Policy', *Critical Policy Studies* 8, 2 227–34.

Laferrière, E. and Stoett, P. (1999) *International Relations Theory and Ecological Thought: Towards a Synthesis*, London: Routledge.

Laferrière, E. and Stoett, P. (eds.) (2006) *International Ecopolitical Theory: Critical Approaches*, Toronto: UBC Press.

Lang, T. and Hines, C. (1993) *The New Protectionism: Protecting the Future against Free Trade*, London: Earthscan.

Latouche, S. (2009) *Farewell to Growth*, Cambridge: Polity Press.

Latour, B. (2009) *Politics of Nature: How to Bring the Sciences into Democracy*, 2nd edition, Harvard: Harvard University Press.

Lawson, N. (2009) *All Consuming*, London: Penguin.

Leach, M. (2014) 'Resilience 2014: Limits Revisited? Planetary Boundaries, Justice and Power', https://steps-centre.org/blog/resilience2014-leach/.

Leach, M. and Scoones, I. (2015) *Carbon Conflicts and Forest Landscapes in Africa*, London: Routledge/Earthscan.

Leach, M. and Scoones, I. (2006) *The Slow Race: Making Technology Work for the Poor*, London: Demos.

Leach, M., Scoones, I. and Wynne, B. (eds.) (2005) *Science and Citizens: Globalization and the Challenge of Engagement*, London: Zed Press.

Lee, K., Humphreys, D. and Pugh, M. (1997) '"Privatisation" in the United Nations System: Patterns of Influence in Three Intergovernmental Organisations', *Global Society: Journal of Interdisciplinary International Relations* 11, 3: 339–57.

Lenin, V. I. (1996) [1916] *Imperialism: The Highest Stage of Capitalism*, London: Pluto Press.

Leopold, A. (1968) *A Sand County Almanac*, Oxford: Oxford University Press.

LeQuesne, C. (1996) *Reforming World Trade: The Social and Environmental Priorities*, Oxford: Oxfam Publishing.

Les Verts (1994) 'Programme politique des Verts pour les elections Européennes de juin 1994', *Vert Contact supplément* no. 333.

Levy, D. and Newell, P. (2002) 'Business Strategy and International Environmental Governance: Toward a Neo-Gramscian Synthesis', *Global Environmental Politics* 3, 4: 84–101.

Levy, D. and Newell, P. (eds.) (2005) *The Business of Global Environmental Governance*, Cambridge, MA: MIT Press.

Lewis, S. and Maslin, M. (2015) 'Defining the Anthropocene', *Nature* 519: 171–80.

Lewis, S. and Maslin, M. (2018a) 'Scorched Earth', *Red Pepper* 221 Autumn: 59–61.

Lewis, S. and Maslin, M. (2018b) *The Human Planet: How We Created the Anthropocene*, London: Penguin.

Linklater, A. (1990) *Beyond Realism and Marxism: Critical Theory and International Relations*, London: Palgrave.

Linklater, A. (1998) *The Transformation of Political Community: Ethical Foundations of the Post-Westphalian Era*, Cambridge: Polity Press.

Lister, J. and Dauvergne, P. (2011) *Timber*, Cambridge: Polity Press.

Lohmann, L. (2006) *Carbon Trading: A Critical Conversation on Climate Change, Privatisation and Power*, Dorset: The Corner House.

Lovelock, J. (1979) *Gaia: A New Look at Life on Earth*, Oxford: Oxford University Press.

Lovins, A. (1977) *Soft Energy Paths: Towards a Durable Peace*, Harmondsworth: Penguin.

Lucas, C. (2015) *Honourable Friends? Parliament and the Fight for Change*, London: Portobello Books.

Mabee, B. and Vucetic, S. (2018) 'Varieties of Militarism: Towards a Typology', *Security Dialogue* 49, 1–2: 96–108.

Madeley, J. (2000) *Hungry for Trade: How the Poor Pay for Free Trade*, London: Zed Books.

Malm, A. (2016) *Fossil Capital: The Rise of Steam Power and the Roots of Global Warming*, London: Verso.

Malm, A. and Hornborg, A. (2014) 'The Geology of Mankind? A Critique of the Anthropocene Narrative', *The Anthropocene Review* 1, 1: 62–9.

Maniates, M. and Meyer, J. (2010) *The Environmental Politics of Sacrifice*, Cambridge, MA: MIT Press.

Mann, M. (1987) 'The Roots and Contradictions of Modern Militarism', *New Left Review* I, 162: 35–50.

Mann, G. (2009) 'Should Political Ecology be Marxist? A Case for Gramsci's Historical Materialism', *Geoforum* 40, 3: 335–44.

Mansfield, B. (2004) 'Neoliberalism in the Oceans: "Rationalization", Property Rights, and the Commons Question', *Geoforum* 35, 3: 313–26.

Manzo, K. (1995) 'Black Consciousness and the Quest for a Counter-Modernist Development', in J. Crush (ed.), *Power of Development*, London and New York: Routledge, 228–52.

Martell, L. (1994) *Ecology and Society: An Introduction*, Cambridge: Polity Press.

Martínez-Alier, J. (2002) *The Environmentalism of the Poor: A Study of Ecological Conflicts and Valuation*, Cheltenham: Edward Elgar.

Martínez-Alier, J. (2012) 'Environmental Justice and Economic Degrowth: An Alliance between Two Movements', *Capitalism Nature Socialism* 23, 1: 51–73.

Mason, M. (2005) *The New Accountability: Environmental Responsibility Across Borders*, London: Earthscan.

Marx, K. (1974) *Capital*, London: Lawrence and Wishart.

Marx, K. (1975) *The German Ideology*, vol. 5, London: Lawrence and Wishart.

Marx, K. and Engels, F. (1998) [1848] *The Communist Manifesto*, Verso, London.

Mathie, A. and Gaventa, J. (eds.) (2015) *Citizen-Led Innovation for a New Economy*, Nova Scotia: Fernwood Publishing.

Matthew, R. A., Barnett, J., McDonald, B. and O'Brien, K. (eds.) (2010) *Global Environmental Change and Human Security*, Cambridge, MA: MIT Press.

Matthews, F. (1991) *The Ecological Self*, London: Routledge.

Matus, M. and Rossi, E. (2002) 'Trade and Environment in the FTAA: A Chilean Perspective', in C. L. Deere and D. Esty (eds.), *Greening the Americas: NAFTA's Lessons for Hemispheric Trade*, Cambridge: MIT Press, 259–73.

Mazzucato, M. (2015) 'The Green Entrepreneurial State', in I. Scoones, M. Leach and P. Newall (eds.), *The Politics of Green Transformations*, London: Routledge/Earthscan, 134–53.

McAfee, K. (1999) 'Selling Nature to Save It? Biodiversity and Green Developmentalism', *Environment and Planning D* 17: 133–54.

McCully, P. (1996) *Silenced Rivers: The Ecology and Politics of Large Dams*, London: Zed Books.

McDonald, M. (2002) 'Human Security and the Construction of Security', *Global Society* 16, 3: 277–95.

McDonald, M. (2012) *Security, the Environment and Emancipation: Contestation over Environmental Change*, Abingdon: Routledge.

McDonald, M. (2013) 'Discourses of Climate Security', *Political Geography* 33: 43–51.

McGlade, C. and Ekins, P. (2015) 'The Geographical Distribution of Fossil Fuels Unused When Limiting Global Warming to 2°C', *Nature* 517, 7533: 187–90.

McLuhan, T. C. (1973) *Touch the Earth*, London: Abacus.

Meadowcroft, J. (2004) 'From Welfare State to Ecostate', in J. Barry and R. Eckersley (eds.), *The State and the Global Ecological Crisis*, Cambridge, MA: MIT Press, 63–87.

Meadows, D., Meadows, D., Randers, J. and Behrens, W. (1972) *The Limits to Growth*, London: Pan Books.

Meadows, D., Meadows, D., Randers, J. and Behrens, W. (1974) *The Dynamics of Growth in a Finite World*, Cambridge, MA: Wright-Allen Press.

Meadows, D., Meadows, D. and Randers, J. (1992) *Beyond the Limits: Global Collapse or a Sustainable Future*, London: Earthscan.

Meadows, D., Randers, J. and Meadows, D. (2004) *Limits to Growth: The 30-Year Update*, London: Earthscan.

Mellor, M. (1992) *Breaking the Boundaries: Towards a Feminist Green Socialism*, London: Virago Press.

Mellor, M. (2015) *Debt or Democracy: Public Money for Sustainability and Social Justice*, London: Pluto Press.

Merchant, C. (1990) *The Death of Nature: Women, Ecology and the Scientific Revolution*, New York: Harper and Row.

Merrifield, J. (1993) 'Putting Scientists in Their Place: Participatory Research in Environmental and Occupational Health', in P. Park, M. Brydon-Miller, B. Hall and T. Jackson (eds.), *Voices of Change: Participatory Research in the United States and Canada*, Toronto: OISE Press.

Mies, M. and Shiva, V. (1993) *Ecofeminism*, London: Zed Books.

Mishan, E. J. (1967) *The Costs of Economic Growth*, Oxford: Oxford University Press.

Mitchell, A. (2014) 'Only Human? A Worldly Approach to Security', *Security Dialogue* 45, 1: 5–21.

Mitchell, T. and Maxwell, S. (2010) 'Defining Climate Compatible Development', *CDKN Policy Briefing*, November.

Mol, A. (2003) *Globalization and Environmental Reform: The Ecological Modernization of the Global Economy*, Cambridge, MA: MIT Press.

Mol, A. P. J. and Spaargaren, G. (eds.) (2000) *Ecological Modernisation around the World: Perspectives and Critical Debates*, London and Portland: Frank Cass Publishers.

Monbiot, G. (2000) *Captive State: The Corporate Takeover of Britain*, London: Pan Macmillan.

Monbiot, G. (2017) *Out of the Wreckage: A New Politics for an Age of Crisis*, London: Verso.

Moore, J. W. (2011a) Transcending the Metabolic Rift: A Theory of Crises in the Capitalist World Ecology, *The Journal of Peasant Studies* 38, 1: 1–46.

Moore, J. W. (2011b) 'Ecology, Capital, and the Nature of Our Times: Accumulation and Crisis in the Capitalist World Ecology, *Journal of World-Systems Research* 17, 1: 108–47.

Moore, J. (2013) 'Anthropocene or Capitalocene?' 13 May, http://jasonwmoore.wordpress.com/2013/05/13/anthropocene-or-capitalocene/.

Moore, J. W. (2014) *The Capitalocene Part I*, www.jasonwmoore.com/uploads/The_Capitalocene___Part_I__June_2014.pdf.

Moore, J. (2015) *Capitalism in the Web of Life: Ecology and the Accumulation of Capital*, London: Verso.

Morgenthau, H. J. (1948) *Power among Nations: The Struggle for Power and Peace*, New York: Alfred Knopf.

Naess, A. (1972) 'The Shallow and the Deep, Long-Range Ecology Movement: A Summary', *Inquiry* 16: 95–100.

Naess, A. (1989) *Ecology, Community and Lifestyle*, Cambridge: Cambridge University Press.

Narayan, D., Patel, R., Schafft, K., Rademacher, A. and Koch-Schulte, S. (2000) *Voices of the Poor: Can Anyone Hear Us?*, New York: Oxford University Press.

NCE (New Carbon Economy) (2018) *Unlocking the Inclusive Growth Story of the 21st Century: Accelerating Climate Action in Urgent Times*, https://newclimateeconomy.report/2018/executive-summary/.

NEF (New Economics Foundation) (2016) *The Happy Planet Index 2016: A Global Index of Sustainable Wellbeing*, London: NEF.

Newell, P. (2001a) 'New Environmental Architectures and the Search for Effectiveness', *Global Environmental Politics* 1, 1: 35–44.

Newell, P. (2001b) 'Managing Multinationals: The Governance of Investment for the Environment', *Journal of International Development* 13: 907–19.

Newell, P. (2002) 'A World Environment Organisation: The Wrong Solution to the Wrong Problem', *The World Economy* 25, 5: 659–71.

Newell, P. (2003) 'Globalization and the Governance of Biotechnology', *Global Environmental Politics* 3, 2: 56–72.

Newell, P. (2005) 'Race, Class and the Global Politics of Environmental Inequality', *Global Environmental Politics* 5, 3: 70–94.

Newell, P. (2007) 'Trade and Environmental Justice in Latin America', *New Political Economy* 12, 2: 237–59.

Newell, P. (2008a) 'The Marketisation of Global Environmental Governance: Manifestations and Implications', in J. Parks, K. Conca and M. Finger (eds.), *The Crisis of Global Environmental Governance: Towards a New Political Economy of Sustainability*, London: Routledge, 77–96.

Newell, P. (2008b) 'The Political Economy of Global Environmental Governance', *Review of International Studies* 34, 3: 507–29.

Newell, P. (2010) 'Democratising Biotechnology? Deliberation, Participation and Social Regulation in a Neo-Liberal World', *Review of International Studies* 36: 471–91.

Newell, P. (2012) *Globalization and the Environment: Capitalism, Ecology and Power*, Cambridge: Polity.

Newell, P. (2014) 'Dialogue of the Deaf? The CDM's Legitimation Crisis', in B. Stephan and R. Lane (eds.), *The Politics of Carbon Markets*, London: Routledge, 212–36.

Newell, P. (2015) 'The Politics of Green Transformations in Capitalism', in I. Sconnes, M. Leach and P. Newell (eds.), *The Politics of Green Transformations*, London: Routledge, 68–86.

Newell, P. (2018) 'Labour's Low-Carbon Plan Is a Good Start – But a "Green Transformation" Must Go Further', *The Conversation*, 4 October, https://theconversation.com/labours-low-carbon-plan-is-a-good-start-but-a-green-transformation-must-go-further-104052.

Newell, P. and Bumpus, A. (2012) 'The Global Political Ecology of the CDM', *Global Environmental Politics* 12, 4: 49–68.

Newell, P. and Lane, R. (2018a) 'A Climate for Change? The Impacts of Climate Change on Energy Politics', *Cambridge Review of International Affairs* (forthcoming)

Newell, P. and Lane, R. (2018b) 'IPE and the Environment in the Age of the Anthropocene', in O. Corry and H. Stevenson (eds.), *Global Environmental Politics: International Relations of the Earth*, Oxon: Routledge/Earthscan, 136–54.

Newell, P. and MacKenzie, R. (2004) 'Whose Rules Rule? Development and the Global Governance of Biotechnology', *IDS Bulletin* 35, 1: 82–92.

Newell, P. and Mulvaney, D. (2013) 'The Political Economy of the Just Transition', *The Geographical Journal* 197, 2: 132–40.

Newell, P. and Paterson, M. (1998) 'Climate for Business: Global Warming, the State and Capital', *Review of International Political Economy* 5, 4: 679–704.

Newell, P. and Simms, A. (2019) 'Towards a Fossil Fuel Non-Proliferation Treaty', *Climate Policy*. doi: 10.1080/14693062.2019.1636759.

Newell, P. and Taylor, O. (2018) 'Contested Landscapes: The Global Political Economy of Climate Smart Agriculture', *Journal of Peasant Studies* 45, 1–2: 108–30.

Newman, J. (2011) *Green Ethics and Philosophy: An A-Z Guide*, Thousand Oaks, CA: Sage.

Nixon, R. (2011) *Slow Violence and the Environmentalism of the Poor*, Harvard: Harvard University Press.

North, P., (1996) 'LETS: A Policy for Community Empowerment in the Inner City?', *Local Economy* 11, 3: 268–77.

North, P. (2007) *Money and Liberation: The Micro-Politics of Alternative Currency Movements*, Minneapolis: University of Minnesota Press.

Obach, B. (2004) *Labor and the Environmental Movement: The Quest for Common Ground*, Cambridge, MA: MIT Press.

O'Brien, K. (2006). 'Are We Missing the Point? Global Environmental Change as an Issue of Human Security', *Global Environmental Change* 16: 1–3.

O'Connor, J. (1991) 'On the Two Contradictions of Capitalism', *Capitalism Nature Socialism*, 2, 3: 107–9.

O'Connor, J. (ed.) (1994) *Is Capitalism Sustainable? Political Economy and the Politics of Ecology*, New York: Guilford Press.

O'Connor, J. (1998) *Natural Causes: Essays in Ecological Marxism*, London: Guildford Press.

Odum, P. and Barrett, G. W. (2004) *Fundamentals of Ecology*, Pacific Grove, CA: Brooks Cole.

OECD (2011) *Towards Green Growth*, Paris: Organisation for Economic Co-operation and Development.

Ophuls, W. (1973) 'Leviathan or Oblivion?', in H. Daly (ed.), *Toward a Steady State Economy*, San Francisco: W. H. Freeman and Co.

Ophuls, W. (1977) *Ecology and the Politics of Scarcity*, San Francisco: W. H. Freeman and Co.

Ophuls, W. (2011) *Plato's Revenge: Politics in the Age of Ecology*, Cambridge, MA: MIT Press.

O'Riordan, T. (1981) *Environmentalism*, London: Pion

Paehlke, R. (2004) *Democracy's Dilemma: Environment, Social Equity and the Global Economy*, Cambridge, MA: MIT Press.

Paehlke, R. C. (1989) *Environmentalism and the Future of Progressive Politics*, New Haven, CT: Yale University Press.

Panitch, L. and Gindin, S. (2012) *The Making of Global Capitalism*, London: Verso.

Park, S. (2011) *The World Bank Group and Environmentalists: Changing International Organisation Identities*, Manchester: Manchester University Press.

Patel, R. and J. Moore (2018) *A History of the World in Seven Cheap Things*, London: Verso.

Paterson, M. (1999) 'Green Political Strategy and the State', in B. Fairweather, S. Elworthy, M. Stroh and P. Stephens (eds.), *Environmental Futures*, Basingstoke: Macmillan, 73–87.

Paterson, M. (2001) *Understanding Global Environmental Politics: Domination, Accumulation, Resistance*, Basingstoke: Palgrave.

Paterson, M. (2009) 'Green Politics', in S. Burchill, et al. (eds.), *Theories of International Relations*, Basingstoke: Palgrave Macmillian.

Paterson, M. (2010) 'Legitimation and Accumulation in Climate Change Governance', *New Political Economy* 15, 3: 345–68.

Pearce, D., Markandya, A. and Barbier, E. (1989) *Blueprint for a Green Economy*, London: Earthscan.

Peet, R., Robbins, P. and Watts, M. (eds.) (2011) *Global Political Ecology*, London: Routledge.

Peet, R. and Watts, M. (eds.) (2004) *Liberation Ecologies: Environment, Development, Social Movements*, 2nd edition, London: Routledge.

Pegels, A. (ed.) (2014) *Green Industrial Policy in Emerging Countries*, London: Routledge.

Pegels, A. and Lütkenhorst, W. (2014). 'Is Germany's Energy Transition a Case of Successful Green Industrial Policy? Contrasting Wind and Solar PV', *Energy Policy* 74: 522–34.

Pepper, D. (1984) *The Roots of Modern Environmentalism*, London: Routledge.

Pepper, D. (1986) 'Radical Environmentalism and the Labour Movement', in J. Weston (ed.), *Red and Green: The New Politics of the Environment*, London: Pluto, 115–39.

Pepper, D. (1993) *Eco-socialism: From Deep Ecology to Social Justice*, London: Routledge.

Pepper, D. (1995) *Eco-socialism: From Deep Ecology to Social Justice*, 2nd edition, London: Routledge.

Perez, C. (2002) *Technological Revolutions and Financial Capital: The Dynamics of Bubbles and Golden Ages*, Cheltenham: Edward Elgar Publishing.

Piketty, T. (2014) *Capital in the Twenty-First Century*, Padstow: TJ International.

Pirages, D. (ed.) (1977) *The Sustainable Society: Implications for Limited Growth*, London and New York: Praeger.

Pirages, D. (1984) 'An Ecological Approach', in S. Strange (ed.), *Paths to International Political Economy*, London: George Allen and Unwin, 53–69.

Pirages, D. (1997) 'Ecological Theory and International Relations', *Indiana Journal of Global Legal Studies* 5, 1: 53–63.

Pirages, D. and Cousins, K. (eds.), (2005) *From Resource Scarcity to Ecological Security*, Cambridge, MA: MIT Press.

Plumwood, V. (1993) *Feminism and the Mastery of Nature*, London: Routledge.

Plumwood, V. (1996) 'Has Democracy Failed Ecology? An Ecofeminist Perspective', *Environmental Politics* 4, 4: 134–68.

Plumwood, V. (2002) *Environmental Culture: The Ecological Crisis of Reason*, London: Routledge.

Poguntke, T. (1989) 'The 'New politics' Dimension in European Green Parties', in F. Müller-Rommel (ed.), *New Politics in Western Europe: The Rise and Success of Green Parties and Alternative Lists*, Boulder, CO: Westview Press, 175–94.

Polanyi, K. (1980) [1944] *The Great Transformation*, Boston, MA: Beacon Press.

Ponting, C. (2007) *A New History of the World: The Environment and the Collapse of Great Civilisations*, London: Vintage.

Porritt, J. (1989) *Seeing Green: The Politics of Ecology Explained*, Oxford: Basil Blackwell.

Porritt, J. and Winner, D. (1988) *The Coming of the Green*, London: Fontana.

Poulantzas, N. (2014) *State, Power, Socialism*, London: Verso.

Power, M., Newell, P., Baker, L., Bulkeley, H., Kirshner, J. and Smith, A. (2016) 'The Political Economy of Energy Transitions in Mozambique and South Africa: The Role of the Rising Powers', *Energy Research and Social Sciences* 17: 10–19.

Prahalad, C. K. (2005) *The Fortune at the Bottom of the Pyramid: Eradicating Poverty through Profits*, Upper Saddle River, NJ: Wharton School Publishing.

Prakash, A. (2000) *Greening the Firm: The Politics of Corporate Environmentalism*, Cambridge: Cambridge University Press.

Princen, T. (2005) *The Logic of Sufficiency*, Cambridge: MIT Press.

Pressenza (2017) '75% of Brits Support UN Nuclear Ban Talks', www.pressenza.com/2017/03/75-brits-support-un-nuclear-ban-talks/.

Raftery, A., Zimmer, A., Frierson, D., Startz, R. and Liu, P. (2017) 'Less Than 2°C Warming by 2100 Unlikely', *Nature Climate Change*, letter doi: 10.1038/nclimate3352.

Raventos, D. (2005) *Basic Income. The Material Conditions of Freedom*, London: Pluto Press.

Raworth, K. (2014) 'Must the Anthropocene Be a Manthropocene?', 20 October, www.theguardian.com/commentisfree/2014/oct/20/anthropocene-working-group-sci ence-gender-bias.

Raworth, K. (2017a) 'Doughnut Economics', www.humansandnature.org/economy-kate-raworth

Raworth, K. (2017b) *Doughnut Economics: Seven Ways to Think Like a 21st-Century Economist*, New York: Random House Business Books.

Read, R. (2012) *Guardians of the Future: A Constitutional Case for Representing and Protecting Future People*, Greenhouse Report.

The Real World Coalition (2001) *From Here to Sustainability: Politics in the Real World*. London: Earthscan.

Re: Common (2018) www.recommon.org/eng/recommon-presentation-english/

Redclift, M. (1987) *Sustainable Development: Exploring the Contradictions*, London: Methuen.

Redclift, M. and Benton T. (1994) *Social Theory and the Global Environment*, London: Routledge.

Rees, J. (2001) 'Imperialism: Globalization, the State and War', *International Socialism* 2: 93.

Regan, T. (1988) *The Case for Animal Rights*, London and New York: Routledge.

Rich, B. (1994) *Mortgaging the Earth: The World Bank, Environmental Imperialism and the Crisis of Development*, London: Earthscan.

Richardson, D. (1995) 'The Green Challenge', in D. Richardson and C. Rootes (eds.), *The Green Challenge: The Development of Green Parties in Europe*, London: Routledge, 3–23.

Richardson, D. and Rootes, C. (eds.) (1995) *The Green Challenge: The Development of Green Parties in Europe*, London: Routledge.

Ritzer, G. (1993) *The McDonaldization of Society*, Thousand Oaks, CA: Pine Forge Press.

Roberts, J. T. and Parks, B. C. (2008) 'Fuelling Injustice: Globalization, Ecologically Unequal Exchange and Climate Change', in J. Ooshthoek and B. Gills (eds.), *The Globalization of Environmental Crises*, London: Routledge, 169–87.

Robbins, P. (2004) *Political Ecology: A Critical Introduction*, Oxford: Blackwell.

Robbins, P., Hintz, J. and Moore, S. (2010) *Environment and Society*, Oxford: Wiley Blackwell.

Robinson, J. (2006) *Economic Philosophy*, London: Aldine.

Rocheleau, D., Thomas-Slayter, B. and Wangari, E. (eds.) (1995) *Feminist Political Ecology*, London: Routledge.

Rockström, J., Klum, M. and Miller, P. (2015) *Big World, Small Planet: Abundance within Planetary Boundaries*, New Haven, CT: Yale University Press.

Rockström, J., Steffen, W., Noone, K., Persson, Å., Chapin, III, F. S., Lambin, E. F., Lenton, T. M., Scheffer, M., Folke, C., Schellnhuber, H. J., Nykvist, B., de Wit, C. A., Hughes, T., van der Leeuw, S., Rodhe, H., Sörlin, S., Snyder, P. K., Costanza, R., Svedin, U., Falkenmark, M., Karlberg, L., Corell, R. W., Fabry, V. J., Hansen, J., Walker, B., Liverman, D., Richardson, K., Crutzen, P. and Foley, J. A. (2009) 'A Safe Operating Space for Humanity', *Nature* 461: 472–5.

Rodrik, D. (1999) *Making Openness Work: The New Global Economy and the Developing Countries*, Washington, DC: Overseas Development Council.

Rosenau, J. (1997) *Along the Domestic–Foreign Frontier: Exploring Governance in a Turbulent World*, Cambridge: Cambridge University Press.

Ross, M. (2012) *The Oil Curse: How Petroleum Wealth Shapes the Development of Nations*, Princeton, NJ: Princeton University Press.

Rostow, W. (1960) *The Stages of Economic Growth*, Cambridge: Cambridge University Press.

RTA (Rapid Transition Alliance) (2019) www.rapidtransition.org/.

Rüdig, W. (1990) 'Explaining Green Party Development', *Strathclyde Papers on Government and Politics* No. 71. https://strathprints.strath.ac.uk/29236/.

Rupert, M. (1995) *Producing Hegemony: The Politics of Mass Production and American Global Power*, Cambridge: Cambridge University Press.

Ryle, M. (1988) *Ecology and Socialism*, London: Radius.

Sachs, W. (1988) 'The Gospel of Global Efficiency' *IFDA Dossier* no. 68: 33–9. www.jstor.org/stable/23002421?seq=1#page_scan_tab_contents

Sachs, W. (ed.) (1992) *The Development Dictionary: A Guide to Knowledge as Power*, London: Zed Books.

Sachs, W. (ed.) (1993) *Global Ecology: A New Arena of Political Conflict*, London: Zed Books.

Said, E. (1979) *Orientalism*, New York: Random House.

Sale, K. (1985) *Dwellers in the Land: The Bioregional Vision*, Philadelphia: New Society.

Santarius, T. (2012) *Green Growth Unravelled: How Rebound Effects Baffle Sustainability Targets When the Economy Keeps Growing*, Berlin: Heinrich Böll Foundation.

Sarkar, S. (1999) *Eco-socialism or Eco-capitalism? A Critical Analysis of Humanity's Fundamental Choices*, London: Zed Books.

Satgar, V. (2014) *The Solidarity Economy Alternative: Emerging Theory and Practice*, Pietermaritzburg, South Africa: University of KwaZulu-Natal Press.

Saurin, J. (1996) 'International Relations, Social Ecology and the Globalization of Environmental Change', in J. Vogler and M. Imber (eds.), *The Environment in International Relations*, London: Routledge, 77–99.

Saurin, J. (2001) 'Global Environmental Crisis as "Disaster Triumphant": The Private Capture of Public Goods', *Environmental Politics* 10, 4 63–84.

Saward, M. (1998) 'Green State/Democratic State', *Contemporary Politics* 4: 345–56.

Schmelzer, M. (2015) 'The Growth Paradigm: History, Hegemony, and the Contested Making of Economic Growthmanship', *Ecological Economics* 118: 262–71.

Schmelzer, M. (2016) *The Hegemony of Growth: The OECD and the Making of the Economic Growth Paradigm*, Cambridge: Cambridge University Press.

Schmidheiny, S. (1992) *Changing Course*, Cambridge, MA: MIT Press.

Schnaiberg, A. (1980) *The Environment – From Surplus to Scarcity*, New York: Oxford University Press.

Scholte, J. A. (ed.) (2011) *Building Global Democracy? Civil Society and Accountable Global Governance*, Cambridge: Cambridge University Press.

Schumacher, E. F. (1974) *Small Is Beautiful*, London: Abacus.

Scoones, I., Leach, M. and Newell, P. (eds.) (2015) *The Politics of Green Transformations*, London: Routledge.

Seel, B. (1997) 'Strategies of Resistance at the Pollok Free State Road Protest Camp', *Environmental Politics* 6, 4: 108–39.

Selby, J. (2014) 'Positivist Climate Conflict Research: A Critique', *Geopolitics* 19, 4: 829–56.

Sell, S. K. (2003) *Private Power, Public Law: The Globalization of Intellectual Property Rights*, Cambridge: Cambridge University Press.

Selwyn, B. (2014) *The Global Development Crisis*, Cambridge: Polity Press.

Sen, A. (1999) *Development as Freedom*, Oxford: Oxford University Press.

Sessions, G. (ed.) (1995) *Deep Ecology for the Twenty-First Century*, Boston: Shambhala Publications.

Seyfang, G. and Longhurst, N. (2013) 'Growing Green Money? Mapping Community Currencies for Sustainable Development', *Ecological Economics* 86: 65–77.

Sharp, G. (1960) *Gandhi Wields the Weapon of Modern Power: Three Case Histories*, Ahmedabad, India: Navajivan Trust.

Shaw, M (1988) *Dialectics of War: An Essay in the Social Theory of Total War and Peace*, London: Pluto Press.

Shiva, V. (1998) *Staying Alive: Women, Ecology and Development*, London: Zed Books.

Shiva, V. (2011) *Monocultures of the Mind: Perspectives on Biodiversity*, Delhi: Natraj Publishers.

Shiva, V. and Moser, I. (eds.) (1995) *Biopolitics: A Feminist and Ecological Reader on Biotechnology*, London: Zed Books.

Simms, A. (2005) *Ecological Debt: The Health of the Planet and the Wealth of Nations*, London: Pluto Press.

Simms, A. (2007) *Tescopoly*, London: Constable and Robinson.

Simms, A. (2013) *Cancel the Apocalypse: The New Path to Prosperity*, London: Little Brown.

Simms, A. and Newell, P. (2017) *How Did We Do That? The Possibility of Rapid Transitions*, Brighton: STEPS Centre.

Simms, A. and Newell, P. (2018) 'We Need a Fossil Fuel Non-Proliferation Treaty – and We Need It Now', *The Guardian*, 23 October, www.theguardian.com/commentisfree/2018/oct/23/fossil-fuel-non-proliferation-treaty-climate-breakdown.

Simon, K. (2016) 'The European Patient: A Diagnosis of the EU's Maladies', *Working Paper*, Brussels: Green European Foundation.

Singer, P. (1995) *Animal Liberation*, 2nd edition, London: Pimlico.

SIPRI (Stockholm International Peace Research Institute) (2018) 'Global Military Spending Remains High at $1.7 Trillion', www.sipri.org/media/press-release/2018/global-military-spending-remains-high-17-trillion.

Smith, A. (2014) *The Wealth of Nations*, London: Shine Classics.

Smith, A. (2016) 'From Arms to Renewables', *GreenWorld*, 2 February.

Smith, D. and Vivekananda, J. (2007) *A Climate of Conflict: The Links between Climate Change, Peace and War*, London: International Alert.

Smith, K. (2007) *The Carbon Neutral Myth – Offset Indulgences for Your Climate Sins*, Barcelona: Carbon Trade Watch.

Smith, M. (1998) *Ecologism: Towards Ecological Citizenship*, Buckingham: Open University Press.

Smith, N. (2006) 'Nature as Accumulation Strategy', in L. Panitch and C. Leys (eds.), *Coming to Terms with Nature*, Monmouth: The Merlin Press, 16–37.

Smith, S. (1993) 'The Environment on the Periphery of International Relations: An Explanation', *Environmental Politics* 2, 4: 28–45.

Søby, C. (2018) 'The Diplomacy of Transitioning: The EU Management of Globalisation in UN Negotiations on Sustainable Development', PhD thesis, Department of Political Science, University of Copenhagen.

Söderbaum, P. (2000) *Ecological Economics*, London: Earthscan.

Sovacool, B. (2016) 'How Long Will It Take? Conceptualizing the Temporal Dynamics of Energy Transitions', *Energy Research & Social Science* 13: 202–15.

Schumpeter, J. A. (1942) *Capitalism, Socialism and Democracy*, 2nd edition, Floyd, VA: Impact Books.

Sikor, T. and Newell, P. (2014) 'Globalizing Environmental Justice?', *Geoforum* 54: 151–7.

Skocpol, T. (1979) *States and Social Revolutions*, Cambridge: Cambridge University Press.

Speth, G. J. (2003) *Worlds Apart: Globalization and Environment*, Washington, DC: Island Press.

Speth, G. J. (2008) *The Bridge at the Edge of the World: Capitalism, the Environment and Crossing from Crisis to Sustainability*, New Haven, CT: Yale University Press.

Spretnak, C. and Capra, F. (1984) *Green Politics: The Global Promise*, London: Paladin Grafton Books.

Sprout, H. and Sprout, M. (1965) *Ecological Perspectives on Human Affairs: With Special Reference to International Politics*, Princeton, NJ: Princeton University Press.

Standing, G. (2008) 'How Cash Transfers Promote the Case for Basic Income', *Basic Income Studies* 3, 1: 1–30.

Stavrianakis, A. (2010) *Taking Aim at the Arms Trade. NGOs, Global Civil Society and the World Military Order*, London: Zed Books.

Stavrianakis, A. (2016) 'Legitimising Liberal Militarism: Politics, Law and War in the Arms Trade Treaty', *Third World Quarterly* 37, 5: 840–65.

Stavrianakis, A. and Selby, J. (eds.) (2013) *Militarism and International Relations: Political Economy, Security, Theory*, London: Routledge.

Stavrianakis, A. and Stern, M. (2018) 'Militarism and Security: Dialogue, Possibilities and Limits', *Security Dialogue* 49, 1–2: 3–18.

Steffen, W., Broadgate, W., Deutsch, L., Gaffney, O. and Ludwig, C. (2015a) 'The Trajectory of the Anthropocene: The Great Acceleration', *The Anthropocene Review* 2, 1: 81–98.

Steffen, W., Crutzen, P. J. and McNeill, J. R. (2007) 'The Anthropocene: Are Humans Now Overwhelming the Great Forces of Nature?', *Ambio*, 36, 8: 614–21.

Steffen, W., Richardson, K., Rockström, J., Cornell, S. E., Fetzer, I., Bennett, E. M., Biggs, R., Carpenter, S. R., de Vries, W., de Wit, C. A., Folke, C., Gerten, D., Heinke, J., Mace, G. M., Persson, L. M., Ramanathan, V., Reyers, B. and Sörlin, S. (2015b) 'Planetary Boundaries: Guiding Human Development on a Changing Planet', *Science* 347, doi: 10.1126/science.1259855.

Stern, N. (2007) *The Economics of Climate Change: The Stern Review*, Cambridge and New York: Cambridge University Press.

Stevenson, H. and Dryzek, J. (2014) *Democratizing Global Climate Governance*, Cambridge: Cambridge University Press.

Stevis, D. and Assetto, V. (eds.) (2001) *The International Political Economy of the Environment: Critical Perspectives*, Boulder, CO: Lynne Rienner.

Stewart, B. (2015) *Don't Trust, Don't Fear, Don't Beg: The Extraordinary Story of the Arctic Thirty*, London: Faber.

Stirling, A. (2010) 'Keep It Complex', *Nature*, 468, 7327: 1029–31.

Stirling, A. (2011) 'Pluralising Progress: From Integrative Transitions to Transformative Diversity', *Environmental Innovation and Societal Transitions* 1, 1: 82–8.

Stirling, A. (2014) *Emancipating Transformations: From Controlling 'the Transition' to Culturing Plural Radical Progress*, STEPS Working Paper 64, Brighton: STEPS Centre.

Stirling, A. (2015) 'Time to Rei(g)n back the Anthropocene' STEPS blog, 16 October, https://steps-centre.org/blog/time-to-reign-back-the-anthropocene/.

Stott, P. and Sullivan, S. (2000) *Political Ecology: Science, Myth and Power*, Oxford: Oxford University Press.

Strange, S. (1996) *The Retreat of the State*, Cambridge: Cambridge University Press.

Strange, S. (1998) *States and Markets*, 2nd edition, London: Continnuum.

Suganami, H. (1996) *On the Causes of War*, Oxford: Clarendon Press.

Sullivan, S. (2013) 'Banking Nature? The Spectacular Financialisation of Environmental Conservation', *Antipode* 45, 1: 198–217.

Swilling, M. and Annecke, E. (2012) *Just Transitions: Explorations of Sustainability in an Unfair World*, South Africa: UCT Press.

Swyngedouw, E. (2010) 'Apocalypse Forever?: Post-Political Populism and the Spectre of Climate Change', *Theory, Culture & Society* 27, 2–3: 213–32.

Swyngedouw, E. (2013) 'The Non-political Politics of Climate Change', *ACME* 12, 1: 1–8.

Swyngedouw, E. and Heynen, N. C. (2003) 'Urban Political Ecology, Justice and the Politics of Scale', *Antipode*, Boulder, CO: Lynne Rienner.

Tatchell, P. (1985) *Democratic Defence: A Non-nuclear Alternative*, London: GMP Publishers.

Tellam, I. (ed.) (2000) *Fuel for Change: World Bank Energy Policy – Rhetoric and Reality*, London: Zed Books.

Tharoor, S. (2016) *Inglorious Empire: What the British Did to India*, London: Hurst and Company.

Thomas, C. (1996) 'Unsustainable Development?', *New Political Economy* 1, 3: 404–7.

Tilly, C. (1993) *Coercion, Capital, and European States, AD 990–1990*, Oxford: Wiley Blackwell.

Toke, D. (2000) *Green Politics and Neo-Liberalism*, Basingstoke: Macmillan.

Tong, R. (1992) *Feminist Thought: A Comprehensive Introduction*, London: Routledge.

Torgerson, D. (1999) *The Promise of Green Politics: Environmentalism and the Public Sphere*, Durham: Duke University Press.

Torry, M. (2013) *Money for Everyone: Why We Need a Citizen's Income*, Bristol: Policy Press.

Trainer, T. (1985) *Abandon Affluence!*, London: Zed Books.

Trainer, T. (1995) *The Conserver Society: Alternatives for Sustainability*, London: Zed Books.

Trainer, T. (1996) *Towards a Sustainable Economy: The Need for Fundamental Change*, Oxford: Jon Carpenter.

Transitions Network (2017) 'Transition Initiatives Directory', https://transitionnetwork.org/?s=transition+initiatives+directory.

TRWC Real World Coalition (2001) *From Here to Sustainability: Politics in the Real World*, London: Earthscan.

UNDP (1994) *New Dimensions of Human Security*, New York: Oxford University Press.

UNDP (2007) *Fighting Climate Change: Human Solidarity in a Divided World*, New York: Palgrave.

UNEP (2011) *Towards a Green Economy: Pathways to Sustainable Development and Poverty Eradication*, Nairobi: UNEP.

UNEP (2015) *The Financial System We Need*, Nairobi: UNEP.

UNEP (2018) *The Emissions Gap Report 2016: A UNEP Synthesis Report*, Nairobi: UNEP.

Union of Concerned Scientists (2017) 'The US Military and Oil', www.ucsusa.org/clean_vehicles/smart-transportation-solutions/us-military-oil-use.html#.WLAzTstvi.

Van Appeldoorn, B. and de Graaff, N. (2015) *American Grand Strategy and Corporate Elite Networks. The Open Door and Its Variations since the End of the Cold War*, London: Routledge.

Van der Pijl, K. (1998) *Transnational Classes and International Relations*, London: Routledge.

Van der Pijl, K. (2014) *The Discipline of Western Supremacy: Modes of Foreign Relations and Political Economy*, vol. III, London: Pluto Press.

Van Gelder, S. (2017) *The Revolution Where You Live*, Oakland, CA: Berrett-Koehler Publishers.

Vanhulst, J. and Beling, A. (2014) 'Buen vivir: Emergent Discourse Within or Beyond Sustainable Development', *Ecological Economics* 101: 54–63.

Van Parijs, P. (2004) 'Basic Income: A Simple and Powerful Idea for the Twenty-First Century', *Politics and Society* 32: 7–39.

Vergara-Camus, L. (2017) 'Capitalism, Democracy, and the Degrowth Horizon', *Capitalism Nature Socialism*, doi: 10.1080/10455752.2017.1344868.

Victor, P. A. (2008) *Managing without Growth: Slower by Design, Not Disaster*, Cheltenham: Edward Elgar.

Vincent, A. (1993) 'The Character of Ecology', *Environmental Politics* 2, 2: 248–76.

Vinthagen, S. (2015) *A Theory of Nonviolent Action – How Civil Resistance Works*, London: Zed Books.

Visvanathan, S. (1991) 'Mrs. Bruntland's Disenchanted Cosmos', *Alternatives: Global, Local, Political* 16, 3: 377–84.

Vlachou, A. (2004) 'Capitalism and Ecological Sustainability: The Shaping of Environmental Policies', *Review of International Political Economy* 11, 5: 926–52.

Von Weizsacker, E., Lovins, A. and Hunter Lovins, L. (1997) *Factor 4: Doubling Wealth, Halving Resource Use*, Sydney: Allen and Unwin.

Wall, D. (1990) *Getting There: Steps towards a Green Society*, London: Merlin Press.

Wall, D. (2017) 'Not Red Yet', *Red Pepper*, London: Socialist Newspaper Publications, 32–3.

Wæver, O. (1993) 'Securitization and Desecuritization', in *COPRI Working Papers* 5/1993, Copenhagen: Copenhagen Peace Research Institute.

Wallerstein, I. (1979) *The Capitalist World Economy: Essays by Immanuel Wallerstein*, Cambridge: Cambridge University Press.

Walker, R. B. J. (1993) *Inside/Outside: International Relations as Political Theory*, Cambridge: Cambridge University Press.

Waltz, K. (1959) *Man, the State and War: A Theoretical Analysis*, New York: Columbia University Press.

Wanner, T. (2015) 'The New "Passive Revolution" of the Green Economy and Growth Discourse: Maintaining the "Sustainable Development" of Neoliberal Capitalism', *New Political Economy* 20, 1: 21–41.

Wapner, P. (2010) *Living through the End of Nature*, Cambridge, MA: MIT Press.

Ward, H. (2002) *Corporate Accountability in Search of a Treaty? Some Insights from Foreign Direct Liability*, Briefing Paper No. 4 Chatham House. London: RIIA.

Ward, J., Sutton, P., Werner, A., Costanza, R., Mohr, S. and Simmons C. (2016) 'Is Decoupling GDP Growth from Environmental Impact Possible?, *PLoS ONE* 11, 10: 1–14.

Watts, M. (2009) 'Oil, Development and the Politics of the Bottom Billion', *MacCalaster International* 24: 79–130.

WCED (World Commission on Environment and Development) (1987) *Our Common Future: Report of the Brundtland Commission on Environment and Development*, Oxford: Oxford University Press.

Weale, A. (1992) *The Politics of Pollution*, Manchester: Manchester University Press.

Weber, M. (1978) *Economy and Society: An Outline of Interpretive Sociology*, Berkeley: University of California Press.

Weber, M. (2005) 'The "Nature" of Environmental Services: GATS, the Environment and the Struggle over the Global Institutionalization of Private Law', *Review of International Political Economy* 12, 3: 456–83.

Welzer, H. (2012) *Climate Wars: Why People Will Be Killed in the 21st Century*, Cambridge: Polity Press.

Weston, J. (ed.) (1986) *Red and Green: The New Politics of the Environment*, London: Pluto Press

Weyler, R. (2004) *Greenpeace*, Vancouver: Raincoast Books.

Whalley, J. and Zissimos, B. (2001) 'What Could a World Environment Organisation Do?', *Global Environmental Politics* 1, 1: 29–35.

Whatmore, S. (2002) *Hybrid Geographies: Natures Cultures Spaces*, London: Sage.

Whatmore, S. (2006) 'Materialist Returns: Practising Cultural Geographies in and for a More-than-Human World', *Cultural Geographies* 13, 4: 600–10.

Whitley, S. and van der Burg, L. (2015) *Fossil Fuel Subsidy Reform: From Rhetoric to Reality*, London: Overseas Development Institute.

Wight, M. (1977) *Systems of States*, Leicester: Leicester University Press.

Wilkinson, R. (2002) 'The Contours of Courtship: The WTO and Civil Society', in R. Wilkinson (ed.), *Global Governance: Critical Perspectives*, London: Routledge, 193–212.

Wilkinson, R. and Pickett, L. (2009) *The Spirit Level: Why Equality Is Better for Everyone*, London: Allen Lane.

Williams, M. (1994) *International Economic Organisations and the Third World*, Hemel Hempstead: Harvester Wheatsheaf.

Williams, M. (1996) 'International Political Economy and Global Environmental Change', in J. Vogler and M. F. Imber (eds.), *The Environment and International Relations*, London: Routledge, 41–58.

Williams, R. (n.d.) *Socialism and Ecology*, London: Socialist Environment and Resources Association.

Williams, R. (1989) *Resources of Hope: Culture, Democracy, Socialism*, London: Verso.

Wissenburg, M. (1998) *Green Liberalism: The Free and the Green Society*, London: UCL Press.

Wood, E. M. (2002) *The Origin of Capitalism: A Longer View*, London: Verso.

Woodcock, G. (ed.) (1983) *The Anarchist Reader*, London: Fontana.

Woodin, M. and Lucas, C. (2004) *Green Alternatives to Globalisation: A Manifesto*, London: Pluto Press.

World Bank (2003) *World Development Report: Dynamic Development in a Sustainable World: Transformation in the Quality of Life, Growth, and Institutions*, New York: Oxford University Press.

World Coal Institute (2018) 'Improving Access to Energy', www.worldcoal.org/sustain able-societies/improving-access-energy.

World Future Council (2012) 'Proposal for a High Commissioner/Ombudsperson for Future Generations: Reflections on the Negotiation Process', http://sdg.iisd.org/com mentary/guest-articles/proposal-for-a-high-commissionerombudsperson-for-future-generations-reflections-on-the-negotiation-process/

Yashar, D. (2005) *Contesting Citizenship in Latin America*, Cambridge: Cambridge University Press.

Youatt, R. (2014) 'Interspecies Relations, International Relations: Rethinking Anthropocentric Politics', *Millennium: Journal of International Studies* 43, 1: 207–23.

Young, O. (1998) *Global Governance: Learning Lessons from the Environmental Experience*, Cambridge, MA: MIT Press.

Young, O. (2010) *Institutional Dynamics: Emergent Patterns in International Environmental Governance*, Cambridge, MA: MIT Press.

Young, S. (ed.) (2000) *The Emergence of Ecological Modernization. Integrating the Environment and the Economy?*, New York: Routledge.

Young, Z. (2002) *A New Green Order? The World Bank and the Politics of the Global Environment Facility*, London: Pluto Press.

Younis, A. S. (2015) 'A True Green Foreign Policy – From Advocacy to Human Empowerment', *Green European Journal* 10, March: 105–10.

Zalasiewicz, J. (2015) 'Epochs: Disputed Start Dates for Anthropocene', *Nature* 520, 7548: 436.

Index

environmentalism of the
  poor, 205
  rich, 1, 205, 223
Extinction Rebellion, 46, 205, 210

finance, 33–4, 76, 83, 103, 106–7, 109, 117, 120, 125,
    132, 141–2, 152, 154, 200, 218–19, 224
financial
  transaction taxes, 109, 165, 179
food. *See* agriculture
Fordism, 21, 95
fracking, 116, 122, 162, 205
fundi, 169

geo-engineering, 117, 191, 197
global governance, 33, 139, 155, 158
globalisation, 11, 13, 143, 145, 155, 164, 173, 185
GNP, 85, 101
Goldsmith, Edward, 25
Gorz, André, 100
great acceleration, 15
Green, ix–x, 1–9, 12–13, 15–19, 21–2, 24–7, 29, 31–3,
    35, 37, 40–1, 43–6, 48–52, 54, 57, 60, 62, 66,
    69–75, 77, 79, 82–3, 85, 88–90, 92, 94, 98–100,
    103–4, 106, 108–11, 113, 117–18, 121, 123,
    125–6, 128–32, 134, 137–44, 146–7, 150, 152,
    154, 157–8, 160–2, 165, 167–9, 171–3, 175,
    177–8, 180–2, 184, 186–7, 189, 194–5, 198–202,
    205–6, 208, 210–13, 215, 217, 219–22, 224–5
Green development, 181, 199
Green economy, 13, 20, 25, 62, 72, 75, 82, 84–5, 92,
    98, 100, 110, 120, 132, 135–6, 144, 159, 179,
    199, 217
Green global governance, 139, 158, 171
Green Growth, 13, 82–3, 159, 168, 173, 223
Green New Deal, 99, 219
Green party, 2, 17, 19, 25, 100, 160–1, 186–7
Green security, 72–3, 129, 199
Green state, 20, 111, 124–5, 138, 169, 174, 184, 199–200
Green Sustainability, 189
Greenhouse, x, 92, 153, 206
Greenpeace, 51, 61

human rights, 22, 73, 122, 127, 137, 141, 147, 153,
    160, 163, 165, 168–9, 171, 182, 186, 208

Icke, David, 187
IMF, xii, 109, 129, 139–41, 146, 149, 152, 177, 186,
    199, 201, 208
industrial revolution, 190
industrialism, 7, 18, 21, 25, 29–31, 35, 37, 46, 55, 76,
    115, 120, 122, 126, 136, 158, 180, 195, 198–9, 220
intergenerational justice, 135
intermediate technology, 98

Jackson, Tim, 86
Just Transition, 95, 102, 183–4, 218, 220

Kelly, Petra, 161

land
  distribution, 217
  tax, 108
limits to growth, 12, 24, 30, 32, 79, 82, 89, 149–50,
    194
localism, 2, 135, 160, 163, 183, 214
Lucas, Caroline, 86

manocene, 36
marketization, 131, 192
markets, 77, 83, 85, 92, 144, 155, 170, 175, 178, 181,
    183–4, 191, 193, 222
Mellor, Mary, 108
militarism, 7, 18, 21, 37, 50–1, 53–5, 57–8,
    67, 90, 122, 125, 157, 173, 196,
    199
modernity, 13, 22, 39, 112, 115, 214
multinational companies (MNCs), 149
mutual aid, 37, 39, 41–2, 45, 126, 129

Naess, Arne, 43
NATO, 51, 72, 144, 170
neoliberalism, 13, 120, 145, 160
New Economics Foundation, 92, 101
nuclear
  energy, 54, 125
  waste, 51
  weapons, 56, 67–8, 72, 165

Ombudsperson for future generations, 167

Paterson, Matthew, x, 2, 140
patriarchy, 13, 16, 18, 27, 42, 52
planetary boundaries, 1, 18, 29, 59, 83, 109, 133,
    141, 151, 154–6, 167, 189, 197–8, 206–7, 213,
    223
Plumwood, Val, 81, 97
Porritt, Jonathan, 29–30
poverty, 1, 8, 34, 57, 74, 78, 96, 101, 107, 123, 142,
    152, 159, 164, 172, 176, 180, 184–5, 187, 192,
    194
prosperity
  without growth, 19, 86, 93, 98, 178,
  223

Rapid Transition Alliance, 222
Raworth, Kate, 109, 154, 198, 206
Read, Rupert, 202
Real World Coalition, 159, 179, 200, 221
realo, 169, 209
republicanism, 128

Sachs, Wolfgang, 46, 175, 194
Schumacher, E.F, x, 97, 211
security, 2–3, 7–8, 10, 16, 19, 23, 27, 38, 49–51, 53–4,
    56–60, 62–3, 65–6, 68, 71–3, 97, 112, 114, 128,
    130, 139, 154, 157, 159, 163, 165–6, 172, 174,
    177, 180, 184, 186, 189, 198, 200, 209, 212, 216,
    224